ROME

THE AUTOBIOGRAPHY

Edited by JON E. LEWIS

ROBINSON

RUNNING PRESS
PHILADELPHIA · LONDON

Constable & Robinson Ltd
3 The Lanchesters
162 Fulham Palace Road
London W6 9ER
www.constablerobinson.com

First published in the UK as *The Mammoth Book of Eyewitness
Ancient Rome* by Robinson,
an imprint of Constable & Robinson, 2003

This updated and revised edition published by Robinson,
an imprint of Constable & Robinson Ltd, 2010

A copy of the British Library Cataloguing in
Publication data is available from the British Library

ISBN: 978-1-84901-083-2

1 3 5 7 9 10 8 6 4 2

First published in the United States in 2009 by Running Press Book Publishers

9 8 7 6 5 4 3 2 1

Digit on the right indicates the number of this printing

US Library of Congress Control Number: 2009920968
US ISBN 978-0-7624-3736-8

Running Press Book Publishers
2300 Chestnut Street
Philadelphia, PA 19103-4371

Visit us on the web!
www.runningpress.com

Printed and bound in the EU

CONTENTS

Part Two   Empire: Rome 30 BC–AD 180   119

Part Three   Fall: Rome AD 181–476   313

Part Four   Epilogue:
The Roman Empire in the East, AD 477–565   **395**

INTRODUCTION

Rome was one of the three pillars of Western civilization. Of the other two, Rome subsumed one (Greece) and succoured the last (Christianity).

It is little surprise, then, that Rome still looms so large in the landscape of Western culture: *Roman* Catholic; modern legal systems (based on Justininian's *Corpus Juris Civilis*); the month of "July" (after Julius Caesar); the tradition of carrying brides across the threshold (a Roman rite); the Latin-derived languages of Italy, France, Portugal and Spain. Even English, the language of the Anglo-Saxons, is 33 per cent based on Latin.

Meanwhile, the physical landscape of the West bears countless imprints of Rome: the ruler-straight road that is the Fosse Way, the aquaduct at Nimes, the Colosseum in Rome, the amphitheatre at Caerleon, the baths at Bath. And when real Roman buildings have fallen to dust, generations of architects have revived the "Classical" style. There are middle-class housing projects the Western world over which have fake Roman columns around the portal.

If the sheer legacy of Rome is taken away, then there is the fascination of Ancient Rome itself. How did a hick village on some undulations beside the Tiber come to build the greatest empire of antiquity? Why did it last so long (nearly a thousand years)? Was it civilized – or was it debauched?

Ancient Rome, if you like, is plain interesting. Ancient Rome, if you must, is a necessary object of study in any understanding of the modern world in which we live.

This book of eye-witness accounts differs from the recorded histories of Rome. There are many of these, Gibbon's *History of the Decline and Fall of the Roman Empire* and Michael Grant's *History of Rome* being exemplars from vastly different times and perspectives. Recorded histories offer analysis and explanation. An anthology of first-hand reports gives something entirely different but complementary: the vicarious experience of "being there". Since many of the events included are actually written by their movers and shakers (Caesar on the invasion of Britain, Augustus on his empire-building achievements, for instance), eye-witness history also allows intimate access to the mind-frame of the great men and women of the past. In other words, it's the inside track.

There are two more virtues of this type of "personal" history. First, it's invariably more vivid than recorded history. Second, it's the actual basic building material of history books. Eye-witness report is what historians use to make their histories. Thus an anthology of eye-witness accounts also enables the reader to make his or her own interpretation. DIY history, perhaps.

An obvious difficulty in compiling such an anthology of Ancient Rome is the paucity of sources. By legend Rome was founded in 753 BC and by historians' agreement it fell in AD 476. Probably the first true first-hand recorder of Rome was Cato the Elder (234–149 BC), and not until the 1st century AD do sources begin to proliferate. Or, at least, begin to survive the accidents of history; many of these records have been lost to invasion, fire, natural disasters, house-cleaning. Accordingly, the compiler of an eye-witness anthology of Rome is obliged to use a little licence. While most accounts are first-hand, some are "second hand", by men and women who lived in the relevant time, or just after, and who can reasonably be supposed to have consulted direct eye-witnesses. Into this category falls Nicolaus of Damascus on Caesar's assassination and Tacitus on Britain (his father-in-law was Agricola, a governor of the isles). On very few occasions I have employed accounts by Ancient historians – notably Suetonius – who flourished after the event because their words closely echo original sources. Suetonius, being a court historian, had access to all extant records, including original letters. Plutarch's account of the slave revolt of Spartacus is allowed because, although hostile to Spartacus, his careful history at least allows the slaves of Ancient Rome to make an appearance in this book in the guise of something other than passive *instrumentum vocale*.

Because, of course, it should never be forgotten that the ancient records which do survive the vicissitudes of time tend to be those of the VIPs of politics and war. The voice of ordinary Romans is more difficult to call, despite the fantastic – by ancient standards – literacy of the Roman people. Graffiti (see pp 40–41, 210–211), and letters, mostly from Romanized Egypt and Britain, offer some glimpses of the lot of "ordinary" people and soldiers. I have supplemented this with excerpts from poetry and plays which depict everyday Rome, at work and at play.

Part One

Rise

Rome 753 BC–31 BC

INTRODUCTION

Rome was not built in a day. Otherwise, little can be said with certainty about the city's foundation. The Romans themselves, following the 1st century BC writer Varro, liked to date the beginning of Rome to 753 BC and ascribe the act to Romulus. This was pure invention. The trowel of the archaelogist suggests that humans inhabited the banks of Tiber as long ago as Neanderthal times. More systematic settlement came 1000 years BC with a minor migration of Iron Age people from nearby "Latium". They were clearly drawn to Rome's natural advantages: its seven hills were easily defended and the Tiber easily crossed there, thanks to a fortuitous island in the middle of the riverine flow. The transformation of Rome, however, from a collection of huts on hills and a rickety wooden bridge into something approaching an urban centre would have to wait until the 7th century BC and the domination of the city by the Etruscans.

The Etruscans were a mystery to the Romans. Modern scholarship is hardly more enlightened. Probably the Etruscans hailed originally from Asia Minor (Turkey) and their culture was obviously influenced by the Greeks. They colonized northern Italy *circa* 700 BC and soon cast a covetous eye at Rome, since it straddled the main trade route between their wealthy cities and trading colonies in the south of the peninsula. Around 625 BC Rome came under the rule of the Etruscan monarch Tarquinius Priscus. Since the Etruscans were inveterate urbanites, they immediately set about big-time town-planning.

Swamps were drained by canals making the Forum habitable, a giant sewer (the Cloaca Maxima) dug, and a temple to Jupiter, Juno and Minerva erected on Capitoline Hill.

The Etruscans also bequeathed the Latin natives of Rome their alphabet, their ceremonies, their pictorial art, and even perhaps their means of organizing the state: the division into units known as tribes (*tribus*), the sub-division into wards (*curiae*), and from both the selection of 300 men who formed the Senate.

These cultural and architectural gifts notwithstanding, the Romans never learned to love the Etruscans and when Etruscan power dwindled on the geopolitical vine, the Romans unceremoniously ejected them, traditionally in 510 BC. In place of the Etruscan monarchy (and the Roman monarchy which had preceded Etruscan rule), the Romans now installed a republican system of government. This consisted of the Senate, plus two consuls – of equal status – who were elected annually. More minor posts were held by elected magistrates.

Public office was the exclusive right of the aristocracy or "patrician" class, the same class which also filled the regalia of religious office and administered the major cults. Roman religion, which borrowed gods from the Etruscans and Greeks to add to its collection of (largely rustic) homegrown divinities, was a curiously business-like affair in which the worshipper promised X to a god in return for Y. Their was little opacity, less mystery, and nothing to inspire the soul (hence the dearth of Roman religious works). The sole virtue of Roman religion was the sense of dutiful respect, *pietas*, it demanded.

Pietas was also central to another facet of Roman life, the institution of *clientela*, which divided society into *patroni* and their dependent *clientes*. Every Roman had a patron, one social gradation above him, from whom came protection (including legal and financial support) in return for unstinting respect. The streets of Rome were jammed every morning with Romans scurrying to make courtesy calls on their patrons.

It might be said that the patron–client relationship was but a minor reflection of the major division in Roman society – that between the patricians and the plebeians (*plebs*). Plebeians were free Romans, but powerless ones. Until, that is, the plebeians –

who constituted more than 90 per cent of Roman society exclusive of slaves – indulged in a spot of ancient class warfare and withdrew not only their labour but their entire beings from Rome in several "secessions". The most obvious result of these secessions was the creation in 494 BC of small numbers of "tribunes" to represent plebeian interests (further, in 471 BC, a plebeian council was allowed) and the writing down in 451 BC of a transparent collection of laws applicable to all freeborn: the Twelve Tables (see pp 13–18). Within a hundred years, social mobility was so developed in Rome that plebeians were allowed into some of the highest offices of the land, including the consulship and censorship. This social mobility, in turn, produced social unity in the face of Rome's enemies.

These were many. An expansionist Republican Rome soon hit up against the rival city states of Italy – those of the Sabines, the Samnites, the Latins and the Etruscans – yet quashed them all on the battlefield. The reasons for the superiority of Roman arms were several. Firstly, in battlefield organization, the Romans dispensed with the "phalanx" in favour of more manoeuverable "maniples", and more or less simultaneously substitued a throwing javelin – *pilum* – for the thrusting spear; after throwing his *pilum*, the Roman soldier followed up the attack with a sword. Secondly, the Romans instituted a basis of service in which legionaries were paid a daily stipend; this was more dependable an income for the legionary than the old self-sustaining-by-looting system. Thirdly, there was the matter of the Roman mind: patriotic but controlled, thanks to the discipline learned in the family home under the iron rule of *paterfamilas*. It might also be added that the Romans were uncommonly bloodthirsty in their waging of war. (The same streak of cruelty surfaced in their "entertainments", particularly the gladiatorial shows beloved of the Roman crowds.)

By 272 BC, after nigh on 250 years of incessant fighting, Rome had subjugated the whole of peninsular Italy. The city-state had become an empire. It was perhaps inevitable that Rome would then come into conflict with the existing super-power of the Mediterranean, the North African merchant state of Carthage. The three Punic Wars between Rome and Carthage were a close-run thing, but eventually Rome emerged triumphant and burnt Carthage to the ground in 146 BC, ploughing the ruins into the ground and then spreading salt into the furrows so that nothing would ever grow there again.

The Punic Wars also taught the Romans something of sea warfare. While they would never be a nation of sailors (when Julius Caesar tried his first invasion of Britain in 55 BC, the legionaries had to be forced into boats for the Channel crossing) they were now more able to export war, and did so all around the Mediterranean. State after state fell to Roman arms, from Spain to Judea, from Macedonia to Numidia. With justification, the Romans began to call the Mediterranean *Mare Nostrum*. Our Sea.

Yet success abroad brought troubles at home. There was a subtle shift in power in the Republic from the elected officials to the military men who brought the victories. Some Roman generals commanded what were virtually personal armies. Moreover, the political machinery which ran a small city-state would not stretch to the running of an empire.

The Republic was doomed. In 60 BC three generals, Pompey, Crassus and Caesar combined in the autocratic "First Triumvirate" against the Senate. The generals promptly fell out and Roman society fell apart. The fatal moment for the Republic came on the night of 10 January 49 BC when Caesar broke Roman law by leading troops outside his province. He led them across the River Rubicon, towards Rome and towards dictatorship. That Caesar was assassinated within five years hardly mattered. The Republic was dead, and could not be revived. More military dictatorship and civil war followed under Mark Antony, until Octavian, Caesar's named heir, usurped him and installed an entirely novel regime. He declared himself Emperor.

NUMA ORDAINS THE VESTAL VIRGINS, C. 680 BC

Plutarch

By legend, Numa Pompilius was the second king of Rome. Whether he lived or not, the religious institutions ascribed to him persisted until the triumph of Christianity under Constantine in AD 324. Plutarch penned this account of the vestal virgins and roman temple rites in the 1st century AD.

The original constitution of the priests, called Pontifices, is ascribed unto Numa, and he himself was, it is said, the first of them; and that they have the name of Pontifices from *potens*, powerful, because they attend the service of the gods, who have power and command over all. The most common opinion is the most absurd, which derives this word from *pons*, and assigns the priests the title of bridge-makers. The sacrifices performed on the bridge were amongst the most sacred and ancient, and the keeping and repairing of the bridge attached, like any other public sacred office, to the priesthood. It was accounted not simply unlawful, but a positive sacrilege, to pull down the wooden bridge; which moreover is said, in obedience to an oracle, to have been built entirely of timber and fastened with wooden pins, without nails or cramps of iron. The stone bridge was built a very long time after, when Æmilius was quæstor, and they do, indeed, say also that the wooden bridge was not so old as Numa's time . . .

The office of Pontifex Maximus, or chief priest, was to declare and interpret the divine law . . . he not only prescribed rules for public ceremony, but regulated the sacrifices of private persons, not suffering them to vary from established custom, and giving information to every one of what was requisite for purposes of worship or supplication. He was also guardian of the vestal virgins, the institution of whom, and of their perpetual fire, was attributed to Numa, who, perhaps, fancied the charge of pure and uncorrupted flames would be fitly entrusted to chaste and unpolluted persons, or that fire, which consumes, but produces nothing, bears an analogy to the virgin estate.

Some are of opinion that these vestals had no other business than the preservation of this fire; but others conceive that they were keepers of other divine secrets, concealed from all but themselves. Gegania and Verenia, it is recorded, were the names of the first two virgins consecrated and ordained by Numa; Canuleia and Tarpeia succeeded; Servius Tullius afterwards added two, and the number of four has been continued to the present time.

The Term of Service for the Vestals
The statutes prescribed by Numa for the vestals were these: that they should take a vow of virginity for the space of thirty years,

the first ten of which they were to spend in learning their duties, the second ten in performing them, and the remaining ten in teaching and instructing others. Thus the whole term being completed, it was lawful for them to marry, and leaving the sacred order, to choose any condition of life that pleased them; but of this permission few, as they say, made use; and in cases where they did so, it was observed that their change was not a happy one, but accompanied ever after with regret and melancholy; so that the greater number, from religious fears and scruples, forbore, and continued to old age and death in the strict observance of a single life.

For this condition he compensated by great privileges and prerogatives; as that they had power to make a will in the lifetime of their father; that they had a free administration of their own affairs without guardian or tutor, which was the privilege of women who were the mothers of three children; when they go abroad, they have the fasces carried before them; and if in their walks they chance to meet a criminal on his way to execution, it saves his life, upon oath being made that the meeting was accidental, and not concerted or of set purpose. Anyone who presses upon the chair on which they are carried is put to death.

Punishment of Unfaithful Vestals

If these vestals commit any minor fault, they are punishable by the high-priest only, who scourges the offender, sometimes with her clothes off, in a dark place, with a curtain drawn between; but she that has broken her vow is buried alive near the gate called Collina, where a little mound of earth stands, inside the city, reaching some little distance, called in Latin *agger*; under it a narrow room is constructed, to which a descent is made by stairs; here they prepare a bed, and light a lamp, and leave a small quantity of victuals, such as bread, water, a pail of milk, and some oil; that so that body which had been consecrated and devoted to the most sacred service of religion might not be said to perish by such a death as famine. The culprit herself is put in a litter, which they cover over, and tie her down with cords on it, so that nothing she utters may be heard. They then take her to the forum; all people silently go out of the way as she passes, and such as follow accompany the bier with solemn and speechless sorrow; and, indeed, there is not any spectacle more appalling, nor any day observed by the city with greater appearance of gloom and sadness. When they come to the place of execution, the officers loose the cords, and then the high-priest, lifting his hands to heaven, pronounces certain prayers to himself before the act; then he brings out the prisoner, being still covered, and placing her upon the steps that lead down to the cell, turns away his face with the rest of the priests; the stairs are drawn up after she has gone down, and a quantity of earth is heaped up over the entrance to the cell, so as to prevent it from being distinguished from the rest of the mound. This is the punishment of those who break their vow of virginity.

THE TWELVE TABLES, c. 450 BC

Anon

As a result of plebeian *pressure, the patricians of the early Roman Republic were obliged into the formulation of a set of laws transparent to all (hitherto, the law, unwritten, was arcanely and biasedly interpreted by upper-class priests or* pontifices*). The ensuing Twelve Tables, published on stone and displayed in the Forum for all to see, codified the civil laws regarding the rights and duties of Roman citizens. They also formed the basis of Roman law for the next thousand years. Something of the regard with which later Roman citizens beheld the Twelve Tables is captured in the remark of Cicero (106–43 BC) that "the Twelve Tables . . . seems to me, assuredly to surpass the libraries of all the philosophers, both in weight of authority, and in plentitude of utility".*

Table I

1. If anyone summons a man before the magistrate, he must go. If the man summoned does not go, let the one summoning him call the bystanders to witness and then take him by force.

2. If he [the defendant] shirks or runs away, let the summoner lay hands on him.

3. If disease or old age is the hindrance, let the summoner provide a team. He need not provide a covered carriage with a pallet unless he chooses.

4. Let the protector of a landholder be a landholder; for one of the proletariat, let anyone that cares, be protector.

6–9. When the parties settle their case by compromise, let the magistrate announce it. If they do not compromise, let them state each his own side of the case, in the *comitium* of the forum before noon. Afterwards let them talk it out together, while both are present. After noon, in case either party has failed to appear, let the magistrate pronounce judgment in favor of the party who is present. If both are present the trial may last until sunset but no later.

Table II
2. He whose witness has failed to appear may summon him by loud calls before his house every third day.

Table III
1–6. One who has confessed a debt, or against whom judgment has been pronounced, shall have thirty days to pay it in. After that forcible seizure of his person is allowed. The creditor shall bring him before the magistrate. Unless he settles the amount of the judgment or someone in the presence of the magistrate interferes in his behalf as protector the creditor so shall take him home and fasten him in stocks or fetters. He shall fasten him with not less than fifteen pounds of weight or, if he choose, with more. If the prisoner choose, he may furnish his own food. If he does not, the creditor must give him a pound of meal daily; if he choose he may give him more.

2. On the third market day let them divide his body among them. If they cut more or less than each one's share it shall be no crime.

3. Against a foreigner the right in property shall be valid forever.

Table IV

1. A dreadfully deformed child shall be quickly killed.

2. If a father surrenders his son three times, the son shall be free from his father.

3. As a man has provided in his will in regard to his money and the care of his property, so let it be binding. If he has no heir and dies intestate, let the nearest agnate have the inheritance. If there is no agnate, let the members of his gens have the inheritance.

4. If one is mad but has no guardian, the power over him and his money shall belong to his agnates and the members of his *gens*.

5. A child born after ten months since the father's death will not be admitted into a legal inheritance.

Table V

1. Females should remain in guardianship even when they have attained their majority.

Table VI

1. When one makes a bond and a conveyance of property, as he has made formal declaration so let it be binding.

3. A beam that is built into a house or a vineyard trellis one may not take from its place.

5. *Usucapio* of movable things requires one year's possession for its completion; but *usucapio* of an estate and buildings two years.

6. Any woman who does not wish to be subjected in this manner to the hand of her husband should be absent three nights in succession every year, and so interrupt the *usucapio* of each year.

Table VII

1. Let them keep the road in order. If they have not paved it, a man may drive his team where he likes.

9b. Should a tree on a neighbour's farm be bent crooked by the wind and lean over your farm, you may take legal action for removal of that tree.

10. A man might gather up fruit that was falling down onto another man's farm.

Table VIII

2. If one has maimed a limb and does not compromise with the injured person, let there be retaliation. 23. If one has broken a bone of a freeman with his hand or with a cudgel, let him pay a penalty of three hundred coins. If he has broken the bone of a slave, let him have one hundred and fifty coins. If one is guilty of insult, the penalty shall be twenty-five coins.

3. If one is slain while committing theft by night, he is rightly slain.

4. If a patron shall have devised any deceit against his client, let him be accursed.

5. If one shall permit himself to be summoned as a witness, or has been a weigher, if he does not give his testimony, let him be noted as dishonest and incapable of acting again as witness.

10. Any person who destroys by burning any building or heap of corn deposited alongside a house shall be bound, scourged, and put to death by burning at the stake provided that he has committed the said misdeed with malice aforethought; but if he shall have committed it by accident, that is, by negligence, it is ordained that he repair the damage or, if he be too poor to be competent for such punishment, he shall receive a lighter punishment.

12. If the theft has been done by night, if the owner kills the thief, the thief shall be held to be lawfully killed.

13. (It is unlawful for a thief to be) killed by day . . . unless he defends himself with a weapon; even though he has come with a weapon, unless he shall use the weapon and fight back, you shall not kill him. And even if he resists, first call out (so that someone may hear and come up).

23. A person who has been found guilty of giving false witness shall be hurled down from the Tarpeian Rock.

26. No person shall hold meetings by night in the city.

Table IX
4. The penalty shall be capital for a judge or arbiter legally appointed who has been found guilty of receiving a bribe for giving a decision.

5. Treason: he who shall have roused up a public enemy or handed over a citizen to a public enemy must suffer capital punishment.

6. Putting to death of any man, whosoever he might be unconvicted is forbidden.

Table X
1. None is to bury or burn a corpse in the city.

3. The women shall not tear their faces nor wail on account of the funeral.

5. If one obtains a crown himself, or if his chattel does so because of his honour and valour, if it is placed on his head, or the head of his parents, it shall be no crime.

Table XI
1. Marriages should not take place between plebeians and patricians.

Table XII

2. If a slave shall have committed theft or done damage with his master's knowledge, the action for damages is in the slave's name.

5. Whatever the people had last ordained should be held as binding by law.

INSTRUCTIONS ON FARMING, c. 400 BC

Anon

For all Ancient Rome's martial grandeur and high civilization, Italy remained stubbornly rural. Below is a farmer's planting-and-husbandry calendar for the month of May. Etched onto a marble cube (along with injunctions for the remainder of the agrarian year), it dates from the 5th century BC but might have come from any point in the millennium of Roman history before Christianization.

The month of May

Thirty-one days, with the nones falling on the seventh day. The day has fourteen and one half hours. The night has nine and one half hours. The sun is under the sign of Taurus. The month of May is under the protection of Apollo.

    The corn is weeded.

    The sheep are shorn.

    The wool is washed.

    The young steers are put under the yoke.

    The vetch in the meadows is cut.

    The lustration of the crops is made. Sacrifices (ought to be made) to Mercury and to Flora.

PUNIC WARS: HANNIBAL ADDRESSES HIS SOLDIERS, 218 BC

Anon

From 264 BC the Romans fought three wars against the North African merchant state of Carthage. These Punic wars – Poeni being Latin for Phoenicians, the founders of Carthage – lasted for nigh on a century, and were almost lost for the Romans when the Carthaginian general Hannibal (247–182 BC) took his elephants over the Pyrenees and Alps and invaded Italy. Here is his speech to his soldiers on their entry into Italy.

If, soldiers, you shall by and by, in judging of your own fortune, preserve the same feelings which you experienced a little before in the example of the fate of others, we have already conquered; for neither was that merely a spectacle, but, as it were, a certain representation of your condition. And I know not whether fortune has not thrown around you still stronger chains and more urgent necessities than around your captives. On the right and left two seas enclose you, without your possessing even a single ship for escape. The river Po around you, the Po larger and more impetuous than the Rhone; the Alps behind, scarcely passed by you when fresh and vigorous, hem you in.

Here, soldiers, where you have first met the enemy, you must conquer or die; and the same fortune which has imposed the necessity of fighting holds out to you, if victorious, rewards than which men are not wont to desire greater, even from the immortal gods. If we were only about to recover by our valour Sicily and Sardinia, wrested from our fathers, the recompense would be sufficiently ample; but whatever, acquired and amassed by so many triumphs, the Romans possess, all, with its masters themselves, will become yours. To gain this rich reward, hasten, then, and seize your arms, with the favour of the gods.

Long enough, in pursuing cattle among the desert mountains of Lusitania and Celtiberia, you have seen no emolument from so many toils and dangers; it is time to make rich and profitable campaigns, and to gain the great reward of your labours, after having accomplished such a length of journey over so many mountains and rivers; and so many nations in arms. Here fortune has granted you the termination of your labors; here she will bestow a reward worthy of the service you have undergone. Nor, in proportion as the war is great in name, ought you to consider that the victory will be difficult. A despised enemy has often maintained a sanguinary contest, and renowned States and kings have been conquered by a very slight effort.

For, setting aside only the splendour of the Roman name, what remains in which they can be compared to you? To pass over in silence your service for twenty years, distinguished by such valour and success, you have made your way to this place from the pillars of Hercules, from the ocean and the remotest limits of the world, advancing victorious through so many of the fiercest nations of Gaul and Spain; you will fight with a raw army, which this very summer was beaten, conquered, and surrounded by the Gauls, as yet unknown to its general, and ignorant of him. Shall I compare myself – almost born, and certainly bred, in the tent of my father, that most illustrious commander, myself the subjugator of Spain and Gaul, the conqueror too not only of the Alpine nations, but, what is much more, of the Alps themselves – with this six-months' general, the deserter of his army? – to whom, if anyone, having taken away their standards, should today show the Carthaginians and Romans, I am sure that he would not know of which army he was consul.

I do not regard it, soldiers, as of small account that there is not a man among you before whose eyes I have not often achieved some military exploit; and to whom, in like manner, I, the spectator and witness of his valour, could not recount his own gallant deeds, particularized by time and place. With soldiers who have a thousand times received my praises and gifts, I, who was the pupil of you all before I became your commander, will march out in battle-array against those who are unknown to and ignorant of each other.

On whatever side I turn my eyes I see nothing but what is full of courage and energy: a veteran infantry; cavalry, both those with and those without the bridle, composed of the most gallant nations, – you, our most faithful and valiant allies, you Carthaginians, who are about to fight as well for the sake of your country as from the justest resentment. We are the assailants in the war, and descend into Italy with hostile standards, about to engage so much more boldly and bravely than the foe, as the confidence and courage of the assailants are greater than those of him who is defensive. Besides, suffering, injury, and indignity inflame and excite our minds: they first demanded me, your leader, for punishment, and then all of you who had laid siege to

Saguntum; and had we been given up they would have visited us with the severest tortures.

That most cruel and haughty nation considers everything its own, and at its own disposal; it thinks it right that it should regulate with whom we are to have war, with whom peace; it circumscribes and shuts us up by the boundaries of mountains and rivers which we must not pass, and then does not adhere to those boundaries which it appointed. Pass not the Iberius; have nothing to do with the Saguntines. Saguntum is on the Iberius; you must not move a step in any direction. Is it a small thing that you take away my most ancient provinces – Sicily and Sardinia? Will you take Spain also? And should I withdraw thence, will you cross over into Africa?

Will cross, did I say? They have sent the two consuls of this year, one to Africa, the other to Spain: there is nothing left to us in any quarter, except what we can assert to ourselves by arms. Those may be cowards and dastards who have something to look back upon; whom, flying through safe and unmolested roads, their own lands and their own country will receive: there is a necessity for you to be brave, and, since all between victory and death is broken off from you by inevitable despair, either to conquer, or if fortune should waver, to meet death rather in battle than in flight. If this be well fixed and determined in the minds of you all, I will repeat, you have already conquered; no stronger incentive to victory has been given to man by the immortal gods.

PUNIC WARS: THE CHARACTER OF HANNIBAL

Polybius

Hannibal's victory at Cannae in 216 BC almost brought Roman power to ruin but troop-shortage prevented him pressing the advantage. He maraudered around Italy for another thirteen years before being recalled to Carthage to repel – unsuccessfully – the Roman invasion under Scipio. Hannibal later committed suicide. Polybius (c. 205–c. 123 BC) was a Greek taken as hostage to Rome, where he became friendly with Scipio Aemilianus, the eventual destroyer of Carthage.

Of all that befell the Romans and Carthaginians, good or bad, the cause was one man and one mind – Hannibal. For it is notorious that he managed the Italian campaigns in person, and the Spanish by the agency of the elder of his brothers, Hasdrubal, and subsequently by that of Mago, the leaders who killed the two Roman generals in Spain about the same time. Again, he conducted the Sicilian campaign first through Hippocrates and afterwards through Myttonus the Libyan. So also in Greece and Illyria: and, by brandishing before their faces the dangers arising from these latter places, he was enabled to distract the attention of the Romans thanks to his understanding with King Philip [of Macedon]. So great and wonderful is the influence of a Man, and a mind duly fitted by original constitution for any undertaking within the reach of human powers.

But since the position of affairs has brought us to inquiry into the genius of Hannibal, the occasion seems to me to demand that I should explain in regard to him the peculiarities of his character which have been especially the subject of controversy. Some regard him as having been extraordinarily cruel, some exceedingly grasping of money. But to speak the truth of him, or of any person engaged in public affairs, is not easy. Some maintain that men's natures are brought out by their circumstances, and that they are detected when in office, or as some say when in misfortunes, though they have up to that time completely maintained their secrecy. I, on the contrary, do not regard this as a sound dictum. For I think that men in these circumstances are compelled, not occasionally but frequently, either by the suggestions of friends or the complexity of affairs, to speak and act contrary to real principles.

And there are many proofs of this to be found in past history if anyone will give the necessary attention. Is it not universally stated by the historians that Agathocles, tyrant of Sicily, after having the reputation of extreme cruelty in his original measures for the establishment of his dynasty, when he had once become convinced that his power over the Siceliots was firmly established, is considered to have become the most humane and mild of rulers? Again, was not Cleomenes of Sparta a most excellent king, a most cruel tyrant, and then again as a private individual most obliging and benevolent? And yet it is not reasonable to suppose the most opposite dispositions to exist in the same nature. They are compelled to change with the changes of circumstances: and so some rulers often display to the world a disposition as opposite as possible to their true nature. Therefore, the natures of men not only are not brought out by such things, but on the contrary are rather obscured. The same effect is produced also not only in commanders, despots, and kings, but in states also, by the suggestions of friends. For instance, you will find the Athenians responsible for very few tyrannical acts, and of many kindly and noble ones, while Aristeides and Pericles were at the head of the state: but quite the reverse when Cleon and Chares were so. And when the Lacedaemonians were supreme in Greece, all the measures taken by King Cleombrotus were conceived in the interests of their allies, but those by Agesilaus not so. The characters of states therefore vary with the variations of their leaders. King Philip again, when Taurion and Demetrius were acting with him, was most impious in his conduct, but when Aratus or Chrysogonus, most humane.

The case of Hannibal seems to me to be on a par with these. His circumstances were so extraordinary and shifting, his closest friends so widely different, that it is exceedingly difficult to estimate his character from his proceedings in Italy. What those circumstances suggested to him may easily be understood from what I have already said, and what is immediately to follow; but it is not right to omit the suggestions made by his friends either, especially as this matter may be rendered sufficiently clear by one instance of the advice offered him. At the time that Hannibal was meditating the march from Iberia to Italy with his army, he was confronted with the extreme difficulty of providing food and securing provisions, both because the journey was thought to be of insuperable length, and because the barbarians that lived in the intervening country were numerous and savage. It appears that at that time the difficulty frequently came on for discussion at the council; and that one of his friends, called Hannibal Monomachus, gave it as his opinion that there was one and only one way by which it was possible to get as far as Italy. Upon Hannibal bidding him speak out, he said that they must teach the army to eat human flesh, and make them accustomed to it. Hannibal could say nothing against the boldness and effectiveness of the idea, but was unable to persuade himself or his friends to entertain it. It is this man's acts in Italy that they say were attributed to Hannibal, to maintain the accusation of cruelty, as well as such as were the result of circumstances.

Fond of money indeed he does seem to have been to a conspicuous degree, and to have had a friend of the same character – Mago, who commanded in Bruttium. That account I got from the Carthaginians themselves; for natives know best not only which way the wind lies, as the proverb has it, but the characters also of their fellow-countrymen. But I heard a still more detailed story from Massanissa, who maintained the charge of money-loving against all Carthaginians generally, but especially against Hannibal and Mago called the Samnite. Among other stories, he told me that these two men had arranged a most generous subdivision of operations between each other from their earliest youth; and though they had each taken a very large number of cities in Iberia and Italy by force or fraud, they had never taken part in the same operation together; but had always schemed against each other, more than against the enemy, in order to prevent the one being with the other at the taking of a city: that they might neither quarrel in consequence of a thing of this sort nor have to divide the profit on the ground of their equality of rank.

The influence of friends then, and still more that of circumstances, in doing violence to and changing the natural character of Hannibal, is shown by what I have narrated and will be shown by what I have to narrate. For as soon as Capua fell into the hands of the Romans, the other cities naturally became restless, and began to look round for opportunities and pretexts for revolting back again to Rome. It was then that Hannibal seems to have been at his lowest point of distress and despair. For neither was he able to keep a watch upon all the cities so widely removed from each other – while he remained entrenched at one spot, and the enemy were manoeuvering against him with several armies – nor could he divide his force into many parts; for he would have put an easy victory into the hands of the enemy by becoming inferior to them in numbers, and finding it impossible to be personally present at all points.

Wherefore he was obliged to completely abandon some of the cities, and withdraw his garrisons from others: being afraid lest, in the course of the revolutions which might occur, he should lose his own soldiers as well. Some cities again he made up his mind to treat with treacherous violence, removing their inhabitants to other cities, and giving their property up to plunder; in consequence of which many were enraged with him, and accused him of impiety or cruelty. For the fact was that these movements were accompanied by robberies of money, murders, and violence, on various pretexts at the hands of the outgoing or incoming soldiers in the cities, because they always supposed that the inhabitants that were left behind were on the verge of turning over to the enemy. It is, therefore, very difficult to express an opinion on the natural character of Hannibal, owing to the influence exercised on it by the counsel of friends and the force of circumstances. The prevailing notion about him, however, at Carthage was that he was greedy of money, at Rome that he was cruel.

PUNIC WARS: THE VIEW OF A SOLDIER POET, C. 210 BC

Quintus Ennius

Ennius was a poet. He was also a footsoldier in the army of Rome which seized much of the Mediterranean and fought the Carthaginians. The bulk of his epic poem Annales, *together with its narrative coherence is lost; but the surviving lines show well the martial culture and burgeoning confidence of the early Romans.*

To men of fortitude is fortune granted.

The bristling spears of the warriors crowded thick upon the plain.

The line of lancers scattered its lances; came a rain-storm of iron.

These the Poeni[1] houghed, wicked haughty foes.

They gave chase: with mightiest clatter their hoofs shook the ground.

[1] "Poeni" – Carthaginians

"Many things does one day bring about in war . . . and many fortunes through chance sink low again. In no wise has fortune followed any man all his days."

The soldiers struggled with sturdy strength.

Go on, O Muse, to tell what each commander of the Romans wrought with his troops in war with King Philip.

He was watching the mettle of his army, waiting to see if they would grumble, saying "what rest will there be at last from our fighting, or end to our hard toil?"

The commander . . . cheers and cheers them on.

Then he led some eight thousand warriors, wearing badges, chosen men, strong to bear war well.

Says he, "Give them destruction, Jupiter, with utter hell!"

Then the round shields resounded, and the iron spear-points whizzed; and the spear, shot into his breast, whizzed as it sped through.

One man by his delays restored the state;
Hearsay he would not put before our safety;
Hence to this day the warrior's glory shines—
In after time, and more than it shone once.
Yes, all those victors, every single soul,
Contented from the bottom of their hearts—
Sleep on a sudden, over all the plain,
Most soft thrilled tingling through them, tended well
By wine.

"It is the part of commanders who are men of deeds, to keep discipline . . . in the place where my very duty displays itself and commands me."

From all sides the javelins like a rain-storm showered in upon the tribune, and pierced his buckler; then jangled the emboss-ment under spears, the helmet too with brassy clang; but not one of them, though strain they did from every side, could rend apart his body with the iron. Every time he shakes and breaks the waves of lances; sweat covers all his body; he is hard distressed; to breathe he has not a chance. The iron came flying as the Histrians cast the spears from their hands to harass him.

He tumbled and withal his armour dinned over him.

The horsemen charged, and the beating of their hollow hoofs shook the ground.

They rushed together as when the breath of the showery Wind of the South and the Wind of the North with his counterblast strive to upheave billows on the mighty main.

Uproars to heaven the shout that rose from either side.

No, it is not meet that good warriors should mumble; warriors who, straining in the toil of battle-fields, have given birth to deeds.

Nor do their firm bodies languish at all.

When the sunny days shall make them lengthen long.

On manners and on men of good old time
Stands firm the Roman State.

Brave are the Romans as the sky's profound
When the commander sets forth with his hosts,
Nor any fear holds them; trusting in their valiance, they rest.

"He who has conquered is not conqueror
Unless the conquered one confesses it"

The best youth of Rome with fine spirit
Sword-girt and slender round the waist.
girt round their hearts with broadswords.
and the light-armed followed in lances.

The skirmishers, holding broad cutting-spears, advanced in a body.

. . . which come sturdily; the fire-spear was hurled

Blunted back were spears that clashed against oncoming spears

And when his head was falling, the trumpet finished alone its tune; and even as the warrior did perish, a hoarse blare sped from the brass.

Hereupon foot pressed foot and weapons weapons rubbed, and warrior warrior thronged.

Here now our men gave way a little while.

"Whither go you all so rashly?"

Order was given to stand and delve into their bodies with spears.

Let chariots of wrathfulness loose like a flood.

PORTRAIT OF A SLAVE-OWNER, c. 201 BC

Titus Maccius Plautus

The great expansion in slavery, which had been known to Rome's remotest past, came with the Roman victories of the third and second centuries BC. The First Punic War alone provided 75,000 prisoners who were sold to Roman masters. At one stage, the slave pens at the market of Capua were handling 20,000 instrumentum vocale (literally "talking tools") a day. As Plautus' comedy Pseudolus makes plain, the enslaved were routinely meted out brutal, and capricious treatment. In all probability, Roman treatment of slaves became progressively worse in the centuries after Plautus.

Ballio [A cruel slave-owner addressing his servants]

Get out, come, out with you, you rascals; kept at a loss, and bought at a loss. Not one of you dreams minding your business, or being a bit of use to me, unless I carry on thus! [*He strikes his whip around on all of them.*] Never did I see men more like asses than you! Why, your ribs are hardened with the stripes. If one flogs you, he hurts himself the most. [*Aside.*] Regular whipping posts are they all, and all they do is to pilfer, purloin, prig, plunder, drink, eat, and abscond! Oh! they *look* decent enough; but they're cheats in their conduct.

[*Addresses the slaves again.*] Now unless you're all attention, unless you get that sloth and drowsiness out of your breasts and eyes, I'll have your sides so thoroughly marked with thongs, that you'll outvie those Campanian coverlets in colour, or a regular Alexandrian tapestry, purple-broidered all over with beasts. Yesterday I gave each of you his special job, but you're so worthless, neglectful, stubborn, that I must remind you with a good basting. So you think, I guess, you'll get the better of this whip and of me – by your stout hides! Zounds! But your hides won't prove harder than my good cowhide. [*He flourishes it.*] Look at this, please! Give heed to this! [*He flogs one slave.*] Well? Does it hurt? . . . Now stand all of you here, you race born to be thrashed! Turn your ears this way! Give heed to what I say. You fellow that's got the pitcher, fetch the water. Take care the kettle's full instanter. You who's got the ax, look after chopping the wood.

Slave. But this ax's edge is blunted.

Ballio. Well; be it so! And so are you blunted with stripes, but is that any reason why you shouldn't work for me? I order that you clean up the house. You know your business; hurry indoors. [*Exit first slave.*]

Now you [*to another slave*] smooth the couches, [for the dinner party]. Clean the plate and put in proper order. Take care that when I'm back from the Forum I find things *done*, – all swept, sprinkled, scoured, smoothed, cleaned, and set in order. To-day's my birthday. You should all set to and celebrate it. Take care – do you hear – to lay the salted bacon, the brawn, the collared neck, and the udder in water. I want to entertain some fine gentlemen in real style, to give the idea that I'm rich. Get in doors, and get these things ready, so there's no delay when the cook comes. I'm going to market to buy what fish is to be had. Boy, you go ahead [*to a special valet*], I've got to take care that no one cuts off my purse.

HOW TO KEEP A SLAVE, C. 170 BC

Cato the Elder

From Cato's farming treatise De Agri Cultura, *the oldest complete work of Latin prose extant. In it Cato recommends that slaves be kept to the same standards as livestock. On his own estate he allowed slaves to copulate with each other – in return for a fee or service paid to himself.*

Country slaves ought to receive in the winter, when they are at work, four modii[1] of grain; and four modii and a half during the summer. The superintendent, the housekeeper, the watchman, and the shepherd get three modii; slaves in chains four pounds of bread in winter and five pounds from the time when the work of training the vines ought to begin until the figs have ripened.

Wine for the slaves. After the vintage let them drink from the sour wine for three months. The fourth month let them have a

---

[1] Modius = about a quarter bushel.

hemina (about half a pint) per day or two *congii* and a half (over seven quarts) per month. During the fifth, sixth, seventh, and eighth months let them have a *sextarius* (about a pint) per day or five congii per month. Finally, in the ninth, tenth, and the eleventh, let them have three *heminæ* (three fourths of a quart) per day, or an *amphora* (about six gallons) per month. On the Saturnalia and on "Compitalia" each man should have a *congius* (something under three quarts).

To feed the slaves. Let the olives that drop of themselves be kept so far as possible. Keep too those harvested olives that do not yield much oil, and husband them, for they last a long time. When the olives have been consumed, give out the brine and vinegar. You should distribute. to every one a sextarius (about a pint) of oil per month. A modius (quarter bushel) of salt apiece is enough for a year.

As for clothes, give out a tunic of three feet and a half, and a cloak (*sagum*) once in two years. When you give a tunic or cloak take back the old ones, to make cassocks (?) out of. Once in two years, good shoes should be given.

Winter wine for the slaves. Put in a wooden cask ten parts of must (non-fermented wine) and two parts of very pungent vinegar, and add two parts of boiled wine and fifty of sweet water. With a paddle mix all these thrice per day for five days in succession. Add one forty-eighth of sea-water drawn some time earlier. Place the lid on the cask and let it ferment for ten days. This wine will last until the solstice. If any remains after that time, it will make very sharp excellent vinegar.

PURCHASING A FARM, C. 170 BC

Cato the Elder

The Roman senator Cato came of peasant stock, which partly explains his long interest in farming, epitomised by the treatise De Agri Cultura. *Another reason was more compelling; farming was the only lawful business activity allowed to senators of Rome.*

When you are thinking of buying a farm, be sure not to complete the purchase over-hastily, take every trouble to visit it, and do not be satisfied with a single tour of inspection. If it is a good property, the more often you go, the more satisfaction it will give you. Pay attention to how the neighbours' farms look. In a good district they ought to look very well. Be sure not to commit yourself, but go into the farm and inspect it, leaving yourself a way of getting out of the deal. It should have a good climate and be free from storms, and the soil should be naturally fertile. If possible, the foot of a hill is best, facing south in a healthy spot, with a good supply of labourers. The water supply must be plentiful, and it must be near a large town, or the sea or a navigable river, or a good well-used road. You want your farm to be in a district where land does not frequently change hands, and where people regret having sold their property. Be sure that the buildings are in good condition, and do not be over-hasty in rejecting a former owner's advice or methods. A better purchase can be made from a man who is a good farmer and a good builder. When you visit the property, look around to see how many oil-presses and wine-vats there are. If the number is small, then you will know that the harvest is proportionately meagre. The farm should not necessarily have masses of equipment, but it must be well-sited. Take care to see that equipment is kept to a minimum to avoid extravagance on the land. Remember that fields are like men; however much profit they make, if they are extravagant, not much is left.

If I were asked what is the best kind of farm, I would suggest a vineyard of about 65 acres in the best situation with various types of soil, if, that is, the wine is good and plentiful. Next to it comes a watered garden, third an osier-bed, fourth an olive grove, fifth pasturage, sixth arable land, seventh a wood for timber, eighth an orchard and ninth a wood for acorns for feed.

Tunics, togas, cloaks, aprons and clogs can be bought at Rome; caps, iron tools, scythes, spades, hoes, axes, harness, ornaments and chains at Cales or Minturnae; spades at Venafrum; carts and drags at Suessa or in Lucania; jars and pots at Alba Longa or Rome; tiles at Venafrum. Ploughs bought at Rome are best for tough soil, Campanian ones for rich dark soil. Roman yokes are the best. Detachable plough-shares are preferable. It is better to buy oil-mills at Pompeii and at Rufus's yard at Nola; nails and bars at Rome; pails, olive vessels, water pitchers, wine urns and other bronze vessels at Capua or Nola. Campanian baskets from Capua are useful. Pulley ropes and all other ropes can be had from Capua, and Roman baskets at Suessa. Lucius Tunnius of Casinum and Gaius, son of Lucius Mennius, of Venafrum make the best ropes for the wine-press.

BRINGING UP CHILDREN, C. 166 BC

Terence

Terence was a North African slave who was educated by his master, Senator P. Terentius Lucanus, and eventually freed by him. Six of Terence's dramatic comedies are extant, among them The Brothers. *The speaker is Micio, a gadabout bachelor who has brought up his nephew as his adoptive son.*

Micio. In my view honour and gentlemanly feeling are better curbs on a gentleman's son than fear. My brother and I disagree in this, he is quite against this view. He comes to me perpetually, crying, "What are you about, Micio? Why are you bringing the boy to ruin on our hands? Why this licence? Why these drinking parties? Why do you pile him up the guineas for such a life and let him spend so much at the tailor's? It's extremely silly of you." He himself is extremely hard, past right and sense, and in my opinion it's a great mistake to suppose that the authority which is founded on force has more weight and stability than that which hangs by the link of friendliness. My system, my theory, is this: he who does his duty under the lash of punishment has no dread except in the thought of detection; if he thinks he won't be found out, back he goes to his natural bent. When you link a son to you by kindness, there is sincerity in all his acts, he sets himself to make a return, and will be the same behind your back as to your face. That's the spirit of a true father, to accustom his son to do right rather by his own inclination than by fear of another, and that's the difference between the parent of sons and the owner of slaves.

THE HARVEST RITUAL, C. 160 BC

Cato the Elder

Before the harvest the sacrifice of the pig must be offered in this manner: Offer a sow as *porca praecidanea* to Ceres before you harvest spelt, wheat, barley, beans, and rape seed. Offer a prayer, with incense and wine, to Janus, Jupiter and Juno, before offering the sow. Offer a pile of cakes to Janus, saying, "Father Janus, in offering these cakes to you, I humbly pray that you will be propitious and merciful to me and my children, my house and my household." Then make an offering of cake to Jupiter with these words: "In offering you this cake, O Jupiter, I humbly pray that you, pleased with this offering, will be propitious and merciful to me and my children, my house and my household." Then present the wine to Janus, saying: "Father Janus, as I have prayed humbly in offering you the cakes, so may you in the same way be honoured by this wine now placed before you." Then pray to Jupiter thus: "Jupiter, may you be honoured in accepting this cake; may you be honoured in accepting the wine placed before you." Then sacrifice the *porca praecidanea*. When the entrails have been removed, make an offering of cakes to Janus, and pray in the same way as you have prayed before. Offer a cake to Jupiter, praying just as before. In the same way offer wine to Janus and offer wine to Jupiter, in the same way as before in offering the pile of cakes, and in the consecration of the cake. Afterward offer the entrails and wine to Ceres.

REWARD FOR CAPTURE: RUNAWAY SLAVES, 156 BC

Anon

Ill-treatment caused many slaves to abscond and live underground. The high reward for the return of the runaways below suggests they were unusually valuable instrumentum vocale.

A slave named Hermon, also answering to Nilos, belonging to Aristognus, the son of Chrysippus, the Alabandan ambassador in Alexandria, has run away. A Syrian by birth from Bombyce, he is eighteen years old, of medium height, clean shaven, thin legged, with a dimple on his chin, a mole on the left side of his nose, and a scar on the left of his face above the lips, with two foreign signs tattoed on his right wrist. He took with him three boxes of coined gold, ten pearls, and an iron ring on which were a flask and strigils. He was wearing a chlamys and a loin-cloth. Anyone who apprehends him shall receive three talents, two talents for pointing him out in sanctuary, or five talents for showing him to be at the house of a man answerable at law. Information should be lodged with the general's secretary.

Another slave, Bion, the property of Callicrates, a chief equerry at court, ran away with him. He is short in stature, broad across the shoulders, with fat legs and bright eyes. When he left he was wearing an himation and a slave's cloak, and took a woman's dress worth nearly seven talents of copper. The same rewards as above are offered for his arrest. Information to be lodged with the general's secretary.

THE PUNIC WARS: SCIPIO DELIVERS THE FINAL ATTACK ON CARTHAGE, 146 BC

Polybius

Having got within the walls, while the Carthaginians still held out on the citadel, Scipio found that the arm of the sea which intervened was not at all deep; and upon Polybius advising him to set it with iron spikes or drive sharp wooden stakes into it, to prevent the enemy crossing it and attacking the mole [the mole of huge stones constructed to block up the mouth of the harbour], he said that, having taken the walls and got inside the city, it would be ridiculous to take measures to avoid fighting the enemy . . .

The pompous Hasdrubal threw himself on his knees before the Roman commander, quite forgetful of his proud language . . . When the Carthaginian commander thus threw himself as a suppliant at Scipio's knees, the proconsul with a glance at those present said: "See what Fortune is, gentlemen! What an example she makes of irrational men! This is the Hasdrubal who but the other day disdained the large favours which I offered him, and said that the most glorious funeral pyre was one's country and its burning ruins. Now he comes with suppliant wreaths, beseeching us for spare life and resting all his hopes on us. Who would not learn from such a spectacle that a mere man should never say or do anything presumptuous?" Then some of the deserters came to the edge of the roof and begged the front ranks of the assailants to hold their hands for a little; and, on Scipio ordering a halt, they began abusing Hasdrubal, some for his perjury, declaring that he had sworn again and again on the altars that he would never abandon them, and others for his cowardice and utter baseness: and they did this in the most unsparing language, and with the bitterest terms of abuse. And just at this moment Hasdrubal's wife, seeing him seated in front of the enemy with Scipio, advanced in front of the deserters, dressed in noble and dignified attire herself, but holding in her hands, on either side, her two boys dressed only in short tunics and shielded under her own robes. First she addressed Hasdrubal by his name, and when he said nothing but remained with his head bowed to the ground, she began by calling on the name of the gods, and next thanked Scipio warmly because, as far as he could secure it, both she and her children were saved. And then, pausing for a short time, she asked Hasdrubal how he had had the heart to secure this favour from the Roman general for himself alone, and, leaving his fellow-citizens who trusted in him in the most miserable plight, had gone over secretly to the enemy? And how he had the assurance to be sitting there holding suppliant boughs, in the face of the very men to whom he had frequently said that the day would never come in which the sun would see Hasdrubal alive and his native city in flames . . .

After an interview with [Scipio], in which he was kindly treated, Hasdrubal desired leave to go away from the town . . .

At the sight of the city utterly perishing amidst the flames Scipio burst into tears, and stood long reflecting on the inevitable change which awaits cities, nations, and dynasties, one and all, as it does every one of us men. This, he thought, had befallen Ilium, once a powerful city, and the once mighty empires of the Assyrians, Medes, Persians, and that of Macedonia lately so splendid. And unintentionally or purposely he quoted – the words perhaps escaping him unconsciously –

"The day shall be when holy Troy shall fall
And Priam, lord of spears, and Priam's folk."

And on my asking him boldly (for I had been his tutor) what he meant by these words, he did not name Rome distinctly, but was evidently fearing for her, from this sight of the mutability of human affairs . . . Another still more remarkable saying of his I may record . . . When he had given the order for firing the town he immediately turned round and grasped me by the hand and said: "O Polybius, it is a grand thing, but, I know not how, I feel a terror and dread, lest some one should one day give the same order about my own native city." . . . Any observation more practical or sensible it is not easy to make. For in the midst of supreme success for one's self and of disaster for the enemy, to take thought of one's own position and of the possible reverse which may come, and in a word to keep well in mind in the midst of prosperity the mutability of Fortune, is the character-istic of a great man, a man free from weaknesses and worthy to be remembered.

"MEN READY TO ENDURE ANYTHING": THE SUPERIORITY OF THE ROMANS, c. 140 BC

Polybius

A Romanophile, the Greek historian Polybius intended his History *to explain Rome's dominance over the civilized world.*

52. If we look however at separate details, for instance at the provisions for carrying on a war, we shall find that whereas for a naval expedition the Carthaginians are the better trained and prepared, – as it is only natural with a people with whom it has been hereditary for many generations to practise this craft, and to follow the seaman's trade above all nations in the world, – yet, in regard to military service on land, the Romans train themselves to a much higher pitch than the Carthaginians. The former bestow their whole attention upon this department:

whereas the Carthaginians wholly neglect their infantry, though they do take some slight interest in the cavalry. The reason of this is that they employ foreign mercenaries, the Romans native and citizen levies. It is in this point that the latter polity is preferable to the former. They have their hopes of freedom ever resting on the courage of mercenary troops: the Romans on the valour of their own citizens and the aid of their allies. The result is that even if the Romans have suffered a defeat at first, they renew the war with undiminished forces, which the Carthaginians cannot do. For, as the Romans are fighting for country and children, it is impossible for them to relax the fury of their struggle; but they persist with obstinate resolution until they have overcome their enemies. What has happened in regard to their navy is an instance in point. In skill the Romans are much behind the Carthaginians, as I have already said; yet the upshot of the whole naval war has been a decided triumph for the Romans, owing to the valour of their men. For although nautical science contributes largely to success in seafights, still it is the courage of the marines that turns the scale most decisively in favour of victory. The fact is that Italians as a nation are by nature superior to Phoenicians and Libyans both in physical strength and courage; but still their habits also do much to inspire the youth with enthusiasm for such exploits. One example will be sufficient of the pains taken by the Roman state to turn out men ready to endure anything to win a reputation in their country for valour.

53. Whenever one of their illustrious men dies, in the course of his funeral, the body with all its paraphernalia is carried into the forum to the Rostra, as a raised platform there is called, and sometimes is propped upright upon it so as to be conspicuous, or, more rarely, is laid upon it. Then with all the people standing round, his son, if he has left one of full age and he is there, or, failing him, one of his relations, mounts the Rostra and delivers a speech concerning the virtues of the deceased, and the successful exploits performed by him in his lifetime. By these means the people are reminded of what has been done, and made to see it with their own eyes, – not only such as were engaged in the actual transactions but those also who were not; – and their sympathies are so deeply moved, that the loss

appears not to be confined to the actual mourners, but to be a public one affecting the whole people. After the burial and all the usual ceremonies have been performed, they place the likeness of the deceased in the most conspicuous spot in his house, surmounted by a wooden canopy or shrine. This likeness consists of a mask made to represent the deceased with extraordinary fidelity both in shape and colour. These likenesses they display at public sacrifices adorned with much care. And when any illustrious member of the family dies, they carry these masks to the funeral, putting them on men whom they thought as like the originals as possible in height and other personal peculiarities. And these substitutes assume clothes according to the rank of the person represented: if he was a consul or praetor, a toga with purple stripes; if a censor, whole purple; if he had also celebrated a triumph or performed any exploit of that kind, a toga embroidered with gold. These representatives also ride themselves in chariots, while the fasces and axes, and all the other customary insignia of the particular offices, lead the way, according to the dignity of the rank in the state enjoyed by the deceased in his lifetime; and on arriving at the Rostra they all take their seats on ivory chairs in their order. There could not easily be a more inspiring spectacle than this for a young man of noble ambitions and virtuous aspirations. For can we conceive any one to be unmoved at the sight of all the likenesses collected together of the men who have earned glory, all as it were living and breathing? Or what could be a more glorious spectacle?

54. Besides the speaker over the body about to be buried, after having finished the panegyric of this particular person, starts upon the others whose representatives are present, beginning with the most ancient, and recounts the successes and achievements of each. By this means the glorious memory of brave men is continually renewed; the fame of those who have performed any noble deed is never allowed to die; and the renown of those who have done good service to their country becomes a matter of common knowledge to the multitude; and part of the heritage of posterity. But the chief benefit of the ceremony is that it inspires young men to shrink from no exertion for the general welfare, in the hope of obtaining the glory which awaits the brave. And what I say is confirmed by

this fact. Many Romans have volunteered to decide a whole battle by single combat; not a few have deliberately accepted certain death, some in time of war to secure the safety of the rest, some in time of peace to preserve the safety of the common-wealth. There have also been instances of men in office putting their own sons to death, in defiance of every custom and law, because they rated the interests of their country higher than those of natural ties even with their nearest and dearest. There are many stories of this kind, related of many men in Roman history; but one will be enough for our present purpose . . . When Hannibal, after conquering the Romans in the battle at Cannae, got possession of the eight thousand who were guard-ing the Roman camp, he made them all prisoners of war, and granted them permission to send messages to their relations that they might be ransomed and return home. They accordingly selected ten of their chief men, whom Hannibal allowed to depart after binding them with an oath to return. But one of them, just as he had got outside the palisade of the camp, saying that he had forgotten something, went back; and, having got what he had left behind, once more set out, under the belief that by means of this return he had kept his promise and discharged his oath. Upon the arrival of the envoys at Rome, imploring and beseeching the Senate not to grudge the captured troops their return home, but to allow them to rejoin their friends by paying three minae each for them, – for these were the terms, they said, granted by Hannibal, – and declaring that the men deserved redemption, for they had neither played the coward in the field, nor done anything unworthy of Rome, but had been left behind to guard the camp; and that, when all the rest had perished, they had yielded to absolute necessity in surrendering to Hannibal: though the Romans had been severely defeated in the battles, and though they were at the time deprived of, roughly speaking, all their allies, they neither yielded so far to misfortune as to disregard what was becoming to themselves, nor omitted to take into account any necessary consideration. They saw through Hannibal's purpose in thus acting, – which was at once to get a large supply of money, and at the same time to take away all enthusiasm from the troops opposed to him, by showing that even the conquered had a hope of getting safe home again. Therefore the Senate, far from acceding to the request, refused all pity even to their own relations, and disregarded the services to be expected from these men in the future: and thus frustrated Hannibal's calculations, and the hopes which he had founded on these prisoners, by refusing to ransom them; and at the same time established the rule for their own men, that they must either conquer or die on the field, as there was no other hope of safety for them if they were beaten. With this answer they dismissed the nine envoys who returned of their own accord; but the tenth who had put the cunning trick in practice for discharging himself of his oath they put in chains and delivered to the enemy. So that Hannibal was not so much rejoiced at his victory in the battle, as struck with astonishment at the unshaken firmness and lofty spirit displayed in the resolutions of these senators.

"I APPEAL TO YOU TO ELECT": ELECTION GRAFFITI, POMPEII, C. 80 BC

Anon

Pompeii was buried by volcanic lava and ash in AD 79. Below are wall graffiti found in the excavated ruins of Pompeii, announcing the various attributes (or not) of candidates for the annual magistracy of c. 80 BC.

1. Numerius Barcha, a fine man; I appeal to you to elect him member of the Board of Duoviri. So may Venus of Pompeii, holy, hallowed goddess, be kind to you.
2. Numerius Veius Barcha, may you rot!
3. Numerius Veius, a fine man; settlers, I appeal to you to elect him member of the Board of Duoviri.
4. Your best friend – Marcus Marius. Elect him Aedile.
5. Marcus Marius, a fine man: I appeal to you, settlers.
6. Quintus Caecilius, a generous man. To be Quaestor, I appeal to you.
7. Quintus Caecilius, a fair and generous man. To be Quaestor.

The below election daubings are from a much later date.

8. The muleteers ask for Gaius Julius Polybius as a member of the Board of Duoviri.

9. I appeal to you to elect Gaius Julius Polybius Aedile: he makes good bread.

10. I appeal to you to elect Marcus Cerrenius Vatia Aedile; all members of the "late-drinkers" club ask for this.

SPARTACUS REVOLTS, 73 BC

Plutarch

Slave disturbances were a fact of Roman life from 198 BC onwards. The most dangerous of the revolts came in 73 BC, under the leadership of a Thracian gladiator named Spartacus.

The insurrection of the gladiators and the devastation of Italy, commonly called the war of Spartacus, began upon this occasion. One Lentulus Batiates trained up a great many gladiators in Capua, most of them Gauls and Thracians, who, not for any fault by them committed, but simply through the cruelty of their master, were kept in confinement for the object of fighting one with another. Two hundred of these formed a plan to escape, but their plot being discovered, those of them who became aware of it in time to anticipate their master, being seventy-eight, got out of a cook's shop chopping knives and spits, and made their way through the city, and lighting by the way on several wagons that were carrying gladiators' arms to another city, they seized upon them and armed themselves. And seizing upon a defensible place, they chose three captains, of whom Spartacus was chief, a Thracian of one of the nomad tribes, and a man not only of high spirit and valiaut, but in understanding, also, and in gentleness, superior to his condition, and more of a Grecian than the people of his country usually are.

First, then, routing those that came out of Capua against them, and thus procuring a quantity of proper soldiers' arms, they gladly threw away their own as barbarous and dishonorable. [Two prætors who were sent against them with small armies were defeated, while a third general's army was routed and himself slain.] After many successful skirmishes with Varinus, the prætor, himself, in one of which Spartacus took his lictors and his own horse, he began to be great and terrible; but wisely considering that he was not to expect to match the force of the empire, he marched his army towards the Alps, intending, when he had passed them, that every man should go to his own home, some to Thrace, some to Gaul. But they, grown confident in their numbers, and puffed up with their success, would give no obedience to him, but went about and ravaged Italy; so that now the Senate was not only moved at the indignity and baseness, both of the enemy and of the insurrection, but, looking upon it as a matter of alarm and of dangerous consequence, sent out both the consuls to it, as to a great and difficult enterprise. The consul Gellius, falling suddenly upon a party of Germans, who through contempt and confidence had straggled from Spartacus, cut them all to pieces. But when Lentulus with a large army besieged Spartacus, he sallied out upon him, and, joining battle, defeated his chief officers, and captured all his baggage. As he made towards the Alps, Cassius, who was prætor of that part of Gaul that lies about the Po, met him with ten thousand men, but being overcome in battle, he had much ado to escape himself, with the loss of a great many of his men.

The Senate in disgust now sent Crassus against the rebels. Spartacus, however, defeated Mummius, Crassus's lieutenant, and the general had to restore discipline among the demoralized Romans by executing fifty who had begun the flight; later he advanced again . . . but Spartacus retreated through Lucania toward the sea, and in the straits, meeting with some Cilician pirate ships, he had thoughts of attempting Sicily, where, by landing two thousand men, he hoped to kindle anew the war of the slaves, which was but lately extinguished, and seemed to need but a little fuel to set it burning again. But after the pirates had struck a bargain with him, and received his earnest, they deceived him and sailed away. He thereupon retired again from the sea, and established his army in the peninsula of Rhegium. Here Crassus tried to blockade him. Spartacus escaped with part of his army to Lucania, but some of Spartacus's followers mutinied, and left him. This division of malcontents was soon destroyed by Crassus.

Spartacus, after this discomfiture, retired to the mountains of Petelia, but Quintius, one of Crassus's officers, and Scrofa, the quæstor, pursued and overtook him. But when Spartacus rallied and faced them, they were utterly routed and fled, and had much ado to carry off their quæstor, who was wounded. This success, however, ruined Spartacus, because it encouraged the slaves, who now disdained any longer to avoid fighting, or to obey their officers, but as they were upon their march, they came to them with their swords in their hand, and compelled them to lead them back again through Lucania, against the Romans, the very thing which Crassus was eager for. For news was already brought that Pompey [Crassus's rival for military glory] was at hand; and people began to talk openly that the honour of this war was reserved for him, who would come and at once oblige the enemy to fight and put an end to the war. Crassus, therefore, eager to fight a decisive battle, encamped very near the enemy, and began to make lines of circumvallation; but the slaves made a sally, and attacked the pioneers. As fresh supplies came in on either side, Spartacus, seeing there was no avoiding it, set all his army in array, and when his horse was brought him, he drew out his sword and killed him, saying, if he got the day, he should have a great many better horses of the enemies, and if he lost it, he should have no need of this. And so making directly towards Crassus himself, through the midst of arms and wounds, he missed him, but slew two centurions that fell upon him together. At last, being deserted by those that were about him, he himself stood his ground, and, surrounded by the enemy, bravely defending himself, was cut in pieces.

"SURELY NOTHING CAN BE SWEETER THAN LIBERTY": CICERO ON THE REPUBLIC, c. 70 BC

Cicero

The orator and advocate Marcus Tullius Cicero (106–43 BC) was a leading defender of the Republic in its twilight. His famous treatise on the constitution, De Republica, *took the form of an imaginary dialogue between men of the previous generation. Scipio Aemilianus was the voice of Cicero himself.*

XXXI. SCIPIO: . . . and every State is such as its ruler's character and will make it. Hence liberty has no dwelling-place in any State except that in which the people's power is the greatest, and surely nothing can be sweeter than liberty; but if it is not the same for all, it does not deserve the name of liberty. And how can it be the same for all, I will not say in a kingdom, where there is no obscurity or doubt about the slavery of the subject, but even in States where everyone is ostensibly free? I mean States in which the people vote, elect commanders and officials, are canvassed for their votes, and have bills proposed to them, but really grant only what they would have to grant even if they were unwilling to do so, and are asked to give to others what they do not possess themselves. For they have no share in the governing power, in the deliberative function, or in the courts, over which selected judges preside, for those privileges are granted on the basis of birth or wealth. But in a free nation, such as the Rhodians or the Athenians, there is not one of the citizens who [may not hold the offices of State and take an active part in the government.] . . .

XXXII. Our authorities say [that] when one person or a few stand out from the crowd as richer and more prosperous, then, as a result of the haughty and arrogant behaviour of these, there arises [a government of one or a few], the cowardly and weak giving way and bowing down to the pride of wealth. But if the people would maintain their rights, they say that no form of government would be superior, either in liberty or happiness, for they themselves would be masters of the laws and the courts, of war and peace, of international agreements, and of every citizen's life and property; this government alone, they believe, can rightly be called a commonwealth, that is, "the property of the people". And it is for that reason, they say, that "the property of the people" is often liberated from the domination of kings or senators, while free peoples do not seek kings or the power and wealth of aristocracies. And indeed they claim that this free popular government ought not to be entirely rejected on account of the excesses of an unbridled mob, for, according to them, when a sovereign people is pervaded by a spirit of harmony and tests every measure by the standard of their own safety and liberty, no form of government is less subject to change or more stable. And they insist that harmony is very easily obtainable in a State where the interests of all are the same, for discord arises from conflicting interests, where different measures are advantageous to different citizens. Therefore they maintain that when a senate has been supreme, the State has never had a stable government, and that such stability is less attainable by far in kingdoms . . . Therefore, since law is the bond which unites the civic association, and the justice enforced by law is the same for all, by what justice can an association of citizens be held together when there is no equality among the citizens? For if we cannot agree to equalize men's wealth, and equality of innate ability is impossible, the legal rights at least of those who are citizens of the same commonwealth ought to be equal. For what is a State except an association or partnership in justice? . . .

XXXIII . . . Indeed they think that States of the other kinds have no right at all to the names which they arrogate to themselves. For why should I give the name of king, the title of Jupiter the Best, to a man who is greedy for personal power and absolute authority, a man who lords it over an oppressed people? Should I not rather call him tyrant? For tyrants may be merciful as well as oppressive; so that the only difference between the nations governed by these rulers is that between the slaves of a kind and those of a cruel master; for in any case the subjects must be slaves. And how could Sparta, at the time when the mode of life inculcated by her constitution was considered so excellent, be assured of always having good and just kings, when a person of any sort, if he was born of the royal family, had to be accepted as king? As to aristocrats, who could tolerate men that have claimed the title without the people's acquiescence, but merely by their own will? For how is a man adjudged to be "the best"? On the basis of knowledge, skill, learning, [and similar qualities surely, not because of his own desire to possess the title] . . .

XXXIV . . . If [the State] leaves [the selection of its rulers] to chance, it will be as quickly overturned as a ship whose pilot should be chosen by lot from among the passengers. But if a free people chooses the men to whom it is to entrust its fortunes, and, since it desires its own safety, chooses the best men, then certainly the safety of the State depends upon the wisdom of its best men, especially since Nature has provided not only that those men who are superior in virtue and in spirit should rule the weaker, but also that the weaker should be willing to obey the stronger.

But they claim that this ideal form of State has been rejected on account of the false notions of men, who, through their ignorance of virtue – for just as virtue is possessed by only a few, so it can be distinguished and perceived by only a few – think that the best men are those who are rich, prosperous, or born of famous families. For when, on account of this mistaken notion of the common people, the State begins to be ruled by the riches, instead of the virtue, of a few men, these rulers tenaciously retain the title, though they do not possess the character, of the "best". For riches, names, and power, when they lack wisdom and the knowledge of how to live and to rule over others, are full of dishonour and insolent pride, nor is there any more depraved type of State than that in which the richest are accounted the best. But what can be nobler than the government of the State by virtue? For then the man who rules others is not himself a slave to any passion, but has already acquired for himself all those qualities to which he is training and summoning his fellows. Such a man imposes no laws upon the people that he does not obey himself, but puts his own life before his fellow-citizens as their law. If a single individual of this character could order all things properly in a State, there would be no need of more than one ruler; or if the citizens as a body could see what was best and agree upon it, no one would desire a selected group of rulers. It has been the difficulty of formulating policies that has transferred the power from a king to a larger number; and the perversity and rashness of popular assemblies that have transferred it from the many to the few. Thus, between the weakness of a single ruler and the rashness of the many, aristocracies have occupied that intermediate position which represents the utmost moderation; and in a State ruled by its best men, the citizens must necessarily enjoy the greatest happiness, being freed from all cares and worries, when once they have entrusted the preservation of their tranquillity to others, whose duty it is to guard it vigilantly and never to allow the people to think that their interests are being neglected by their rulers. For that equality of legal rights of which free peoples are so fond cannot be maintained (for the people themselves, though free and unrestrained, give very many special powers to many individuals, and create great distinctions among men and the honours granted to them), and what is called equality is really most inequitable. For when equal honour is given to the highest and the lowest – for men of both types must exist in every nation – then this very "fairness" is most unfair; but this cannot happen in States ruled by their best citizens. These arguments and others like them, Laelius, are approximately those which are advanced by men who consider this form of government the best.

XXXV. LAELIUS: But what about yourself, Scipio? Which of these three forms do you consider the best?

SCIPIO: You are right to ask which I consider the best of the three, for I do not approve of any of them when employed by itself, and consider the form which is a combination of all of them superior to any single one of them. But if I were compelled to approve one single unmixed form, [I might choose] the kingship . . . the name of king seems like that of father to us, since the king provides for the citizens as if they were his own children, and is more eager to protect them than . . . to be sustained by the care of one man who is the most virtuous and most eminent. But here are the aristocrats, with the claim that they can do this more effectively, and that there will be more wisdom in the counsels of several than in those of one man, and an equal amount of fairness and scrupulousness. And here also are the people, shouting with a loud voice that they are willing to obey neither one nor a few, that nothing is sweeter than liberty even to wild beasts, and that all who are slaves, whether to a king or to an aristocracy, are deprived of liberty. Thus kings attract us by our affection for them, aristocracies by their wisdom, and popular governments by their freedom, so that in comparing them it is difficult to say which one prefers.

XLII. When I have set forth my ideas in regard to the form of State which I consider the best, I shall have to take up in greater detail those changes to which States are liable, though I think it will not be at all easy for any such changes to take place in the State which I have in mind. But the first and most certain of these changes is the one that takes place in kingships: when the king begins to be unjust, that form of government is immediately at an end, and the king has become a tyrant. This is the worst sort of government, though closely related to the best. If the best men overthrow it, as usually happens, then the State is in the second of its three stages; for this form is similar to a kingship, being one in which a paternal council of leading men makes good provision for the people's welfare. But if the people themselves have killed or driven out the tyrant, they govern rather moderately, as long as they are wise and prudent, and, delighting in their exploit, they endeavour to maintain the government they have themselves set up. But if the people ever rebel against a just king and deprive him of his kingdom, or, as happens more frequently, taste the blood of the aristocracy and subject the whole State to their own caprices (and do not dream, Laelius, that any sea or any conflagration is so powerful that it cannot be more easily subdued than an unbridled multitude enjoying unwonted power), then we have a condition which is splendidly described by Plato, if only I can reproduce his description in Latin; it is difficult, but I will attempt it. XLIII. He says: "When the insatiable throats of the people have become dry with the thirst for liberty, and, served by evil ministers, they have drained in their thirst a draught of liberty which, instead of being moderately tempered, is too strong for them, then, unless the magistrates and men of high rank are very mild and indulgent, serving them with liberty in generous quantities, the people persecute them, charge them with crime and impeach them, calling them despots, kings, and tyrants." I think you are acquainted with this passage.

Laelius: It is very familiar to me.

Scipio: He continues thus: "Those who follow the lead of prominent citizens are persecuted by such a people and called willing slaves; but those who, though in office, try to act like private citizens, and those private citizens who try to destroy all distinction between a private citizen and a magistrate are praised to the skies and loaded with honours. It necessarily follows in such a State that liberty prevails everywhere, to such an extent that not only are homes one and all without a master, but the vice of anarchy extends even to the domestic animals, until finally the father fears his son, the son flouts his father, all sense of shame disappears, and all is so absolutely free that there is no distinction between citizen and alien; the schoolmaster fears and flatters his pupils, and pupils despise their masters; youths take on the gravity of age, and old men stoop to the games of youth, for fear they may be disliked by their juniors and seem to them too serious. Under such conditions even the slaves come to behave with unseemly freedom, wives have the same rights as their husbands, and in the abundance of liberty even the dogs, the horses, and the asses are so free in their running about that men must make way for them in the streets. Therefore," he concludes, "the final result of this boundless licence is that the minds of the citizens become so squeamish and sensitive that, if the authority of government is exercised in the smallest degree, they become angry and cannot bear it. On this account they begin to neglect the laws as well, and so finally are utterly without a master of any kind."

XLIV. LAELIUS: You have given us his description with great exactness.

SCIPIO: Well, to return now to my own style of discourse, he also says that from this exaggerated licence, which is the only thing such people call liberty, tyrants spring up as from a root, and are, as it were, engendered. For just as an excess of power in the hands of the aristocrats results in the overthrow of an aristocracy, so liberty itself reduces a people who possess it in too great degree to servitude. Thus everything which is in excess – when, for instance, either in the weather, or in the fields, or in men's bodies, conditions have been too favourable – is usually changed into its opposite; and this is especially true in States, where such excess of liberty either in nations or in individuals turns into an excess of servitude. This extreme liberty gives birth to a tyrant and the utterly unjust and cruel servitude of the tyranny. For out of such an ungoverned, or rather, untamed, populace someone is usually chosen as leader against those leading citizens who have already been subjected to persecution and cast down from their leadership – some bold and depraved man, who shamelessly harasses oftentimes even those who have deserved well of the State, and curries favour with the people by bestowing upon them the property of others as well as his own.

To such a man, because he has much reason to be afraid if he remains a private citizen, official power is given and continually renewed; he is also surrounded by armed guards, as was Pisistratus at Athens; and finally he emerges as a tyrant over the very people who have raised him to power. If the better citizens overthrow such a tyrant, as often happens, then the State is re-established; but if it is the bolder sort who do so, then we have that oligarchy which is only a tyranny of another kind. This same form of government also arises from the excellent rule of an aristocracy, when some bad influence turns the leading citizens themselves from the right path. Thus the ruling power of the State, like a ball, is snatched from kings by tyrants, from tyrants by aristocrats or the people, and from them again by an oligarchical faction or a tyrant, so that no single form of government ever maintains itself very long.

XLV. Since this is true, the kingship, in my opinion, is by far the best of the three primary forms, but a moderate and balanced form of government which is a combination of the three good simple forms is preferable even to the kingship. For there should be a supreme and royal element in the State, some power also ought to be granted to the leading citizens, and certain matters should be left to the judgment and desires of the masses. Such a constitution, in the first place, offers in a high degree a sort of equality, which is a thing free men can hardly do without for any considerable length of time, and, secondly, it has stability. For the primary forms already mentioned degenerate easily into the corresponding perverted forms, the king being replaced by a despot, the aristocracy by an oligarchical faction, and the people by a mob and anarchy; but whereas these forms are frequently changed into new ones, this does not usually happen in the case of the mixed and evenly balanced constitution, except through great faults in the governing class. For there is no reason for a change when every citizen is firmly established in his own station, and there underlies it no perverted form into which it can plunge and sink.

XLVI. But I am afraid that you, Laelius, and you, my very dear and learned friends, may think, if I spend more time upon this aspect of the subject, that my discourse is rather that of a master or teacher than of one who is merely considering these matters in company with yourselves. Therefore I will pass to a topic which is familiar to everyone, and which we ourselves discussed some time ago. For I am convinced, I believe, and I declare that no other form of government is comparable, either in its general character, in its distribution of powers, or in the training it gives, with that which our ancestors received from their own forefathers, and have handed down to us. Therefore, if you have no objection – since you have desired to hear me discourse upon matters with which you are already familiar – I will explain the character of this constitution and show why it is the best; and, using our own government as my pattern, I will fit to it, if I can, all I have to say about the ideal State. If I can keep to this intention and carry it through, the task that Laelius has imposed upon me will, in my opinion, have been abundantly accomplished.

XLVII. LAELIUS: The task is yours indeed, Scipio, and yours alone; for who is better qualified than yourself to speak of the institutions of our ancestors, since you yourself are descended from most famous fore-fathers? Or who is better able to speak of the ideal State? For if we are to have such a constitution (surely at present that is not the case), who would be more prominent in its administration than yourself? Or who is better qualified to speak of provisions for the future, when you have provided for all future time by freeing our city from the two dangers that threatened it?

PIRACY IN SICILY, 71 BC

Marcus Cicero

Piracy was a constant problem under the Republic. Eventually, in 67 BC, Pompey was given special powers under Gabinian Law (plus millions of sesterces) and cleared the Mediterranean of sea robbers in three months. Cicero's account of piracy in Sicilian waters is from his prosecution speech against Verres, the governor of Sicily, for extortion.

Cleomenes left harbour on board the quadrireme from Centuripa, followed by ships from Segesta, Tyndaris, Herbita, Heraclea, Apollonia and Haluntium. It had all the appearance of a fine fleet, but was actually feeble and weak because of the leave of absence given to the marines and sailors. Our wonderful, industrious governor only had his eyes on this fleet of his command for as long as it sailed past his notorious debauch. He had not been seen for several days, but he allowed the sailors a brief look at him then, as he, a governor of the Roman people, stood in sandals, a purple cloak and a tunic that reached the ankles, leaning on a woman on the beach. This was the dress in which very many Sicilians and Roman citizens had seen him.

The fleet moved on and finally reached Pachynus after four days' sailing, where the sailors in their agony of hunger collected the roots of the wild palms, which are very plentiful there as in most of Sicily, and on these the poor desperate men fed. Cleomenes, on the other hand, who considered himself a second Verres in point of luxury, wickedness and leadership, drank himself silly all day long in his tent erected on the shore. While he was incapable and the rest starving, news suddenly came of a pirate vessel in the port of Odyssea (our fleet still being at Pachynus). Cleomenes was relying on the theoretical but far from actual existence of some land forces to bring his complement of sailors and oarsmen up to strength. But the same greedy method of Verres was found to have been applied to these as well as to the fleets and there were only a few left, for most had been dismissed. First Cleomenes gave orders for the mast to be raised in his own ship, sails to be set, anchors to be weighed, and instructed the signal to be given for the rest to follow him. This vessel from Centuripa had a remarkable turn of speed under canvas, though no one knew a ship's potential under oars during Verres's governorship, in spite of the fact that Cleomenes was short of fewer oarsmen and marines as a mark of special honour and favour.

The quadrireme quickly disappeared as if in flight, while the remaining ships were struggling in one spot. But they had more courage. Although they were few and their situation critical, they shouted out that they were prepared to fight, and were willing to offer in battle the part of their lives and strength still left to them by hunger. If Cleomenes had not fled so far in front, there could have been some plan for resistance, for his was the only decked ship; it was of such a size that it could have protected the rest, and in a pirate battle would have seemed like a city among those pirate sloops. But hungry, in want, and deserted by their leader and admiral, they could do nothing except begin to follow him on the same course. Like Cleomenes, they made for Helorus, not so much in flight from the pirates' attack as in pursuit of their commander. As each dropped back last of the column, so it came first into danger, as the pirates attacked the rear ship . . . While all this was happening, Cleomenes had reached the shore at Helorus, where he jumped out, leaving the quadrireme wallowing in the sea. The remaining commanders, once their admiral had gone ashore, could not fight back or make their escape by sea, and so they followed Cleomenes to Helorus. Then Heracleo, the pirate chief, suddenly finding himself the victor quite beyond his expectation, not by any valour of his own but because of the greed and wickedness of Verres, gave orders for the glorious fleet of the Roman people to be set on fire and burnt as it lay drawn up on the beach. The time was early evening . . .

News of this dreadful tragedy was brought to Syracuse late at night. Everyone converged on the governor's residence . . . Cleomenes, in spite of the dark, did not dare to show his face in public, but shut himself up at home, without even the company of his wife, who could perhaps have consoled her husband in his misfortune [she was with Verres]. The domestic discipline of our singular governor was so strict that in such a crisis and at the receipt of such momentous news, no one was allowed in, and no one dared to wake Verres from his sleep or interrupt him if awake. When the news was known throughout the city, a great crowd gathered . . . The governor was asked for, and when it was agreed that no one had told him the news, there was a sudden rush on the house . . . While he was still half-asleep in a drunken stupor, the crowd gained control of themselves, took their arms and manned the Forum and the Island, which comprises a great part of the city.

The pirates waited for just one night at Helorus, then left our ships still smouldering and proceeded on their way to Syracuse. The first part they approached was the summer quarters of the governor, that part of the beach where throughout those days he had placed his tents and camp of luxury. They found the spot deserted and, realizing that the governor had moved, they at once began to penetrate quite fearlessly into the harbour itself. When I say the harbour, I mean that the pirates entered the city and the inmost part of the city. For at Syracuse the buildings do not come to an end at the harbour, but the harbour is surrounded by and contained in the town, which means that the edges of the walls are washed by the sea, and the water, as it were, ebbs into a bay formed by the town. Here, under your governorship, Verres, the pirate Heracleo sailed at his fancy with his four little pirate sloops . . . And as he passed the Island, the roots of the wild palms found in our ships were thrown out to let everyone know of the crimes of Verres and the disaster that had come upon Sicily.

LETTER OF MITHRIDATES, C. 69 BC

Sallust

Most of Rome's writers lauded the city's besandalled march to empire. Sallust was one who did not. Roman victories in the East, Sallust recognized, had brought suffering to the conquered. The Letter of Mithridates *is an invention of Sallust's, but the anti-Roman feeling attributed to the king of Pontus is accurate enough. In 69 BC the real Mithridates and his ally Tigranes of Armenia sought succour in their struggle against Rome from Arsaces of Parthia. Sallust imagines what Mithridates' missive to Arsaces might have contained.*

King Mithridates to King Arsaces, Greeting. All those who in the time of their prosperity are asked to form an offensive alliance ought to consider, first, whether it is possible for them to keep peace at that time; and secondly, whether what is asked of them is wholly right and safe, honourable or dishonourable. If it were possible for you to enjoy lasting peace, if no treacherous foes were near your borders, if to crush the Roman power would not bring you glorious fame, I should not venture to sue for your alliance, and it would be vain for me to hope to unite my misfortunes with your prosperity. But the considerations which might seem to give you pause, such as the anger against Tigranes inspired in you by the recent war, and my lack of success, if you but consent to regard them in the right light, will be special incentives. For Tigranes is at your mercy and will accept an alliance on any terms which you may desire, while so far as I am concerned, although Fortune has deprived me of much, she has bestowed upon me the experience necessary for giving good advice; and since I am no longer at the height of my power, I shall serve as an example of how you may conduct your own affairs with more prudence, a lesson highly advantageous to the prosperous.

In fact, the Romans have one inveterate motive for making war upon all nations, peoples and kings; namely, a deep-seated desire for dominion and for riches. Therefore they first began a war with Philip, king of Macedonia, having pretended to be his friends as long as they were hard pressed by the Carthaginians. When Antiochus came to his aid, they craftily diverted him from his purpose by the surrender of Asia, and then, after Philip's power had been broken, Antiochus was robbed of all the territory this side Taurus, and of ten thousand talents. Next Perses, the son of Philip, after many battles with varying results, was formally taken under their protection before the gods of Samothrace; and then those masters of craft and artists in treachery caused his death from want of sleep, since they had made a compact not to kill him. Eumenes, whose friendship they boastfully parade, they first betrayed to Antiochus as the price of peace; later, having made him the guardian of a captured territory, they transformed him by means of imposts and insults from a king into the most wretched of slaves. Then, having forged an unnatural will, they led his son Aristonicus in triumph like an enemy, because he had tried to recover his father's realm. They took possession of Asia, and finally, on the death of Nicomedes, they seized upon all Bithynia, although Nysa, whom Nicomedes had called queen, unquestionably had a son.

Why should I mention my own case? Although I was separated from their empire on every side by kingdoms and tetrarchies, yet because it was reported that I was rich and that I would not be a slave, they provoked me to war through Nicomedes. And I was not unaware of their design, but I had previously given warning of what afterwards happened, both to the Cretans, who alone retained their freedom at that time, and to king Ptolemy. But I took vengeance for the wrongs inflicted upon me; I drove Nicomedes from Bithynia, recovered Asia, the spoil taken from king Antiochus, and delivered Greece from cruel servitude. Further progress was frustrated by Archelaus, basest of slaves, who betrayed my army; and those whom cowardice or misplaced cunning kept from taking up arms, since they hoped to find safety in my misfortunes, are suffering most cruel punishment. For Ptolemy is averting hostilities from day to day by the payment of money, while the Cretans have already been attacked once and will find no respite from war until they are destroyed. As for me, I soon learned that the peace afforded by civil dissensions at Rome was really only a postponement of the struggle, and although Tigranes refused to join with me (he now admits the truth of my prediction when it is too late), though you were far away, and all the rest had submitted, I nevertheless renewed the war and routed Marcus Cotta, the Roman general, on land at Chalcedon, while on the sea I stripped him of a fine fleet. During the delay caused by my siege of Cyzicus with a great army provisions failed me, since no one in the neighbourhood rendered me aid and at the same time winter kept me off the sea. When I, therefore, without compulsion from the enemy, attempted to return into my kingdom, I lost the best of my soldiers and my fleets by shipwrecks at Parium and at Heraclea. Then when I had raised a new army at Cabira and engaged with Lucullus with varying success, scarcity once more attacked us both. He had at his command the kingdom of Ariobarzanes, unravaged by war, while I, since all the country about me had been devastated, withdrew into Armenia. Thereupon the Romans followed me, or rather followed their custom of over-throwing all monarchies, and because they were able to keep from action a huge force hemmed in by narrow defiles, boasted of the results of Tigranes' imprudence as if they had won a victory.

I pray you, then, to consider whether you believe that when we have been crushed you will be better able to resist the Romans, or that there will be an end to the war. I know well that you have great numbers of men and large amounts of arms and gold, and it is for that reason that I seek your alliance and the Romans your spoils. Yet my advice is, while the kingdom of Tigranes is entire, and while I still have soldiers who have been trained in warfare with the Romans, to finish far from your homes and with little labour, at the expense of our bodies, a war in which we cannot conquer or be conquered without danger to you. Do you not know that the Romans turned their arms in this direction only after Ocean had blocked their westward progress? That they have possessed nothing since the beginning of their existence except what they have stolen: their home, their wives, their lands, their empire? Once vagabonds without fatherland, without parents, created to be the scourge of the whole world, no laws, human or divine, prevent them from seizing and destroying allies and friends, those near them and those afar off, weak or powerful, and from considering every government which does not serve them, especially monarchies, as their enemies.

Of a truth, few men desire freedom, the greater part are content with just masters; we are suspected of being rivals of the Romans and future avengers. But you, who possess Seleucea, greatest of cities, and the realm of Perses famed for its riches, what can you expect from them other than guile in the present and war in the future? The Romans have weapons against all men, the sharpest where victory yields the greatest spoils; it is by audacity, by deceit, and by joining war to war that they have grown great. Following their usual custom, they will destroy everything or perish in the attempt . . . and this is not difficult if you on the side of Mesopotamia and we on that of Armenia surround their army, which is without supplies and without allies, and has been saved so far only by its good fortune or by our own errors. You will gain the glory of having rendered aid to great kings and of having crushed the plunderers of all the nations. This is my advice and this course I urge you to follow; do not prefer by our ruin to put off your own for a time rather than by our alliance to conquer.

HOW TO BECOME CONSUL, 64 BC

Quintus Cicero

Advice from Quintus Cicero to his brother, the advocate and orator Marcus Cicero on the latter's candidature for the Consulship. Before the dictatorship

*and the Empire, the Consuls – two were elected annually for a year's service –
were the most important individuals in Rome, invested with command of the
army and execution of the law. Marcus Cicero was successful in his
candidature.*

Almost every day as you go down to the Forum you must say to
yourself, "I am a *novus homo* [i.e. without noble ancestry]." "I
am a candidate for the consulship." "This is Rome." For the
"newness" of your name you will best compensate by the
brilliance of your oratory. This has ever carried with it great
political distinction. A man who is held worthy of defending ex-
consuls, cannot be deemed unworthy of the constitution itself.
Therefore approach each individual case with the persuasion
that on it depends as a whole your entire reputation. For you
have, as few *novi homines* have had – all the tax-syndicate
promoters, nearly the whole equestrian *ordo*, and many municipal towns, especially devoted to you, many people who have
been defended by you, many trade guilds, and besides these a
large number of the rising generation, who have become
attached to you in their enthusiasm for public speaking, and
who visit you daily in swarms, and with such constant regularity!

See that you retain these advantages by reminding these
persons, by appealing to them, and by using every means to
make them understand that this, and this only, is the time for
those who are in your debt now, to show their gratitude, and for
those who wish for your services in the future, to place you
under an obligation. It also seems possible that a *novus homo* may
be much aided by the fact that he has the good wishes of men of
high rank, and especially of ex-consuls. It is a point in your
favour that you should be thought worthy of this position and
rank by the very men to whose position you are wishing to
attain.

All these men must be canvassed with care, agents must be
sent to them, and they must be convinced that we have always
been at one with the *Optimates*, that we have never been
dangerous demagogues in the very least. Also take pains to
get on your side the young men of high rank, and keep the
friendship of those whom you already have. They will con-

tribute much to your political position. Whosoever gives any sign of inclination to you, or regularly visits your house, you must put down in the category of friends. But yet the most advantageous thing is to be beloved and pleasant in the eyes of those who are friends on the more regular grounds of relationship by blood or marriage, the membership in the same club, or some close tie or other. You must take great pains that these men should love you and desire your highest honour.

In a word, you must secure friends of every class, magistrates, consuls and their tribunes to win you the vote of the centuries: men of wide popular influence. Those who either have gained or hope to gain the vote of a tribe or a century, or any other advantage, through your influence, take all pains to collect and to secure. So you see that you will have the votes of all the centuries secured for you by the number and variety of your friends. The first and obvious thing is that you embrace the Roman senators and *equites*, and the active and popular men of all the other orders. There are many city men of good business habits, there are many freedmen engaged in the Forum who are popular and energetic: these men try with all your might, both personally and by common friends, to make eager in your behalf. Seek them out, send agents to them, show them that they are putting you under the greatest possible obligation. After that, review the entire city, all guilds, districts, neighbourhoods. If you can attach to yourself the leading men in these, you will by their means easily keep a hold upon the multitude. When you have done that, take care to have in your mind a chart of all Italy laid out according to the tribes in each town, and learn it by heart, so that you may not allow any chartered town, colony, prefecture – in a word, any spot in Italy to exist, in which you have not a firm foothold.

Trace out also individuals in every region, inform yourself about them, seek them out, secure that in their own districts they shall canvas for you, and be, as it were, candidates in your interest.

After having thus worked for the "rural vote", the centuries of the *equites* too seem capable of being won over if you are careful. And you should be strenuous in seeing as many people as possible every day of every possible class and order, for from the mere numbers of these you can make a guess of the amount of support you will get on the balloting. Your visitors are of three kinds: one consists of morning callers who come to your house, a second of those who escort you to the Forum, the third of those who attend you on your canvass. In the case of the mere morning callers, who are less select, and according to present-day fashion, are decidedly numerous, you must contrive to think that you value even this slight attention very highly. It often happens that people when they visit a number of candidates, and observe the one that pays special heed to their attentions, leave off visiting the others, and little by little become real supporters of this man.

Secondly, to those who escort you to the Forum: since this is a much greater attention than a mere morning call, indicate clearly that they are still more gratifying to you; and with them, as far as it shall lie in your power, go down to the Forum at fixed times, for the daily escort by its numbers produces a great impression and confers great personal distinction.

The third class is that of people who continually attend you upon your canvass. See that those who do so spontaneously understand that you regard yourself as forever obliged by their extreme kindness; from these on the other hand who *owe* you the attention for services rendered frankly demand that so far as their age and business allow they should be constantly in attendance, and that those who are unable to accompany you in person, should find relatives to substitute in performing this duty. I am very anxious and think it most important that you should always be surrounded with numbers. Besides, it confers a great reputation, and great distinction to be accompanied by those whom you have defended and saved in the law courts. Put this demand fairly before them – that since by your means, and without any fee – some have retained property, others their honour, or their civil rights, or their entire fortunes – and since there will never be any other time when they can show their gratitude, they now should reward you by this service.

THE CATILINE CONSPIRACY: THE CHARACTER AND CAREER OF CATILINE, 63 BC

Sallust

Lucius Catilina (Catiline) was a discontented, impoverished patrician who had stood unsuccessfully against Marcus Cicero for the consulship in 64 BC. Catiline tried for the office again in 63 BC, this time on a programme of radical land redistribution and debt cancellation – he was himself an undischarged embezzler – designed to appeal to the displaced and disaffected. When he was rebuffed electorally for a second time, he commenced plotting the Republic's overthrow.

In so populous and corrupt a city [as Rome] Catiline easily kept about him, as a bodyguard, crowds of the lawless and desperate. All the shameless libertines and profligate rascals were his associates and intimate friends, – the men who had squandered their paternal estates by gaming, luxury, sensuality, and all too who had plunged heavily into debt to buy immunity for crimes; all assassins or sacrilegious persons from every quarter, convicted, or dreading conviction for their misdeeds; all, likewise, for whom their tongue or hand won a livelihood by perjury or bloodshed; all, in short, whom wickedness, poverty, or a guilty conscience goaded were friends to Catiline.

If any man of character as yet unblemished fell into his society, he presently rendered him by daily intercourse and temptation like to and equal to the rest. But it was the young whose acquaintance he chiefly courted and easily ensnared. For as the passions of each, according to his years, were aroused, he furnished mistresses to some, bought horses and dogs for others, and spared, in a word, neither his purse nor his character, if he could make them his devoted and trustworthy supporters.

Catiline was alleged to have corrupted a Vestal Virgin, and wrought many vile crimes; at last, smitten with a passion for a certain Aurelia, he murdered his own grown-up son, because she objected to marrying him and having in the house a grown-up stepson. And this crime seems to me to have been the chief cause of hurrying forward his conspiracy. For his guilty mind, at peace neither with gods nor men, found no comfort either waking or sleeping, so utterly did conscience desolate his tortured spirit. His complexion, in consequence, was pale, his eyes haggard, his walk sometimes quick and sometimes slow, and distraction was plainly evident in every feature and look.

The young men (his boon companions) . . . he enticed by various methods into evil practices. From among them he furnished false witnesses and forgers of signatures; and he taught them all to regard with equal unconcern property and danger. At length when he had stripped them of all character and shame he led them to other and greater iniquities. When there was no ready motive for crime, he nevertheless stirred them up to murder quite inoffensive persons, just as if they had injured him, lest their hand or heart should grow torpid for want of employment.

Trusting to such confederates and comrades, and knowing that the load of debt was everywhere great, and that the veterans of Sulla, having spent their [bounty] money too freely, now were longing for a civil war, remembering their spoils and former victory, Catiline accordingly formed the design of over-throwing the government.

THE CATILINE CONSPIRACY: CATILINE ROUSES HIS ACCOMPLICES, 63 BC

Lucius Catilina

In late summer 63 BC Catiline began the organisation of a coup d'etat, the centrepiece of which was to be a march on Rome by a rabble of yokel supporters from Etruria. The main plotters, however were young, listless Roman patricians like Catiline himself. Here is Catiline's speech to them from a secret conference at his mansion.

If your courage and fidelity had not been sufficiently proved by me, this favourable opportunity would have occurred to no purpose; mighty hopes, absolute power, would in vain be within our grasp; nor should I, depending on irresolution or fickle-mindedness, pursue contingencies instead of certainties. But as I have, on many remarkable occasions, experienced your bravery and attachment to me, I have ventured to engage in a most important and glorious enterprise. I am aware, too, that whatever advantages or evils affect you, the same affect me;

and to have the same desires and the same aversions is assuredly a firm bond of friendship.

What I have been meditating you have already heard separately. But my ardour for action is daily more and more excited when I consider what our future condition of life must be unless we ourselves assert our claims to liberty. For since the government has fallen under the power and jurisdiction of a few, kings and princes have constantly been their tributaries; nations and states have paid them taxes; but all the rest of us, however brave and worthy, whether noble or plebeian, have been regarded as a mere mob, without interest or authority, and subject to those to whom, if the state were in a sound condition, we should be a terror. Hence all influence, power, honour, and wealth, are in their hands, or where they dispose of them; to us they have left only insults, dangers, persecutions, and poverty. To such indignities, O bravest of men, how long will you submit? Is it not better to die in a glorious attempt, than, after having been the sport of other men's insolence, to resign a wretched and degraded existence with ignominy?

But success (I call gods and men to witness!) is in our own hands. Our years are fresh, our spirit is unbroken; among our oppressors, on the contrary, through age and wealth a general debility has been produced. We have, therefore, only to make a beginning; the course of events will accomplish the rest.

Who in the world, indeed, that has the feelings of a man, can endure that they should have a superfluity of riches, to squander in building over seas and levelling mountains, and that means should be wanting to us even for the necessaries of life; that they should join together two houses or more, and that we should not have a hearth to call our own? They, though they purchase pictures, statues, and embossed plate; though they pull down new buildings and erect others, and lavish and abuse their wealth in every possible method, yet cannot, with the utmost efforts of caprice, exhaust it. But for us there is poverty at home, debts abroad; our present circumstances are bad, our prospects much worse; and what, in a word, have we left, but a miserable existence?

Will you not, then, awake to action? Behold that liberty, that liberty for which you have so often wished, with wealth, honour, and glory, are set before your eyes. All these prizes fortune offers to the victorious. Let the enterprise itself, then, let the opportunity, let your property, your dangers, and the glorious spoils of war, animate you far more than my words. Use me either as your leader or your fellow soldier; neither my heart nor my hand shall be wanting to you. These objects I hope to effect, in concert with you, in the character of consul; unless, indeed, my expectation deceives me, and you prefer to be slaves rather than masters.

THE CATILINE CONSPIRACY: CICERO SPEAKS TO THE SENATE, 63 BC

Sallust

When rumours of Catiline's intended coup reached the Senate it passed an emergency decree allowing consul Cicero to take extreme measures against the culprits. Yet Catiline himself, due to the influence of high-powered friends and relatives, was left at large – until Cicero delivered before the Senate his damning "First Oration against Catiline".

A few days later, in a meeting of the senate, Lucius Saenius, one of its members, read a letter which he said had been brought to him from Faesulae, stating that Gaius Manlius[1] had taken the field with a large force on the twenty-seventh day of October. At the same time, as is usual in such a crisis, omens and portents were reported by some, while others told of the holding of meetings, of the transportation of arms, and of insurrections of the slaves at Capua and in Apulia.

Thereupon by decree of the senate Quintus Marcius Rex was sent to Faesulae and Quintus Metellus Creticus to Apulia and its neighbourhood.

These precautions struck the community with terror, and the aspect of the city was changed. In place of extreme gaiety and frivolity, the fruit of long-continued peace, there was sudden and general gloom. Men were uneasy and apprehensive, put little confidence in any place of security or in any human being, were neither at war nor at peace, and measured the peril each

[1] Gaius Manlius was a co-conspirator with Catiline.

by his own fears. The women, too, whom the greatness of our country had hitherto shielded from the terrors of war, were in a pitiful state of anxiety, raised suppliant hands to heaven, bewailed the fate of their little children, asked continual questions, trembled at everything, and throwing aside haughtiness and self-indulgence, despaired of themselves and of their country.

But Catiline's pitiless spirit persisted in the same attempts, although defences were preparing, and he himself had been arraigned by Lucius Paulus under the Plautian law. Finally, in order to conceal his designs or to clear himself, as though he had merely been the object of some private slander, he came into the senate. Then the consul Marcus Tullius, either fearing his presence or carried away by indignation, delivered a brilliant speech of great service to the state, which he later wrote out and published.

When he took his seat, Catiline, prepared as he was to deny everything, with downcast eyes and pleading accents began to beg the Fathers of the Senate not to believe any unfounded charge against him; he was sprung from such a family, he said, and had so ordered his life from youth up, that he had none save the best of prospects. They must not suppose that he, a patrician, who like his forefathers had rendered great service to the Roman people, would be benefited by the overthrow of the government, while its saviour was Marcus Tullius, a resident alien in the city of Rome. When he would have added other insults, he was shouted down by the whole body, who called him traitor and assassin. Then in a transport of fury he cried: "Since I am brought to bay by my enemies and driven desperate, I will put out my fire by general devastation."

With this he rushed from the senate-house and went home. There after thinking long upon the situation, since his designs upon the consul made no headway and he perceived that the city was protected against fires by watchmen, believing it best to increase the size of his army and secure many of the necessities of war before the legions were enrolled, he left for the camp of Manlius with a few followers in the dead of night.

"FIELD FARES STUFFED WITH ASPARAGUS, FATTENED FOWLS, OYSTER AND MUSSEL PASTIES . . .": THE BILL OF FARE AT A ROMAN BANQUET, 63 BC

Macrobius

The Romans considered cooking to be an art to rival sculpture. No peoples before or since have given such importance to the satisfaction of the palate. The feast below was held by Mucius Lentulus Niger on his elevation to pontifex (priest).

Before the dinner proper came sea hedgehogs; fresh oysters, as many as the guests wished; large mussels; sphondyli; field fares with asparagus; fattened fowls; oyster and mussel pasties; black and white sea acorns; sphondyli again; glycimarides; sea nettles; becaficoes; roe ribs; boar's ribs; fowls dressed with flour; becaficoes; purple shellfish of two sorts. The dinner itself consisted of sows' udder; boar's head; fish-pasties; boar-pasties; ducks; boiled teals; hares; roasted fowls; starch pastry; Pontic pastry.

THE CATILINE CONSPIRACY: THE LAST STAND OF CATILINE, JANUARY 62 BC

Sallust

After Cicero's "First Oration Against Catiline" the latter fled Rome to place himself at the head of his supporters in Etruria. The government accordingly sent two armies against him, at which Catiline abandoned his insurrection and tried instead to escape the Italian peninsula northwards. He was trapped and destroyed, along with his followers, near Pistoria (Pistoia).

When Petreius, after making all his preparations, gave the signal with the trumpet, he ordered his cohorts to advance slowly; the army of the enemy followed their example. After they had reached a point where battle could be joined by the skirmishers, the hostile armies rushed upon each other with loud shouts, then threw down their pikes and took to the sword. The veterans, recalling their old-time prowess, advanced bravely to close quarters; the enemy, not lacking in courage, stood their ground, and there was a terrific struggle.

Meanwhile Catiline, with his light-armed troops, was busy in the van, aided those who were hard pressed, summoned fresh troops to replace the wounded, had an eye to everything, and at the same time fought hard himself, often striking down the foe – thus performing at once the duties of a valiant soldier and of a skilful leader.

When Petreius saw that Catiline was making so much stronger a fight than he had expected, he led his praetorian cohort against the enemy's centre, threw them into confusion, and slew those who resisted in various parts of the field; then he attacked the rest on both flanks at once. Manlius and the man from Faesulae were among the first to fall, sword in hand. When Catiline saw that his army was routed and that he was left with a mere handful of men, mindful of his birth and former rank he plunged into the thickest of the enemy and there fell fighting, his body pierced through and through.

When the battle was ended it became evident that boldness and resolution had pervaded Catiline's army. For almost every man covered with his body, when life was gone, the position which he had taken when alive at the beginning of the conflict. A few, indeed, in the centre, whom the praetorian cohort had scattered, lay a little apart from the rest, but the wounds even of these were in front. But Catiline was found far in advance of his men amid a heap of slain foemen, still breathing slightly, and showing in his face the indomitable spirit which had animated him when alive. Finally, out of the whole army not a single citizen of free birth was taken during the battle or in flight, showing that all had valued their own lives no more highly than those of their enemies.

But the army of the Roman people gained no joyful or bloodless victory, for all the most valiant had either fallen in the fight or come off with severe wounds. Many, too, who had gone from the camp to visit the field or to pillage, on turning over the bodies of the rebels found now a friend, now a guest or kinsman; some also recognized their personal enemies. Thus the whole army was variously affected with sorrow and grief, rejoicing and lamentation.

JURY CORRUPTION, ROME, 61 BC

Cicero

Cicero relates the trial of Clodius for impersonating a woman and attending the Festival of the Good Goddess from which men were excluded.

So if you want – *pour en revenir* – to know the cause of the acquittal – it was the empty pockets and itching palms of our jurymen . . . When the challenging had taken place amid loud outcries, the prosecutor like a scrupulous censor rejecting the infamous characters, and the defendant like a kind-hearted exhibitor of gladiators putting aside the most respectable, from the moment the jury had gone into the box, the hearts of good people began indeed to fail them. Greater rascals, in fact, never sat round the table of a gambling hell. There were seedy senators and needy knights, and tribunes who may be called paymasters, but are not masters of much pay. Yet here and there among them were respectable people whom the defendant had been unable to get rid of by his challenge. There they sat, looking as sad as they felt, among companions who formed the strongest contrast to them, and sorely troubled at their contact with such pollution. Well, as point after point was submitted to the bench on the preliminary applications, the uprightness they showed was utterly unexpected, and that without a single dissentient voice. The defendant did not gain a point: the prosecutor was allowed more than he ventured to claim; in a word, Hortensius was beginning to be triumphant at his own penetration. Nobody looked on Clodius as now on his trial, but rather as condemned a thousand times over. But when they called me as a witness, I suppose the uproar of the partisans of Clodius must have been enough to tell you how the jury rose as one man, how they took their stand by me, how they showed themselves to Clodius in the court ready for my life to offer their throats to the sword. This circumstance seems to me more complimentary than either the famous one when you Athenians made Xenocrates give his evidence without oath, or when in our own country a jury refused to inspect the accounts of Metellus Numidicus on their being handed round as usual: this tribute to myself is, I repeat, even more remarkable.

Thanks therefore to these utterances from the jurors, since they rallied round me thus as the saviour of the country, the defendant was utterly smashed, and he and all his supporters gave in, while next day I was met at my house by as great a crowd as that which escorted me home in triumph when I laid down my consulship . . . Not a soul thought the fellow would have any defence to make. But now *musa, mihi caussas memora*. You know whom I mean by "Baldhead" – one of the Nanneian set – that late panegyrist of mine about whose speech and its compliments to me I have already told you – well, in a couple of days, with the help of a single slave, one fetched too from the nearest training-school, he had the whole business settled: he had sent for them all, promised the money, given security, and paid the bribe down . . . In the end, though there was a complete disappearance of the better sort, and the forum was crowded with gladiators, there were still twenty-five on the bench resolute enough, even in face of this extreme danger, to be willing to lose their lives rather than live and be lost; while thirty-one of them cared little about being famous, but much about being famished. When Catulus met one of them afterwards, "Why was it"; says he, "you demanded a guard from us? Were you afraid of being robbed of your wages?"

Here then you have, as shortly as I can put it, the kind of trial there was, and the reason of the acquittal.

POMPEY ENTERS ROME IN TRIUMPH, 30 SEPTEMBER 61 BC

Appian

Pompey began his military career at 17, fighting the Social War against the would-be dictator Marius. Thereafter, he proceeded from one dazzling martial endeavour to the next, annihilating Spartacus, the Mediterranean pirates, Mithridates of Pontus, Tigranes of Armenia and Antiochus of Syria. These latter victories, which consolidated Roman power in Asia Minor and the Middle East, caused something like "Pompey-mania" in Rome.

At the end of the winter [63–62 BC] Pompey distributed rewards to the army, 1,500 Attic drachmas to each soldier, and in like proportion to the oficers, the whole, it was said, amounting to

16,000 talents. Then he marched to Ephesus, embarked for Italy, and hastened to Rome, having dismissed his soldiers at Brundisium to their homes, by which act his popularity was greatly increased among the Romans.

As he approached the city he was met by successive processions, first of youths, farthest from the city; then bands of men of different ages came out as far as they severally could walk; last of all came the Senate, which was lost in wonder at his exploits, for no one had ever before vanquished so powerful an enemy and at the same time brought so many great nations under subjection and extended the Roman rule to the Euphrates.

He was awarded a triumph exceeding in brilliancy any that had gone before. It occupied two successive days; and many nations were represented in the procession from Pontus, Armenia, Cappadocia, Cilicia, all the peoples of Syria, besides Albanians, Heniochi, Achæans, Scythians, and Eastern Iberians; 700 complete ships were brought into the harbour;[1] in the triumphal procession were two-horse carriages and litters laden with gold or with other ornaments of various kinds, also the couch of Darius, the son of Hystaspes, the throne and sceptre of Mithridates Eupator himself, and his image, eight cubits high, made of solid gold, and 75,000,000 drachmæ of silver coin. The number of wagons carrying arms was infinite and the number of prows of ships. After these came the multitude of captives and pirates, none of them bound, but all arrayed in their native costume.

Before Pompey himself were led the satraps, sons and generals of the kings against whom he had fought, who were present – some having been captured, some given as hostages to the number of 324. Among them were five sons of Mithridates, and two daughters; also Aristobulus, king of the Jews; the tyrants of the Cilicians, and other potentates.

There were carried in the procession images of those who were not present, of Tigranes [king of Armenia] and of Mithridates, representing them as fighting, as vanquished, and as fleeing. Even the besieging of Mithridates and his silent flight by night were represented. Finally, it was shown how he died, and

---

[1] Probably of Ostia.

the daughters who perished with him were pictured also, and there were figures of the sons and daughters who died before him, and images of the barbarian gods decked out in the fashion of their countries. A tablet was borne, also, inscribed thus:—

SHIPS WITH BRAZEN BEAKS CAPTURED DCCC:

CITIES FOUNDED IN CAPPADOCIA VIII:

IN CILICIA AND COELE-SYRIA XX:

IN PALESTINE THE ONE NOW CALLED SELEUCIS.

KINGS CONQUERED: TIGRANES THE ARMENIAN: ARTOCES THE IBERIAN: OROEZES THE ALBANIAN: ARETAS THE NABATÆAN: DARIUS THE MEDE: ANTIOCHUS OF COMMAGENE.

Pompey himself was borne in a chariot studded with gems, wearing, it is said, the cloak of Alexander the Great, if any one can believe that. This was supposed to have been found among the possessions of Mithridates . . . His chariot was followed by the officers who had shared the campaigns with him, some on horseback, and others on foot. When he reached the Capitol, he did not put any prisoners to death, as had been customary at other triumphs, but sent them all home at the public expense, except the kings. Of these Aristobulus alone was shortly put to death, and Tigranes [son of the king of Armenia] some time later.

Such was Pompey's triumph!

JULIUS CAESAR DEFEATS THE NERVII, 57 BC

Julius Caesar

Born of an ancient patrician family, Caesar was infinitely ambitious and through guile, drive and some minor military accomplishments climbed to the top of the greasy pole. He was elected to the consulship for 59 BC. Even this was not enough. Along with Crassus and Pompey, he formed an autocratic alliance ("The First Triumvirate") which effectively turned the Assembly and Senate into rubber-stamp institutions. Yet Caesar had no intention of sharing supreme power: He wanted to be sole dictator. To achieve this, he had to win a military renown to rival Pompey's. Obtaining the governorship of Cisalpine Gaul (northern Italy), Illyricum (Dalmatia) and Transalpine

Gaul (southern France), Caesar accordingly began a nine-year (58–50 BC) campaign to extend Roman hegemony in the West. The Belgic Nervii were among the most powerful of the tribes rallied against him.

The Ambiani were neighbours of the Nervii, about whose character and habits Caesar made enquiries. He learned that they did not admit traders into their country and would not allow the importation of wine or other luxuries, because they thought such things made men soft and took the edge off their courage; that they were a fierce, warlike people, who bitterly reproached the other Belgae for throwing away their inheritance of bravery by submitting to the Romans, and vowed that they would never ask for peace or accept it on any terms. After three days' march through Nervian territory, Caesar learned from prisoners that the river Sambre was not more than ten miles from the place where he was encamped, and that all the Nervian troops were posted on the farther side of it, awaiting the arrival of the Romans. Already with them in the field, he was told, were their neighbours the Atrebates and the Viromandui, whom they had persuaded to try the fortune of war along with them; and they were expecting to be joined by the forces of the Atuatuci, which were already on the way. They had hastily thrust their women, and all who were thought too young or too old to fight, into a place which marshes made inaccessible to an army.

On receiving this information Caesar sent forward a reconnoitring party, accompanied by some centurions, to choose a good site for a camp. A large number of Gauls, including some of the Belgae who had surrendered, had attached themselves to Caesar and were marching with the troops. Some of these, as was afterwards ascertained from prisoners, had observed the order in which our army marched during the previous days, and at night made their way to the Nervii and explained to them that each legion was separated from the following one by a long baggage-train, so that when the first reached camp the others would be far away; it would be quite easy to attack it while the men were still burdened with their packs, and when it was routed and its baggage plundered, the others would not dare to make a stand. There was one thing that favoured the execution of the plan suggested by these deserters. The Nervii, having virtually no cavalry, long ago devised a method of hindering their neighbours' cavalry when it made plundering raids into their territory. They cut off the tops of saplings, bent them over, and let a thick growth of side branches shoot out; in between them they planted briars and thorns, and thus made hedges like walls, which gave such protection that no one could even see through them, much less penetrate them. As these obstacles hindered the march of our column, the Nervii thought the proposed plan too good to leave untried.

At the place that the Romans had chosen for their camp a hill sloped down evenly from its summit to the Sambre. Opposite it, on the other side of the river, rose another hill with a similar gradient, on the lower slopes of which were some three hundred yards of open ground, while the upper part was covered by a wood which it was not easy to see into. In this wood the main part of the enemy's forces lay concealed, while on the open ground along the river bank a few pickets of cavalry were visible. The depth of the river was about three feet.

Caesar had sent his cavalry a little in advance and was following with the rest of his forces. But the column was formed up in a different manner from that which the Belgic deserters had described to the Nervii. In accordance with his usual practice when approaching an enemy, Caesar marched at the head of the column with six legions, unencumbered by heavy baggage; then came the transport of the entire army, protected by the two newly-enrolled legions, which brought up the rear. First of all, our cavalry crossed the river with the slingers and archers and engaged the enemy's horsemen. These kept on retiring into the wood where their comrades were and then reappearing to charge our troops, who dared not pursue them beyond the end of the open ground. Meanwhile the six legions that were the first to arrive measured out the ground and began to construct the camp. The Gauls concealed in the wood had already formed up in battle-order and were waiting full of confidence. As soon as they caught sight of the head of the baggage-train – the moment which they had agreed upon for starting the battle – they suddenly dashed out in full force and swooped down on our cavalry, which they easily routed. Then they ran down to the river at such an incredible speed that almost at the same instant they seemed to be at the edge of the wood, in the water, and already upon us. With equal rapidity they climbed the hill towards our camp to attack the men who were busy entrenching it.

Caesar had everything to do at once – hoist the flag which was the signal for running to arms, recall the men from their work on the camp, fetch back those who had gone far afield in search of material for the rampart, form the battle-line, address the men, and sound the trumpet-signal for going into action. Much of this could not be done in the short time left available by the enemy's swift onset. But the situation was saved by two things – first, the knowledge and experience of the soldiers, whose training in earlier battles enabled them to decide for themselves what needed doing, without waiting to be told; secondly, the order which Caesar had issued to all his generals, not to leave the work, but to stay each with his own legion until the camp fortifications were completed. As the enemy was so close and advancing so swiftly, the generals did not wait for further orders but on their own responsibility took the measures they thought proper.

After giving the minimum of essential orders, Caesar hastened down to the battlefield to address the troops and happened to come first upon the 10th legion, to which he made only a short speech, urging them to live up to their tradition of bravery, to keep their nerve, and to meet the enemy's attack boldly. Then, as the Nervii were within range, he gave the signal for battle. On going to the other side of the field to address the troops there, he found them already in action. The soldiers were so pushed for time by the enemy's eagerness to fight, that they could not even take the covers off their shields or put on helmets – not to speak of fixing on crests or decorations. Each man, on coming down from his work at the camp, went into action under the first standard he happened to see, so as not to waste time searching for his own unit. The battle-front was not formed according to the rules of military theory, but as necessitated by the emergency and the sloping ground of the hill-side. The legions were facing different ways and fighting separate actions, and the thick hedges obstructed their view.

The result was that Caesar could not fix upon definite points for stationing reserves or foresee what would be needed in each part of the field, and unity of command was impossible. In such adverse circumstances there were naturally ups and downs of fortune.

The 9th and 10th legions were on the left, and discharged a volley of spears at the Atrebates, who happened to be facing them. Breathless and exhausted with running, and many of them now wounded, the Atrebates were quickly driven down to the river, and when they tried to cross it our soldiers with their swords attacked them at a disadvantage and destroyed a large number. Crossing the river themselves without hesitation and pushing forward up the steep slope, they renewed the fight when the enemy began to resist once more, and again put them to flight. Meanwhile in another part of the field, on a front facing in a slightly different direction, the 11th and 8th legions engaged the Viromandui, drove them down the hill, and were now fighting right on the river banks. By this time, however, the Roman camp was almost entirely exposed in front and on the left, and the 12th and 7th legions, which were posted fairly close together on the right, were attacked by the whole force of the Nervii, led in a compact mass by their commander-in-chief Boduognatus. Some of them began to surround the legions on their right flank, while the rest made for the hill-top where the camp stood.

At the same time, the Roman cavalry and light-armed troops, routed by the first attack, were in the act of retreating into the camp, when they found themselves face to face with the Nervii and took to flight again in a different direction. The servants, too, who from the back gate on the summit of the hill had seen our victorious troops cross the river, and had gone out to plunder, on looking back and seeing the enemy in the camp immediately ran for their lives. Meanwhile shouting and din arose from the drivers coming up with the baggage, who rushed panic-stricken in every direction. With the army were some auxiliary cavalry sent by the Treveri, a people with a unique reputation for courage among the Gauls. When these horsemen saw the Roman camp full of the enemy, the legions hard pressed and almost surrounded, and the non-combatants, cavalry, slingers, and Numidians scattered and stampeding in every direction, they decided that our case was desperate, and, riding off home in terror, reported that the Romans were utterly defeated and their camp and baggage captured.

After addressing the 10th legion Caesar had gone to the right wing, where he found the troops in difficulties. The cohorts of the 12th legion were packed together so closely that the men were in one another's way and could not fight properly. All the centurions of the 4th cohort, as well as a standard-bearer, were killed, and the standard was lost; nearly all the centurions of the other cohorts were either killed or wounded, including the chief centurion Publius Sextius Baculus, a man of very great courage, who was so disabled by a number of severe wounds that he could no longer stand. The men's movements were slow, and some in the rear, feeling themselves abandoned, were retiring from the fight and trying to get out of range. Meanwhile the enemy maintained unceasing pressure up the hill in front, and were also closing in on both flanks. As the situation was critical and no reserves were available, Caesar snatched a shield from a soldier in the rear (he had not his own shield with him), made his way into the front line, addressed each centurion by name, and shouted encouragement to the rest of the troops, ordering them to push forward and open out their ranks, so that they could use their swords more easily. His coming gave them fresh heart and hope; each man wanted to do his best under the eyes of his commander-in-chief, however desperate the peril, and the enemy's assault was slowed down a little.

Noticing that the 7th legion, which stood close by, was likewise hard put to it, Caesar told the military tribunes to join the two legions gradually together and adopt a square formation, so that they could advance against the enemy in any direction. By this manoeuvre the soldiers were enabled to support one another, and were no longer afraid of being surrounded from behind, which encouraged them to put up a bolder resistance. Meanwhile the two legions which had acted as a guard to the baggage at the rear of the column, having received news of the battle, had quickened their pace, and now appeared on the hill-top, where the enemy could see them; and Labienus, who had captured the enemy's camp, and from the high ground on which it stood could see what was going on in ours, sent the 10th legion to the rescue. The men of the 10th, who could tell from the flight of the cavalry and the non-combatants how serious things were, and what peril threatened the camp, the legions, and their commander-in-chief, strained every nerve to make the utmost speed.

Their arrival so completely changed the situation that even some of the Roman soldiers who had lain down, exhausted by wounds, got up and began to fight again, leaning on their shields. The non-combatants, observing the enemy's alarm, stood up to their attack, unarmed as they were; and the cavalry, anxious to wipe out the disgrace of their flight, scoured the whole battlefield and tried to outdo the legionaries in gallantry. But the enemy, even in their desperate plight, showed such bravery that when their front ranks had fallen those immediately behind stood on their prostrate bodies to fight; and when these too fell and the corpses were piled high, the survivors still kept hurling javelins as though from the top of a mound, and flung back the spears intercepted by their shields. Such courage accounted for the extraordinary feats they had performed already. Only heroes could have made light of crossing a wide river, clambering up the steep banks, and launching themselves on such a difficult position.

So ended this battle, by which the tribe of the Nervii was almost annihilated and their name almost blotted out from the face of the earth.

DRUIDS IN GAUL, 54 BC

Julius Caesar

The Druids officiate at the worship of the gods, regulate public and private sacrifices, and give rulings on all religious questions. Large numbers of young men flock to them for instruction, and they are held in great honour by the people. They act as judges in practically all disputes, whether between tribes or between individuals; when any crime is committed, or a murder takes place, or a dispute arises about an inheritance or a boundary, it is they who adjudicate the matter and appoint the compensation to be paid and received by the parties concerned. Any individual or tribe failing to accept their award is banned from taking part in sacrifice – the heaviest punishment that can be inflicted upon a Gaul. Those who are laid under such a ban are regarded as impious criminals. Everyone shuns them and avoids going near or speaking to them, for fear of taking some harm by contact with what is unclean; if they appear as plaintiffs, justice is denied them, and they are excluded from a share in any honour. All the Druids are under one head, whom they hold in the highest respect. On his death, if any one of the rest is of outstanding merit, he succeeds to the vacant place; if several have equal claims, the Druids usually decide the election by voting, though sometimes they actually fight it out. On a fixed date in each year they hold a session in a consecrated spot in the country of the Carnutes, which is supposed to be the centre of Gaul. Those who are involved in disputes assemble here from all parts, and accept the Druids' judgments and awards. The Druidic doctrine is believed to have been found existing in Britain and thence imported into Gaul; even today those who want to make a profound study of it generally go to Britain for the purpose.

The Druids are exempt from military service and do not pay taxes like other citizens. These important privileges are naturally attractive: many present themselves of their own accord to become students of Druidism, and others are sent by their parents or relatives. It is said that these pupils have to memorize a great number of verses – so many, that some of them spend twenty years at their studies. The Druids believe that their religion forbids them to commit their teachings to writing, although for most other purposes, such as public and private accounts, the Gauls use the Greek alphabet. But I imagine that this rule was originally established for other reasons – because they did not want their doctrine to become public property, and in order to prevent their pupils from relying on the written word and neglecting to train their memories; for it is usually found that when people have the help of texts, they are less diligent in learning by heart, and let their memories rust. A lesson which they take particular pains to inculcate is that the soul does not perish, but after death passes from one body to another; they think that this is the best incentive to bravery, because it teaches men to disregard the terrors of death. They also hold long discussions about the heavenly bodies and their movements, the size of the universe and of the earth, the physical constitution of the world, and the power and properties of the gods; and they instruct the young men in all these subjects . . .

As a nation the Gauls are extremely superstitious; and so persons suffering from serious diseases, as well as those who are exposed to the perils of battle, offer, or vow to offer, human sacrifices, for the performance of which they employ Druids. They believe that the only way of saving a man's life is to propitiate the god's wrath by rendering another life in its place, and they have regular state sacrifices of the same kind. Some tribes have colossal images made of wickerwork, the limbs of which they fill with living men; they are then set on fire, and the victims burnt to death. They think that the gods prefer the execution of men taken in the act of theft or brigandage, or guilty of some offence; but when they run short of criminals, they do not hesitate to make up with innocent men.

GANG-WARFARE IN ROME, NOVEMBER 57 BC

Marcus Cicero

To protect his interests in Rome whilst on campaign, Caesar recruited the young hoodlum Clodius. One of Clodius's prime targets was the statesman Cicero, who had once sought to convict him for wearing women's clothing in a gatecrash of a religious ceremony (see pp 68–69). In revenge, Clodius achieved the exile of Cicero on a legal technicality relating to the Catiline insurrection. Cicero returned to Rome after a year. His reception by Clodius was predictable. Yet the matter was not personal, it was political. Cicero was a supporter of Pompey, Clodius was Caesar's enforcer. The Republic was slipping into factional intrigue and ultimately civil war.

I am sure you are dying to know what's afoot here, and also to know it from me – not that news of what goes on in full public view is any more reliable from my pen than when it comes to you from the letters or reports of others, but I should like you to see from a letter of my own how I react to developments, and my attitude of mind and general state of being at the present time.

On 3 November an armed gang drove the workmen from my site, threw down Catulus' portico which was in process of restoration by consular contract under a senatorial decree and had nearly reached the roof stage, smashed up my brother's house by throwing stones from my site, and then set it on fire. This was by Clodius' orders, with all Rome looking on as the firebrands were thrown, amid loud protest and lamentation – I won't say from honest men, for I doubt whether they exist, but from all and sundry. Clodius was running riot even before, but after this frenzy he thinks of nothing but massacring his enemies, and goes from street to street openly offering the slaves their freedom. Earlier on, when he would not stand trial, he had a difficult, obviously bad case, but still a case. He could have denied the charges or blamed others or even have defended this or that action as legitimate. But after this orgy of wrecking, arson, and loot, his followers have left him. It is all he can do to keep Decius (?) the undertaker or Gellius, and he takes slaves for his advisers. He sees that if he slaughters everybody he chooses in broad daylight, his case, when it comes to court, won't be a jot worse than it is already.

Accordingly, on 11 November as I was going down the Via Sacra, he came after me with his men. Uproar! Stones flying, cudgels and swords in evidence. And all like a bolt from the blue! I retired into Tettius Damio's forecourt, and my companions had no difficulty in keeping out the rowdies. Clodius himself could have been killed, but I am becoming a dietician, I'm sick of surgery. When he found that everyone was calling for him to be bundled off to trial or rather to summary execution, his subsequent behaviour was such as made every Catiline look like an Acidinus. On 12 November he tried to storm and burn Milo's house in the Cermalus, bringing out fellows with drawn swords and shields and others with lighted firebrands, all in full view at eleven o'clock in the morning. He himself had made P. Sulla's house his assault base. Then out came Q. Flaccus with some stout warriors from Milo's other house, the Anniana, and killed off the most notorious bandits of the whole Clodian gang. He had every wish to kill their principal, but *he* had gone to earth in the recesses (?) of Sulla's house.

JULIUS CAESAR INVADES BRITAIN, 55 BC

Julius Caesar

Caesar's invasion was intended to prevent the Britons from aiding their subjugated kinsmen in Gaul.

. . . and so it was about 10 a.m. when Caesar arrived off Britain with the leading ships. Armed men could be seen stationed on all the heights, and the nature of the place was such, with the shore edged by sheer cliffs, that missiles could be hurled onto the beach from the top. Caesar considered this a totally unsuitable place for disembarkation, and waited at anchor till 3 p.m. for the rest of his invasion fleet to assemble. He then summoned a meeting of his brigade and battalion commanders, revealed the news he had from Volusenus, and outlined his orders. He wanted them to be ready to act immediately, on the slightest sign from him. For military practice demanded this, especially in a naval attack, which was liable to rapid, unexpected changes of circumstance. Dismissing his officers, he waited for a favourable combination of wind and tide, and then gave the signal to weigh anchor. Sailing on for about seven miles, he halted his line opposite an open, level beach.

The barbarians had discovered Caesar's plan by sending forward cavalry units and charioteers (a very common method of fighting with them). Their main force which had followed later was now in a position to prevent our men from disembarking. This caused considerable difficulty. The ships could only be drawn up in deep water because of their draught. The soldiers were faced with unknown ground and had their hands impeded, while they were burdened with a very heavy load of arms. And yet they had to leap down from the ships, keep their footing in the waves and fight the enemy. The latter, on the other hand, could either resist from dry land or by moving just a little forward into the shallows. So, completely unencumbered and with full knowledge of the ground, they boldly hurled their missiles, badly disturbing the horses which were totally unused to the conditions. Our men were shaken by these circumstances through lack of experience of this style of warfare, and failed to show the same dash and enthusiasm as they did in land battles.

As Caesar noticed this, he gave orders to the warships to row off slightly to the enemy's open flank away from the cargo ships. These ships were less well known to the barbarians and much more manoeuvrable. They were to halt, attack and move the enemy back by the use of slings, arrows and other missiles. All this helped our men considerably. The barbarians were affected by the strange shape of the ships, by the motion of the oars and the unusual type of catapult. Halting their advance, they slowly began to retire.

Our troops, however, were still hesitating, largely because of the depth of the sea, when the standard-bearer of the Tenth legion, with a prayer to the gods for a happy outcome for his legion, shouted, "Jump down, men, unless you want the enemy to get your standard. You will not find me failing in my duty to my country or my leader." This he yelled at the top of his voice, and then springing off the boat began to bear the eagle forward against the enemy. Our troops, with mutual words of encouragement not to commit a terrible wrong, all jumped down into the sea. Their fellows in the next boats saw what they were doing, followed suit and came to grips with the enemy . . .

Fighting was tough on both sides. My men could not keep in line, get a firm foothold or keep to their own standards. Each man joined the nearest unit irrespective of his ship and chaos reigned. The enemy knew the lie of the shoals and when they saw from the beach isolated groups disembarking they made a mounted charge and attacked them in their difficulties. These they outnumbered and surrounded, while their comrades raked the main party with an enfilade. Caesar assessed the situation and had both the boats of the warships and the sloops packed with soldiers to help wherever he saw need. Our men reached the land and were there reinforced by all those behind.

Then came the assault which routed the enemy, but we could not follow up satisfactorily as the cavalry had failed to hold its course and make the island. The enemy lost the day. As soon as they could stop bolting they sent a peace delegation to Caesar. Commius, the Atrebatian, came along with it. It was he whom

Caesar had sent to Britain to bring that general's instructions; but they had seized him as soon as he stepped ashore and clapped him in irons. The outcome of our victory was his release. In sueing for peace they attributed this outrage to the lower classes and asked him to let it pass as an act of their folly. Caesar protested at their unprovoked aggression after they had taken it upon themselves to send a delegation over to the continent to make peace with him. Yet he forgave their folly and demanded hostages. Some they delivered on the spot but promised to send for the others from up-country in a few days. Meanwhile they demobilized the tribesmen, and the chiefs came in from all quarters to surrender themselves and their countries to Caesar. Thus peace was made within four days of the landing in Britain.

The pax *proved temporary and the British resumed campaigning.*

A CHARIOT FIGHT, 55 BC

Julius Caesar

Meanwhile the Seventh legion was out on a routine foraging mission without any thought of action as there were still people on the farms and traffic in and out of the camp. Suddenly the guards at the gate reported to Caesar an exceptional quantity of dust where the legion had gone. Caesar rightly sensed a new native stratagem. He told the two duty cohorts to follow him and the other two to relieve them, and the rest to arm and follow at once. After a short march he saw his troops pressed by the enemy almost to breaking point with the legion unde-ployed and subject to crossfire. For the corn had been reaped in every district except one and the enemy had guessed they would go there and had prepared an ambush by night in the woods. Our men were scattered, busy reaping with arms piled, when the attack began. They killed some, put the others into confusion and surrounded them with both cavalry and char-iots.

A chariot fight is like this: first they scour the field shooting and this often breaks the line just with the fear of the horses and the din of wheels. When they have infiltrated among the cavalry units they jump down and fight as infantry. Meanwhile the drivers withdraw a bit to wait where they can quickly escape to base if compelled by weight of numbers. Thus they show the dash of cavalry and the steadiness of infantry in action. Daily drill teaches them the habit of checking their steeds even in full career down a steep slope, of lightning turns and of running along the pole, standing on the yoke and getting back quickly into the chariot.

Caesar brought help in the nick of time to our men for they were dismayed by such novel tactics.

Caesar withdrew from Britain in 55 BC, only to reinvade in the following year.

THE BRITONS, 54 BC

Julius Caesar

The population is exceedingly large, the ground thickly studded with homesteads, closely resembling those of the Gauls, and the cattle very numerous. For money they use either bronze, or gold coins, or iron ingots of fixed weights. Tin is found inland, and small quantities of iron near the coast; the copper that they use is imported. There is timber of every kind, as in Gaul, except beech and fir. Hares, fowl, and geese they think it unlawful to eat, but rear them for pleasure and amusement. The climate is more temperate than in Gaul, the cold being less severe.

By far the most civilized inhabitants are those living in Kent (a purely maritime district), whose way of life differs little from that of the Gauls. Most of the tribes in the interior do not grow corn but live on milk and meat, and wear skins. All the Britons dye their bodies with woad, which produces a blue colour, and this gives them a more terrifying appearance in battle. They wear their hair long, and shave the whole of their bodies except the head and the upper lip. Wives are shared between groups of ten or twelve men, especially between brothers and between fathers and sons; but the offspring of these unions are counted as the children of the the man with whom a particular woman cohabited first.

Troubles in Gaul forced Caesar to retreat from Britain again. It was not until AD 43, under Emperor Claudius, that the Romans successfully colonized England and Wales. Scotland remained unconquered.

ELECTORAL BRIBERY, ROME, 54 BC

Marcus Cicero

There is a fearful recrudescence of bribery. Never was there anything like it. On 15 July the rate of interest rose from four to eight per cent, owing to the compact made by Memmius with the consul Domitius. I am not exaggerating. They offer as much as 10,000,000 sesterces for the vote of the first century [in the consular elections]. The matter is a burning scandal. The candidates for the tribuneship have made a mutual compact; having deposited 500,000 sesterces apiece with Cato, they agree to conduct their canvass according to his directions, with the understanding that any one offending against it will be condemned to forfeit by him.

If this election [for tribunes] then turns out to be pure, Cato will have been of more avail than all the laws and jurors put together.

AN AEDILE REQUESTS PANTHERS, ROME, 51 BC

Caelius

Caelius as aedile was expected to provide the populace with a wild beast show. The recipient of the request was his friend Cicero, the new governor of Cilicia.

To Cicero, from Caelius.   *Rome, 2 September* (51 BC)
In nearly all my letters I have mentioned the panthers. It will be a disgrace to you if, while Patiscus has sent Curio ten panthers, you do not send a great many more. Those ten, and ten others from Africa, Curio has presented to me, so you need not think he only gives away country houses. If only you'll remember and send for some from Cibyra, and also from Pamphylia (where they tell me more are caught), you'll get what you want. I am all the more exercised about it now because I think I shall have to make all the preparations

without my colleague. For old friendship's sake, do make yourself do this. You always like taking trouble, as much as I hate it. The only trouble this business entails is speaking a few words, that is, giving the necessary orders.

(ii)

To Caelius, from Cicero.   *Laodicea, 4 April* (50 BC)

About the panthers, energetic steps are being taken on my instructions by those who regularly hunt them; but there is a remarkable scarcity, and they say that such as there are complain bitterly that no traps are laid for anyone in my province but them; so they are reported to have decided to emigrate to Caria. However, great efforts are being made, especially by Patiscus. Any products shall be yours, but what they will amount to I have no idea. I assure you I have your aedileship very much at heart, and I am reminded of it by today's date, this being the festival of the Great Mother.

Please write to me very carefully about the political situation, as I shall place most reliance on what I hear from you.

CICERO TAKES PINDENISSUM, CILICIA, DECEMBER 51 BC

Cicero

In 51 BC, by Senatorial decree, Cicero found himself reluctantly drawing a lot for the governorship of a province. He got Cilicia, which comprised much of southern Asia Minor. His year's gubernatorial sojourn saw him lead a military campaign against the untamed tribes of the mountains. He writes to Titus Pomponius Atticus, a friend since schooldays.

Camp at Pindenissum, 19 December [51 BC]

Pindenissum surrendered to me on the Saturnalia, eight weeks after we began the siege. "Pindenissum?" you'll say, "And what the deuce may that be? Never heard of it." Well, that's no fault of mine. I couldn't make Cilicia into Aetolia or Macedonia. You can take it from me here and now: at this time, with this army, and in this place, just so much could be done. Let me give you a *résumé*, as you permit in your last letter.

You know about my arrival in Ephesus, indeed you have congratulated me on the assemblage that day, one of the most flattering experiences of my life. From there, getting wonderful welcomes in such towns as there were, I reached Laodicea on 31 July. There I spent two days with great *réclame*, and by dint of courteous speeches effaced all earlier grievances. I did the same at Apamea, where I spent five days, and at Synnada (three days), at Philomelium (five days), at Iconium (ten). My administration of justice in these places lacked neither impartiality nor mildness nor responsibility.

Thence I arrived in camp on 24 August, and on the 28th reviewed the army near Iconium. As grave reports were coming in about the Parthians, I marched from camp there to Cilicia through that part of Cappadocia which borders Cilicia, so that Artavasdes of Armenia and the Parthians themselves would feel that their way to Cappadocia was blocked. After encamping for five days at Cybistra in Cappadocia I received intelligence that the Parthians were a long way away from that approach to Cappadocia and that the threat was rather to Cilicia. I therefore marched forthwith into Cilicia through the Gates of Taurus.

I reached Tarsus on 5 October and pressed on to the Amanus which separates Syria from Cilicia at the watershed, a mountain range full of enemies of Rome from time immemorial. Here on 13 October we made a great slaughter of the enemy, carrying and burning places of great strength, Pomptinus coming up at night and myself in the morning. I received the title of general from the army. For a few days we encamped near Issus in the very spot where Alexander, a considerably better general than either you or I, pitched his camp again Darius. There we stayed five days, plundering and laying waste the Amanus, and then left. Meanwhile – you have heard tell of panics and of nerve-warfare – the rumour of my advent encouraged Cassius, who was shut up in Antioch, and struck terror into the Parthians. Cassius pursued their retreat from the town and gained a success. Osaces, the celebrated Parthian general, died a few days later of a wound received in the flight. My name stood high in Syria.

Bibulus arrived meanwhile. I suppose he wanted to be even

with me over this bauble of a title – he started looking for a scrap of laurel in the wedding cake* in these same mountains of Amanus. The result was that he lost his entire First Cohort, including a Chief-Centurion, Asinius Dento, a distinguished man in his own class, and the other Centurions of the Cohort, also a Military Tribune, Sex. Lucilius, whose father T. Gavius Caepio is a man of wealth and standing. It was certainly a nasty reverse, both in itself and as coming when it did.

For my part I marched on Pindenissum, a strongly fortified town of the Free Cilicians which had been in arms as long as anyone can remember. The inhabitants were wild, fierce folk, fully equipped to defend themselves. We drew a rampart and moat round the town, erected a huge mound with penthouses and a high tower, plenty of siege artillery and a large number of archers. In the end, with a great deal of labour and apparatus and many of our own men wounded but none killed, we finished the job. The Saturnalia was certainly a merry time, for men as well as officers. I gave them the whole of the plunder excepting the captives, who are being sold off today, 19 December. As I write there is about HS 120,000 on the stand. I am handing over the army to my brother Quintus, who will take it into winter quarters in unsettled country. I myself am returning to Laodicea.

RESTRAINTS IN THE LIFE OF THE PRIEST OF JUPITER, ROME, c. 50 BC

Marcus Cicero

A *Flamen Dialis was the priest assigned to the worship of Jupiter. In the hierarchy of Roman state religion, only the* Pontifex Maximus *and* Rex Sacrorum *outranked him.*

A great many ceremonies are imposed upon the *Flamen Dialis* [the priest of Jupiter], and also many restraints, about which we read in the books *On The Public Priesthoods* and also in Book I of Fabius Pictor's work. Among them I recall the following:

---

* i.e., to look for glory (the victor's, or Triumphator's, laurel crown) on easy terms. The elder Cato's recipe for a wedding-cake contains laurel bark and the cake was cooked on laurel leaves (*De re rustica*, 121).

1) It is forbidden the Flamen Dialis to ride a horse;

2) It is likewise forbidden him to view the classes arrayed outside the *pomerium* [the boundary of Rome], i.e., armed and in battle order – hence only rarely is the Flamen Dialis made a Consul, since the conduct of wars is entrusted to the Consuls;

3) It is likewise forbidden for him ever to take an oath by Jupiter;

4) It is likewise forbidden for him to wear a ring, unless it is cut through and empty;

5) It is also forbidden to carry out fire from the *flaminia, i.e.,* the Flamen Dialis's house, except for a sacral purpose;

6) if a prisoner in chains enters the house he must be released and the chains must be carried up through the opening in the roof above the atrium or living room onto the roof tiles and dropped down from there into the street;

7) He must have no knot in his head gear or in his girdle or in any other part of his attire;

8) If anyone is being led away to be flogged and falls at his feet as a suppliant, it is forbidden to flog him that day;

9) The hair of the Flamen Dialis is not to be cut, except by a freeman;

10) It is customary for the Flamen neither to touch nor even to name a female goat, or raw meat, ivy, or beans;

11) He must not walk under a trellis for vines;

12) The feet of the bed on which he lies must have a thin coating of clay, and he must not be away from this bed for three successive nights, nor is it lawful for anyone else to sleep in this bed;

13) At the foot of his bed there must be a box containing a little pile of sacrificial cakes;

14) The nail trimmings and hair of the Dialis must be buried in the ground beneath a healthy tree;

15) Every day is a holy day for the Dialis;

16) He must not go outdoors without a head-covering – this is now allowed indoors, but only recently by decree of the pontiffs, as Masurius Sabinus has stated; it is also said that some of the other ceremonies have been remitted and cancelled;

17) It is not lawful for him to touch bread made with yeast;

18) His underwear cannot be taken off except in covered places, lest he appear nude under the open sky, which is the same as under the eye of Jove;

19) No one else outranks him in the seating at a banquet except the *Rex Sacrorum;*

20) If he loses his wife, he must resign his office;

21) His marriage cannot be dissolved except by death;

22) He never enters a burying ground, he never touches a corpse – he is, however, permitted to attend a funeral.

Almost the same ceremonial rules belong to the *Flaminica Dialis* [*i.e.*, his wife]. They say that she observes certain other and different ones, for example, that she wears a dyed gown, and that she has a twig from a fruitful tree tucked in her veil, and that it is forbidden for her to ascend more than three rungs of a ladder and even that when she goes to the *Argei* Festival [in which puppets were thrown into the Tiber] she must neither comb her head nor arrange her hair.

CIVIL WAR: THE BATTLE OF PHARSALUS, 48 BC

Julius Caesar

The death of Crassus in battle against the Parthians in 53 BC left Pompey and Caesar in direct rivalry for supreme control of Rome. Three years of stand-off, compromise, and manoeuvering ensued before Pompey chose, or allowed, a direct breach with his erstwhile partner. In December the consuls appointed Pompey as commander of all the forces of the Republic. An emergency Senate decree against Caesar was also passed. Caesar's hand was forced (though he hardly complained); on the night of 10 January 49 BC he crossed the small River Rubicon which formed the border between Cisalpine Gaul and eastern Italy. In the moment he crossed the Rubicon's bridge he broke Rome's law of treason, which forbade a governor to lead troops outside his own province. The Civil War had begun. The military advantage lay with Caesar, for many of Pompey's troops were in far-flung corners of the Empire. Neither were they as battle-hardened as Caesar's Gallic-War veterans. In 65 days Caesar was master of Italy and Pompey fled to his powerbase in the East. Fifteen months later Pompey and Caesar met at Pharsalus in Greece for the endgame of their Civil War.

When Caesar approached Pompey's army, he observed his line drawn up as follows. On the left wing were the two legions which had been handed over by Caesar in accordance with the decree of the Senate at the beginning of the troubles. One was named the First, the other the Third. Pompey himself was there. Scipio was holding the centre of the line with his legions from Syria. The legion from Cilicia together with the Spanish cohorts which, as we said, were brought over by Afranius, was stationed on the right wing. Pompey believed that these were his strongest troops. The rest he had stationed between the centre and the wings and had made up 110 cohorts. There were 45,000 men, plus about 2,000 time-expired veterans from the special-duty corps of the earlier armies who had come to join him. These he dispersed throughout the battle-line. The remaining seven cohorts he had posted to guard the camp and the near-by forts. His right wing was protected by a stream with steep banks[1], and he had therefore put all the cavalry, archers and slingers on the left wing.

Caesar, keeping his previous order of battle, had stationed the Tenth legion on the right wing and the Ninth on the left, although the latter had been sorely depleted by the battle at Dyrrachium. To it he added the Eighth legion, so as almost to make one legion out of two, and ordered them to cooperate. He had eighty cohorts stationed in the line, totalling 22,000 men. He had left two cohorts to guard the camp. He had put Antony on the left wing, Sulla on the right and Gnaeus Domitius in the centre. He himself took up his position opposite Pompey. At the same time, he observed the dispositions described above, and fearing that his right wing might be surrounded by the large numbers of the Pompeian cavalry, he quickly took one cohort from each legion from his third line and formed them into a fourth line, which he stationed opposite the cavalry. He gave them their instructions, and warned them that that day's victory would depend on the valour of those cohorts. He also ordered the third line and the army as a whole not to charge without his command, saying that he would give a signal with his flag when he wished them to do so.

[1] The Enipeus.

In giving the usual address of encouragement to the troops, in which he related the good service they had done him at all times, he recalled above all that he could call the troops to witness the earnestness with which he had sought peace, his attempts to negotiate through Vatinius by personal interviews and, through Aulus Clodius, with Scipio, and his efforts at Oricum to negotiate with Libo for the sending of envoys. It had never been his wish to expose his troops to bloodshed, nor to deprive the State of either army. After this speech, at the insistence of his troops, who were afire with enthusiasm, he gave the signal by trumpet.

In Caesar's army there was a recalled veteran named Crastinus, who in the previous year had been chief centurion of the Tenth legion in his service, a man of outstanding valour. When the signal was given, he said: "Follow me, you who were formerly in my company, and give your general the service you have promised. Only this one battle remains; after it, he will recover his position, and we our freedom". Looking at Caesar, "General," he said, "today I shall earn your gratitude, either dead or alive." So saying, he ran out first from the right wing, followed by about 120 crack troops, volunteers from the same century.

Between the two armies there was just enough space left for them to advance and engage each other. Pompey, however, had told his men to wait for Caesar's onset, and not to move from their positions or allow the line to be split up. He was said to have done this on the advice of Gaius Triarius, with the intention of breaking the force of the first impact of the enemy and stretching out their line, so that his own men, who were still in formation, could attack them while they were scattered. He also thought that the falling javelins would do less damage if the men stood still than if they were running forward while the missiles were discharged. Moreover, Caesar's troops, having to run twice the distance, would be out of breath and exhausted. It appears to us that he did this without sound reason, for there is a certain eagerness of spirit and an innate keenness in everyone which is inflamed by desire for battle. Generals ought to encourage this not repress it; nor was it for nothing that the practice began in antiquity of giving the signal on both sides and everyone's raising a war-cry: this was believed both to frighten the enemy and to stimulate one's own men.

Our men, on the signal, ran forward with javelins levelled; but when they observed that Pompey's men were not running to meet them, thanks to the practical experience and training they had had in earlier battles they checked their charge and halted about half-way, so as not to approach worn out. Then after a short interval they renewed the charge, threw their javelins and, as ordered by Caesar, quickly drew their swords. Nor indeed did the Pompeians fail to meet the occasion. They stood up to the hail of missiles and bore the onset of the legions; they kept their ranks, threw their javelins, and then resorted to their swords. At the same time the cavalry all charged forward, as instructed, from Pompey's left wing, and the whole horde of archers rushed out. Our cavalry failed to withstand their onslaught; they were dislodged from their position and gave ground a little. Pompey's cavalry thereupon pressed on the more hotly and began to deploy in squadrons and surround our line on its exposed flank. Observing this, Caesar gave the signal to the fourth line which he had formed of single cohorts. They ran forward swiftly to the attack with their standards and charged at Pompey's cavalry with such force that none of them could hold ground. They all turned, and not only gave ground but fled precipitately to the hilltops. Their withdrawal left all the archers and slingers exposed and, unarmed and unprotected, they were killed. In the same charge the cohorts surrounded the Pompeians who were still fighting and putting up a resistance on the left wing, and attacked them in the rear.

At the same time Caesar gave the order to advance to the third line, which had done nothing and had stayed in its position up till then. As a result, when fresh and unscathed troops took the place of the weary, while others were attacking from the rear, the Pompeians could not hold out, and every one of them turned tail and fled. Caesar was not wrong in thinking that the victory would originate from those cohorts which had been stationed in a fourth line to counteract the cavalry, as he had declared in cheering on his men; for it was by these first that the cavalry were repulsed, it was by these that the slingers and archers were massacred, and it was by these that the Pompeian left wing was surrounded and the rout started. When Pompey, however, saw his cavalry routed, and observed that part of his forces on which he most relied in a state of panic, having no confidence in the rest he left the field; he rode straight to the camp and said to the centurions he had posted on guard at the praetorian gate, loudly, so that the soldiers could hear: "Watch the camp and defend it strenuously, if there should be any reverse. I am going round to the other gates to make sure of the guard on the camp". So saying, he went to his tent, doubting his chances of success and yet awaiting the outcome.

The Pompeians were driven back in their retreat inside the rampart. Caesar, thinking that they should be given no respite in their panic, urged his men to take advantage of the generosity of fortune and storm the camp. Even though it was extremely hot – for the engagement had gone on until midday – his men were ready to undertake any toil and obeyed his order. The camp was being zealously defended by the cohorts left to guard it, and more fiercely still by the Thracian and native auxiliaries. For the troops who had fled from the field, terrified and exhausted, mostly dropped their weapons and military standards and had more thought for continuing their flight than for the defence of the camp. Nor indeed could those who had taken up their position on the rampart hold out any longer against the hail of missiles. Overcome by their wounds, they abandoned their posts and at once, led by their centurions and tribunes, fled to the hilltops near the camp.

In Pompey's camp could be seen artificial arbours, a great weight of silver plate laid out, tents spread with fresh turf, those of Lucius Lentulus and several others covered with ivy, and many other indications of extravagant indulgence and confidence in victory; so that it could readily be judged that they had had no fears for the outcome of the day, in that they were procuring unnecessary comforts for themselves. Yet these were the men who taunted Caesar's wretched and long-suffering army with self-indulgence, although the latter had always been short of all kinds of necessities. When our men were already inside the rampart, Pompey got a horse, removed his general's insignia, rushed out of the camp by the rear gate and galloped off to Larissa. He did not stop there, but with a few of his men whom he had picked up in his flight he went on through the night without stopping, accompanied by thirty cavalrymen, until he reached the sea. There he embarked on a grain-ship, with, it was said, frequent laments that he should have been so grossly mistaken, that he appeared almost tò have been betrayed by the very group of men whom he had hoped would secure victory but who had in fact started the flight.

Once Caesar had taken possession of the camp, he urged the soldiers not to let preoccupation with plundering render them incapable of attending to the tasks that remained. They obeyed, and he began building fortifications round the hill. Since the hill had no water, Pompey's men had no confidence in this position and leaving the mountain they all began retreating towards Larissa over its foothills. Caesar observed what they intended to do, and dividing his own forces he ordered part of the legions to stay behind in Pompey's camp and sent part back to his own camp; he took four legions with him and started along a more convenient route, to intercept the Pompeians. After advancing six miles he drew up his battle line. Observing this, the Pompeians halted on a hill, close under which ran a river. Caesar spoke encouragingly to his troops and though they were tired with continual exertion all during the day, and night was already approaching, he constructed a fortification cutting off the river from the hill, so that Pompey's men should not be able to get water during the night. When this was complete, the Pompeians sent a deputation and began to negotiate a surrender. A few of the senatorial order who had joined them sought to save themselves by fleeing during the night.

At dawn Caesar ordered all those who had settled on the hill to come down from the higher ground on to the plain and throw down their weapons. They did this without demur; then they threw themselves to the ground with their hands outstretched, weeping, and begged him for their lives. He reassured them, told them to get up, and spoke briefly to them about his own leniency, to alleviate their fears. He spared them all and charged his own soldiers to see to it that none of them suffered any physical violence or lost any part of his property. These matters taken care of, he ordered the other legions to come from the camp to join him, and the ones which he brought with him to go back to camp and rest in their turn. He arrived at Larissa on the same day.

Pompey himself escaped the battle to Egypt, where he was promptly assassinated: The Egyptians had no intention of aiding the loser in their hegemonic neighbour's power struggle.

A DICTATOR COMES TO DINNER, DECEMBER 45 BC

Marcus Cicero

Caesar ruled as dictator – sometimes a benevolent one, certainly an efficient one – from 49 BC until his assassination in 44 BC. Cicero had sided with Pompey in the Civil War, hence the tone of wary, amused cynicism in his letter recounting Caesar's dropping in for dinner.

To Atticus

Oh, what a formidable guest to have had! and yet *je ne m'en plains pas*, because he was in a very agreeable mood. But after his arrival at Philippus's house on the evening of the second day of the Saturnalia the whole establishment was so crowded with soldiers that even the room where Caesar himself was to dine could hardly be kept clear from them; it is a fact that there were two thousand men! Of course I was nervous about what might be the case with me next day, and so Cassius Barba came to my assistance; he set some men on guard. The camp was pitched out of doors; my villa was made secure. On the third day of the Saturnalia he stayed at Philippus's till near one, and admitted nobody (accounts with Balbus, I suppose); then took a walk on the beach. After two to the bath: then he heard about Mamurra; he made no objection. After the toilet he sat down to dinner. He was under the "emetic cure", and consequently he ate and drank *sans peur*, and with much satisfaction. And certainly everything was very good, and well served; nay more, I may say that

    "Though the cook was good,
    'Twas Attic salt that flavoured best the food."

There were three dining-rooms besides, where there was a very hospitable reception for the gentlemen of his *suite*; while the inferior class of freedmen and slaves had abundance at any rate; for as to the better class, they had a more refined table. In short, I think I acquitted myself like a man. The guest however was not the sort of person to whom you would say "I shall be most delighted if you will come here again on your way back"; once is enough. Nothing was said *au grand sérieux*; much on "literary" chat. In short, he was greatly pleased, and seemed to enjoy himself. He told me that he should be one day at Puteoli, and the next near Baiae. Here you have the story of his visit – or, I may call it, his *billeting* – which, as I told you, was a thing one would shrink from, but did not give much trouble. I am for Tusculum next after a short stay here.

When he was passing Dolabella's house, but nowhere else, the whole guard was paraded in arms on either side of him as he rode; I have it from Nicias.

"EVERY-WOMAN'S HUSBAND AND EVERY MAN'S WIFE": THE PERSONAL TRAITS OF JULIUS CAESAR

Suetonius

Though not a contemporary of Caesar, Suetonius (c. AD 72–130) provides the most informed witness to the dictator's habits and character. Suetonius was variously Director of the Imperial Library, Secretary of Studies and Secretary of Correspondence under Hadrian and thus had free access to state papers and records.

His stature is said to have been tall, his complexion light and clear, with eyes black, lively, and quick, set in a face somewhat full; his limbs were round and strong, and he was also very healthy, except towards his latter days when he was given to sudden swoons and disturbance in his sleep; and twice in the conduct of military affairs, he was seized with the falling sickness. In the care of his person, his scrupulousness almost approached the fantastical; for he not only kept the hair of his head closely cut and had his face smoothly shaved, but even had the hair on other parts of his body plucked out by the roots, a whim for which he was often twitted. Moreover, finding by experience that his baldness exposed him many times to the jibes of his enemies, he was much cast down because of it, and was wont to bring forward the thin growth of hair from his crown to his forehead; hence, of all the honours bestowed upon him by the senate and people, there was none which he accepted or used with greater alacrity than the privilege of wearing constantly a laurel crown. It is said also that in his apparel he was noted for a certain singularity; for he wore his senatorial purple-bordered robe trimmed with fringes about the wrists, and always had it girded about him, though rather loosely. This habit gave rise to the saying of Sulla, who admonished the nobles often to "beware of the ill-girt boy".

He dwelt at first in the Suburra, but after he was raised to the pontificate he occupied a palace belonging to the state in the Via Sacra. Many writers say that he was exceedingly addicted to elegance in his house and sumptuous fare at his table; and that he entirely demolished a villa near the grove of Aricia, which he had built from the foundation and finished at great cost, because it did not exactly realise his taste, although at that time he possessed but slender means and was deeply in debt. Finally, it is said that in his military expeditions he carried about him tessellated and marble slabs to grace the floor of his tent.

He made a voyage (as they say) into Britain in the hope of finding pearls; for the rumour was current that excellent pearls of all colours, but chiefly white, were found in the British seas; and he would compare the size of these and poise them in his hand to ascertain their weight. He was most eager, also, to purchase, at any cost, gems, carved works, statues, and pictures, executed by the eminent masters of antiquity. And for young, finely set-up slaves, he would pay a price so great that out of shame for his own extravagance he forbad its being recorded in the diary of his accounts.

It is reported of him that in all the provinces he governed, he feasted continually and maintained two tables, one for the officers of the army and the gentry of the country, and the other for Romans of the highest rank and provincials of the first distinction. He was so precise in his domestic arrangements, both great and small, that he once imprisoned a baker for serving to his guests bread of a lesser quality than to himself; and he put to death a freedman who was a particular favourite, for dishonouring the wife of a Roman knight, although no complaint had been made to him of the matter.

His reputation for continence and a clean life was unblemished save by the occasion of his intimacy with Nicomedes; but that was a foul stain that remained with him always and provoked many taunts and reproaches. I will not dwell at length on the notorious verses of Calvus Licinius, beginning:

Whate'er Bithynia and her lord possess'd, –
Her lord who Caesar in his lust caress'd –

I pass over the invectives and accusations of Dolabella, and Curio the father; in which Dolabella dubs him "the queen's rival, and the inner side of the royal couch", and Curio, "the brothel of Nicomedes, and the Bithynian stew". I likewise pass over the edicts of Bibulus, wherein he proclaimed his colleague under the name of "the queen of Bithynia", adding that "he had formerly been in love with a king, but now coveted a kingdom". At which time, as Marcus Brutus relates, there was one Octavius, a man of disordered brain and one given to overbroad jests, who, in a crowded assembly, after he had saluted Pompey by the title of king, addressed Caesar as queen. Caius Memmius likewise upbraided him with serving the king at table among the rest of his catamites, in the presence of a large company in which were some merchants from Rome, the names of whom he mentions.

But Cicero, not content with writing in certain of his letters that Caesar, having been conducted by the royal attendants from his own bedchamber to that of the king, was there laid upon a bed of gold with a covering of purple, where the flower of youth and innocence of him who was descended from Venus became defiled in Bithynia; but upon Caesar's pleading the cause of Nysa, the daughter of Nicomedes, before the senate, and there recounting the king's kindnesses to him, he replied: "Pray tell us no more of that; for it is well known, both what he bestowed upon you and also what you gave to him." Finally, in the Gallic triumph, his soldiers recited these verses among the others which they chanted merrily upon such occasions, and they have since that time become commonly current:

> The Gauls to Caesar yield, Caesar to Nicomede,
> Lo! Caesar triumphs for his glorious deed,
> But Caesar's conqueror gains no victor's meed.

It was generally believed that he was given to carnal pleasures and in this way spent much of his substance; also, that he dishonoured many ladies of noble houses, among whom were Postumia, the wife of Servius Sulpicius, Lollia, the wife of Aulus Gabinius, Tertulla, the wife of Marcus Crassus, and Mucia, the wife of Cnaeus Pompey. Certain it is, that not only the Curios, both father and son, but many others also reproached Pompey. "That to gratify his ambition, he married the daughter of a man upon whose account he had divorced his wife, after having had three children by her, and whom he used, with a deep sigh, to call Aegisthus." For it was Aegisthus who, like Caesar, was a pontiff, and who dishonoured Clytemnestra while Agamemnon was engaged in the Trojan war; in like manner did Caesar to Mucia, the wife of Pompey. But above all the rest, he loved Servilia, the mother of Marcus Brutus, for whom he purchased, in his first consulship after the commencement of their intrigue, a pearl that cost him six millions of sesterces; and also to whom, during the civil war, in addition to many other gifts, he sold for a very trifling consideration, some valuable farms that were offered at public auction. And when many persons marvelled that they went so cheap, Cicero pointedly remarked: "To acquaint you with the real value of the purchase (between ourselves), Tertia was deducted." For Servilia was thought to have prostituted her own daughter to Caesar; and her name, signifying "a third", gives added grace to the jest.

Nor did he avoid the wives of men in the provinces which he governed, as appears from this distich, which was as much repeated in the Gallic triumph as the other:

> Look to your wives, ye citizens, a lecher bald we bring,
> In Gaul adultery cost thee gold, here 'tis but borrowing.

For, as Caesar "borrowed" of other men, so he also "loaned", in that his own wife, Pompeia, as is thought, was maintained by P. Claudius.

He was enamoured also of certain queens, among whom was Eunoë, a Moor, the wife of Bogudes, to whom and her husband he made, as Naso reports, many handsome presents. But among these his liveliest fancy was for Cleopatra, with whom he often revelled all night until break of day; and he would have accompanied her through Egypt in dalliance as far as Ethiopia, in her luxurious galley, had not the army refused point blank to follow. He afterwards received her in Rome, whence he sent her back rich with honours and presents, and also gave her permission to name after him a son which she bore, and who, according to Greek historians of the times, was very like him both in shape and gait. Mark Antony avowed in the senate that Caesar had acknowledged the child to be his own; and that Caius Matias, Caius Oppius, and the rest of Caesar's friends knew it to be true. Of these, Caius Oppius, (as if the matter were so weighty as to require some apology) issued a book designed to show "that the child which Cleopatra fathered upon Caesar was not his". Helvius Cinna, tribune of the people, confessed to many persons that he had a law drawn out and in readiness, which Caesar had ordered him to prepare in his absence, to the effect that it might be lawful for him to take any wife he pleased, and as many as he desired, for the purpose of leaving issue. And that no man might have any doubt how infamous he was for sodomy and adulteries, Curio, the father, calls him in one of his orations, "Every woman's husband and every man's wife."

That he was a most sparing drinker of wine, his very enemies did not deny. Whereupon arose the remark of Marcus Cato, "that Caesar was the only sober man among all those who tried to overthrow the state". In the matter of diet, Caius Oppius reports him so indifferent, that when a person in whose house he was entertained, had served him with rancid instead of fresh, sweet oil for his vegetables, and the rest of the company would not touch it, he alone partook heartily that he might not be thought to blame his host either for negligence or rusticity.

From other men's goods, however, he did not abstain, neither when he had the command of armies abroad, nor when he held

office at Rome; for (as some have recorded), he took money
from the proconsul, Tubero, who was his predecessor in Spain,
and from the Roman allies in that quarter, for the discharge of
his debts; and certain towns of the Lusitanians, he sacked at the
point of the sword, although they did not rebel at his commands
but opened their gates to him upon his arrival. In Gaul he
robbed and spoiled the very chapels and temples of the gods,
which were full of rich gifts and oblations. As for cities, he
demolished them more often for the sake of their spoil, than for
any ill they had committed. In this way, he got such an
abundance of gold, that he exchanged it through Italy and
the provinces of the empire for three thousand sesterces the
pound. In his first consulship, he stole out of the Capitol three
thousand pounds' weight of gold, and left in its place the same
quantity of gilt brass. He bartered likewise to foreign nations
and princes, for gold, the titles of allies and kings, with the
honours and privileges that accompanied them; and he exacted
from Ptolemy alone nearly six thousand talents, in the name of
himself and Pompey. He afterwards supported the expense of
the civil wars, and of his triumphs and public spectacles, by the
most flagrant rapine and sacrilege.

CLEOPATRA IN ROME, C. 45 BC

Cicero

The Egyptian queen had been brought to Rome by Caesar as his mistress.

. . . I detest the Queen: let Hammonius, the voucher for her
promises, vouch that I have good cause for saying so.[1] For all
the presents she promised were things of a learned kind, and
consistent with my character, such as I could proclaim on the
housetops. As for Sara, I know him to be not only an unprincipled rascal but aggressively insolent to me. Only once have I
seen him at my house, and when I asked him politely what I
could do for him, he said he was looking for Atticus. And the
insolence of the Queen herself when she was living in Caesar's
trans-Tiberine villa, the recollection of it is painful to me. So I

---

[1] Presents from Cleopatra to Cicero had miscarried.

will have nothing to do with any of them. They think me devoid
not only of spirit, but of the ordinary feelings of a human being.

THE ASSASSINATION OF JULIUS CAESAR, ROME, 15 MARCH 44 BC

Nicolaus of Damascus

*Caesar was assassinated by an aristocratic conspiracy which sought to restore
republican freedom. The actual result was to plunge Rome into another bout
of civil war.*

The conspirators never met openly, but they assembled a few at
a time in each other's homes. There were many discussions and
proposals, as might be expected, while they investigated how
and where to execute their design. Some suggested that they
should make the attempt as he was going along the Sacred
Way, which was one of his favourite walks. Another idea was for
it to be done at the elections during which he had to cross a
bridge to appoint the magistrates in the Campus Martius; they
should draw lots for some to push him from the bridge and for
others to run up and kill him. A third plan was to wait for a
coming gladiatorial show. The advantage of that would be that,
because of the show, no suspicion would be aroused if arms were
seen prepared for the attempt. But the majority opinion favoured killing him while he sat in the Senate, where he would
be by himself since non-Senators would not be admitted, and
where the many conspirators could hide their daggers beneath
their togas. This plan won the day. Chance, too, played a part,
for it made him settle on a definite day for the Senate to meet to
discuss his intended measures.

When the day came, they assembled, with everything ready,
in Pompey's Stoa, their normal meeting-place. The impression
might be gained from his evil genius that all this was quite by
accident and subject to chance, but in fact it led him into his
enemy's place, in which he was to lie dead in front of Pompey's
statue, and be murdered near the image of a man now dead
whom, when alive, he had defeated. But if any attention is paid
to such things, his destiny had the stronger force. For his friends
were alarmed at certain rumours and tried to stop him going to

the Senate-house, as did his doctors, for he was suffering from one of his occasional dizzy spells. His wife, Calpurnia, especially, who was frightened by some visions in her dreams, clung to him and said that she would not let him go out that day. But Brutus, one of the conspirators who was then thought of as a firm friend, came up and said, "What is this, Caesar? Are you a man to pay attention to a woman's dreams and the idle gossip of stupid men, and to insult the Senate by not going out, although it has honoured you and has been specially summoned by you? But listen to me, cast aside the forebodings of all these people, and come. The Senate has been in session waiting for you since early this morning." This swayed Caesar and he left.

While this was happening, the conspirators were making their preparations and arranging their seats, some next to him, some facing him and some behind. Before he entered the chamber, the priests brought up the victims for him to make what was to be his last sacrifice. The omens were clearly unfavourable. After this unsuccessful sacrifice, the priests made repeated other ones, to see if anything more propitious might appear than what had already been revealed to them. In the end they said that they could not clearly see the divine intent, for there was some transparent, malignant spirit hidden in the victims. Caesar was annoyed and abandoned divination till sunset, though the priests continued all the more with their efforts. Those of the murderers present were delighted at all this, though Caesar's friends asked him to put off the meeting of the Senate for that day because of what the priests had said, and he agreed to do this. But some attendants came up, calling him and saying that the Senate was full. He glanced at his friends, but Brutus approached him again and said, "Come, good sir, pay no attention to the babblings of these men, and do not postpone what Caesar and his mighty power has seen fit to arrange. Make your own courage your favourable omen." He convinced Caesar with these words, took him by the right hand, and led him to the Senate which was quite near. Caesar followed in silence.

The Senate rose in respect for his position when they saw him entering. Those who were to have part in the plot stood near him. Right next to him went Tillius Cimber, whose brother had been exiled by Caesar. Under pretext of a humble request on behalf of this brother, Cimber approached and grasped the mantle of his toga, seeming to want to make a more positive move with his hands upon Caesar. Caesar wanted to get up and use his hands, but was prevented by Cimber and became exceedingly annoyed. That was the moment for the men to set to work. All quickly unsheathed their daggers and rushed at him. First Servilius Casca struck him with the point of the blade on the left shoulder a little above the collar-bone. He had been aiming for that, but in the excitement he missed. Caesar rose to defend himself, and in the uproar Casca shouted out in Greek to his brother. The latter heard him and drove his sword into the ribs. After a moment, Cassius made a slash at his face, and Decimus Brutus pierced him in the side. While Cassius Longinus was trying to give him another blow, he missed and struck Marcus Brutus on the hand. Minucius also hit out at Caesar and hit Rubrius in the thigh. They were just like men doing battle against him. Under the mass of wounds, he fell at the foot of Pompey's statue. Everyone wanted to seem to have had some part in the murder, and there was not one of them who failed to strike his body as it lay there, until, wounded thirty-five times, he breathed his last.

AFTER THE DEED: THE CONPIRATORS MEET, ANTIUM, 8 JUNE 44 BC

Cicero

Cicero was not directly involved in the assassination of Caesar, but met with the "liberators" afterwards. In truth, these were a rag-bag of republicans, careerists and slighted nobles who, having dispatched Caesar, were goalless thereafter. Their indecision is manifest in Cicero's account. Noteworthy is the role played by women in the proceedings, particularly Brutus' mother, Servilia.

To Atticus

I came to Antium today (the eighth). Brutus was pleased I had come. Then, before a large audience – Servilia, Tertulla, Porcia – he asked me what I advised. Favonius was also there. My advice, which I had been thinking out on the journey, was that he should accept the directorship of the corn-supply from Asia. The only thing left for us to do, I said, was to ensure his safety, since that was equivalent to safeguarding the Republic itself. While I was talking, Cassius came in. I repeated what I had been saying. At that point Cassius, with a fierce look in his eye, and practically breathing fire and slaughter, declared that he would not go to Sicily. "Am I to take an insult as a favour?" "Then what will you do?" I enquired. He said he would go to Achaia. "What about you, Brutus?" I asked. "I will go to Rome," he said, "if you think that is the right thing to do." "On the contrary," I replied; "you would not be safe there." "But if I could be safe there, would you think I should go?" "Yes," I said; "I am against your going to a province either now or after your praetorship, but I do not advise you to risk going to Rome." I gave the reasons – which no doubt occur to you – why he would not be safe there.

Then they went on talking for a long time and lamenting their lost chances, Cassius in particular, and they bitterly attacked Decimus Brutus. I offered the opinion that they ought to stop harping on the past, but I expressed agreement with what they said. When I went on to suggest what ought to have been done, saying nothing new but what everyone says every day, and not touching on the question whether anyone besides Caesar ought to have been dealt with, but observing that the Senate should have been summoned and that more should have been done to rouse the excited populace, your friend Servilia exclaimed. "Well, I never heard anyone . . .!" I stopped short. However, I think Cassius will go; for Servilia has promised she will see that the appointment to the corn-supply is erased from the senatorial decree. And our friend soon dropped his foolish talk about wanting to be in Rome. So he has decided that the Games[1] shall be held in his absence but under his name. Nevertheless, I believe he intends to go to Asia, embarking from Antium.

---

[1] Brutus, owing to the political danger which had kept him and Cassius out of Rome until the second week of April, decided not to hold the Games of Apollo (6–13 July) incumbent on him as city-praetor, but to have them held by another praetor in his name.

EVERYDAY LIFE: A ROMAN STUDENT WRITES HOME, ATHENS, 44 BC

Marcus Tullius Cicero

It was commonplace for male Roman youth to complete their education at the feet of a Greek tutor. Cicero's son (and namesake) writes home to his father's amanuensis.

After I had been anxiously expecting letter-carriers day after day, at length they arrived 46 days after they left you. Their arrival was most welcome to me: for while I took the greatest possible pleasure in the letter of the kindest and most beloved of fathers, still your most delightful letter put a finishing stroke to my joy. So I no longer repent of having suspended writing for a time, but am rather rejoiced at it; for I have reaped a great reward in your kindness from my pen having been silent. I am therefore exceedingly glad that you have unhesitatingly accepted my excuse. I am sure, dearest Tiro, that the reports about me which reach you answer your best wishes and hopes. I will make them good and will do my best that this belief in me, which day by day be comes more and more in evidence, shall be doubled. Wherefore you may with confidence and assurance fulfill your promise of being the trumpeter of my reputation.

For the errors of my youth have caused me so much remorse and suffering, that not only does my heart shrink from what I did, my very ears abhor the mention of it. And for this anguish and sorrow I know and am assured that you have taken your share. And I don't wonder at it! for while you wished me all success for my sake, you did so also for your own; for I have ever meant you to be my partner in all my good fortunes. Since, therefore, you have suffered sorrow through me, I will now take care that through me your joy shall be doubled. Let me assure you that my very close attachment to Cratippus is that of a son rather than a pupil: for though I enjoy his lectures, I am also specially charmed with his delightful manners. I spend whole days with him, and often part of the night: for I induce him to dine with me as often as possible. This intimacy having been established, he often drops in upon us unexpectedly while we are at dinner, and laying aside the stiff airs of a philosopher joins in our jests with the greatest possible freedom. He is such a man – so delightful, so distinguished – that you should take pains to make his acquaintance at the earliest possible opportunity. I need hardly mention Bruttius, whom I never allow to leave my side. He is a man of a strict and moral life, as well as being the most delightful company. For in him fun is not divorced from literature and the daily philosophical enquiries which we make in common. I have hired a residence next door to him, and as far as I can with my poor pittance I subsidize his narrow means. Furthermore, I have begun practising declamation in Greek with Cassius; in Latin I like having my practice with Bruttius. My intimate friends and daily companions are those whom Cratippus brought with him from Mitylene – good scholars, of whom he has the highest opinion. I also see a great deal of Epicrates, the leading man at Athens, and Leonides, and other men of that sort. So now you know how I am going on.

You remark in your letter on the character of Gorgias. The fact is, I found him very useful in my daily practice of declamation; but I subordinated everything to obeying my father's injunctions, for he had written ordering me to give him up at once. I would not shilly-shally about the business, for fear my making a fuss should cause my father to harbour some suspicion. Moreover, it occurred to me that it would be offensive for me to express an opinion on a decision of my father's. However, your interest and advice are welcome and acceptable. Your apology for lack of time I quite accept; for I know how busy you always are. I am very glad that you have bought an estate, and you have my best wishes for the success of your purchase. Don't be surprised at my congratulations coming in at this point in my letter, for it was at the corresponding point in yours that you told me of your purchase. You are a man of property! You must drop your city manners: you have become a Roman country gentleman. How clearly I have your dearest face before my eyes at this moment! For I seem to see you buying things for the farm, talking to your bailiff, saving the seeds at dessert in the corner of your cloak. But as to the matter of money, I am as sorry as you that I was not on the spot to help you. But do not doubt, my dear Tiro, of my assisting you in the future, if fortune does but stand by me; especially as I know that this estate has been purchased for our joint advantage.

As to my commissions about which you are taking trouble – many thanks! But I beg you to send me a secretary at the earliest opportunity – if possible a Greek; for he will save me a great deal of trouble in copying out notes. Above all, take care of your health, that we may have some literary talk together hereafter. I commend Anteros to you.

CIVIL WAR: A POET CELEBRATES AN OUTBREAK OF PEACE, 40 BC

Virgil

After Caesar's murder, his henchmen Mark Antony, Lepidus and Octavian (Caesar's adoptive son) assumed power in the so-called "Second Triumvirate". The triumvirs massacred their enemies – which included Cicero, beheaded and behanded – before falling out with each other. Publius Vergilius Maro here celebrates the reconciliation of Octavian and Mark Antony (Lepidus having been forcibly retired from power) and thus the descent of peace on his beloved Italian countryside. The child referred to was not as some Medieval scholars believed an anticipation of Christ but the hoped-for offspring between Antony and Octavian's sister. Civil war resumed six years later.

Sicilian Muse, I would try now a somewhat grander
    theme.
Shrubberies or meek tamarisks are not for all: but if it's
Forests I sing, may the forests be worthy of a consul.
    Ours is the crowning era foretold in prophecy:
Born of Time, a great new cycle of centuries
Begins. Justice returns to earth, the Golden Age
Returns, and its first-born comes down from heaven
    above.
Look kindly, chaste Lucina, upon this infant's birth,
For with him shall hearts of iron cease, and hearts of
    gold
Inherit the whole earth – yes, Apollo reigns now.
And it's while you are consul – you, Pollio – that this
    glorious

Age shall dawn, the march of its great months begin.
You at our head, mankind shall be freed from its
   age-long fear,
All stains of our past wickedness being cleansed away.
This child shall enter into the life of the gods, behold
   them
Walking with antique heroes, and himself be seen of
   them,
And rule a world made peaceful by his father's virtuous
   acts.
   Child, your first birthday presents will come from
     nature's wild –
Small presents: earth will shower you with romping ivy,
   foxgloves,
Bouquets of gipsy lilies and sweetly-smiling acanthus.
Goats shall walk home, their udders taut with milk, and
   nobody
Herding them: the ox will have no fear of the lion:
Silk-soft blossom will grow from your very cradle to lap
   you.
But snakes will die, and so will fair-seeming, poisonous
   plants.
Everywhere the commons will breathe of spice and
   incense.
   But when you are old enough to read about famous
     men
And your father's deeds, to comprehend what manhood
   means,
Then a slow flush of tender gold shall mantle the great plains,
Then shall grapes hang wild and reddening on
   thorn-trees,
And honey sweat like dew from the hard bark of oaks.
Yet there'll be lingering traces still of our primal
   error,
Prompting us to dare the seas in ships, to girdle
Our cities round with walls and break the soil with
   plough-shares.
A second Argo will carry her crew of chosen heroes,
A second Tiphys steer her. And wars – yes, even wars

There'll be; and great Achilles must sail for Troy again.
  Later, when the years have confirmed you in full
  manhood,
Traders will retire from the sea, from the pine-built
  vessels
They used for commerce: every land will be self-
  supporting.
The soil will need no harrowing, the vine no pruning-
  knife;
And the tough ploughman may at last unyoke his oxen.
We shall stop treating wool with artificial dyes,
For the ram himself in his pasture will change his
  fleece's colour,
Now to a charming purple, now to a saffron hue,
And grazing lambs will dress themselves in coats of
  scarlet.
    "Run, looms, and weaves this future!" – thus have
      the Fates spoken,
In unison with the unshakeable intent of Destiny.
    Come soon, dear child of the gods, Jupiter's great
      viceroy!
Come soon – the time is near – to begin your life
  illustrious!
Look how the round and ponderous globe bows to
  salute you,
The lands, the stretching leagues of sea, the unplumbed sky!
Look how the whole creation exults in the age to come!
    If but the closing days of a long life were prolonged
For me, and I with breath enough to tell your story,
Oh then I should not be worsted at singing by Thracian
  Orpheus
Or Linus – even though Linus were backed by Calliope
His mother, and Orpheus by his father, beauteous
  Apollo.
Should Pan compete with me, and Arcady judge us, even
Pan, great Pan, with Arcadian judges, would lose the
  contest.
    Begin, dear babe, and smile at your mother to show
    you know her –

This is the tenth month now, and she is sick of waiting.
Begin, dear babe. The boy who does not smile at his
    mother
Will never deserve to sup with a god or sleep with a
    goddess.

A JOURNEY TO BRUNDUSIUM, 38 BC

Horace

From Horace's Satires. *Brundusium is nowadays Brindisi.*

Having left mighty Rome, Aricia received me in but a middling inn: Heliodorus the rhetorician, most learned in the Greek language, was my fellow-traveller: thence we proceeded to Forum-Appî, stuffed with sailors and surly landlords. This stage, but one for better travellers than we, being laggard we divided into two; the Appian Way is less tiresome to bad travellers. Here I, on account of the water, which was most vile, proclaim war against my belly, waiting not without impatience for my companions whilst at supper. Now the night was preparing to spread her shadows upon the earth, and to display the constellations in the heavens. Then our slaves began to be liberal of their abuse to the watermen, and the watermen to our slaves. "Here bring to." "You are stowing in hundreds; hold, now sure there is enough." Thus while the fare is paid and the mule fastened, a whole hour is passed away. The cursed gnats, and frogs of the fens, drive off repose, while the waterman and a passenger, well soaked with plenty of thick wine, vie with one another in singing the praises of their absent mistresses. At length the passenger, being fatigued, begins to sleep, and the lazy waterman ties the halter of the mule turned out a-grazing to a stone, and snores, lying flat on his back.

And now the day approached, when we saw the boat made no way, until a choleric fellow, one of the passengers, leaps out of the boat, and drubs the head and sides of both mule and waterman with a willow cudgel. At last we were scarcely set ashore at the fourth hour. We wash our faces and hands in thy water, O Feronia. Then, having dined, we crawled on three miles; and arrive under Anxur, which is built upon rocks that look white to a great distance. Mæcenas was to come here, as was the excellent Cocceius, both sent ambassadors on matters of great importance, having been accustomed to reconcile friends at variance. Here, having got sore eyes, I was obliged to use the black ointment. In the meantime came Mæcenas and Cocceius, and Fonteius Capito along with them, a man of perfect polish, and intimate with Mark Antony, no man more so.

Without regret we passed Fundi, where Aufidius Luscus was prætor, laughing at the honours of that crazy scribe, his prætexta, laticlave, and pan of incense. At our next stage, being weary, we tarry in the city of the Mamurræ, Murena complimenting us with his house, and Capito with his kitchen.

The next day arises, by much the most agreeable to all, for Plotius and Varius and Virgil met us at Sinuessa; souls more candid ones than which the world never produced, nor is there a person in the world more bound to them than myself. Oh what embraces and what transports were there! While I am in my senses, nothing can I prefer to a pleasant friend. The village, which is next adjoining to the bridge of Campania, accommodated us with lodging at night, and the public officers with such a quantity of fuel and salt as they are obliged to by law.

From this place the mules deposited their pack-saddles at Capua betimes in the morning. Mæcenas goes to play at tennis, but I and Virgil to our repose, for to play at tennis is hurtful to weak eyes and feeble constitutions.

From this place the villa of Cocceius, situated above the Caudian inns, which abounds with plenty receives us. Now, my muse, I beg of you briefly to relate the engagement between the buffoon Sarmentus and Messius Cicirrus, and from what ancestry descended each began the contest. The illustrious race of Messius – Oscan; Sarmentus's mistress is still alive. Sprung from such families as these, they came to the combat.

First, Sarmentus: "I pronounce thee to have the look of a mad horse."

We laugh, and Messius himself says:

"I accept your challenge," and wags his head.

"Oh!" cries Sarmentus, "if the horn were not cut off your forehead, what would you not do, since, maimed as you are, you bully at such a rate?"

For a foul scar has disgraced the left part of Messius's bristly forehead. Cutting many jokes upon his Campanian disease and upon his face, Sarmentus desired him to exhibit Polyphemus's dance, that he had no occasion for a mask or the tragic buskins.

Cicirrus retorted largely to these: he asked whether he had consecrated his chain to the household gods according to his vow, though he was a scribe, he told him, his mistress's property in him was not the less. Lastly he asked him how he ever came to run away, such a lank meagre fellow, for whom a pound of corn a-day would be ample. We were so diverted that we continued that supper to an unusual length.

Hence we proceed straight on for Beneventum, where the bustling landlord almost burned himself in roasting some lean thrushes, for the fire falling through the old kitchen floor, the spreading flame made a great progress towards the highest part of the roof. Then you might have seen the hungry guests and frightened slaves snatching their supper out of the flames, and every body endeavouring to extinguish the fire.

After this Apulia began to discover to me her well-known mountains, which the Atabulus scorches with his blasts, and through which we should never have crept unless the neighbouring village of Trivicus had received us, not without a smoke that brought tears into our eyes – occasioned by a hearth's burning some green boughs with the leaves upon them. Here, like a great fool as I was, I wait till midnight for a deceitful mistress; sleep, however, overcomes me whilst meditating love, and disagreeable dreams make me ashamed of myself and every thing about me.

Hence we were bowled away in chaises twenty-four miles, intending to stop at a little town, which one cannot name in a verse,[1] but it is easily enough known by description; for water is sold here, though it is the worst in the world; but their bread is exceedingly fine, insomuch that the wary traveller is used to carry it willingly on his shoulders, for the bread of Canusium is gritty, which place was formerly built by the valiant Diomedes. Here Varius departs dejected from his weeping friends.

Hence we came to Rubi, fatigued, because we made a long journey, and it was rendered still more troublesome by the

[1] Equotuticum.

rains. Next day the weather was better, the road worse, even to the very walls of Barium that abounds in fish. In the next place, Egnatia, which seems to have been built on troubled waters, gave us occasion for jests and laughter, for they wanted to persuade us that at this sacred portal the incense melted without fire. The Jew, Apella, may believe this, not I! For I have learned from Epicurus that the gods dwell in a state of tranquillity; nor, if nature effect any wonder, that the anxious gods sent it from the high canopy of the heavens.

Brundusium ends both my journey and my paper.

ON GOING TO BED WITH CLEOPATRA, 33 BC

Mark Antony

The rivalry between Octavian and Antony was embittered particularly by Antony's affair with Cleopatra, queen of Egypt. Antony happened, simultaneously, to be married to Octavian's sister, Octavia. When Antony divorced Octavia in 33 BC, so that he could enjoy the charms of Cleopatra unencumbered, it provided a filip for renewed war between the two men.

To Octavianus Augustus
What's upset you? Because I go to bed with Cleopatra? But she's my wife, and I've been doing so for nine years, not just recently. And, anyway, is Livia *your* only pleasure? I expect that you will have managed, by the time you read this, to have hopped into bed with Tertulla, Terentilla, Rufilla, Salvia Titisenia, or the whole lot of them. Does it really matter where, or with what women, you get your excitement?

OCTAVIAN'S VICTORY AT ACTIUM, 31 BC

Horace

In 32 BC Octavian went to war against Cleopatra, a clever ruse which avoided direct declaration of hostilities against compatriot Antony but would surely bring him to the fray. It did. At Actium, Greece, a joint Egyptian–Antonian naval force was defeated by Octavian and his nautical genius Agrippa; Antony and Cleopatra fled back to Egypt, where they committed suicide.

Horace's ode Cleopatra, *written in 30* BC, *shows something of the relief Rome felt at the Egyptians' defeat.*

Now 'tis the hour for wine, now without check
To trip it gaily, now with feasts sublime
   Worthy a Salian board, 'twas time
      Each deity's place to deck!

Who could till now his Caecuban exhume
From bins ancestral, while a queen designed
   For Rome's high seat destruction blind,
      And for Rome's empire doom,

She, and her plague-scarred crew of evil fame,
Reckless enough to dream joys without bound,   10
   And in sweet fortune's frenzies drowned?
      But pause to madness came,

When scarce one ship from burning she could save!
Her soul, with Mareotic wine o'erwrought,
   Caesar to real terrors brought,
      When he from Italy drave

Her flight, and tracked her o'er the sea (as track
Hawks the soft dove, or as swift hunters ply
   A hare in snow-clad Thessaly),
      Minded a plague so black   20

To enchain. But she, seeking her end to grace
By nobler dying, feared not as woman might
   The sword's keen edge, nor sought by flight
      Some seaward hiding-place;

Dared ev'n to look upon her Court o'erthrown
With eye serene, and with untrembling lip
   The deadly hissing asps to grip,
      And drink their venom down.

With death resolved upon, more proud her mien;
Scorning that such as she, in hostile sloop   30
  Her foes like some poor trull should coop
    For triumph, her, a queen!

Part Two

Empire
Rome 30 BC–AD 180

INTRODUCTION

After seizing power, Octavian was astute enough to leave the trappings of the Republic in place. The Senate still met, consuls and magistrates were still elected. But it was *de facto* one-man rule: Octavian had the power, and exercised it through a new caste of imperial officials. Few objected, even when Octavian elevated himself into a god and rebranded himself "Augustus" (sacred). The alternative was a return to the civil war of the last decades. Augustan stability, moreover, allowed the wealth of the widespread Roman empire to flow to the eternal city. There was chattering among intellectuals and artists of a new golden age. (Meanwhile the poor in Roman society, who tended to remain poor, had their minds more on the dole of bread or the state-sponsored diversion of the circus.) Virgil's epic poem the *Aeneid*, which traced the story of Rome back to its origins, posited the enticing notion that Rome had been born again in more glorious form under Augustus.

Augustus' successors in the Julio–Claudian dynasty perpetuated and expanded imperial rule. Yet the monarchy remained capriciously dependent on the personality of the individual emperor. A bad emperor made for a bad reign. Moreover, the exalted status of "the purple" tended to go to the incumbent's head, ego and libido, so that even those who began well ended debauched, despotic and entirely free of beneficence (Tiberius, for instance). Most Julio–Claudians were also morbidly afflicted with paranoia – not that their ravings entirely lacked justification, for plots for replacements abounded, within the palace and without. The emperor's personal army of protection, the Praetorian Guard, in particular, possessed the unhappy belief that it should make or break an emperor. Thus the Praetorian Guard installed Caligula on Tiberius' death in AD 37 but when Caligula displeased they murdered him in AD 41 (plus his wife and infant daughter). They then dragged the spastic Claudius out of his hiding place behind a curtain and set him on the throne.

If anything, the emperors who immediately followed the Julio–Claudians had a harder task in keeping the throne, since the Julio–Claudians had basked in Augustus' reflected popular glory. In AD 69 there were no less than four emperors installed – and uninstalled – on the throne because they failed to please. Only an exceptional figure like Vespasian, an ascetic, intelligent soldier, was able to rule long and wisely (AD 69–79). It was Vespasian who restored government finances, extended and consolidated the conquests in Judea, Britain and Germany, and embarked on an ambitious building programme in Rome itself, the centrepiece of which was the Colosseum. Arguably, however, the peak of imperial rule came in AD 98–180, with the back-to-back reigns of Trajan (a Spaniard), Hadrian (another Spaniard), Antonius (the "Pius") and Marcus Aurelius, the Stoic philosopher. The four shared a policy of establishing secure borders for the empire against the "barbarians", butressed by permanent military fortifications, epitomised by Hadrian's Wall in the north of England. No less than 30 legions of between 3,000–6,000 men each, plus tens of thousands of auxiliaries (hired, Romanized natives) were engaged in the empire's defence.

At its greatest extent, under Trajan, the empire stretched from the Atlantic coast of Spain in the west to Babylonia in the east, from England in the north to Egypt in the south east – an area of 2,000,000 square miles. This vast territory the Romans not only pacified (the so-called *Pax Romana*) but Romanized. No matter the geographical point in the empire, be it Colchester in England or Timgad in Algeria, the Romans installed straight roads (for defensive purposes mainly, enabling infantry to march at 20 miles a day), erected civilized public amenities (notably bath-houses), built amphitheatres (all modelled on the Colosseum in Rome, all showing the same bloody bill of gladiators and wild animals in deadly combinations; some circuses slew 5,000 wild animals per day), forums, and temples. To most subject peoples the Romans also extended the rights of citizenship, and thus the protection of Roman law. "I am a Roman born" declared St Paul (born in Cilicia, now Turkey) to his Jewish accusers in Jerusalem, and accordingly demanded – and got – his citizen's right to trial in the imperial capital. It was, incidentally, *Pax Romana*'s very stability and expansive road-network which allowed the obscure sect known as Christians, after their crucified Judean leader, to spread The Word and eventually convert the empire from paganism.

This spiritual dimension notwithstanding, *Pax Romana* gave Rome a material prosperity unrivalled in the Ancient World. This was not only because peace allowed uninterrupted production, but because the demolition of internal barriers within the empire allowed a continental-sized expansion of trade. As the hub of the imperial trading network, Rome – which was on a navigable stretch of the Tiber and only 20 miles from the sea – grew phenomenally, to reach a million-plus population.

Yet the wealth of Rome was always relative. The last of the "four good emperors", Marcus Aurelius, faced a desperate financial crisis at the very moment he needed money most. For in the 160s, German tribesmen – "barbarians" to the Romans – began to pour across the Danubian frontier and even penetrate into Italy itself. The Emperor negated the incursions, partly through military means, partly by allowing some tribes to settle inside the empire. But, as was obvious to all, the barbarians would come again. The death of Marcus Aurelius was regarded, correctly, as a national disaster. His son, Commodus, was a lightweight savage, his father's opposite in every respect. After Commodus' assassination in AD 180 the empire was sold off at auction. The long and spectacular decline of Rome had begun.

THE DEEDS OF AUGUSTUS, 44 BC–AD 14

Augustus

After Actium, Octavian became the sole ruler of the Roman world, initially robing his dictatorship in republican forms. The cloth grew increasingly thin and in 27 BC he received the name "Augustus" (sacred) in recognition of his status as both emperor and divinity. Although Augustus' own Autobiography *is lost, a record of his public achievements – as written by Augustus himself, and originally set in bronze before his Mausoleum in Rome – is extant in copies in both Greek and Latin. The most famous of these copies is inscribed in temple to Augustus in Ankara, Turkey.*

Below is a copy of the deeds of the divine Augustus, by which he subjected the whole world to the dominion of the Roman People, and of the sums of money he spent upon the Republic and the Roman People, even as they are graven on the two brazen columns which are set up in Rome.

In my twentieth year [44 BC], acting on my own initiative and at my own charges, I raised an army wherewith I brought again liberty to the Republic oppressed by the dominance of a faction. Therefore did the Senate admit me to its own order by honorary decrees, in the consulship of Gaius Pansa and Aulus Hirtius. At the same time they gave unto me rank among the consulars in the expressing of my opinion in the Senate;[1] and they gave unto me the *imperium*.[2] It also voted that I, as proprætor, together with the consuls, should "see to it that the state suffered no harm." In the same year, too, when both consuls had fallen in battle, the people made me consul and triumvir for the reestablishing of the Republic.

The men who killed my father [Julius Cæsar] I drove into exile by strictly judicial process,[3] and then, when they took up arms against the Republic, twice I overcame them in battle.[4]

I undertook civil and foreign wars both by land and by sea; as victor therein I showed mercy to all surviving Roman citizens. Foreign nations, that I could safely pardon, I preferred to spare rather than to destroy. About 500,000 Roman citizens took the military oath of allegiance to me. Rather over 300,000 of these have I settled in colonies, or sent back to their home towns

---

1 He could speak in the Senate when the presiding officer summoned the ex-consuls to speak, *i.e.* among the first.
2 In Angustus's case this amounted to confirming him in his exceptional command over an army raised by him without public authority.
3 Augustus wants to pose as a close adherent to legal processes – not martial power.
4 Not actually true; in the first battle at Philippi Augustus was worsted, though Antonius's half of the army succeeded.

(municipia) when their term of service ran out; and to all of these I have given lands bought by me, or the money for farms – and this out of my private means. I have taken 600 warships, besides those smaller than triremes.

Offices and Honours given to Augustus

Twice have I had the lesser triumph [ovation]; thrice the [full] curule triumph; twenty-one times have I been saluted as "Imperator". After that, when the Senate voted me many triumphs, I declined them. Also I often deposited the laurels in the Capitol, fulfilling the vows which I had made in battle. On account of the enterprises brought to a happy issue on land and sea by me, or by my legates, under my auspices, fifty-five times has the Senate decreed a thanksgiving unto the Immortal Gods. The number of days, too, on which thanksgiving was professed, fulfilling the Senate's decrees, was 890. Nine kings, or children of kings, have been led before my car in my triumphs. And when I wrote these words, thirteen times had I been consul, and for the thirty-seventh year was holding the tribunician power.

The dictatorship which was offered me by the People and by the Senate, both when I was present and when I was absent, I did not accept. The annual and perpetual consulship I did not accept.

Ten years in succession I was one of the "triumvirs for the reestablishing of the Republic." Up to the day that I wrote these words I have been *princeps* of the Senate forty years. I have been *pontifex maximus*, augur, member of the "College of XV for the Sacred Rites" and of the other religious brotherhoods.

Augustus' Acts as Censor

In my fifth consulship, by order of the People and the Senate, I increased the number of patricians. Three times I revised the Senate list. In my sixth consulship, with my colleague, Marcus Agrippa, I made a census of the People. By it the number of Roman citizens was 4,063,000. Again in the consulship of Gaius Censorinus and Gaius Asinus [8 BC] I took the census, when the number of Roman citizens was 4,230,000. A third time . . . in the consulship of Sextus Pompeius and Sextus Appuleius [AD 14], with Tiberius Cæsar as colleague, I took the census when the number of Roman citizens was 4,937,000. By new legislation I have restored many customs of our ancestors which had begun to fall into disuse, and I have myself also set many examples worthy of imitation by those to follow me.

By decree of the Senate my name has been included in the hymn of the Salii,[5] and it has been enacted by law that as long as I live I shall be invested with the tribunician power. I refused to be *pontifex maximus* in place of a colleague still living, when the people proffered me that priesthood which my father had held.

Benefactions and Public Works conducted by Augustus

The temple of Janus Quirinus, which it was the purpose of our fathers to close when there was a victorious peace throughout the whole Roman Empire, – by land and sea, – and which – before my birth – had been alleged to have been closed only twice at all, since Rome was founded: thrice did the Senate order it closed while I was princeps.[6]

To each of the Roman plebs I paid 300 sesterces in accord with the last will of my father [Cæsar]. In my own name in my fifth consulship [29 BC] I gave 400 sesterces from the spoils of war. Again in my tenth consulship [24 BC] I gave from my own estate to every man among the Romans 400 sesterces as a donative. In my eleventh, twelve times I made distributions of food, buying grain at my own charges. And I made like gifts on several other occasions. The sum which I spent for Italian farms for the veterans was about 600,000,000 sesterces and for lands in the provinces about 260,000,000 . . . Four times have I aided the public treasury from my own means, to such extent that I furnished to those managing the treasury department 150,000,000 sesterces.

I built the Curia [Senate House], and the Chalcidicum adjacent thereunto, the temple of Apollo on the Palatine with its porticoes, the temple of the deified Julius [Cæsar], the Lupercal, the portico to the Circus of Flaminius and a vast number of other public buildings and temples.

5 As if Augustus were a god.
6 29 BC, 25 BC, and probably again in 8 BC.

Aqueducts which have crumbled through age I have restored, and I have doubled the water in the aqueduct called the Marcian by turning a new stream into its course. The Forum Julium and the basilica which was between the temple of Castor and the temple of Saturn, works begun and almost completed by my father, I finished.

Three times in my own name and five times in that of my adoptive sons or my grandsons I have given gladiator exhibitions; in these exhibitions about 10,000 men have fought. Besides other games twenty-six times in my own name, or in that of my sons and grandsons I have given hunts of African wild beasts in the circus, the Forum, the amphitheaters – and about 3,500 wild beasts have been slain.

I gave the people the spectacle of a naval battle beyond the Tiber where is now the grove of the Cæsars. For this purpose an excavation was made 1,800 feet long and 1,200 wide. In this contest thirty warships – triremes or biremes – took part, and many others smaller. About 3,000 men fought on these craft beside the rowers.

Conquests wrought by Augustus

I have cleared the sea from pirates. In that war with the slaves[7] I delivered to their masters for punishment 80,000 slaves who had fled their masters and taken up arms against the Republic. The provinces of Gaul, Spain, Africa, Sicily, and Sardinia swore the same allegiance to me. I have extended the boundaries of all the provinces of the Roman People which were bordered by nations not yet subjected to our sway. My fleet has navigated the ocean from the mouth of the Rhine as far as the boundaries of the Cimbri where aforetime no Roman had ever penetrated by land or by sea. The German peoples there sent their legates, seeking my friendship, and that of the Roman people. At almost the same time, by my command and under my auspices two armies have been led into Ethiopia and into Arabia, which is called "The Happy", and very many of the enemy of both peoples have fallen in battle, and many towns have been captured.

7 The reference is to Sextus Pompeius's forces overthrown in 36 BC which were largely recruited from runaway slaves.

I added Egypt to the Empire of the Roman People. When the king of Greater Armenia was killed I could have made that country a province, but I preferred after the manner of our fathers to deliver the kingdom to Tigranes [a vassal prince] . . . I have compelled the Parthians to give up to me the spoils and standards of three Roman armies, and as suppliants to seek the friendship of the Roman people. Those recovered standards, moreover, I have deposited in the sanctuary located in the temple of Mars the Avenger.

In my sixth and seventh consulships [28 and 27 BC] when I had put an end to the civil wars, after having obtained complete control of the government, by universal consent I transferred the Republic from my own dominion back to the authority of the Senate and Roman People. In return for this favour by me, I received by decree of the Senate the title *Augustus*, the door-posts of my house were publicly decked with laurels, a civic crown[8] was fixed above my door, and in the Julian Curia [Senate-house] was set a golden shield, which by its inscription bore witness that it was bestowed on me, by the Senate and Roman People, on account of my valour, clemency, justice, and piety. After that time I excelled all others in dignity, but of power I held no more than those who were my colleagues in any magistracy.

AN ESTATE OWNER'S WILL, 8 BC

Gaius Isidorus

Gaius Caecilius Claudius Isidorus in the consulship of Gaius Asinius Gallus and Gaius Marcius Censorinus [8 BC] upon the sixth day before the kalends of February declared by his will, that though he had suffered great losses by the civil wars, he was still able to leave behind him 4,116 slaves, 3,600 yoke of oxen, and 257,000 head of other kinds of cattle, besides in ready money 60,000,000 sesterces. Upon his funeral he ordered 1,100,000 sesterces to be expended.

8 A "civic crown" was given for saving a citizen. Augustus had saved the state.

HOUSEKEEPING RECORD, C. AD 1

Anon

From Romanized Egypt. The attention to the diet of children is an historical transcendent.

		drachmas	obols
Jan. 16	Coraxian cloak	10	
	Turnips for preserving	1	2
	Hire of copper vessel for dyeing		2
	Salt		1
	Grinding 1 artaba of wheat on the 13th		3
	Rushes for the bread baking		2
	Wages for repair of Coraxian cloak		1½
	Entertaining the wife of Gemellus		4
	Myrrh for the burial of Phna's daughter		4
Jan. 17	Chous of olive-oil	1	4
	Wax and stilus for the children		1
	Pure bread for Prima		½
	Entertaining Tyche		3
Feb. 4	Lunch for the weaver		1
	For the Serapeum		2
	Pure bread for the children		½
	Beer for the weaver		2
	Leeks for the weaver's lunch		1
	A pigeon		1
	To Antas	2	2
	Grinding 2 artabae of wheat for flour through Isas in town	1	2
5	Grinding 1 artaba of wheat for flour in encampment		4
	Weaver's lunch		1
	Asparagus for Antas' dinner at the feast of the fuller		½
	Cabbage for the boys' dinner	½	
10	Savoury		½
	Rushes for the loaves		2½

11	Milk for the children		½
	Pure bread		½
12	To Secundus for a cake		
	for the children		½
13	Barley gruel for the children		½
14	Sauce		1
	Pure bread		½
	Entertaining Antonia		2
	Entertaining Taptollous		3
	Garlands for the birthday of		
	Tryphas		2
	Birthday garlands		2
15	Pomegranates for the children		1
	Toys etc. for the children		½
	Beer		3
	Sauce		1
Feb. 16	Sauce		1
	Thaesis – 2 days (? stay or work)		5
	Taarpaesis – 2 days		5
	Berous – 10 days	4	1
18	Grinding 1 artaba of wheat		4
	2 measures of salt for pickling		2
	Salt		1
	Needle and thread		1
	Grinding 1 artaba of wheat		
	(through Theodorus)		4
	Weaving of a cloak	1	2
	White loaves	1	
	Pigeon for the children		1
	Pure bread for the children		½
	To Secundus for a cake for the children		½
	Dry finest flour		½
	Milk		½
	Myrrh for the burial of the daughter		
	of Pasis	1	

EGYPT UNDER THE RULE OF ROME, c. AD 1

Strabo

Unlike other Roman territories, Egypt was the personal domain of the Emperor. Strabo – the name means "squint-eyed" – was a Greek geographer and explorer who eventually settled in Rome.

At present [in Augustus' time] Egypt is a Roman province, and pays considerable tribute, and is well governed by prudent persons sent there in succession. The governor thus sent out has the rank of king. Subordinate to him is the administrator of justice, who is the supreme judge in many cases. There is another officer called the Idologus whose business is to inquire into property for which there is no claimant, and which of right falls to Cæsar. These are accompanied by Cæsar's freedmen and stewards, who are intrusted with affairs of more or less importance.

Three legions are stationed in Egypt, one in the city [of Alexandria], the rest in the country. Besides these, there are also nine Roman cohorts quartered in the city, three on the borders of Ethiopia in Syene, as a guard to that tract, and three in other parts of the country. There are also three bodies of cavalry distributed at convenient posts.

Of the native magistrates in the cities, the first is the "Expounder of the Law" – who is dressed in scarlet. He receives the customary honours of the land, and has the care of providing what is necessary for the city. The second is the "Writer of the Records"; the third is the "Chief Judge"; the fourth is the "Commander of the Night Guard". These officials existed in the time of the [Ptolemaic] kings, but in consequence of the bad administration of the public affairs by the latter, the prosperity of the city of Alexandria was ruined by licentiousness. Polybius expresses his indignation at the state of things when he was there. He describes the inhabitants of Alexandria as being composed of three classes, – first the Egyptians and natives, acute in mind, but very poor citizens, and wrongfully meddlesome in civic affairs. Second were the mercenaries, – a numerous and undisciplined body, – for it was an old custom to keep foreign soldiers – who from the worthlessness of their sovrans

knew better how to lord it than to obey. The third were the so-
called "Alexandrines", who, for the same reason, were not
orderly citizens; however they were better than the mercenaries, for although they were a mixed race, yet being of Greek
origin they still retained the usual Hellenic customs.

Such, then, if not worse, were the social conditions of Alexandria under the last kings. The Romans, as far as they were
able, corrected – as I have said – many abuses, and established
an orderly government – by setting up vice-governors, "no-
marchs," and "ethnarchs," whose business it was to attend to
the details of administration.

AUGUSTUS AT THE GAMING BOARD, c. AD 5

Augustus

A letter to Tiberius, Augustus' adoptive son and heir.

I have spent, my dear Tiberius, a most enjoyable festival of
Minerva. I played every day, and made the gaming-board quite
hot. Your brother* was very noisy over a desperate run of ill-luck,
but on the whole he did not lose much, for, though he lost
enormously at first, he gradually made an unhoped-for recovery.
I lost 20,000 sesterces, for my part, but this was due to the
extravagant generosity which I make a habit of showing at play.
For if I had called in all the debts I forgave, or even merely kept
what I gave away, I should have won 50,000. But I prefer to do
thus, in order to exalt my reputation for generosity to the skies.

ARMINIUS FORCES THE ROMAN EAGLES BACK, GERMANY, AD 9

Velleius Paterculus

*Between 12 and 9 BC Germany as far as the Elbe was conquered by Nero
Drusus, stepson of Augustus. However, in AD 9 the Roman governor, Varus,
was defeated by the patriotic chieftain Arminius, leaving Germany outside
Roman control for evermore.*

---

* Claudius

Quintilius Varus [the new governor of Germany] was born of a noble rather than an illustrious family; he was of a mild disposition, and of a sedate manner, and being rather indolent both in mind and body was more accustomed to ease in a camp than action in the field. How far he was from despising money, Syria – where he had been governor – gave the proof; for when he went there the province was rich and he was poor; when he departed it was poor and he was rich! On appointment to the command in Germany, he imagined that the inhabitants had nothing human but their voice and limbs, and that creatures who could be tamed by the sword might be civilized by the intricacies of law. With this notion, once in the heart of Germany, as if among a most peace-loving folk, he spent the summer deciding litigation, and ordering the pleadings before a tribunal. The Germans, though exasperated by such strange proceedings, pretended to be grateful for them and they at length lulled Varus into such a perfect security that he fancied himself a city prætor [at Rome] handing out justice in the Forum, instead of commanding an army in the middle of Germany.

It was at this time, that a young man of high birth, Arminius, son of the German prince, Segimer, – brave in action, quick in understanding and with an activity of mind far beyond his barbarian condition, a youth who had regularly accompanied our army in the former war, and had been made a Roman citizen and even an eques, – took advantage of the general's indolence to perpetrate an act of atrocity; cleverly judging that a man is most easily destroyed when he is most secure, and that security very often is the commencement of calamity. He communicated his thoughts at first to a few, then to more friends, assuring them that the Romans might readily be surprised. Then he proceeded to add action to resolution, and fixed a time for executing the plot. Notice of his intent was given to Varus by Segestes, a German of high credit and rank; but fate was not to be opposed by warnings, and had already darkened the Roman general's vision . . . Varus refused to credit the information, asserting that "he felt a trust in the good will of the subject people, proportioned to his kindness to them." And after this first warning there was no time for a second.

The Roman army was therefore surprised in the forest by the Germans of Arminius. An army unrivalled in bravery, the flower of the Roman troops in discipline, vigour and military experience, was thus brought through supine leadership, the perfidy of the foe, and a cruel Fortune into an utterly desperate situation. The troops did not even have the opportunity of fighting as they wished . . . and hemmed in by woods, lakes and the bands of ambushed enemies, were entirely cut off by those foes, whom they had used to slaughter like cattle. Their leader, Varus, showed some spirit in dying, though none in fighting – for, imitating the example of his father and grandfather, he ran himself through with his sword. Of the two præfects of the camp Lucius Eggius gave an honourable example, but Ceionius one of baseness, for after the bulk of the army had perished, Ceionius advised a surrender, preferring to die by the executioner than in battle. Numonius Vala, Varus' lieutenant, a man hitherto of good reputation, this time proved guilty of foul treachery, for leaving the infantry unguarded he fled with the allied cavalry, trying to reach the Rhine. But Fortune avenged his crime; he perished in this act of deserting his countrymen. The savage enemy mangled the half-burned body of Varus. His head was cut off and sent to Marobodus [a barbarian king] and by him sent to the Emperor; and so at length received honourable burial in the sepulchre of his family.

THE EDUCATION OF CLAUDIUS, C. AD 10

Augustus

The Emperor writes to his wife, Livia. The subject of the letter, Claudius, was assumed (wrongly) to be an imbecile. He was twenty at the time of the epistle. Thirty-one years later, on Caligula's assassination, he was dragged out of hiding to become the fourth Roman emperor.

I have had some conversation with Tiberius[1], according to your desire, my dear Livia, as to what must be done with your grandson, Claudius, at the games of Mars. We are both agreed in this, that once for all we ought to determine what course to

---

[1] Tiberius was Livia's son and Augustus' adoptive son.

take with him. For if he be really sound and, so to speak, quite right in his intellects, why should we hesitate to promote him by the same steps and degrees as we did his brother? But if we find him below par and deficient both in body and mind, we must beware of giving occasion for him and ourselves to be laughed at by the world, which is ready enough to make such matters the subject of mirth and derision. For we never shall be easy, if we are always to be debating upon every occasion of this kind, without settling, in the first instance, whether he be really capable of public offices or not. Concerning the things about which you consult me at the present moment, I am not averse to his taking charge of the priests' dining chamber, in the games of Mars, if he will suffer himself to be governed by his kinsman, Silanus' son, that he may do nothing to make the people stare, and deride him. But I do not approve of his witnessing the Circensian games from the Pulvinar. He will be there exposed to view in the very front of the theatre. Nor do I like that he should go to the Alban Mount, or be at Rome during the Latin festival. For if he be capable of attending his brother to the mount, why is he not made prefect of the city? Thus, my dear Livia, you have my thoughts upon the matter. In my opinion, we ought to settle this affair once for all, that we may not be always in suspense between hope and fear. You may, if you think proper, give your kinsman Antonia this part of my letter to read.

HOW TO COOK RISSOLES . . . SEA FOOD FRICASEE . . . SUCKLING PIG, c. AD 15

Apicius

Put in a mortar pepper, lovage, and origan; pound, moisten with *liquamen* [sauce], add cooked brains, pound thoroughly to dissolve lumps. Add five eggs and beat well to work all into a smooth paste. Blend with *liquamen*, place in a metal pan, and cook. When it is cooked turn out on a clean board and dice. Put in the mortar pepper, lovage, origan; pound, mix together; pour in *liquamen* and wine, put in a saucepan and bring to the boil. When boiling crumble in pastry to thicken, stir vigorously, and pour in the serving-dish over the diced rissoles; sprinkle with pepper and serve.

Put fish in a saucepan, add *liquamen*, oil, wine, stock. Finely chop leeks with their heads [i.e., green and white parts] and coriander, make tiny fishballs, and chop up fillets of cooked fish, and add sea-urchins, having washed them well. When all this is cooked crush pepper, lovage, origan, pound thoroughly, moisten with *liquamen*, and some of the cooking liquor, and put into the saucepan. When it bubbles crumble pastry into it to bind, and stir well. Sprinkle with pepper and serve.

Brown the pig and truss. Put in the pan (in which you cook the pig) oil, *liquamen*, wine water, and a bouquet of leeks and coriander. Halfway through the cooking add *defrutum* to colour. Put in the mortar pepper, lovage, caraway, origan, celery-seed, asafoetida root; pound, moisten with *liquamen*, and some of the cooking-liquor. Blend with wine and *passum* [raisin wine]. Empty this into the pan, bring to the boil, and when it boils thicken with cornflour. Dress the pig on a shallow dish and pour the sauce over. Sprinkle with pepper and serve.

A PICTURE OF ROME, c. AD 15

Strabo

The Greek cities are thought to have flourished mainly on account of the felicitous choice made by their founders, in regard to the beauty and strength of their sites, their proximity to some haven, and the fineness of the country. But the Roman prudence was more particularly employed on matters which have received but little attention from the Greeks, – such as paving their roads, constructing aqueducts, and sewers. In fact they have paved the roads, cut through hills, and filled up valleys, so that the merchandise may be conveyed by carriage from the ports. The sewers, arched over with hewn stones, are large enough in parts for actual hay wagons to pass through, while so plentiful is the supply of water from the aqueducts, that rivers may be said to flow through the city and the sewers, and almost every house is furnished with water pipes and copious fountains.

We may remark that the ancients of Republican times bestowed little attention upon the beautifying of Rome. But their successors, and especially those of our own day, have at the same time embellished the city with numerous and splendid objects. Pompey, the Divine Cæsar [*i.e.* Julius Cæsar], and Augustus, with his children, friends, wife, and sister have surpassed all others in their zeal and munificence in these decorations. The greater number of these may be seen in the Campus Martius which to the beauties of nature adds those of art. The size of the plain is remarkable, allowing chariot races and the equestrian sports without hindrance, and multitudes here exercise themselves with ball games, in the Circus, and on the wrestling grounds. The structures that surround the Campus, the greensward covered with herbage all the year around, the summit of the hills beyond the Tiber, extending from its banks with panoramic effect, present a spectacle which the eye abandons with regret.

Near to this plain is another surrounded with columns, sacred groves, three theatres, an amphitheatre, and superb temples, each close to the other, and so splendid that it would seem idle to describe the rest of the city after it. For this cause the Romans esteeming it the most sacred place, have erected funeral monuments there to the illustrious persons of either sex. The most remarkable of these is that called the "Mausoleum" [the tomb of Augustus] which consists of a mound of earth raised upon a high foundation of white marble, situated near the river, and covered on the top with evergreen shrubs. Upon the summit is a bronze statue of Augustus Cæsar, and beneath the mound are the funeral urns of himself, his relatives, and his friends. Behind is a large grove containing charming promenades. In the center of the plain [the Campus Martius] is the spot where the body of this prince was reduced to ashes. It is surrounded by a double inclosure, one of marble, the other of iron, and planted within with poplars. If thence you proceed to visit the ancient Forum, which is equally filled with basilicas, porticoes, and temples, you will there behold the Capitol, the Palatine, and the noble works that adorn them, and the piazza of Livia [Augustus' Empress], – each successive work causing you speedily to forget that which you have seen before. Such then is Rome!

JESUS CHRIST IS CRUCIFIED, JERUSALEM, C. AD 30

St John

One of the Twelve Apostles, St John – by tradition, at least – composed the Gospel which bears his name before dying at an advanced age near Ephesus.

Then Pilate therefore took Jesus, and scourged *him*.

2 And the soldiers platted a crown of thorns, and put *it* on his head, and they put on him a purple robe,

3 And said, Hail, King of the Jews! and they smote him with their hands.

4 Pilate therefore went forth again, and saith unto them, Behold, I bring him forth to you, that ye may know that I find no fault in him.

5 Then came Jesus forth, wearing the crown of thorns, and the purple robe. And *Pilate* saith unto them, Behold the man!

6 When the chief priests therefore and officers saw him, they cried out, saying, Crucify *him*, crucify *him*. Pilate saith unto them, Take ye him, and crucify *him*: for I find no fault in him.

7 The Jews answered him, We have a law, and by our law he ought to die, because he made himself the Son of God.

8 When Pilate therefore heard that saying, he was the more afraid;

9 And went again into the judgment hall, and saith unto Jesus, Whence art thou? But Jesus gave him no answer.

10 Then saith Pilate unto him, Speakest thou not unto me? Knowest thou not that I have power to crucify thee, and have power to release thee?

11 Jesus answered, Thou couldest have no power *at all* against me, except it were given thee from above: therefore he that delivered me unto thee hath the greater sin.

12 And from thenceforth Pilate sought to release him: but the Jews cried out, saying, If thou let this man go, thou art not Cæsar's friend: whosoever maketh himself a king speaketh against Caesar.

13 When Pilate therefore heard that saying, he brought Jesus forth, and sat down in the judgment seat in a place that is called the Pavement, but in the Hebrew, Gabbatha.

14 And it was the preparation of the passover, and about the sixth hour: and he saith unto the Jews, Behold your King!

15 But they cried out, Away with *him*, away with *him*, crucify him, Pilate saith unto them, Shall I crucify your King? The chief priests answered, We have no king but Caesar.

16 Then delivered he him therefore unto them to be crucified. And they took Jesus, and led *him* away.

17 And he bearing his cross went forth into a place called *the place* of a skull, which is called in the Hebrew Golgotha:

18 Where they crucified him, and two other with him, on either side one, and Jesus in the midst.

19 And Pilate wrote a title, and put *it* on the cross. And the writing was, JESUS OF NAZARETH THE KING OF THE JEWS.

20 This title then read many of the Jews: for the place where Jesus was crucified was nigh to the city: and it was written in Hebrew, *and* Greek, *and* Latin.

21 Then said the chief priests of the Jews to Pilate, Write not, The King of the Jews; but that he said, I am King of the Jews.

22 Pilate answered, What I have written I have written.

23 Then the soldiers, when they had crucified Jesus, took his garments, and made four parts, to every soldier a part; and also *his* coat: now the coat was without seam, woven from the top throughout.

24 They said therefore among themselves, Let us not rend it, but cast lots for it, whose it shall be: that the scripture might be fulfilled, which saith, They parted my raiment among them, and for my vesture they did cast lots. These things therefore the soldiers did.

25 Now there stood by the cross of Jesus his mother, and his mother's sister, Mary the *wife* of Cleophas, and Mary Magdalene.

26 When Jesus therefore saw his mother, and the disciple standing by, whom he loved, he saith unto his mother, Woman, behold thy son!

27 Then saith he to the disciple. Behold thy mother! And from that hour that disciple took her unto his own *home*.

28 After this, Jesus knowing that all things were now accomplished, that the scripture might be fulfilled, saith, I thirst.

29 Now there was set a vessel full of vinegar: and they filled a sponge with vinegar, and put *it* upon hyssop, and put *it* to his mouth.

30 When Jesus therefore had received the vinegar, he said, It is finished: and he bowed his head, and gave up the ghost.

THE WHIMSICAL CRUELTIES OF EMPEROR CALIGULA, AD 37–41

Suetonius

*Caligula was born Gaius Caesar Augustus Germanicus; Caligula was a nickname from the soldier's boots (*caligae*) he wore as child in the camps of his father. He ingratiated himself with Tiberius, and was eventually appointed co-heir with the emperor's grandson Gemellus. The Senate, however, conferred the purple on Caligula alone. The capricious, despotic nature of his reign ensured that it was but brief. He was assassinated by his own bodyguards.*

His deeds, horrible as they were, he augmented with words equally outrageous. "There is nothing in my nature," he would say, "that I commend or approve so much, as my inflexible rigour." When his grandmother Antonia gave him some advice, he said to her (as though it were not enough to disregard it), "Remember that all things are lawful for me." When about to murder his brother, whom he suspected of taking antidotes against poison, he said, "See then, an antidote against Caesar!" And when he banished his sisters, he told them in a menacing tone that he had not only islands at command, but likewise swords. One of praetorian rank having sent several times from Anticyra, whither he had gone for his health, to have his leave of absence prolonged, he ordered him to be put to death; adding these words: "Bleeding is necessary for one that has taken hellebore so long, and found no benefit." It was his custom every tenth day to sign the lists of prisoners appointed for execution; and this he called "clearing his accounts". And having condemned several Gauls and Greeks at one time, he boasted that he had subdued Gallograecia.

He would not permit any to die quickly, but only after many strokes, and those dealt softly, this being his well-known and constant order: "Strike so that he may feel that he is dying." He once executed a person whom he had not appointed to die, by mistaking him for the one condemned; "But it makes no difference," said he, "this one deserved it quite as much." He had many times upon his tongue these words of the tragedian,

Oderint dum metuant

I scorn their hatred, if they do but fear me.

[. . .]

Even in the midst of his recreations, while gaming or feasting, his cruelty of word and deed was never mitigated one whit. Often as he sat at dinner, persons were put to the torture in his presence; and a soldier, who was skilled in the art of beheading, used at such times to take off the heads of prisoners who were brought in for that purpose. At Puteoli, when he dedicated the bridge which he planned, as already described, he invited a number of people to come to him from the shore, and then suddenly flung them headlong from the bridge into the water, thrusting down with poles and oars those who, to save themselves, caught at the rudders of the ships. At a public feast in Rome, when a slave stole some thin plates of silver with which the couches were inlaid, he delivered him at once to an executioner, with orders to cut off his hands, hang them from his neck over his breast, together with a written placard declaring the cause of his punishment; and so led around the company as they sat at the board. A gladiator who was practising with him, and voluntarily threw himself at his feet, he stabbed with a poniard, and then ran about with a palm branch in his hand, after the manner of those who are victorious in the games. When a victim was to be offered upon an altar he, clad in the habit of the Popae, and holding the axe aloft for a while, at last slaughtered, instead of the animal, an officer who attended to cut up the sacrifice. And at a sumptuous entertainment, he suddenly burst into immoderate laughter, and upon the consuls, who reclined next to him, respectfully asking him the occasion: "At what else," he retorted, "but this, that upon a single nod of my head, you might both have your throats cut."

A PERSONAL AUDIENCE WITH CALIGULA, ROME, AD 40

Philo

In AD 38 the synagogues of Alexandria were attacked by Roman settlers because of the refusal of the city's Jews to accept the divinity of the Emperor. Philo was part of a Jewish embassy from the city making complaint. The embassy also wished to secure Roman citizenship for Alexandria's Jews.

It is right to recount what we saw and heard when we were summoned to present our case on the question of citizenship. Immediately on entering, we realized from his face and gestures that we were in the presence not of a judge but of a prosecuting counsel, and that we would find him more firmly against us than our actual opponents. A proper judge would have sat with some colleagues chosen on merit, as this was a most important examination which affected many thousands of Jews in Alexandria for the first time in the city's history, after complete silence for nearly 400 years. The litigants would have been standing on either side of him with their advocates, and, after listening in turn for a set time to the cases of the plaintiffs and defendants, he would have risen to discuss with his colleagues what was the fairest public judgement they should give. But the actual events were more like those of a cruel tyrant, with a scowl on his despotic brow.

 He did not do one of the things I have just mentioned, but sent for the stewards of the two gardens belonging to Maecenas and Lamia. These gardens are situated together near the city, and he had been there for the past three or four days. That was the stage on which the drama against our whole race was to be enacted, and we were to be the audience. He gave instructions for all the rooms to be opened, as he wanted to carry out a detailed inspection of each of them.

When we were brought before him, we bowed ourselves to the ground in reverence and care, and saluted him, addressing him as Augustus Autocrator. His answer was couched in terms so kind and gentle that we surrendered any idea not merely of winning our case but even of saving our lives. In a sarcastic, sneering way, he said, "You are the god-haters, who do not consider me to be a god but refuse to accept me as one, although all others have agreed that I am one." Then, stretching his hands to heaven, he gave vent to an appeal which it was sin even to listen to, let alone repeat verbatim. You can imagine the delight which at once filled the delegates on the other side, who thought their case won from the opening remark by Gaius. They waved their arms about, danced around and called him by the name of every god they could think of. The bitter, sycophantic Isidorus saw that he was delighted with these more-than-human names, and said, "Sire, you will find even more cause to hate these men and those of their race when you know of their ill-will and impiety towards you. When the whole world conducted sacrifices of thanksgiving for your recovery, these alone could not bear to join in. When I say 'these', I include the other Jews." We all cried in unison, "Lord Gaius, this is slander. We did sacrifice, hecatombs too, not merely by sprinkling blood on the altar and carrying home the meat for a banquet and party, as is the way of some, but by giving all the offerings to the sacred flame. This we have done not once but three times to date; once when you became Emperor, again when you recovered from that dreadful disease which affected the whole world, and a third time in hope of a victory in Germany." His reply was, "All right, perhaps this is true, that you have sacrificed and on my behalf. But the sacrifices were offered to another god. What good is that if you did not sacrifice to me?" This, coming on top of his earlier remark, caused in us such a deep and immediate shudder that it was clearly visible on our faces.

During this conversation, Gaius was going round the villas, inspecting the men's and women's quarters, ground floor, second floor, everything, with criticism of some things as inadequately prepared and plans for others to be more lavishly equipped. We were tugged along behind as we followed him up and down, scoffed and jeered at by our opponents like knockabout comedians. In fact it was rather like a play. The judge had taken on the role of prosecuting counsel, the prosecuting counsel that of a poor judge who paid attention not to the nature of the truth but only to the dictates of his own personal enmity. When a judge of that sort accuses a man on trial, silence is imperative. For silence can be a defence, especially to those like us, who could make no reply to the questions which he wanted answered, since our customs and laws held our tongues and kept our mouths tightly stitched up.

When he had arranged some of the matters about the buildings, he asked us most importantly and solemnly, "Why don't you eat pork?" A great peal of laughter broke out from our opponents at this question, partly from pleasure and partly from a definite policy to flatter him to make his remark seem witty and graceful. So loud was the laughter that one of his attendants who followed him was amazed at the insult to the Emperor in whose presence even a faint smile is unsafe unless you know him very well. We replied, "Different people have different customs, and both we and our opponents are forbidden to use certain things." Someone said, "Many people don't eat lamb, which is so easy to get." Gaius laughed and said, "Quite right, for it's not nice." We were in despair with these inanities and insults, when he at last said sarcastically, "We wish to know what justice you have in your claim about the citizenship." We started to outline our case, but when he had had a taste of the justice of our plea, and had recognized that it was a good one, he cut us short before we reached the main points and leaped off at the double into a large room, where he rushed about ordering windows to be fitted all round, with translucent stones like clear glass which do not stop the light but block out the wind and the heat of the sun. Then he slowly approached us and said equably enough, "What is your case?" We were just beginning to go on with our points when he ran into another room in which he ordered original pictures to be painted. Thus our claims were scattered, disjointed, virtually amputated and obliterated. We gave up, for we had no strength left, and the only thing we expected was instant death. We had no spirit remaining, but in our agony we went out to pray to the true God that he might check the anger of this man, so falsely called a god. And he, taking pity on us, turned Gaius' wrath to mercy. Becoming gentler, he said, "The men seem misguided rather than wicked, and stupid not to believe that my natural lot was that of a god." Whereupon, he went away, bidding us go too.

CLAUDIUS HARANGUES THE CONSCRIPT FATHERS, AD 48

Claudius

Claudius escaped the periodic terrors of his imperial brother (Tiberius) and nephew (Caligula) because of his presumed imbecility. He was a waste of a plot. This did not prevent the Praetorian Guard from dragging him from hiding on Caligula's assassination in AD 41 and making him Emperor. In fact, Claudius was of sound mind, if weak body, and during his 13-year reign expanded the Empire to include Mauretania, Thrace, England and Wales. He also cleverly integrated provincials into the Empire by extending Roman citizenship. Below is his Senate speech in favour of that integration. Although this policy met Senate approval, the Conscript Fathers were generally antagonistic to Claudius (note the irreverent interruptions to the Claudian oration); his paranoia steadily deepened and he recklessly executed numerous of the political and military classes.

"It is surely an innovation of the divine Augustus, my great-uncle, and of Tiberius Cæsar, my uncle, to desire that particularly the flower of the colonies and of the municipal towns, that is to say, all those that contain men of breeding and wealth, should be admitted to this assembly?"

[*Interruption, seemingly by a senator*]: "How now? Is not an Italian senator to be preferred to a provincial senator?"

"I will soon explain this point to you, when I submit that part of my acts which I performed as censor, but I do not conceive it needful to repel even the provincials who can do honour to the Senate House. Here is this splendid and powerful colony of Vienna;[1] is it so long since it sent to us senators? From that

---

[1] Vienne in Southern France.

colony comes Lucius Vestinus, one of the glories of the equestrian order, my personal friend, whom I keep close to myself for the management of my private affairs. Let his sons be suffered – I pray you – to become priests of the lowest rank, while waiting till, with the lapse of years, they can follow the advancement of their dignity. As for that robber, [Valerius Asiaticus from Vienna] I will pass over his hateful name. For I detest that hero of the gymnasium, who brought the consulship into his family before even his colony had obtained the full rights of Roman citizenship. I could say as much of his brother, stamped as unworthy by this unlucky relationship, and incapable henceforth of being a useful member of your body."

[*Interrupting shout*]: "Here now, Tiberius Cæsar Germanicus! It's time to let the Conscript Fathers understand what your talk is driving at – already you've reached the very limits of Narbonnese Gaul!"

[*Claudius resumes*]: "All these young men of rank, on whom I cast my glance, you surely do not regret to see among the number of the senators; any more than Persicus, that most highborn gentleman and my friend, is ashamed when he meets upon the images of his ancestors the name Allobrogius. And if such is your thought, what would you desire more? Do I have to point it out to you? Even the territory which is located beyond the province of [Gallia] Narbonnensis, has it not already sent you senators? For surely we have no regrets in going clear up to Lugdunum for the members of our order. Assuredly, Conscript Fathers, it is not without some hesitation that I cross the limits of the provinces which are well known and familiar to you, – but the moment is come when I must plead openly the cause of Further Gaul. It will be objected that Gaul sustained a war against the divine Julius for ten years. But let there be opposed to this the memory of a hundred years of steadfast fidelity, and a loyalty put to the proof in many trying circumstances. My father, Drusus, was able to force Germany to submit, because behind him reigned a profound peace assured by the tranquillity of the Gauls. And note well, that at the moment he was summoned to that war, he was busy instituting the census in Gaul, a new institution among them, and contrary to their customs. And how difficult and perilous to us is this business of

the census, although all we require is that our public resources
should be known, we have learned by all too much experience."

MESSALINA PROSTITUTES HERSELF, c. AD 48

Juvenal

Valeria Messalina was the third wife of Emperor Claudius, bearing him the
children Octavia (later wife of Nero) and Britannicus. She was apparently
nymphomaniacal. Juvenal's Satire VI preserved the popular tradition that
Messalina, whilst Empress, spent her nights as common prostitute called
"Lycisca". Messalina was eventually executed by Claudius for going through
a form of public marriage with her favourite, the consul-designate Silius.

And when the hour of business now was spent,
And all the trulls dismissed, repining went.
Yet what she could, she did: slowly she passed,
And saw her man and shut her cell the last,
Still raging with the fever of desire,
Her veins all turgid, and her blood on fire.
With joyless pace the imperial couch she sought,
And to her happy spouse (yet slumbering) brought
Cheeks rank with sweat, limbs drenched with poisonous
     dews,
The steam of lamps, and odour of the stews.
Claudius had scarce begun his eyes to close
Ere from his pillow Messalina rose
(Accustomed long the bed of state to slight
For the coarse mattress and the hood of night),
And with one maid and her dark hair concealed
Beneath a yellow tire, a strumpet veiled,
She slipped into the stews unseen, unknown,
And hired a cell, yet reeking, for her own.
There, flinging off her dress, the imperial whore
Stood, with bare breasts and gilded, at the door,
And showed, Britannicus, to all who came,
The womb that bore thee, in Lycisca's name;
Allured the passers-by with many a wile,
And asked her price, and took it with a smile.

GLADIATORIAL SHOWS, ROME, AD 50

Seneca

Gladiatorial shows dated back to the First Punic War, when the Roman government, in a bid to raise morale (or distract attention from military setbacks), organized exhibitions of mortal combat. Thereafter, gladiatorial games became Rome's national sport, although there was periodic revulsion at their brutality by literrati *such as Seneca the Stoic. From Seneca's* Epistles 7:

I happened to go to one of these shows at the time of the lunch-hour interlude, expecting there to be some light and witty entertainment then, some respite for the purpose of affording people's eyes a rest from human blood. Far from it. All the earlier contests were charity in comparison. The nonsense is dispensed with now: what we have now is murder pure and simple. The combatants have nothing to protect them; their whole bodies are exposed to the blows; every thrust they launch gets home. A great many spectators prefer this to the ordinary matches and even to the special, popular demand ones. And quite naturally. There are no helmets and no shields repelling the weapons. What is the point of armour? Or of skill? All that sort of thing just makes the death slower in coming. In the morning men are thrown to the lions and the bears: but it is the spectators they are thrown to in the lunch hour. The spectators insist that each on killing his man shall be thrown against another to be killed in his turn; and the eventual victor is reserved by them for some other form of butchery; the only exit for the contestants is death. Fire and steel keep the slaughter going. And all this happens while the arena is virtually empty.

"But he was a highway robber, he killed a man." And what of it? Granted that as a murderer he deserved this punishment, what have you done, you wretched fellow, to deserve to watch it? "Kill him! Flog him! Burn him! Why does he run at the other man's weapon in such a cowardly way? Why isn't he less half-hearted about killing? Why isn't he a bit more enthusastic about dying? Whip him forward to get his wounds! Make them each offer the other a bare breast and trade blow for blow on them." And when there is an interval in the show: "Let's have some throats cut in the meantime, so that there's something happening!"

As Seneca noted, many of the slaves and criminals being prepared as gladiators sought suicide as a death preferable to the one awaiting them in the arena.

Men of the meanest lot in life have by a mighty impulse escaped to safety, and when they were not allowed to die at their own convenience, or to suit themselves in their choice of instruments of death, they have snatched up whatever was lying ready to hand, and by sheer strength have turned objects which were by nature harmless into weapons of their own. For example, there was lately in a training-school for wild-beast gladiators a German, who was making ready for the morning exhibition; he withdrew in order to relieve himself – the only thing which he was allowed to do in secret and without the presence of a guard. While so engaged, he seized the stick of wood, tipped with a sponge, which was devoted to the vilest uses, and stuffed it, just as it was, down his throat; thus he blocked up his wind-pipe, and choked the breath from his body. That was truly to insult death! Yes, indeed; it was not a very elegant or becoming way to die: but what is more foolish than to be over-nice about dying? What a brave fellow! He surely deserved to be allowed to choose his fate! How bravely he would have wielded a sword! With what courage he would have hurled himself into the depths of the sea, or down a precipice! Cut off from resources on every hand, he yet found a way to furnish himself with death, and with a weapon for death. Hence you can understand that nothing but the will need postpone death. Let each man judge the deed of this most zealous fellow as he likes, provided we agree on this point – that the foullest death is preferable to the fairest slavery . . .

. . . Lately a gladiator, who had been sent forth to the morning exhibition was being conveyed in a cart along with the other prisoners; nodding as if he were heavy with sleep, he let his head fall over so far that it was caught in the spokes; then he kept his body in position long enough to break his neck by the revolution of the wheel. So he made his escape by means of the very wagon which was carrying him to his punishment . . .

. . . During the second event in a sham sea-fight one of the barbarians sank deep into his own throat a spear which had been given him for use against his foe. "Why, oh why," he said, have I not long ago escaped from all this torture and all this mockery? Why should I be armed and yet wait for death to come?" This exhibition was all the more striking because of the lesson men learn from it that dying is more honourable than killing.

A PORTRAIT OF ITALY, c. AD 50

Pliny the Elder

When we come to Italy, we begin with the Ligures [in the Northwest], after whom we have Etruria, Umbria, Latium, where the mouths of the Tiber are situate, and Rome the "Capital of the World", 16 miles distant from the Sea. We then come to the coasts of the Volsci and Campania, and the districts of Picenum, of Lucania and of Bruttium, where Italy extends the farthest in a southerly direction, and projects into the [two] seas with the chain of the Alps, which there forms pretty nearly the shape of a crescent. Leaving Bruttium we come to the coast of Magna Græcia, then the Apuli, Peligni, Sabini, Picentes, Galli, the Umbri, the Tusci, the Venetes and other peoples.

I am quite aware that I might be justly accused of ingratitude and indolence, were I to describe thus briefly and in so cursory a manner the land which is at once the foster-child and the parent of all lands: chosen by the providence of the Gods to render even heaven itself more glorious, to unite the scattered empires of the earth, to bestow a polish upon men's manners, to unite the discordant and uncouth dialects of so many nations by the powerful ties of one common language, to confer the enjoyments of discourse and of civilization upon mankind, to become, in short, the mother-country of all the nations.

But how shall I begin the task? So vast is the number of celebrated places no one living can name them all. So great is the renown of each spot I feel myself wholly at a loss. The city of Rome alone, which forms a portion of Italy, a face well worthy of shoulders so beauteous, how great a book it would take for a due description! And then too there is the coast of Campania, just taken by itself, – so blessed with natural charms and riches, that it is evident that when nature formed it, she took a delight in accumulating all her blessings in a single spot – how am I to do justice to this?

Again the climate, with its eternal freshness, and so abounding in health and vitality, the sereneness of the weather so enchanting, the fields so fertile, the hill sides so sunny, the thickets so free from every danger, the groves so cool and shady, the forests with a vegetation so varying and luxuriant, the fruitfulness of the grain, the vines, and the admirable olives, the flocks with fleeces so noble, the bulls with necks so sinewy; the lakes with one ever coming after another, the numerous rivers and springs which refresh the land on every side with their waters, the numerous gulfs of the sea with their havens, and the bosom of the lands opening everywhere to the commerce of the wide world, yes, as it were, eagerly reaching out into the very midst of the waves, for the purpose of aiding – so it seems – the efforts of the Immortals!

At present I omit speaking of its genius, its manners, its men, and the nations whom it has conquered by eloquence and the might of arms. The very Greeks – a folk fond mightily of spreading their own praises – have given ample judgment in favour of Italy, when they named simply a small part of it "Magna Græcia". But we must be content in this case, as in our description of the heavens. We must only touch upon these points, and take notice of merely a few of its stars.

I may begin by remarking that this land very much resembles in shape an oak-leaf, being much longer than it is broad; towards the top it inclines to the left if one is facing south, while it terminates in the form of an Amazonian buckler, in which the central projection is called Cocinthos, while it sends forth two horns at the end of its crescent shaped bays – Leucopetra on the right, and Lacinium on the left. It extends in length 1,020 miles, if we measure from the foot of the Alps at Prætoria Augusta through the city of Rome and Capua to Rhegium, – which is situate on the shoulder of the Peninsula, just at the bend of the neck as it were. The distance is much greater if measured to Lacinium, but in that case the line, being drawn obliquely, would incline too much to one side. The breadth of Italy is variable; being 410 miles between the two seas, the Lower Tuscan and the Upper Adriatic, and the rivers Varus by Gaul and Arsia by Istria; at about the middle and in the vicinity of the city of Rome, from the spot where the river Aternus flows into the Adriatic to the mouth of the Tiber, the distance is 136 miles, and a little less from Castrum-Novum on the Adriatic sea to Alsium on the Tuscan;— but at no place does it exceed 200 miles in breadth. The circuit of the whole from the Varus to the Arsia is 3,059 miles.[1]

As to its distance from the countries that surround it, Epirus and Illyricum [nearest points toward Greece] are 50 miles distant, Africa is less than 200, as we are informed by Marcus Varro, and Sicily a mile and a half.

THE PUMPKINIFICATION OF CLAUDIUS, C. AD 54

Anon

The Pumpkinification *of Claudius (Apocolocyntosis Divi Claudii) was a brutal satire on Claudius' funeral and deification. The scenario has the late Emperor brought to heaven to be judged by the Gods. Claudius' speech impediment, his French birth, his shuffling (probably spastic) gait, his judicial murders, the power he granted his freemen – all are mercilessly skewered. Given its seditious whiff, the* Pumpkinification *was presumably published when Claudius was safely poisoned by Agrippina in AD 54. The author may have been Seneca the Stoic philosopher, who was also tutor to Nero, Claudius' adoptive heir.*

What happened next on earth it is mere waste of time to tell, for you know it all well enough, and there is no fear of your ever forgetting the impression which that public rejoicing made on your memory. No one forgets his own happiness. What happened in heaven you shall hear: for proof please apply to my informant. Word comes to Jupiter that a stranger had arrived, a man well set up, pretty grey; he seemed to be threatening something, for he wagged his head ceaselessly; he dragged the right foot. They asked him what nation he was of; he answered something in a confused mumbling voice: his language they did

[1] Actually, 2,500 miles.

not understand. He was no Greek and no Roman, nor of any known race. On this Jupiter bids Hercules go and find out what country he comes from; you see Hercules had travelled over the whole world, and might be expected to know all the nations in it. But Hercules, the first glimpse he got, was really much taken aback, although not all the monsters in the world could frighten him; when he saw this new kind of object, with its extraordinary gait, and the voice of no terrestrial beast, but such as you might hear in the leviathans of the deep, hoarse and inarticulate, he thought his thirteenth labour had come upon him. When he looked closer, the thing seemed to be a kind of man. Up he goes, then, and says what your Greek finds readiest to his tongue:

Who art thou, and what thy people? Who thy parents, where thy home?

Claudius was delighted to find literary men up there, and began to hope there might be some corner for his own historical works. So he caps him with another Homeric verse, explaining that he was Caesar:

Breezes wafted me from Ilion unto the Ciconian land.

But the next verse was more true, and no less Homeric:

Thither come, I sacked a city, slew the people every one.

He would have taken in poor simple Hercules, but that Our Lady of Malaria was there, who left her temple and came alone with him: all the other gods he had left at Rome. Quoth she

The fellow's tale is nothing but lies. I have lived with him all these years, and I tell you, he was born at Lyons. You behold a fellow-burgess of Marcus. As I say, he was born at the sixteenth milestone from Vienne, a native Gaul. So of course he took Rome, as a good Gaul ought to do. I pledge you my word that in Lyons he was born, where Licinus was king so many years. But you that have trudged over more roads than any muleteer that plies for hire, you must have come across the people of Lyons, and you must know that it is a far cry from Xanthus to the Rhone.

At this point Claudius flared up and expressed his wrath with as big a growl as he could manage. What he said nobody understood; as a matter of fact, he was ordering my lady of Fever to be taken away, and making that sign with his trembling hand (which was always steady enough for that, if for nothing else) by which he used to decapitate men. He had ordered her head to be chopped off. For all the notice the others took of him, they might have been his own freedmen.

Then Hercules said, "You just listen to me, and stop playing the fool. You have come to the place where the mice nibble iron. Out with the truth, and look sharp, or I'll knock your quips and quiddities out of you." Then to make himself all the more awful, he strikes an attitude and proceeds in his most tragic vein:

> Declare with speed what spot you claim by birth,
> Or with this club fall stricken to the earth!
> This club hath ofttimes slaughtered haughty kings!
> Why mumble unintelligible things?
> What land, what tribe produced that shaking head?
> Declare it! On my journey when I sped
> Far to the Kingdom of the triple King,
> And from the Main Hesperian did bring
> The goodly cattle to the Argive town,
> There I beheld a mountain looking down
> Upon two rivers: this the Sun espies
> Right opposite each day he doth arise.
> Hence, mighty Rhone, thy rapid torrents flow,
> And Arar, much in doubt which way to go,
> Ripples along the banks which shallow roll,
> Say, is this land, the nurse that bred thy soul?

These lines he delivered with much spirit and a bold front. All the same, he was not quite master of his wits, and had some fear of a blow from the fool. Claudius, seeing a mighty man before him, saw things looked serious and understood that here he had not quite the same pre-eminence as at Rome, where no one was his equal: the Gallic cock was worth most on his own dunghill. So this is what he was thought to say, as far as could be made out:

I did hope, Hercules, bravest of all the gods, that you would take my part with the rest, and if I should need a voucher, I meant to name you who know me so well. Do but call it to mind, how it was I used to sit in judgment before your temple whole days together during July and August. You know what miseries I endured there, in hearing the lawyers plead day and night. If you had fallen amongst these, you may think yourself very strong, but you would have found it worse than the sewers of Augeas: I drained out more filth than you did. But since I want . . .

No wonder you have forced your way into the Senate House: no bars or bolts can hold against you. Only do say what species of god you want the fellow to be made. An Epicurean god he cannot be: for they have no troubles and cause none. A Stoic, then? How can he be globular, as Varro says, without a head or any other projection? There *is* in him something of the Stoic god, as I can see now: he has neither heart nor head. Upon my word, if he had asked this boon from Saturn, he would not have got it, though he kept up Saturn's feast all the year round, a truly Saturnalian prince. A likely thing he will get it from Jove, whom he condemned for incest as far as in him lay: for he killed his son-in-law Silanus, because Silanus had a sister, a most charming girl, called Venus by all the world, and he preferred to call her Juno. Why, you say, I want to know why, his own sister? Read your books, stupid: you may go halfway at Athens, the whole way at Alexandria. Because the mice lick meal at Rome, you say. Is this creature to mend our crooked ways? What goes on in his own closet he knows not; and now he searches the regions of the sky, wants to be a god. Is it not enough that he has a temple in Britain, that savages worship him and pray to him as a god, so that they may find a fool to have mercy upon them?

At last it came into Jove's head, that while strangers were in the House it was not lawful to speak or debate. "My lords and gentlemen," said he, "I gave you leave to ask questions, and you have made a regular farmyard of the place. Be so good as to keep the rules of the House. What will this person think of us, whoever he is?" So Claudius was led out, and the first to be asked his opinion was Father Janus: he had been made consul elect for the afternoon of the next first of July, being as shrewd a man as you could find on a summer's day: for he could see, as they say, before and behind. He made an eloquent harangue, because his life was passed in the forum, but too fast for the notary to take down. That is why I give no full report of it, for I don't want to change the words he used. He said a great deal of the majesty of the gods, and how the honour ought not to be given away to every Tom, Dick, or Harry. "Once," said he,

> it was a great thing to become a god; now you have made it a farce. Therefore; that you may not think I am speaking against one person instead of the general custom, I propose that from this day forward the godhead be given to none of those who eat the fruits of the earth, or whom mother earth doth nourish. After this bill has been read a third time, whosoever is made, said, or portrayed to be god, I vote he be delivered over to the bogies, and at the next public show be flogged with a birch amongst the new gladiators.

The next to be asked was Diespiter, son of Vica Pota, he also being consul elect, and a moneylender; by this trade he made a living, used to sell rights of citizenship in a small way. Hercules trips me up to him daintily, and tweaks him by the ear. So he uttered his opinion in these words:

> Inasmuch as the blessed Claudius is akin to the blessed Augustus, and also to the blessed Augusta, his grandmother, whom he ordered to be made a goddess, and whereas he far surpasses all mortal men in wisdom, and seeing that it is for the public good that there be some one able to join Romulus in devouring boiled turnips, I propose that from this day forth blessed Claudius be a god, to enjoy that honour with all its

appurtenances in as full a degree as any other before him, and
that a note to that effect be added to Ovid's Metamorphoses.

The meeting was divided, and it looked as though Claudius was
to win the day. For Hercules saw his iron was in the fire, trotted
here and trotted there, saying, "Don't deny me; I make a point
of the matter. I'll do as much for you again, when you like; you
roll my log, and I'll roll yours: one hand washes another."

Then arose the blessed Augustus when his turn came, and
spoke with much eloquence. "I call you to witness, my lords and
gentlemen," said he,

that since the day I was made a god I have never uttered one
word. I always mind my own business. But now I can keep
on the mask no longer, nor conceal the sorrow which shame
makes all the greater. Is it for this I have made peace by land
and sea? For this have I calmed intestine wars? For this, laid
a firm foundation of law for Rome, adorned it with buildings,
and all that – my lords, words fail me; there are none can rise
to the height of my indignation. I must borrow that saying of
the eloquent Messala Corvinus, I am ashamed of my authority. This man, my lords, who looks as though he could not
hurt a fly, used to chop off heads as easily as a dog sits down.
But why should I speak of all those men, and such men?
There is no time to lament for public disasters, when one has
so many private sorrows to think of. I leave that, therefore,
and say only this; for even if my sister knows no Greek, I do:
The knee is nearer than the shin. This man you see, who for
so many years has been masquerading under my name, has
done me the favour of murdering two Julias, great-grand-
daughters of mine, one by cold steel and one by starvation;
and one great-grandson, L. Silanus – see, Jupiter, whether he
had a case against him (at least it is your own if you will be
fair). Come tell me, blessed Claudius, why of all those you
killed, both men and women, without a hearing, why you
did not hear their side of the case first, before putting them to
death? Where do we find that custom? It is not done in
heaven. Look at Jupiter: all these years he has been king, and
never did more than once to break Vulcan's leg.

Whom seizing by the foot he cast from the threshold of the
sky, and once he fell in a rage with his wife and strung her up:
did he do any killing? You killed Messalina, whose great-
uncle I was no less than yours. "I don't know," did you say?
Curse you that is just it: not to know was worse than to kill.
Caligula he went on persecuting even when he was dead.
Caligula murdered his father-in-law, Claudius his son-in-law
to boot. Caligula would not have Crassus' son called Great;
Claudius gave him his name back, and took away his head.
In one family he destroyed Crassus Magnus, Scribonia, the
Tristionias, Assario, noble though they were; Crassus indeed
such a fool that he might have been emperor. Is this he you
want now to make a god? Look at his body, born under the
wrath of heaven! In fine, let him say the three words quickly,
and he may have me for a slave. God! Who will worship this
god, who will believe in him? While you make gods of such as
he, no one will believe you to be gods. To be brief, my lords: if
I have lived honourably among you, if I have never given
plain speech to any, avenge my wrongs. This is my motion:

then he read out his amendment, which he had committed to
writing:

Inasmuch as the blessed Claudius murdered his father-in-law
Appius Silanus, his two sons-in-law, Pompeius Magnus and
L. Silanus, Crassus Frugi his daughter's father-in-law, as like
him as two eggs in a basket, Scribonia his daughter's mother-
in-law, his wife Messalina, and others too numerous to
mention; I propose that strong measures be taken against
him, that he be allowed no delay of process, that immediate
sentence of banishment be passed on him, that he be de-
ported from heaven within 30 days, and from Olympus
within 30 hours.

This motion was passed without further debate. Not a moment was lost: Mercury screwed his neck and haled him to the
lower regions, to that bourne "from which they say no traveller
returns." As they passed downwards along the Sacred Way,
Mercury asked what was that great concourse of men? Could it

be Claudius' funeral? It was certainly a most gorgeous spectacle, got up regardless of expense, clear it was that a god was
being borne to the grave: tootling of flutes, roaring of horns, an
immense brass band of all sorts, such a din that even Claudius
could hear it. Joy and rejoicing on every side, the Roman
people walking about like free men. Agatho and a few pettifoggers were weeping for grief, and for once in a way they meant
it. The Barristers were crawling out of their dark corners, pale
and thin, with hardly a breath in their bodies, as though just
coming to life again. One of them when he saw the pettifoggers
putting their heads together, and lamenting their sad lot, up
comes he and says: "Did not I tell you the Saturnalia could not
last for ever?"

When Claudius saw his own funeral train, he understood that
he was dead. For they were chanting his dirge in anapaests,
with much mopping and mouthing:

Pour forth your laments, your sorrow declare,
Let the sounds of grief rise high in the air:
For he that is dead had a wit most keen,
Was bravest of all that on earth have been.
Racehorses are nothing to his swift feet:
Rebellious Parthians he did defeat;
Swift after the Persians his light shafts go:
For he well knew how to fit arrow to bow.
Swiftly the striped barbarians fled:
With one little wound he shot them dead.
And the Britons beyond in their unknown seas,
Blue-shielded Brigantians too, all these
He chained by the neck as the Romans' slaves.
He spake, and the Ocean with trembling waves
Accepted the axe of the Roman law.
O weep for the man! This world never saw
One quicker a troublesome suit to decide,
When only one part of the case had been tried
(He could do it indeed and not hear either side).
Who'll now sit in judgment the whole year round?
Now he that is judge of the shades underground,
Once ruler of fivescore cities in Crete,

Must yield to his better and take a back seat.
Mourn, mourn, pettifoggers, ye venal crew,
And you, minor poets, woe, woe is to you!
And you above all, who get rich quick
By the rattle of dice and the three card trick.

Claudius was charmed to hear his own praises sung, and would have stayed longer to see the show. But the Talthybius of the gods laid a hand on him, and led him across the Campus Martius, first wrapping his head up close that no one might know him, until betwixt Tiber and the Subway he went down to the lower regions. His freedman Narcissus had gone down before him by a short cut, ready to welcome his master. Out he comes to meet him, smooth and shining (he had just left the bath), and says he: "What make the gods among mortals?" "Look alive," says Mercury, "go and tell them we are coming." Away he flew, quicker than tongue can tell. It is easy going by that road, all down hill. So although he had a touch of the gout, in a trice they were come to Dis's door. There lay Cerberus, or, as Horace puts it, the hundred-headed monster. Claudius was a trifle perturbed (it was a little white bitch he used to keep for a pet) when he spied this black shag-haired hound, not at all the kind of thing you could wish to meet in the dark. In a loud voice he cried, "Claudius is coming!" All marched before him singing, "The lost is found, O let us rejoice together!" Here were found C. Silius consul elect, Juncus the ex-praetor, Sextus Traulus, M. Helvius, Trogus, Cotta, Vettius Valens, Fabius, Roman Knights whom Narcissus had ordered for execution. In the midst of this chanting company was Mnester the mime, whom Claudius for honour's sake had made shorter by a head. The news was soon blown about that Claudius had come: to Messalina they throng: first his freedmen, Polybius, Myron, Harpocras, Amphaeus, Pheronactus, all sent before him by Claudius that he might not be unattended anywhere; next two prefects, Justus Catonius and Rufrius Pollio; then his friends, Saturninus Lusius and Pedo Pompeius and Lupus and Celer Asinius, these of consular rank; last came his brother's daughter, his sister's daughter, sons-in-law, fathers and mothers-in-law, the whole family in fact. In a body they came to meet

Claudius; and when Claudius saw them, he exclaimed, "Friends everywhere, on my word! How came you all here?" To this Pedo Pompeius answered, "What, cruel man? How came we here? Who but you sent us, you, the murderer of all the friends that you ever had? To court with you! I'll show you where their lordships sit."

Pedo brings him before the judgment seat of Aeacus, who was holding court under the Lex Cornelia to try cases of murder and assassination. Pedo requests the judge to take the prisoner's name, and produces a summons with this charge: Senators killed, 35; Roman Knights, 221; others as the sands of the sea-shore for multitude. Claudius finds no counsel. At length out steps P. Petronius, an old chum of his, a finished scholar in the Claudian tongue, and claims a remand. Not granted. Pedo Pompeius prosecutes amid loud applause. The counsel for the defense tries to reply; but Aeacus, who is the soul of justice, will not have it. Aeacus hears the case against Claudius, refuses to hear the other side and passes sentence against him, quoting the line:

As he did, so be he done by, this is justice undefiled.

A great silence fell. Not a soul but was stupefied at this new way of managing matters; they had never known anything like it before. It was no new thing to Claudius, yet he thought it unfair. There was a long discussion as to the punishment he ought to endure. Some said that Sisyphus had done his job of porterage long enough; Tantalus would be dying of thirst, if he were not relieved; the drag must be put at last on wretched Ixion's wheel. But it was determined not to let off any of the old stagers, lest Claudius should dare to hope for any such relief. It was agreed that some new punishment must be devised: they must devise some new task, something senseless, to suggest some craving without result. Then Aeacus decreed he should rattle dice for ever in a box with holes in the bottom. At once the poor wretch began his fruitless task of hunting for the dice, which for ever slipped from his fingers.

For when he rattled with the box, and thought he now had got 'em,

The little cubes would vanish thro' the perforated bottom.
Then he would pick 'em up again, and once more set
   a-trying:
The dice but served him the same trick: away they went
   a-flying.
So still he tries, and still he fails; still searching long he
   lingers;
And every time the tricksy things go slipping thro' his fingers.
Just so when Sisyphus at last gets there with his boulder,
He finds the labour all in vain – it rolls down off his shoulder.

All on a sudden who should turn up but Caligula, and claims
the man for a slave: brings witnesses, who said they had seen
him being flogged, caned, fisticuffed by him. He is handed over
to Caligula, and Caligula makes him a present to Aeacus.
Aeacus delivers him to his freedman Menander, to be his
law-clerk.

NERO MURDERS BRITANNICUS, ROME, AD 55

Tacitus

*Nero was declared Emperor by the Praetorian Guards on the death of
Claudius in AD 54. His reign began with promise but helter-skeletered into
debauchery, paranoia and tyranny. Britannicus, the legitimate son of Claudius, was one of Nero's first murder victims. The Emperor was only 18
himself at the time.*

Agrippina, Nero's mother, was disappointed in her hopes of
controlling the government through her son. She complained of
the efforts of his ministers Seneca and Burrhus against her, and
threw out hints that Britannicus, Claudius' real heir, and
stepbrother to Nero, was coming of age and must have his
rights.

   Nero was confounded at this, and as the day was near on
which Britannicus was to complete his fourteenth year, he
reflected on the domineering temper of his mother, and now
again on the character of the young prince, which a trifling
circumstance had lately tested, – trifling, yet sufficient to gain

him wide popularity. During the Saturnalia amid other pastimes of his playmates, at a game of lot drawing for "king" [of the revels], the lot fell upon Nero, upon which he gave all his other companions various orders but of such a character as would not put them to the blush; but when he told Britannicus to step forward and begin a song, hoping for a laugh at the expense of a boy who knew nothing of sober, much less of riotous, society, the lad had with perfect coolness commenced some verses which hinted at his expulsion from his father's house, and from supreme power. This procured him pity, which was all the more conspicuous, as night with its merriment had stripped off all disguise of men's feelings.

Nero saw the reproach and doubled his hate. Pressed by Agrippina's menaces, having no charge against his "brother", and not daring openly to order his murder, he meditated a secret device, and directed poison to be prepared through the agency of Jullius Pollio, a tribune of the prætorians, who had in his custody a woman under sentence for poisoning, – one Locusta, – a person with a vast reputation for crime. That all the people waiting upon Britannicus should care nothing for right or honour had been long since provided for. He actually received his first dose of poison from his tutors but it did not prove deadly, and he suffered no great hurt. But Nero, impatient at such slow progress in crime, threatened the tribune and ordered the prisoner to execution, for prolonging his anxiety while they were thinking of the popular gossip and preparing their own defence. Then they promised that that death should be as sudden as if it were the hurried work of the dagger, and a rapid poison of ingredients previously tested was prepared close to the Emperor's chamber.

It was customary for the young imperial princes to sit during their meals with other nobles of the same age, in the sight of their kinsfolk, but at a table of their own, furnished somewhat frugally. There Britannicus was dining, and as whatever he ate and drank was always tested by the taste of a select attendant, the following device was contrived, that the usage might not be dropped, or the crime betrayed by the death of both prince and attendant. – A cup as yet harmless, but extremely hot and already tested was handed to Britannicus; – then, on his refusing it because of its warmth, poison was poured in with some cold water, and this so penetrated his entire frame that he lost alike voice and breath.

There was a stir among the company; some, taken by surprise, ran hither and thither, while those whose discernment was keener remained motionless, with their eyes fixed on Nero, – who, as he reclined in seeming unconcern, said that, – "this was a common occurrence, from a periodic epilepsy, which had afflicted Britannicus from infancy, and his sight and senses would presently return." As for Agrippina, her terror and confusion, though her countenance struggled to hide it, so visibly appeared, that she was clearly ignorant, as was Octavia, Britannicus' own sister [and Nero's wife]. She saw in fact that she was robbed of her only remaining refuge, and that here was a precedent for parricide. Even Octavia, – notwithstanding her useful inexperience, – had learned to hide her grief, her affection, and indeed every emotion.

And so after a brief pause the company resumed its mirth. One and the same night witnessed Britannicus' death and funeral, preparations having already been made for his obsequies, which were on a humble scale. [A violent storm, testified, in popular opinion, to the wrath of heaven at the whole proceeding.] The emperor apologized for the hasty funeral by reminding people that it was the practice of our ancestors to withdraw from view any grievously untimely death, and not to dwell on it with panegyrics or display.

THE SUICIDE OF SENECA, AD 65

Tacitus

The Stoic philosopher was forced into suicide by the Emperor.

Seneca's death followed. It delighted the emperor. Nero had no proof of Seneca's complicity but was glad to use arms against him when poison had failed. The only evidence was a statement of Antonius Natalis that he had been sent to visit the ailing Seneca and complain because Seneca had refused to receive Piso. Natalis had conveyed the message that friends ought to have friendly meetings; and Seneca had answered that frequent meetings and conversations would benefit neither: but that his own welfare depended on Piso's.

A colonel of the Guard, Gavius Silvanus, was ordered to convey this report to Seneca and ask whether he admitted that those were the words of Natalis and himself. Fortuitously or intentionally, Seneca had returned that day from Campania and halted at a villa four miles from Rome. Towards evening the officer arrived. Surrounding the villa with pickets, he delivered the emperor's message to Seneca as he dined with his wife Pompeia Paulina and two friends. Seneca replied as follows: "Natalis was sent to me to protest, on Piso's behalf, because I would not let him visit me. I answered excusing myself on grounds of health and love of quiet. I could have had no reason to value any private person's welfare above my own. Nor am I a flatterer. Nero knows this exceptionally well. He has had more frankness than servility from Seneca!"

The officer reported this to Nero in the presence of Poppaea and Tigellinus, intimate counsellors of the emperor's brutalities. Nero asked if Seneca was preparing for suicide. Gavius Silvanus replied that he had noticed no signs of fear or sadness in his words or features. So Silvanus was ordered to go back and notify the death-sentence. According to Fabius Rusticus, he did not return by the way he had come but made a detour to visit the commander of the Guard, Faenius Rufus; he showed Faenius the emperor's orders, asking if he should obey them; and Faenius, with that ineluctable weakness which they all revealed, told him to obey. For Silvanus was himself one of the conspirators – and now he was adding to the crimes which he had conspired to avenge. But he shirked communicating or witnessing the atrocity. Instead he sent in one of his staff-officers to tell Seneca he must die.

Unperturbed, Seneca asked for his will. But the officer refused. Then Seneca turned to his friends. "Being forbidden," he said, "to show gratitude for your services, I leave you my one remaining possession, and my best: the pattern of my life. If you remember it, your devoted friendship will be rewarded by a name for virtuous accomplishments. As he talked – and sometimes in sterner and more imperative terms – he checked their tears and sought to revive their courage. Where had their philosophy gone, he asked, and that resolution against impending misfortunes which they had devised over so many years? "Surely nobody was unaware that Nero was cruel!" he added. "After murdering his mother and brother, it only remained for him to kill his teacher and tutor."

These words were evidently intended for public hearing. Then Seneca embraced his wife and, with a tenderness very different from his philosophical imperturbability, entreated her to moderate and set a term to her grief, and take just consolation, in her bereavement, from contemplating his well-spent life. Nevertheless, she insisted on dying with him, and demanded the executioner's stroke. Seneca did not oppose her brave decision. Indeed, loving her wholeheartedly, he was reluctant to leave her behind to be persecuted. "Solace in life was what I commended to you," he said. "But you prefer death and glory. I will not grudge your setting so fine an example. We can die with equal fortitude. But yours will be the nobler end."

Then, each with one incision of the blade, he and his wife cut their arms. But Seneca's aged body, lean from austere living, released the blood too slowly. So he also severed the veins in his ankles and behind his knees. Exhausted by severe pain, he was afraid of weakening his wife's endurance by betraying his agony – or of losing his own self-possession at the sight of her sufferings. So he asked her to go into another bedroom. But even in his last moments his eloquence remained. Summoning secretaries, he dictated a dissertation. (It has been published in his own words, so I shall refrain from paraphrasing it.)

Nero did not dislike Paulina personally. In order, therefore, to avoid increasing his ill-repute for cruelty, he ordered her suicide to be averted. So, on instructions from the soldiers, slaves and ex-slaves bandaged her arms and stopped the bleeding. She may have been unconscious. But discreditable versions are always popular, and some took a different view – that as long as she feared there was no appeasing Nero, she coveted the distinction of dying with her husband, but when better prospects appeared life's attractions got the better of her. She lived on for a few years, honourably loyal to her husband's memory, with pallid features and limbs which showed how much vital blood she had lost.

Meanwhile Seneca's death was slow and lingering. Poison, such as was formerly used to execute State criminals at Athens,[1] had long been prepared; and Seneca now entreated his experienced doctor Annaeus Statius, who was also an old friend, to supply it. But when it came, Seneca drank it without effect. For his limbs were already cold and numbed against the poison's action. Finally he was placed in a bath of warm water. He sprinkled a little of it on the attendant slaves, commenting that this was his libation to Jupiter. Then he was carried into a vapour-bath, where he suffocated. His cremation was without ceremony, in accordance with his own instructions about his death – written at the height of his wealth and power.

AGRIPPINA PLEADS FOR HER LIFE, AD 59

Agrippina the Younger

The third wife of Emperor Claudius, Agrippina the Younger had guilefully won the throne for her son Nero. Her influence – and homicidal habits – proved intolerable, however; five years into his reign Nero ordered her execution for treason. Agrippina's letter below, pleading for clemency from her son, failed. She was strangled shortly afterwards.

I do wonder that barren Silana has no sense of maternal affection. One who has never borne a son naturally would not know how to bear the loss of one. Nature renders either hateful or indifferent those objects that we do not ourselves experience . . . I am amazed that even the most skilful sorcery of words could make you pay the least attention to such barbarous inhumanity . . .

Don't you know, my son, the affection all mothers naturally bear their children? Our love is unbounded, incessantly fed by that tenderness unknown to all but ourselves. Nothing should be more dear to us than what we have bought with the risk of our lives; nothing more precious than what we have endured such grief and pain to procure. These are so acute and unbearable that if it were not for the vision of a successful birth, which makes us forget our agonies, generation would soon cease.

[1] Hemlock was the poison of choice; Socrates was supplied it in his forced suicide.

Do you forget that nine full months I carried you in my womb and nourished you with my blood? How likely is it, then, that I would destroy the dear child who cost me so much anguish to bring into the world? It may be that the just gods were angry at my excessive love of you, and used this way to punish me.

Unhappy Agrippina! You are suspected of a crime of which nobody could really think you guilty . . . What does the title of empress mean to me, if I am accused of a crime that even the basest of women would abhor? Unhappy are those who breathe the air of the court. The wisest of people are not secure from storms in that harbour. There even a calm is dangerous. But why blame the court? Can that be the cause of my being suspected of parricide? . . .

Tell me, why should I plot against your life? To plunge myself into a worse fate? That's not likely. What hopes could induce me to build upon your downfall? I know that the lust for empire often corrupts the laws of nature; that justice has no sword to punish those who offend in this way; and that ambition disregards wrong so long as it succeeds in its aim . . . Nay, to what deity could I turn for absolution after I had committed so black a deed? . . .

What difficulties have I not surmounted to crown your brow with laurels? But I insult your gratitude by reminding you of my services. My innocence ought not to defend itself but to rely wholly on your justice.

Farewell

THE VANITY OF NERO, AD 59

Tacitus

Nero had long desired to drive in four-horse chariot races. Another equally deplorable ambition was to sing to the lyre, like a professional. "Chariot-racing," he said, "was an accomplishment of ancient kings and leaders – honoured by poets, associated with divine worship. Singing, too, is sacred to Apollo: that glorious and provident god is represented in a musician's dress in Greek cities, and also in Roman temples."

There was no stopping him. But Seneca and Burrus tried to prevent him from gaining both his wishes by conceding one of them. In the Vatican valley, therefore, an enclosure was constructed, where he could drive his horses, remote from the public eye. But soon the public were admitted – and even invited; and they approved vociferously. For such is a crowd: avid for entertainment, and delighted if the emperor shares their tastes. However, this scandalous publicity did not satiate Nero, as his advisers had expected. Indeed, it led him on. But if he shared his degradation, he thought it would be less; so he brought on to the stage members of the ancient nobility whose poverty made them corruptible. They are dead, and I feel I owe it to their ancestors not to name them. For though they behaved dishonourably, so did the man who paid them to offend (instead of not to do so). Well-known knights, too, he induced by huge presents to offer their services in the arena. But gifts from the man who can command carry with them an obligation.

However, Nero was not yet ready to disgrace himself on a public stage. Instead he instituted "Youth Games". There were many volunteers. Birth, age, official career did not prevent people from acting – in Greek or Latin style – or from accompanying their performances with effeminate gestures and songs. Eminent women, too, rehearsed indecent parts. In the wood which Augustus had planted round his Naval Lake, places of assignation and taverns were built, and every stimulus to vice was displayed for sale. Moreover, there were distributions of money. Respectable people were compelled to spend it; disreputable people did so gladly. Promiscuity and degradation throve. Roman morals had long become impure, but never was there so favourable an environment for debauchery as among this filthy crowd. Even in good surroundings people find it hard to behave well. Here every form of immorality competed for attention, and no chastity, modesty, or vestige of decency could survive.

The climax was the emperor's stage debut. Meticulously tuning his lyre, he struck practice notes to the trainers beside him. A battalion attended with its officers. So did Burrus, grieving – but applauding. Now, too, was formed the corps of Roman knights known as the Augustiani. These powerful

young men, impudent by nature or ambition, maintained a din
of applause day and night, showering divine epithets on Nero's
beauty and voice. They were grand and respected as if they had
done great things.

But the emperor did not obtain publicity by his theatrical
talents only. He also aspired to poetic taste. He gathered round
himself at dinner men who possessed some versifying ability but
were not yet known. As they sat on, they strung together verses
they had brought with them, or extemporized – and filled out
Nero's own suggestions, such as they were. This method is
apparent from Nero's poems themselves, which lack vigour,
inspiration, and homogeneity. To philosophers, too, he devoted
some of his time after dinner, enjoying their quarrelsome
assertions of contradictory views. There were enough of such
people willing to display their glum features and expressions for
the amusement of the court.

BOUDICCA REVOLTS, BRITAIN, AD 60

Tacitus

*It was not until AD 43, under Claudius, that the Romans began a successful
colonization of England and Wales (Scotland remained unconquered). Their
rule was grasping and in AD 61 the Iceni rose in rebellion. Tacitus noted of
the Britons that they could "bear to be ruled by others but not be their slaves".
Tacitus himself, in all probability, never visited Britannia, but his source
was unimpeachable; it was his father-in-law, Agricola, the most astute of the
island's Roman governors.*

The new imperial governor of Britain was Gaius Suetonius
Paulinus. Corbulo's rival in military science, as in popular talk
– which makes everybody compete – he was ambitious to
achieve victories as glorious as the reconquest of Armenia.
So Suetonius planned to attack the island of Mona, which
although thickly populated had also given sanctuary to many
refugees.

Flat-bottomed boats were built to contend with the shifting
shallows, and these took the infantry across. Then came the
cavalry; some utilized fords, but in deeper water the men swam
beside their horses. The enemy lined the shore in a dense armed

mass. Among them were black-robed women with dishevelled hair like Furies, brandishing torches. Close by stood Druids, raising their hands to heaven and screaming dreadful curses.

This weird spectacle awed the Roman soldiers into a sort of paralysis. They stood still – and presented themselves as a target. But then they urged each other (and were urged by the general) not to fear a horde of fanatical women. Onward pressed their standards and they bore down their opponents, enveloping them in the flames of their own torches. Suetonius garrisoned the conquered island. The groves devoted to Mona's barbarous superstitions he demolished. For it was their religion to drench their altars in the blood of prisoners and consult their gods by means of human entrails.

While Suetonius was thus occupied, he learned of a sudden rebellion in the province. Prasutagus, king of the Iceni, after a life of long and renowned prosperity, had made the emperor co-heir with his own two daughters. Prasutagus hoped by this submissiveness to preserve his kingdom and household from attack. But it turned out otherwise. Kingdom and household alike were plundered like prizes of war, the one by Roman officers, the other by Roman slaves. As a beginning, his widow Boudicca[1] was flogged and their daughters raped. The Icenian chiefs were deprived of their hereditary estates as if the Romans had been given the whole country. The king's own relatives were treated like slaves.

And the humiliated Iceni feared still worse, now that they had been reduced to provincial status. So they rebelled. With them rose the Trinobantes and others. Servitude had not broken them, and they had secretly plotted together to become free again. They particularly hated the Roman ex-soldiers who had recently established a settlement at Camulodunum. The settlers drove the Trinobantes from their homes and land, and called them prisoners and slaves. The troops encouraged the settlers' outrages, since their own way of behaving was the same – and they looked forward to similar licence for themselves. Moreover, the temple erected to the divine Claudius was a blatant stronghold of alien rule, and its observances were a

[1] The spelling "Boadicea" is unauthenticated.

pretext to make the natives appointed as its priests drain the whole country dry.

It seemed easy to destroy the settlement; for it had no walls. That was a matter which Roman commanders, thinking of amenities rather than needs, had neglected. At this juncture, for no visible reason, the statue of Victory at Camulodunum fell down – with its back turned as though it were fleeing the enemy. Delirious women chanted of destruction at hand. They cried that in the local senate-house outlandish yells had been heard; the theatre had echoed with shrieks; at the mouth of the Thames a phantom settlement had been seen in ruins. A blood-red colour in the sea, too, and shapes like human corpses left by the ebb tide, were interpreted hopefully by the Britons – and with terror by the settlers.

Suetonius, however, was far away. So they appealed for help to the imperial agent Catus Decianus. He sent them barely 200 men, incompletely armed. There was also a small garrison on the spot. Reliance was placed on the temple's protection. Misled by secret prorebels, who hampered their plans, they dispensed with rampart or trench. They omitted also to evacuate old people and women and thus leave only fighting men behind. Their precautions were appropriate to a time of un-broken peace.

Then a native horde surrounded them. When all else had been ravaged or burnt, the garrison concentrated itself in the temple. After two days' siege, it fell by storm. The ninth Roman division, commanded by Quintus Petilius Cerialis Caesius Rufus, attempted to relieve the town, but was stopped by the victorious Britons and routed. Its entire infantry force was massacred, while the commander escaped to his camp with his cavalry and sheltered behind its defences. The imperial agent Catus Decianus, horrified by the catastrophe and by his unpopularity, withdrew to Gaul. It was his rapacity which had driven the province to war.

But Suetonius, undismayed, marched through disaffected territory to Londinium. This town did not rank as a Roman settlement, but was an important centre for business-men and merchandise. At first, he hesitated whether to stand and fight there. Eventually, his numerical inferiority – and the price only too clearly paid by the divisional commander's rashness – decided him to sacrifice the single city of Londinium to save the province as a whole. Unmoved by lamentations and appeals, Suetonius gave the signal for departure. The inhabitants were allowed to accompany him. But those who stayed because they were women, or old, or attached to the place, were slaughtered by the enemy. Verulamium suffered the same fate.

The natives enjoyed plundering and thought of nothing else. Bypassing forts and garrisons, they made for where loot was richest and protection weakest. Roman and provincial deaths at the places mentioned are estimated at 70,000. For the British did not take or sell prisoners, or practise other war-time exchanges. They could not wait to cut throats, hang, burn, and crucify – as though avenging, in advance, the retribution that was on its way.

Suetonius collected the fourteenth brigade and detachments of the twentieth, together with the nearest available auxiliaries – amounting to nearly 10,000 armed men – and decided to attack without further delay. He chose a position in a defile with a wood behind him. There could be no enemy, he knew, except at his front, where there was open country without cover for ambushes. Suetonius drew up his regular troops in close order, with the light-armed auxiliaries at their flanks, and the cavalry massed on the wings. On the British side, cavalry and infantry bands seethed over a wide area in unprecedented numbers. Their confidence was such that they brought their wives with them to see the victory, installing them in carts stationed at the edge of the battlefield.

Boudicca drove round all the tribes in a chariot with her daughters in front of her. "We British are used to women commanders in war," she cried. "I am descended from mighty men! But now I am not fighting for my kingdom and wealth. I am fighting as an ordinary person for my lost freedom, my bruised body, and my outraged daughters. Nowadays Roman rapicity does not even spare our bodies. Old people are killed, virgins raped. But the gods will grant us the vengeance we deserve! The Roman division which dared to fight is annihilated. The others cower in their camps, or watch for a chance to escape. They will never face even the din and roar of all our thousands, much less the shock of our onslaught. Consider how many of you are fighting – and why. Then you will win this battle, or perish. That is what I, a woman, plan to do! – let the men live in slavery if they will."

Suetonius trusted his men's bravery. Yet he too, at this critical moment, offered encouragements and appeals. "Disregard the clamours and empty threats of the natives!" he said. "In their ranks, there are more women than fighting men. Unwarlike, unarmed, when they see the arms and courage of the conquerors who have routed them so often, they will break immediately. Even when a force contains many divisions, few among them win the battles – what special glory for your small numbers to win the renown of a whole army! Just keep in close order. Throw your javelins, and then carry on: use shield-bosses to fell them, swords to kill them. Do not think of plunder. When you have won, you will have everything."

The general's words were enthusiastically received: the old battle-experienced soldiers longed to hurl their javelins. So Suetonius confidently gave the signal for battle. At first the regular troops stood their ground. Keeping to the defile as a natural defence, they launched their javelins accurately at the approaching enemy. Then, in wedge formation, they burst forward. So did the auxiliary infantry. The cavalry, too, with lances extended, demolished all serious resistance. The remaining Britons fled with difficulty since their ring of wagons blocked the outlets. The Romans did not spare even the women. Baggage animals too, transfixed with weapons, added to the heaps of dead.

THE BANQUET OF TRIMALCHIO, c. AD 60

Petronius

A picture of Roman hedonism from Petronius' comic romance Satyricon. *Petronius was well acquainted with the excesses of the Roman rich – which he lampooned unsparingly in* Satyricon – being a court favourite of Nero himself. (This did not spare Petronius his life; Nero later ordered him to commit suicide.) Trimalchio is a *noveau riche freedman*.

At last we went to recline at table where boys from Alexandria poured snow water on our hands, while others, turning their attention to our feet, picked our nails, and not in silence did they perform their task, but singing all the time. I wished to try if the whole retinue could sing, and so I called for a drink, and a boy, not less ready with his tune, brought it accompanying his action with a sharp-toned ditty; and no matter what you asked for it was all the same song.

The first course was served and it *was* good, for all were close up at the table, save Trimalchio, for whom, after a new fashion, the place of honour was reserved. Among the first viands there was a little ass of Corinthian bronze with saddle bags on his back, in one of which were white olives and in the other black. Over the ass were two silver platters, engraved on the edges with Trimalchio's name, and the weight of silver. Dormice seasoned with honey and poppies lay on little bridgelike structures of iron; there were also sausages brought in piping hot on a silver gridiron, and under that Syrian plums and pomegranate grains.

We were in the midst of these delights when Trimalchio was brought in with a burst of music. They laid him down on some little cushions, very carefully; whereat some giddy ones broke into a laugh, though it was not much to be wondered at, to see his bald pate peeping out from a scarlet cloak, and his neck all wrapped up and a robe with a broad purple stripe hanging down before him, with tassels and fringes dingle-dangle about him.

Then going through his teeth with a silver pick, "my friends," quoth he, "I really didn't want to come to dinner so soon, but I was afraid my absence would cause too great a delay, so I denied myself the pleasure I was at – at any rate I hope you'll let me finish my game." A slave followed, carrying a checkerboard of turpentine wood, with crystal dice; but one thing in particular I noticed as extra nice – he had gold and silver coins instead of the ordinary black and white pieces. While he was cursing like a trooper over the game and we were starting on the lighter dishes, a basket was brought in on a tray, with a wooden hen in it, her wings spread round, as if she were hatching.

Then two slaves came with their eternal singing, and began searching the straw, whence they rooted out some peahen's eggs, and distributed them among the guests. At this Trimalchio turned around – "Friends," he says, "I had some peahen's eggs placed under a hen, and so help me Hercules! – I hope they're not hatched out; we'd better try if they're still tasty." Thereupon we took up our spoons – they were not less than half a pound weight [of silver] – and broke the eggs that were made of rich pastry. I had been almost on the point of throwing my share away, for I thought I had a chick in it, until hearing an old hand saying, "There must be something good in this," I delved deeper – and found a very fat fig-pecker inside, surrounded by peppered egg yolk.

At this point Trimalchio stopped his game, demanded the same dishes, and raising his voice, declared that if any one wanted more liquor he had only to say the word. At once the orchestra struck up the music, as the slaves also struck up theirs, and removed the first course. In the bustle a dish chanced to fall, and when a boy stooped to pick it up, Trimalchio gave him a few vigorous cuffs for his pains, and bade him to "throw it down again" – and a slave coming in swept out the silver platter along with the refuse. After that two long-haired Ethiopians entered with little bladders, similar to those used in sprinkling the arena in the amphitheater, but instead of water they poured *wine* on our hands. Then glass wine jars were brought in, carefully sealed and a ticket on the neck of each, reading thus:

"Opimian Falernia[1]
One hundred years old."

Presently one of the guests remarks, first on how completely Trimalchio is under the thumb of his wife; next he comments on the gentleman's vast riches.

"So help me Hercules, the tenth of his slaves don't know their own master . . . Some time ago the quality of his wool was not to his liking; so what does he do, but buys rams at Tarentum to improve the breed. In order to have Attic honey at home with him, he has bees brought from Attica to better his stock by crossing it with the Greek. A couple of days ago he had the notion to write to India for mushroom seed. And his freedmen,

---

[1] An extremely choice vintage.

his one-time comrades [in slavery] they are no small cheese either; they are immensely well-off. Do you see that chap on the last couch over there? To-day he has his 800,000 sesterces. He came from nothing, and time was when he had to carry wood upon his back . . . He has been manumitted only lately, but he knows his business. Not long ago he displayed this notice:

CAIUS . POMPEIUS . DIOGENES
HAVING . TAKEN . A . HOUSE . IS . DISPOSED
TO . LET . HIS . GARRET . FROM . THE
KALENDS . OF . JULY.

[After a very long discussion in like vein and a vulgar display of luxuries and riches, Trimalchio condescends to tell the company how he came by his vast wealth.]

"When I came here first as a slave from Asia, I was only as high as yonder candlestick, and I'd be measuring my height on it every day, and greasing my lips with lamp oil to bring out a bit of hair on my snout.

"Well, at last, to make a long story short, as it pleased the gods, I became master in the house, and as you see, I'm chip of the same block. He [my master] made me co-heir with Cæsar, and I came into a royal fortune, but no one ever thinks he has enough. I was mad for trading, and to put it all in a nutshell, bought five ships, freighted them with wine – and wine was as good as coined money at that time – and sent them to Rome. You wouldn't believe it, – every one of those ships was wrecked. In one day Neptune swallowed up 30,000,000 sesterces on me. D'ye think I lost heart? Not much! I took no notice of it, by Hercules! I got more ships made, larger, better, and luckier; that no one might say I wasn't a plucky fellow. A big ship has big strength – that's plain! Well I freighted them with wine, bacon, beans, perfumes, and slaves. Here Fortuna (my consort) showed her devotion. She sold her jewellery and all her dresses, and gave me a hundred gold pieces – that's what my fortune grew from. What the gods ordain happens quickly. For on just one voyage I scooped in 10,000,000 sesterces and immediately started to redeem all the lands that used to be my master's. I built a house, bought some cattle to sell again – whatever I laid my hand to grew like a honeycomb. When I found myself richer than all the country round about wàs worth, in less than no time I gave up trading, and commenced lending money at interest to the freedmen. 'Pon my word, I was very near giving up business altogether, only an astrologer, who happened to come into our colony, dissuaded me.

"And now I may as well tell you it all, – I have thirty years, four months and two days to live, moreover I'm to fall in for an estate, – that's the astrologer's prophecy anyway. If I'm so lucky as to be able to join my domains to Apulia, I'll say I've got on pretty well. Meanwhile under Mercury's fostering, I've built this house. Just a hut once, you know – now a regular temple! It has four dining rooms, twenty bedrooms, two marble porticoes, a set of cells [for the slaves?] upstairs, my own bedroom, a sitting room for this viper [my wife!] here, a very fine porter's room, and it holds guests to any amount. There are a lot of other things too that I'll show you by and by. Take my word for it, if you have a penny you're worth a penny, you are valued for just what you have. Yesterday your friend was a frog, he's a king today – that's the way it goes."

Trimalchio goes on to show off to his guests the costly shroud, perfumes, etc., he has been assembling for his own funeral; and at last we, the guests were already disgusted with the whole affair when Trimalchio, who, by the way, was beastly drunk, ordered in the cornet players for our further pleasure, and propped up with cushions, stretched himself out at full length.

"Imagine I'm dead," says he, "and play something soothing!" Whereat the cornet players struck up a funeral march, and one of them especially – a slave of the undertaker fellow – the best in the crowd, played with such effect that he roused the whole neighbourhood. So the watchmen, who had charge of the district, thinking Trimalchio's house on fire, burst in the door, and surged in – as was their right – with axes and water ready. Taking advantage of such an opportune moment . . . we bolted incontinently, as if there had been a real fire in the place.

LIVING ABOVE ROMAN BATHS, C. AD 60

Seneca

I live over a bathing establishment. Picture to yourself now the assortment of voices, the sound of which is enough to sicken one . . . When the stronger fellows are exercising and swinging heavy leaden weights in their hands, when they are working hard or pretending to be working hard, I hear their groans; and whenever they release their pent-up breath, I hear their hissing and jarring breathing. When I have to do with a lazy fellow who is content with a cheap rubdown, I hear the slap of the hand pummelling his shoulders, changing its sound according as the hand is laid flat or curved. If now a professional ball player comes along and begins to keep score, I am done for. Add to this the arrest of a brawler or a thief, and the fellow who always likes to hear his own voice in the bath, and those who jump into the pool with a mighty plash as they strike the water. In addition to those whose voices are, if nothing else, natural, imagine the hair plucker keeping up a constant chatter in this thin and strident voice, to attract more attention, and never silent except when he is plucking armpits and making the customer yell instead of yelling himself. It disgusts me to enumerate the varied cries of the sausage dealer and confectioner and of all the peddlers of the cook shops, hawking their wares, each with his own peculiar intonation.

THE GREAT FIRE OF ROME, AD 64

Tacitus

Nero now tried to make it appear that Rome was his favourite abode. He gave feasts in public places as if the whole city were his own home. But the most prodigal and notorious banquet was given by Tigellinus. To avoid repetitious accounts of extravagance, I shall describe it, as a model of its kind. The entertainment took place on a raft constructed on Marcus Agrippa's lake. It was towed about by other vessels, with gold and ivory fittings. Their rowers were degenerates, assorted according to age and vice. Tigellinus had also collected birds and animals from remote countries, and even the products of the ocean. On the quays were brothels stocked with high-ranking ladies. Opposite them could be seen naked prostitutes, indecently posturing and gesturing.

At nightfall the woods and houses nearby echoed with singing and blazed with lights. Nero was already corrupted by every lust, natural and unnatural. But he now refuted any surmises that no further degradation was possible for him. For a few days later he went through a formal wedding ceremony with one of the perverted gang called Pythagoras. The emperor, in the presence of witnesses, put on the bridal veil. Dowry, marriage bed, wedding torches, all were there. Indeed everything was public which even in a natural union is veiled by night.

Disaster followed. Whether it was accidental or caused by a criminal act on the part of the emperor is uncertain – both versions have supporters. Now started the most terrible and destructive fire which Rome had ever experienced. It began in the Circus, where it adjoins the Palatine and Caelian hills. Breaking out in shops selling inflammable goods, and fanned by the wind, the conflagration instantly grew and swept the whole length of the Circus. There were no walled mansions or temples, or any other obstructions, which could arrest it. First, the fire swept violently over the level spaces. Then it climbed the hills – but returned to ravage the lower ground again. It outstripped every counter-measure. The ancient city's narrow winding streets and irregular blocks encouraged its progress.

Terrified, shrieking women, helpless old and young, people intent on their own safety, people unselfishly supporting in-valids or waiting for them, fugitives and lingerers alike – all heightened the confusion. When people looked back, menacing flames sprang up before them or outflanked them. When they escaped to a neighbouring quarter, the fire followed – even districts believed remote proved to be involved. Finally, with no idea where or what to flee, they crowded on to the country roads, or lay in the fields. Some who had lost everything – even their food for the day – could have escaped, but preferred to die. So did others, who had failed to rescue their loved ones. Nobody dared fight the flames. Attempts to do so were prevented by menacing gangs. Torches, too, were openly thrown in, by men crying that they acted under orders. Perhaps they had received orders. Or they may just have wanted to plunder unhampered.

Nero was at Antium. He returned to the city only when the fire was approaching the mansion he had built to link the Gardens of Maecenas to the Palatine. The flames could not be prevented from overwhelming the whole of the Palatine, including his palace. Nevertheless, for the relief of the homeless, fugitive masses he threw open the Field of Mars, including Agrippa's public buildings, and even his own Gardens. Nero also constructed emergency accommodation for the destitute multitude. Food was brought from Ostia and neighbouring towns, and the price of corn was cut to less than 1/4 sesterce a pound. Yet these measures, for all their popular character, earned no gratitude. For a rumour had spread that, while the city was burning, Nero had gone on his private stage and, comparing modern calamities with ancient, had sung of the destruction of Troy.

By the sixth day enormous demolitions had confronted the raging flames with bare ground and open sky, and the fire was finally stamped out at the foot of the Esquiline Hill. But before panic had subsided, or hope revived, flames broke out again in the more open regions of the city. Here there were fewer casualties; but the destruction of temples and pleasure arcades was even worse. This new conflagration caused additional ill-feeling because it started on Tigellinus' estate in the Aemilian district. For people believed that Nero was ambitious to found a new city to be called after himself.

Of Rome's fourteen districts only four remained intact. Three were levelled to the ground. The other seven were reduced to a few scorched and mangled ruins.

AFTER THE FIRE: NERO REBUILDS ROME, AD 64

Tacitus

Nero meanwhile availed himself of his country's desolation, and erected a mansion in which the jewels and gold, long familiar objects, quite vulgarized by our extravagance, were not so marvellous as the fields and lakes, with woods on one side to resemble a wilderness, and, on the other, open spaces and extensive views. The directors and contrivers of the work were Severus and Celer, who had the genius and the audacity to attempt by art even what nature had refused, and to fool away an emperor's resources. They had actually undertaken to sink a navigable canal from the lake Avernus to the mouths of the Tiber along a barren shore or through the face of hills, where one meets with no moisture which could supply water, except the Pomptine marshes. The rest of the country is broken rock and perfectly dry. Even if it could be cut through, the labour would be intolerable, and there would be no adequate result. Nero, however, with his love of the impossible, endeavoured to dig through the nearest hills to Avernus, and there still remain the traces of his disappointed hope.

Of Rome meanwhile, so much as was left unoccupied by his mansion, was not built up, as it had been after its burning by the Gauls, without any regularity or in any fashion, but with rows of streets according to measurement, with broad thoroughfares, with a restriction on the height of houses, with open spaces, and the further addition of colonnades, as a protection to the frontage of the blocks of tenements. These colonnades Nero promised to erect at his own expense, and to hand over the open spaces, when cleared of the debris, to the ground landlords. He also offered rewards proportioned to each person's position and property, and prescribed a period within which they were to obtain them on the completion of so many houses or blocks of building. He fixed on the marshes of Ostia for the reception of the rubbish, and arranged that the ships which had brought up corn by the Tiber, should sail down the river with cargoes of this rubbish. The buildings themselves, to a certain height, were to be solidly constructed, without wooden beams, of stone from Gabii or Alba, that material being impervious to fire. And to provide that the water which individual licence had illegally appropriated, might flow in greater abundance in several places for the public use, officers were appointed, and everyone was to have in the open court the means of stopping a fire. Every building, too, was to be enclosed by its own proper wall, not by one common to others. These changes which were liked for their utility, also added beauty to the new city. Some, however, thought that its old arrangement had been more conducive to health, inasmuch as the narrow streets with the elevation of the roofs were not equally penetrated by the sun's heat, while now the open space, unsheltered by any shade, was scorched by a fiercer glow.

AFTER THE FIRE: NERO PERSECUTES THE CHRISTIANS, ROME, AD 64

Tacitus

To divert suspicion that he himself had ordered the firing of Rome, Nero scapegoated the Christians, who were anyway viewed by the majority of citizens as a growing pernicious and radical (being confined largely to the lower orders) sect.

. . . all human efforts, all the lavish gifts of the emperor, and the propitiations of the gods, did not banish the sinister belief that the conflagration was the result of an order. Consequently, to get rid of the report, Nero fastened the guilt and inflicted the most exquisite tortures on a class hated for their abominations, called Christians by the populace. Christus, from whom the name had its origin, suffered the extreme penalty during the reign of Tiberius at the hands of one of our procurators, Pontius Pilatus, and a most mischievous superstition, thus checked for the moment, again broke out not only in Judaea, the first source of the evil, but even in Rome, where all things hideous and shameful from every part of the world find their centre and become popular. Accordingly, an arrest was first made of all who pleaded guilty; then, upon their information, an immense multitude was convicted, not so much of the crime of firing the city, as of hatred against mankind. Mockery of every sort was added to their deaths. Covered with the skins of beasts, they were torn by dogs and perished, or were nailed to crosses, or were doomed to the flames and burned, to serve as a nightly illumination, when daylight had expired.

Nero offered his gardens for the spectacle, and was exhibiting a show in the circus, while he mingled with the people in the dress of a charioteer or stood aloft on a car. Hence, even for criminals who deserved extreme and exemplary punishment, there arose a feeling of compassion; for it was not, as it seemed, for the public good, but to glut one man's cruelty, that they were being destroyed.

THE GLUTTONY OF VITELLIUS, AD 69

Suetonius

The Emperor Vitellius was only notable for his "excessive feeding and cruelty" (Suetonius), the shortness of his reign (less than a year) and the public manner of his murder (see pp 185–187).

He [Vitellius] always ate three meals a day, sometimes four: breakfast, dinner, supper, and a drunken revel after all, which he was able to bear very well, by reason of regular vomiting. His manner was to send word that he would breakfast with one friend, dine with another, etc., and all in one day. None ever entertained him at a cost of less than four hundred thousand sesterces. The most notorious one of all was a set banquet given him by his brother at which, it is said, there were served up no less than two thousand choice fishes and seven thousand birds. Yet even this feast, sumptuous as it was, he himself surpassed at one he gave upon the first use of a dish which had been made for him and which, for its extraordinary size, he called "The Shield of Minerva". In this dish there were tossed up together the livers of charfish, the brains of pheasants and peacocks, with the tongues of flamingos, and the entrails of lampreys, all of which had been brought in ships of war as far as from the Carpathian Sea and the Spanish Straits. He was not only a man of prodigious appetite, but he would gratify it likewise at unseasonable times, and with any gross stuff that came in his way; so that, at a sacrifice, he would snatch from the fire flesh and cakes and devour them on the spot. When he travelled, he would stop at every inn along the road and fall to viands piping hot, or cold and left over from the day before, sometimes half eaten, just as fortune served him.

VITELLIUS: THE END, AD 69

Suetonius

In the eighth month of his reign, the troops both in Moesia and Pannonia revolted from him; as did likewise, of the armies beyond the sea those in Judaea and Syria, some of which swore allegiance to Vespasian as emperor in his own presence, and others in his absence. In order, therefore, to retain the favour and affection of the people, Vitellius lavished on all around whatever he had it in his power to bestow, both publicly and privately, in the most extravagant manner. He also levied soldiers in the city, and promised all who enlisted as volunteers, not only their discharge after the victory was gained, but all the rewards due to veterans who had served their full time in wars. The enemy now pressing hotly forward both by sea and land, on one hand he opposed against them his brother with a fleet, the new levies, and a body of gladiators, and in another quarter the troops and generals who were engaged at Bedriacum. But being discomfited in open field or secretly betrayed at every turn, he agreed with Flavius Sabinus, Vespasian's brother, to abdicate, on condition of having his life spared and a hundred millions of sesterces granted him; and he immediately, upon the palace steps, publicly declared to a large body of soldiers there assembled, "that he resigned the government, which he had accepted against his will"; but they all remonstrating against it, he put off the conclusion of the treaty. Next day, early in the morning, he came down to the Forum in a very mean habit, and with many tears repeated the speech, from a writing which he held in his hand; but the soldiers and people both, interrupting him a second time and exhorting him not to be cast down, but to rely on their zealous assistance, he took courage again, and forced Sabinus, with the rest of the Flavian party, who now thought themselves secure, to retreat into the Capitol where he destroyed them all by setting fire to the temple of Jupiter, while he beheld the contest and the fire from Tiberius' house where he was feasting. Not long after, repenting of what he had done, and laying all the fault upon others, he called a public assembly: where he swore, and compelled all the rest to take the same oath, "that he and they would hold nothing more sacred than the public peace". Then, drawing a dagger from his side, he presented it first to the consul and, upon his refusing it, to the magistrates, and then to every one of the senators; but none of them being willing to accept it, he went away, as if he meant to lay it up in the temple of Concord. But some crying out to him, "You are Concord", he came back again, and said that he would not only keep his weapon, but for the future use the surname of Concord.

He advised the senate to send ambassadors, accompanied by the Vestal Virgins, to crave peace, or at least, some longer time to consult upon the point. The next day, while he was waiting for an answer, word was brought to him by a spy that the enemy was advancing. Immediately, therefore, throwing himself into a small litter, borne by hand, with only two attendants, a baker and a cook, he privately withdrew to his father's house, on the Aventine hill, intending to escape thence into Campania. Soon after, upon a groundless report flying around that the enemy was willing to come to terms, he suffered himself to be brought back to the palace; where, finding nobody, and those who were with him slinking away, he girded round his waist a belt full of gold pieces, and then ran into the porter's lodge, tying the dog before the door, and piling up against it the bed and bedding.

By this time the forerunners of the enemy's army had broken into the palace, and meeting with nobody, searched, as was natural, every corner. Being dragged by them out of his cell, and asked "who he was?" (for they did not recognize him), "and if he knew where Vitellius was?" he deceived them by a lie. But at last being recognized, he begged hard to be detained in custody, even were it in a prison; pretending to have something to say which concerned Vespasian's security. Nevertheless he was dragged half naked into the Forum, with his hands tied behind him, a rope about his neck, and his clothes torn, amid the most scornful abuse, both by word and deed, and then along the Via Sacra; his head being held back by the hair, in the manner of condemned criminals, and the point of a sword put under his chin, that he might hold up his face to public view;

some of the mob, meanwhile, pelting him with dung and mud, while others called him "an incendiary and glutton". They also upbraided him with the defects of his person, for he was monstrously tall, and had a face usually very red with hard drinking, a large belly, and one thigh weak, by reason of a chariot having run against him, during his attendance upon Caius Caligula at a race. At length, upon the Gemonian Steps, he was tortured and mangled by slow degrees, and then dragged by a hook into the Tiber.

Thus he perished, with his brother and son, in the fifty-seventh year of his age, and so verified the prediction of those who had foretold him that by the sign which had been seen at Vienne, as before related, he would fall into the hands of a Gaul. For he was seized by Antoninus Primus, a general of the adverse party, who was born at Toulouse, and, when a boy, had the surname of Becco, which signifies a cock's beak.

THE REBUILDING OF THE TEMPLE OF JUPITER, AD 70

Tacitus

As ordered by Vespasian, Vitellius' successor.

The work of rebuilding the Capitol was assigned by him to Lucius Vestinius, a man of the Equestrian order, who, however, for high character and reputation ranked among the nobles. The soothsayers whom he assembled directed that the remains of the old shrine should be removed to the marshes, and the new temple raised on the original site. The Gods, they said, forbade the old form to be changed. On the 21st of June, beneath a cloudless sky, the entire space devoted to the sacred enclosure was encompassed with chaplets and garlands. Soldiers, who bore auspicious names, entered the precincts with sacred boughs. Then the vestal virgins, with a troop of boys and girls, whose fathers and mothers were still living, sprinkled the whole space with water drawn from the fountains and rivers. After this, Helvidius Priscus, the praetor, first purified the spot with the usual sacrifice of a sow, a sheep, and a bull, and duly placed the entrails on turf; then, in terms dictated by Publius Aelianus, the high-priest, besought Jupiter, Juno, Minerva, and the tutelary deities of the place, to prosper the undertaking, and to lend their divine help to raise the abodes which the piety of men had founded for them. He then touched the wreaths, which were wound round the foundation stone and entwined with the ropes, while at the same moment all the other magistrates of the State, the Priests, the Senators, the Knights, and a number of the citizens, with zeal and joy uniting their efforts, dragged the huge stone along. Contributions of gold and silver and virgin ores, never smelted in the furnace, but still in their natural state, were showered on the foundations. The soothsayers had previously directed that no stone or gold which had been intended for any other purpose should profane the work. Additional height was given to the structure; this was the only variation which religion would permit, and the one feature which had been thought wanting in the splendour of the old temple.

VESPASIAN MARCHES AGAINST THE JEWS, AD 70

Josephus

Judea became a vassal state of Rome in 63 BC. The Jews, however, never reconciled themselves to Roman rule and in AD 66 "Zealots" fomented widespread unrest. Rome's reaction was predictable. Josephus was a Jew who had gone over to the Romans.

But as Vespasian had a great mind to fall upon Galilee, he marched out of Ptolemais, having put his army into that order wherein the Romans used to march. He ordered those auxiliaries which were lightly armed, and the archers, to march first, that they might prevent any sudden insults from the enemy, and might search out the woods that looked suspiciously, and were capable of ambuscades. Next to these followed that part of the Romans which was completely armed, both footmen, and horsemen. Next to these followed ten out of every hundred, carrying along with them their arms, and what was necessary to measure out a camp withal; and after them, such as were to make the road even and straight, and if it were any where rough and hard to be passed over, to plane it, and to cut down the woods that hindered their march, that the army might not be in distress, or tired with their march. Behind these he set such carriages of the army as belonged both to himself and to the other commanders, with a considerable number of their horsemen for their security. After these he marched himself, having with him a select body of footmen, and horsemen, and pikemen. After these came the peculiar cavalry of his own legion, for there were 120 horsemen that peculiarly belonged to every legion. Next to these came the mules that carried the engines for sieges, and the other warlike machines of that nature. After these came the commanders of the cohorts and tribunes, having about them soldiers chosen out of the rest. Then came the ensigns encompassing the eagle, which is at the head of every Roman legion, the king, and the strongest of all birds, which seems to them a signal of dominion, and an omen that they shall conquer all against whom they march; these sacred ensigns are followed by the trumpeters. Then came the main army in their squadrons and battalions, with six men in depth, which were followed at last by a centurion, who, according to custom, observed the rest. As for the servants of every legion, they all followed the footmen, and led the baggage of the soldiers, which was borne by the mules and other beasts of burden. But behind all the legions carne the whole multitude of the mercenaries; and those that brought up the rear came last of all for the security of the whole army, being both footmen, and those in their armour also, with a great number of horsemen.

THE SIEGE OF JERUSALEM: CIVILIAN SUFFERING, AD 70

Josephus

Vespasian himself retired to Rome, leaving the subduing of the Jews and their capital to Titus.

Now of those that perished by famine in the city, the number was prodigious, and the miseries they underwent were unspeakable; for if so much as the shadow of any kind of food did any where appear, a war was commenced presently, and the dearest friends fell a fighting one with another about it, snatching from each other the most miserable supports of life. Nor would men believe that those who were dying had no food, but the robbers would search them when they were expiring, lest any one should have concealed food in their bosoms, and counterfeited dying; nay, these robbers gaped for want, and ran about stumbling and staggering along like mad dogs, and reeling against the doors of the houses like drunken men; they would also, in the great distress they were in, rush into the very same houses two or three times in one and the same day. Moreover, their hunger was so intolerable, that it obliged them to chew every thing, while they gathered such things as the most sordid animals would not touch, and endured to eat them; nor did they at length abstain from girdles and shoes; and the very leather which belonged to their shields they pulled off and gnawed: the very wisps of old hay became food to some; and some gathered up fibres, and sold a very small weight of them for four Attic [drachmae]. But why do I describe the shameless impudence that the famine brought on men in their eating inanimate things, while I am going to relate a matter of fact, the like to which no history relates, either among the Greeks or Barbarians? It is horrible to speak of it, and incredible when heard. I had indeed willingly omitted this calamity of ours, that I might not seem to deliver what is so portentous to posterity, but that I have innumerable witnesses to it in my own age; and besides, my country would have had little reason to thank me for suppressing the miseries that she underwent at this time.

There was a certain woman that dwelt beyond Jordan, her name was Mary; her father was Eleazar, of the village Bethezob, which signifies the *house of Hyssop*. She was eminent for her family and her wealth, and had fled away to Jerusalem with the rest of the multitude, and was with them besieged therein at this time. The other effects of this woman had been already seized upon, such I mean as she had brought with her out of Perea, and removed to the city. What she had treasured up besides, as also what food she had contrived to save, had been also carried off by the rapacious guards, who came every day running into her house for that purpose. This put the poor woman into a very great passion, and by the frequent reproaches and imprecations she east at these rapacious villains, she had provoked them to

anger against her; but none of them, either out of the indignation she had raised against herself, or out of commiseration of
her case, would take away her life; and if she found any food, she
perceived her labours were for others, and not for herself; and it
was now become impossible for her any way to find any more
food, while the famine pierced through her very bowels and
marrow, when also her passion was fired to a degree beyond the
famine itself; nor did she consult with any thing but with her
passion and the necessity she was in. She then attempted a most
unnatural thing; and snatching up her son, who was a child
sucking at her breast, she said, "O thou miserable infant! for
whom shall I preserve thee in this war, this famine, and this
sedition? As to the war with the Romans, if they preserve our
lives, we must be slaves. This famine also will destroy us, even
before that slavery comes upon us. Yet are these seditious rogues
more terrible than both the other. Come on; be thou my food,
and be thou a fury to these seditious varlets, and a by-word to
the world, which is all that is now wanting to complete the
calamities of us Jews." As soon as she had said this, she slew her
son, and then roasted him, and ate the one half of him, and kept
the other half by her concealed. Upon this the seditious came in
presently, and smelling the horrid scent of this food, they
threatened her that they would cut her throat immediately if
she did not show them what food she had gotten ready. She
replied that she had saved a very fine portion of it for them, and
withal uncovered what was left of her son. Hereupon they were
seized with a horror and amazement of mind, and stood
astonished at the sight, when she said to them, "This is mine
own son, and what hath been done was mine own doing! Come,
eat of this food; for I have eaten of it myself! Do not you pretend
to be either more tender than a woman, or more compassionate
than a mother; but if you be so scrupulous, and do abominate
this my sacrifice, as I have eaten the one half, let the rest be
reserved for me also." After which those men went out trembling, being never so much affrighted at any thing as they were
at this, and with some difficulty they left the rest of that meat to
the mother. Upon which the whole city was full of this horrid
action immediately; and while every body laid this miserable
case before their own eyes, they trembled, as if this unheard of

action had been done by themselves. So those that were thus distressed by the famine were very desirous to die, and those already dead were esteemed happy, because they had not lived long enough either to hear or to see such miseries.

THE DESTRUCTION OF THE TEMPLE AT JERUSALEM, AD 70

Josephus

And now two of the legions had completed their banks on the eighth day of the month Lous [Ab]. Whereupon Titus gave orders that the battering rams should be brought, and set over against the western edifice of the inner temple; for before these were brought, the firmest of all the other engines had battered the wall for six days together without ceasing, without making any impression upon it; but the vast largeness and strong connexion of the stones were superior to that engine, and to the other battering rams also. Other Romans did indeed undermine the foundations of the northern gate, and after a world of pains removed the outermost stones, yet was the gate still upheld by the inner stones, and stood still unhurt; till the workmen, despairing of all such attempts by engines and crows, brought their ladders to the cloisters. Now the Jews did not interrupt them in so doing; but when they were gotten up, they fell upon them, and fought with them; some of them they thrust down, and threw them backwards headlong; others of them they met and slew; they also beat many of those that went down the ladders again, and slew them with their swords before they could bring their shields to protect them; nay, some of the ladders they threw down from above when they were full of armed men; a great slaughter was made of the Jews also at the same time, while those that bare the ensigns fought hard for them, as deeming it a terrible thing, and what would tend to their great shame, if they permitted them to be stolen away. Yet did the Jews at length get possession of these engines, and destroyed those that had gone up the ladders, while the rest were so intimidated by what those suffered who were slain, that they retired; although none of the Romans died without having done good service before his death. Of the seditious, those that had fought bravely in the former battles did the like now, as besides them did Eleazar, the brother's son of Simon the tyrant. But when Titus perceived that his endeavors to spare a foreign temple turned to the damage of his soldiers, and then be killed, he gave order to set the gates on fire.

In the meantime, there deserted to him Ananus, who came from Emmaus, the most bloody of all Simon's guards, and Archelaus, the son of Magadatus, they hoping to be still forgiven, because they left the Jews at a time when they were the conquerors. Titus objected this to these men, as a cunning trick of theirs; and as he had been informed of their other barbarities towards the Jews, he was going in all haste to have them both slain. He told them that they were only driven to this desertion because of the utmost distress they were in, and did not come away of their own good disposition; and that those did not deserve to be preserved, by whom their own city was already set on fire, out of which fire they now hurried themselves away. However, the security he had promised deserters overcame his resentments, and he dismissed them accordingly, though he did not give them the same privileges that he had afforded to others. And now the soldiers had already put fire to the gates, and the silver that was over them quickly carried the flames to the wood that was within it, whence it spread itself all on the sudden, and caught hold on the cloisters. Upon the Jews seeing this fire all about them, their spirits sunk together with their bodies, and they were under such astonishment, that not one of them made any haste, either to defend himself or to quench the fire, but they stood as mute spectators of it only. However, they did not so grieve at the loss of what was now burning, as to grow wiser thereby for the time to come; but as though the holy house itself had been on fire already, they whetted their passions against the Romans. This fire prevailed during that day and the next also; for the soldiers were not able to burn all the cloisters that were round about together at one time, but only by pieces.

But then, on the next day, Titus commanded part of his army to quench the fire, and to make a road for the more easy marching up of the legions, while he himself gathered the commanders together. Of those there were assembled the six principal persons: Tiberius Alexander, the commander [under the general] of the whole army; with Sextus Cerealis, the commander of the fifth legion; and Larcius Lepidus, the commander of the tenth legion; and Titus Frigius, the commander of the fifteenth legion: there was also with them Eternius, the leader of the two legions that came from Alexandria; and Marcus Antonius Julianus, procurator of Judea: after these came together all the rest of the procurators and tribunes. Titus proposed to these that they should give him their advice what should be done about the holy house. Now some of these thought it would be the best way to act according to the rules of war, [and demolish it,] because the Jews would never leave off rebelling while that house was standing; at which house it was that they used to get all together. Others of them were of opinion, that in case the Jews would leave it, and none of them would lay their arms up in it, he might save it; but that in case they got upon it, and fought any more, he might burn it; because it must then be looked upon not as a holy house, but as a citadel; and that the impiety of burning it would then belong to those that forced this to be done, and not to them. But Titus said, that "although the Jews should get upon that holy house, and fight us thence, yet ought we not to revenge ourselves on things that are inanimate, instead of the men themselves"; and that he was not in any case for burning down so vast a work as that was, because this would be a mischief to the Romans themselves, as it would be an ornament to their government while it continued. So Fronto, and Alexander, and Cerealis grew bold upon that declaration, and agreed to the opinion of Titus. Then was this assembly dissolved, when Titus had given orders to the commanders that the rest of their forces should lie still; but that they should make use of such as were most courageous in this attack. So he commanded that the chosen men that were taken out of the cohorts should make their way through the ruins, and quench the fire.

Now it is true that on this day the Jews were so weary, and under such consternation, that they refrained from any attacks. But on the next day they gathered their whole force together, and ran upon those that guarded the outward court of the temple very boldly, through the east gate, and this about the second hour of the day. These guards received that their attack with great bravery, and by covering themselves with their shields before, as if it were with a wall, they drew their squadron close together; yet was it evident that they could not abide there very long, but would be overborne by the multitude of those that sallied out upon them, and by the heat of their passion. However, Caesar seeing, from the tower of Antonia, that this squadron was likely to give way, he sent some chosen horsemen to support them. Hereupon the Jews found themselves not able to sustain their onset, and upon the slaughter of those in the forefront, many of the rest were put to flight. But as the Romans were going off, the Jews turned upon them, and fought them; and as those Romans came back upon them, they retreated again, until about the fifth hour of the day they were overborne, and shut themselves up in the inner [court of the] temple.

So Titus retired into the tower of Antonia, and resolved to storm the temple the next day, early in the morning, with his whole army, and to encamp round about the holy house. But as for that house, God had, for certain, long ago doomed it to the fire; and now that fatal day was come, according to the revolution of ages; it was the tenth day of the month Lous, [Ab,] upon which it was formerly burnt by the king of Babylon; although these flames took their rise from the Jews themselves, and were occasioned by them; for upon Titus's retiring, the seditious lay still for a little while, and then attacked the Romans again, when those that guarded the holy house fought with those that quenched the fire that was burning the inner court of the temple; but these Romans put the Jews to flight, and proceeded as far as the holy house itself. At which time one of the soldiers, without staying for any orders, and without any concern or dread upon him at so great an undertaking, and being hurried on by a certain divine fury, snatched somewhat out of the materials that were on fire, and being lifted up by another soldier, he set fire to a golden window, through which there was a passage to the rooms that were round about the holy house, on the north side of it. As the flames went upward, the Jews made a great clamour, such as so mighty an affliction required, and ran together to prevent it; and now they spared not their lives any longer, nor suffered any thing to restrain their force, since that holy house was perishing, for whose sake it was that they kept such a guard about it.

And now a certain person came running to Titus, and told him of this fire, as he was resting himself in his tent after the last battle; whereupon he rose up in great haste, and, as he was, ran to the holy house, in order to have a stop put to the fire; after him followed all his commanders, and after them followed the several legions, in great astonishment; so there was a great clamour and tumult raised, as was natural upon the disorderly motion of so great an army. Then did Caesar, both by calling to the soldiers that were fighting, with a loud voice, and by giving a signal to them with his right hand, order them to quench the fire. But they did not hear what he said, though he spake so loud, having their ears already dimmed by a greater noise another way; nor did they attend to the signal he made with his hand neither, as still some of them were distracted with fighting, and others with passion. But as for the legions that came running thither, neither any persuasions nor any threatenings could restrain their violence, but each one's own passion was his commander at this time; and as they were crowding into the temple together, many of them were trampled on by one another, while a great number fell among the ruins of the cloisters, which were still hot and smoking, and were destroyed in the same miserable way with those whom they had conquered; and when they were come near the holy house, they made as if they did not so much as hear Caesar's orders to the contrary; but they encouraged those that were before them to set it on fire. As for the seditious, they were in too great distress already to afford their assistance [towards quenching the fire]; they were every where slain, and every where beaten; and as for a great part of the people, they were weak and without arms, and had their throats cut wherever they were caught. Now round about the altar lay dead bodies heaped one upon another, as at the steps going up to it ran a great quantity of their blood, whither also the dead bodies that were slain above [on the altar] fell down.

And now, since Caesar was no way able to restrain the enthusiastic fury of the soldiers, and the fire proceeded on more and more, he went into the holy place of the temple, with his commanders, and saw it, with what was in it, which he found to be far superior to what the relations of foreigners contained, and not inferior to what we ourselves boasted of and believed about it. But as the flame had not as yet reached to its inward parts, but was still consuming the rooms that were about the holy house, and Titus supposing what the fact was, that the house itself might yet he saved, he came in haste and endeavoured to persuade the soldiers to quench the fire, and gave order to Liberalius the centurion, and one of those spearmen that were about him, to beat the soldiers that were refractory with their staves, and to restrain them; yet were their passions too hard for the regards they had for Caesar, and the dread they had of him who forbade them, as was their hatred of the Jews, and a certain vehement inclination to fight them, too hard for them also. Moreover, the hope of plunder induced many to go on, as having this opinion, that all the places within were full of money, and as seeing that all round about it was made of gold. And besides, one of those that went into the place prevented Caesar, when he ran so hastily out to restrain the soldiers, and threw the fire upon the hinges of the gate, in the dark; whereby the flame burst out from within the holy house itself immediately, when the commanders retired, and Caesar with them, and when nobody any longer forbade those that were without to set fire to it. And thus was the holy house burned down, without Caesar's approbation.

Now although any one would justly lament the destruction of such a work as this was, since it was the most admirable of all the works that we have seen or heard of, both for its curious structure and its magnitude, and also for the vast wealth bestowed upon it, as well as for the glorious reputation it had for its holiness; yet might such a one comfort himself with this thought, that it was fate that decreed it so to be, which is inevitable, both as to living creatures, and as to works and places also. However, one cannot but wonder at the accuracy of this period thereto relating; for the same month and day were now observed, as I said before, wherein the holy house was burned formerly by the Babylonians. Now the number of years that passed from its first foundation, which was laid by king

Solomon, till this its destruction, which happened in the second year of the reign of Vespasian, are collected to be one thousand one hundred and thirty, besides seven months and fifteen days; and from the second building of it, which was done by Haggai, in the second year of Cyrus the king, till its destruction under Vespasian, there were six hundred and thirty-nine years and forty-five days.

While the holy house was on fire, every thing was plundered that came to hand, and ten thousand of those that were caught were slain; nor was there a commiseration of any age, or any reverence of gravity, but children, and old men, and profane persons, and priests were all slain in the same manner; so that this war went round all sorts of men, and brought them to destruction, and as well those that made supplication for their lives, as those that defended themselves by fighting. The flame was also carried a long way, and made an echo, together with the groans of those that were slain; and because this hill was high, and the works at the temple were very great, one would have thought the whole city had been on fire. Nor can one imagine any thing either greater or more terrible than this noise; for there was at once a shout of the Roman legions, who were marching all together, and a sad clamour of the seditious, who were now surrounded with fire and sword. The people also that were left above were beaten back upon the enemy, and under a great consternation, and made sad moans at the calamity they were under; the multitude also that was in the city joined in this outcry with those that were upon the hill. And besides, many of those that were worn away by the famine, and their mouths almost closed, when they saw the fire of the holy house, they exerted their utmost strength, and brake out into groans and outcries again: Pera did also return the echo, as well as the mountains round about [the city,] and augmented the force of the entire noise. Yet was the misery itself more terrible than this disorder; for one would have thought that the hill itself, on which the temple stood, was seething hot, as full of fire on every part of it, that the blood was larger in quantity than the fire, and those that were slain more in number than those that slew them; for the ground did no where appear visible, for the dead bodies that lay on it; but the soldiers went over heaps of those bodies, as they ran upon such as fled from them. And now it was that the multitude of the robbers were thrust out [of the inner court of the temple by the Romans,] and had much ado to get into the outward court, and from thence into the city, while the remainder of the populace fled into the cloister of that outer court. As for the priests, some of them plucked up from the holy house the spikes that were upon it, with their bases, which were made of lead, and shot them at the Romans instead of darts. But then as they gained nothing by so doing, and as the fire burst out upon them, they retired to the wall that was eight cubits broad, and there they tarried; yet did two of these of eminence among them, who might have saved themselves by going over to the Romans, or have borne up with courage, and taken their fortune with the others, throw themselves into the fire, and were burnt together with the holy house; their names were Meirus the son of Belgas, and Joseph the son of Daleus.

And now the Romans, judging that it was in vain to spare what was round about the holy house, burnt all those places, as also the remains of the cloisters and the gates, two excepted; the one on the east side, and the other on the south; both which, however, they burned afterward. They also burned down the treasury chambers, in which was an immense quantity of money, and an immense number of garments, and other precious goods there reposited; and, to speak all in a few words, there it was that the entire riches of the Jews were heaped up together, while the rich people had there built themselves chambers [to contain such furniture]. The soldiers also came to the rest of the cloisters that were in the outer [court of the] temple, whither the women and children, and a great mixed multitude of the people, fled, in number about six thousand. But before Caesar had determined any thing about these people, or given the commanders any orders relating to them, the soldiers were in such a rage, that they set that cloister on fire; by which means it came to pass that some of these were destroyed by throwing themselves down headlong, and some were burned in the cloisters themselves. Nor did any one of them escape with his life.

THE ROMAN ARMY AT REST: A MILITARY CAMP, AD 70

Josephus

Nor can their [the Romans'] enemies easily surprise them with the suddenness of their incursions; for as soon as they have marched into an enemy's land, they do not begin to fight till they have walled their camp about; nor is the fence they raise rashly made, or uneven; nor do they all abide ill it, nor do those that are in it take their places at random; but if it happens that the ground is uneven, it is first levelled: their camp is also four-square by measure, and carpenters are ready, in great numbers, with their tools, to erect their buildings for them.

As for what is within the camp, it is set apart for tents, but the outward circumference hath the resemblance to a wall, and is adorned with towers at equal distances, where between the towers stand the engines for throwing arrows and darts, and for slinging stones, and where they lay all other engines that can annoy the enemy, all ready for their several operations. They also erect four gates, one at every side of the circumference, and those large enough for the entrance of the beasts, and wide enough for making excursions, if occasion should require. They divide the camp within into streets, very conveniently, and place the tents of the commanders in the middle; but in the very midst of all is the general's own tent, in the nature of a temple, insomuch, that it appears to be a city built on the sudden, with its market-place, and place for handicraft trades, and with seats for the officers superior and inferior, where, if any differences arise, their causes are heard and determined. The camp, and all that is in it, is encompassed with a wall round about, and that sooner than one would imagine, and this by the multitude and the skill of the laborers; and, if occasion require, a trench is drawn round the whole, whose depth is four cubits, and its breadth equal.

When they have thus secured themselves, they live together by companies, with quietness and decency, as are all their other affairs managed with good order and security. Each company hath also their wood, and their corn, and their water brought them, when they stand in need of them; for they neither sup nor dine as they please themselves singly, but all together. Their times also for sleeping, and watching, and rising are notified beforehand by the sound of trumpets, nor is any thing done without such a signal; and in the morning the soldiery go every one to their centurions, and these centurions to their tribunes, to salute them; with whom all the superior officers go to the general of the whole army, who then gives them of course the watchword and other orders, to be by them cared to all that are under their command; which is also observed when they go to fight, and thereby they turn themselves about on the sudden, when there is occasion for making sallies, as they come back when they are recalled in crowds also.

Now when they are to go out of their camp, the trumpet gives a sound, at which time nobody lies still, but at the first intimation they take down their tents, and all is made ready for their going out; then do the trumpets sound again, to order them to get ready for the march; then do they lay their baggage suddenly upon their mules, and other beasts of burden, and stand, as at the place of starting, ready to march; when also they set fire to their camp, and this they do because it will be easy for them to erect another camp, and that it may not ever be of use to their enemies. Then do the trumpets give a sound the third time, that they are to go out, in order to excite those that on any account are a little tardy, that so no one may be out of his rank when the army marches. Then does the crier stand at the general's right hand, and asks them thrice, in their own tongue, whether they be now ready to go out to war or not? To which they reply as often, with a loud and cheerful voice, saying, "We are ready." And this they do almost before the question is asked them: they do this as filled with a kind of martial fury, and at the same time that they so cry out, they lift up their right hands also.

THE GREAT BUILDINGS OF ROME, c. AD 75

Pliny the Elder

In great buildings as well as in other things the rest of the world has been outdone by us Romans. If, indeed, all the buildings in our City are considered in the aggregate, and supposing them – so to say – all thrown together in one vast mass, the united grandeur of them would lead one to imagine that we were describing another world, accumulated in a single spot.

Not to mention among our great works the Circus Maximus, that was built by the Dictator Cæsar – one stadium broad and three in length – and occupying with the adjacent buildings no less than four jugera [about 2½ acres] with room for no less than 160,000 spectators seated, – am I not, however, to include in the number of our magnificent structures the Basilica of Paulus with its admirable Phrygian columns [built also in Julius Cæsar's day], the Forum of the late Emperor Augustus, the Temple of Peace erected by the Emperor Vespasian Augustus – some of the finest work the world has ever seen?

We behold with admiration pyramids that were built by kings, while the very ground alone that was purchased by the Dictator Cæsar, for the construction of his Forum, cost 100,000,000 sesterces. If, too, an enormous expenditure has its attractions for any one whose mind is influenced by money matters, be it known that the house in which Clodius [Cicero's enemy] dwelt ... was purchased by him at a price of 14,800,000 sesterces – a thing which I for my part look upon as no less astonishing than the monstrous follies that have been displayed by kings.

Frequently praise is given to the great sewer system of Rome. There are seven "rivers" made to flow, by artificial channels, beneath the city. Rushing onward like so many impetuous torrents, they are compelled to carry off and sweep away all the sewerage; and swollen as they are by the vast accession of the rain water, they reverberate against the sides and bottoms of their channels. Occasionally too the Tiber, overflowing, is thrown backward in its course, and discharges itself by these outlets. Obstinate is the struggle that ensues between the meeting tides, but so firm and solid is the masonry that it is able to offer an effectual resistance. Enormous as are the accumulations that are carried along above, the work of the channels never gives way. Houses falling spontaneously to ruins, or leveled with the ground by conflagrations are continually battering against them; now and then the ground is shaken by earthquakes, and yet – built as they were in the days of Tarquinius Priscus, 700 years ago – these constructions have survived, all but unharmed.

Passing to the dwellings of the city: in the consulship of Lepidus and Catulus [78 BC] we learn on good authority there was not in all Rome a finer house than that belonging to Lepidus himself, but yet – by Hercules! – within twenty-five years the very same house did not hold the hundredth rank simply in the City! Let anybody calculate – if he please – considering this fact, the vast masses of marble, the productions of painters, the regal treasures that must have been expended in bringing these hundred mansions to vie with one that in its day had been the most sumptuous and celebrated in all the City; and then let him reflect that, since then and down to the present, these houses had all of them been surpassed by others without number. There can be no doubt that the great fires in Rome are a punishment inflicted upon us for our luxury; but such are our habits, that in spite of such warnings, we cannot be made to understand that there are things in existence more perishable than even man himself.

But let us now turn our attention to some marvels that, if justly appreciated, may be pronounced to remain unsurpassed. Quintus Marcius Rex [prætor in 144 BC] upon being commanded by the Senate to repair the Appian Aqueduct and that of the Anio, constructed during his prætorship a new aqueduct that bore his name, and was brought hither by a channel pierced through the very sides of mountains. Agrippa [prime minister of Augustus] during his ædileship, united the Marcian and the "Virgin" Aqueducts and repaired and strengthened the channels of others. He also formed 700 wells, in addition to 500 fountains, and 130 reservoirs, many of them magnificently adorned. Upon these works too he erected 300 statues of marble or bronze, and 400 marble columns, and all this in the space of a single year! In the work which he has written in commemoration of his ædileship, he also informs us that public games were celebrated for the space of 57 days and 170 gratuitous bathing places were opened to the public. The number of these public baths at Rome has vastly increased since his time.

The preceding aqueducts, however, have all been surpassed by the costly work which has more recently been completed by the Emperors Gaius [Caligula] and Claudius. Under these princes the Curtian and the Cærulean Waters with the "New Anio" were brought a distance of forty miles, and at so high a level that all the hills – whereon Rome is built – were supplied with water. The sum expended on these works was 350,000,000 sesterces. If we take into account the abundant supply of water to the public, for baths, ponds, canals, household purposes, gardens, places in the suburbs and country houses, and then reflect upon the distances that are traversed [from the sources on the hills], the arches that have been constructed, the mountains pierced, the valleys leveled, – we must perforce admit that there is nothing more worthy of our admiration throughout the whole universe.

CONCEPTION, CONTRACEPTION AND ABORTION, ROME, AD 1ST CENTURY

Soranus

Conception

One must judge the majority from the ages of 15 to 40 to be fit for conception, if they are not mannish, compact, and oversturdy, or too flabby and very moist. Since the uterus is similar to the whole [body], it will in these cases either be unable, on account of its pronounced hardness, easily to accept the attachment of the seed, or by reason of its extreme laxity and atony [let it fall again]. Furthermore they seem fit if their uteri are neither very moist or dry, nor too lax or constricted, and if they have their catharsis regularly, not through some moisture or ichors of various kinds, but through blood and of this neither too much nor, on the other hand, extremely little. Also those in whom the orifice of the uterus is comparatively far forward and lies in a straight line (for an orifice deviated even in its natural state and lying farther back in the vagina, is less suited for the attraction and acceptance of the seed).

The best time for fruitful intercourse is when menstruation is ending and abating, when urge and appetite for coitus are present, when the body is neither in want nor too congested and heavy from drunkenness and indigestion, and after the body has been rubbed down and a little food been eaten and when a pleasant state exists in every respect. "When menstruation is ending and abating", for the time before menstruation is not suitable, the uterus already being overburdened and in an unresponsive state because of the ingress of material and incapable of carrying on two motions contrary to each other, one for the excretion of material, the other for receiving.

In order that the offspring may not be rendered misshapen, women must be sober during coitus because in drunkenness the soul becomes the victim of strange fantasies; this furthermore, because the offspring bears some resemblance to the mother as well not only in body but in soul . . .

Together with these points it has already been stated that the best time is after a rubdown has been given and a little food been eaten. The food will give the inner turbulence an impetus towards coitus, the urge for intercourse not being diverted by appetite for food; while the rubdown will make it possible to lay hold of the injected seed more readily. For just as the rubdown naturally aids the distribution of food, it helps also in the reception and retention of the seed, yesterday's superfluities, as one may say, being unloaded, and the body thoroughly cleansed and in a sound state for its natural processes. Consequently, as the farmer sows only after having first cleansed the soil and removed any foreign material, in the same manner we too advise that insemination for the production of man should follow after the body has first been given a rubdown.

Contraception

A contraceptive differs from an abortive, for the first does not let conception take place, while the latter destroys what has been conceived . . . And an expulsive some people say is synonymous with an abortive; others, however, say that there is a difference because an expulsive does not mean drugs but shaking and leaping . . . For this reason they say that Hippocrates, although prohibiting abortives, yet in his book "On the Nature of the Child" employs leaping with the heels to the buttocks for the sake of expulsion. But a controversy has arisen. For one party banishes abortives, citing the testimony of Hippocrates who says: "I will give to no one an abortive"; moreover, because it is the specific task of medicine to guard and preserve what has been engendered by nature. The other party prescribes abortives, but with discrimination, that is, they do not prescribe them when a person wishes to destroy the embryo because of adultery or out of consideration for youthful beauty; but only to prevent subsequent danger in parturition if the uterus is small and not capable of accommodating the complete development, or if the uterus at its orifice has knobbly swelling and fissures, or if some similar difficulty is involved. And they say the same about contraceptives as well, and we too agree with them. And since it is safer to prevent conception from taking place than to destroy the foetus, we shall now first discourse upon such prevention.

For if it is much more advantageous not to conceive than to destroy the embryo, one must consequently beware of having sexual intercourse at those periods which we said were suitable for conception. And during the sexual act, at the critical moment of coitus when the man is about to discharge the seed, the woman must hold her breath and draw herself away a little, so that the seed may not be hurled too deep into the cavity of the uterus. And getting up immediately and squatting down, she should induce sneezing and carefully wipe the vagina all round; she might even drink something cold. It also aids in preventing conception to smear the orifice of the uterus all over before with old olive oil or honey or cedar resin or juice of the balsam tree, alone or together with white lead; or with a moist cerate containing myrtle oil and white lead; or before the act with moist alum, or with galbanum together with wine; or to put a lock of fine wool into the orifice of the uterus; or, before sexual relations to use vaginal suppositories which have the power to contract and to condense. For such of these things as are styptic, clogging and cooling cause the orifice of the uterus to shut before the time of coitus and do not let the seed pass into its fundus. [Such, however, as are hot] and irritating not only do not allow the seed of the man to remain in the cavity of the uterus, but draw forth as well another fluid from it.

And we shall make specific mention of some. Pine bark, tanning sumach, equal quantities of each, rub with wine and apply in due measure before coitus after wool has been wrapped around; and after two or three hours she may remove it and have intercourse. Another: of Cimolian earth, root of panax, equal quantities, rub with water separately and together, and when sticky apply in like manner. Or: grind the inside of fresh pomegranate peel with water, and apply. Or: grind two parts of pomegranate peel and one part of oak galls, form small suppositories and insert after the cessation of menstruation. Or: moist alum, the inside of pomegranate rind, mix with water, and apply with wool. Or: of unripe oak galls, of the inside of pomegranate peel, of ginger, of each 2 drachms, mould it with wine to the size of vetch peas and dry indoors and give before coitus, to be applied as a vaginal suppository. Or: grind the flesh of dried figs and apply together with natron. Or: apply pomegranate peel with an equal amount of gum and an equal amount of oil of roses. Then one should always follow with a drink of honey water. But one should beware of things which are very pungent, because of the ulcerations arising from them. And we use all these things after the end of menstruation . . .

Abortion

In order that the embryo be separated, the woman should have [more violent exercise], walking about energetically and being shaken by means of draught animals; she should also leap energetically and carry things which are heavy beyond her strength. She should use diuretic decoctions which also have the power to bring on menstruation, and empty and purge the abdomen with relatively pungent clysters; sometimes using warm and sweet olive oil as injections, sometimes anointing the whole body thoroughly therewith and rubbing it vigorously, especially around the pubes, the abdomen, and the loins, bathing daily in sweet water which is not too hot, lingering in the baths and drinking first a little wine and living on pungent food. If this is without effect, one must also treat locally by having her sit in a bath of a decoction of linseed, fenugreek, mallow, marsh mallow, and wormwood. She must also use poultices of the same substances and have injections of old oil, alone or together with rue juice or maybe with honey, or of iris oil, or of absinthium together with honey, or of panax balm or else of spelt together with rue and honey, or of Syrian unguent. And if the situation remains the same she must no longer apply the common poultices, but those made of meal of lupines together with ox bile and absinthium, [and she must use] plasters of a similar kind.

For a woman who intends to have an abortion, it is necessary for two or even three days beforehand to take protracted baths, little food and to use softening vaginal suppositories; also to abstain from wine; then to be bled and a relatively great quantity taken away. For the dictum of Hippocrates in the Aphorisms, even if not true in a case of constriction, is yet true of a healthy woman: "A pregnant woman if bled, miscarries." For just as sweat, urine or faeces are excreted if the parts containing these substances slacken very much, so the foetus falls out after the uterus dilates. Following the venesection one must shake her by means of draught animals (for now the shaking is more effective on the parts which previously have been relaxed) and one must use softening vaginal suppositories. But if a woman reacts unfavourably to venesection and is languid, one must first relax the parts by means of hip-baths, full baths, softening vaginal suppositories, by keeping her on water and limited food, and by means of aperients and the application of a softening clyster; afterwards one must apply an abortive vaginal suppository. Of the latter one should choose those which are not too pungent, that they may not cause too great a sympathetic reaction and heat. And of the more gentle ones there exist for instance: Of myrtle, wallflower seed, bitter lupines equal quantities, by means of water, mould troches the size of a bean. Or: of rue leaves 3 drachms, of myrtle 2 drachms and the same of sweet bay, mix with wine in the same way, and give her a drink. Another vaginal suppository which produces abortion with relatively little danger: of wallflower, cardamom, brimstone, absinthium, myrrh, equal quantities, mould with water. And she who intends to apply these things should be bathed beforehand or made to relax by hip-baths; and if after some time she brings forth nothing, she should again be relaxed by hip-baths and for the second time a suppository should be applied. In addition, many different things have been mentioned by others; one must, however, beware of things that are too powerful and of separating the embryo by means of something sharp-edged, for danger arises that some of the adjacent parts be wounded.

CHARITY, NORTH AFRICA, AD 2ND CENTURY

P. Licinius Papirianus

To my fellow townsmen of Cirta [Sicca], to my beloved Siccenses, I [P. Licinius Papirianus] wish to give 1,300,000 sesterces. I entrust this sum to you, dearest townsmen, that from the interest of five per cent there may be maintained each year 300 boys and 300 girls, the boys from the age of three to fifteen, each boy receiving 2½ denarii per month, the girls from the age of three to thirteen, each girl receiving 2 denarii. Townsmen and residents likewise should be chosen, provided that the residents shall be dwelling within the buildings which bound our colony, and these, if it shall seem good to you, it will be best for the duoviri of each year to choose; but care should be taken that an immediate replacement is found for any child reaching adult age or dying, so that the full number may always be maintained.

RECIPE FOR HONEY WINE, c. AD 77

Pliny the Elder

From Pliny the Elder's 37-volume Historia Naturalis, *AD 77*

A wine is also made of only water and honey. For this it is recommended that rain-water should be stored for five years. Some who are more expert use rain-water as soon as it has fallen, boiling it down to a third of the quantity and adding one part of old honey to three parts of water, and then keeping the mixture in the sun for 40 days after the rising of the Dog-star. Others pour it off after nine days and then cork it up. This beverage is called in Greek "water-honey"; with age it attains the flavour of wine. It is nowhere rated more highly than in Phrygia. Also honey used even to be mixed with vinegar, so exhaustive have been men's experiments in living. This mixture was called in Greek "sour honey"; it was made with 10 pounds of honey, 2½ pints of old vinegar, 1 pound of sea salt and 5 pints of rain-water, heated to boiling 10 times, after which the liquor was drawn off and so kept till it was old. All these wines are condemned by Themison, who is a very high authority; and, I vow, the employment of them does appear to be a *tour de force*, unless anybody believes that aromatic wine and wines compounded of perfumes are products of nature, or that nature gave birth to shrubs in order for them to be used for drink! Contrivances of this sort are amusing to learn of, owing to the ingenuity of the human mind that investigates everything. There can be no doubt that none of these wines will keep a year, except those which we have stated to be actually the products of age, and that the larger number of them will not keep even a month.

MESSAGES OF LOVE, POMPEII, AD 1ST CENTURY

Anon

Inscriptions and daubings from the walls of Pompeii.

1) Here slept Vibius Restitutus all by himself [,] his heart filled with longing for his Urbana.
2) He who has never been in love can be no gentleman.
3) Romula keep tryst here with Staphylus.
4) If any man seek/My girl from me to turn/On far-off mountains bleak/May Love the scoundrel burn!
5) Restitutus has many times deceived many girls.
6) Health to you, Victoria, and wherever you are may you sneeze sweetly[1]

ADVERTISEMENTS FOR GLADIATORIAL SHOWS, POMPEII, AD 1ST CENTURY

Anon

As scratched on the walls of Pompeii. The town reached a population of around 25,000 before its burial under Vesuvius' laval flows in AD 79 (see pp211–216).

1. Twenty pairs of gladiators provided by Quintus Monnius Rufus are to fight at Nola May First, Second, and Third, and there will be a hunt.

---

[1] Sneezing signified good luck.

2. Thirty pairs of gladiators provided by Gnaeus Alleius Nigidius Maius quinquennial duumvir, together with their substitutes, will fight at Pompeii on November 24, 25, 26. There will be a hunt. Hurrah for Maius the Quinquennial! Bravo, Paris!

3. The gladiatorial troop of the Aedile Aulius Suettius Certus will fight at Pompeii May 31. There will be a hunt, and awnings will be provided.

4. Twenty pairs of gladiators furnished by Decimus Lucretius Satrius Valens perpetual priest of Nero, son of the Emperor, and ten pairs of gladiators furnished by Decimus Lucretius Valens his son, will fight at Pompeii April 8, 9, 10, 11, and 12. There will be a big hunt and awnings. Aemilius Celer wrote this by the light of the moon.

SMALL ADS: ROOMS AND PREMISES TO RENT, POMPEII, AD 1ST CENTURY

Various

Inscriptions from the walls of Pompeii.

1. To rent from the first day of next July, shops with the floors over them, fine upper chambers, and a house, in the Arnius Pollio block, owned by Gnaeus Alleius Nigidius Maius. Prospective lessees may apply to Primus, slave of Gnaeus Alleius Nigidius Maius.

2. To let, for the term of five years, from the thirteenth day of next August to the thirteenth day of the sixth August thereafter, the Venus bath, fitted up for the best people, shops, rooms over shops, and second-story apartments in the property owned by Julia Felix, daughter of Spurius.

THE ERUPTION OF VESUVIUS, BAY OF NAPLES, 4 AUGUST AD 79

Pliny the Younger

My uncle[1] was stationed at Misenum, in active command of the

---

[1] i.e. Pliny the Elder

fleet. On 24 August, in the early afternoon, my mother drew his attention to a cloud of unusual size and appearance. He had been out in the sun, had taken a cold bath, and lunched while lying down, and was then working at his books. He called for his shoes and climbed up to a place which would give him the best view of the phenomenon. It was not clear at that distance from which mountain the cloud was rising (it was afterwards known to be Vesuvius); its general appearance can best be expressed as being like an umbrella pine, for it rose to a great height on a sort of trunk and then split off into branches, I imagine because it was thrust upwards by the first blast and then left unsupported as the pressure subsided, or else it was borne down by its own weight so that it spread out and gradually dispersed. Sometimes it looked white, sometimes blotched and dirty, according to the amount of soil and ashes it carried with it. My uncle's scholarly acumen saw at once that it was important enough for a closer inspection, and he ordered a boat to be made ready, telling me I could come with him if I wished. I replied that I preferred to go on with my studies, and as it happened he had himself given me some writing to do.

As he was leaving the house he was handed a message from Rectina, wife of Tascius whose house was at the foot of the mountain, so that escape was impossible except by boat. She was terrified by the danger threatening her and implored him to rescue her from her fate. He changed his plans, and what he had begun in a spirit of inquiry he completed as a hero. He gave orders for the warships to be launched and went on board himself with the intention of bringing help to many more people besides Rectina, for this lovely stretch of coast was thickly populated. He hurried to the place which everyone else was hastily leaving, steering his course straight for the danger zone. He was entirely fearless, describing each new movement and phase of the portent to be noted down exactly as he observed them. Ashes were already falling, hotter and thicker as the ships drew near, followed by bits of pumice and blackened stones, charred and cracked by the flames: then suddenly they were in shallow water, and the shore was blocked by the debris from the mountain. For a moment my uncle wondered whether to turn back, but when the helmsman advised this he refused, telling him that Fortune stood by the courageous and they must make for Pomponianus at Stabiae. He was cut off there by the breadth of the bay (for the shore gradually curves round a basin filled by the sea) so that he was not as yet in danger, though it was clear that this would come nearer as it spread. Pomponianus had therefore already put his belongings on board ship, intending to escape if the contrary wind fell. This wind was of course full in my uncle's favour, and he was able to bring his ship in. He embraced his terrified friend, cheered and encouraged him, and thinking he could calm his fears by showing his own composure, gave orders that he was to be carried to the bathroom. After his bath he lay down and dined; he was quite cheerful, or at any rate he pretended he was, which was no less courageous.

Meanwhile on Mount Vesuvius broad sheets of fire and leaping flames blazed at several points, their bright glare emphasized by the darkness of night. My uncle tried to allay the fears of his companions by repeatedly declaring that these were nothing but bonfires left by the peasants in their terror, or else empty houses on fire in the districts they had abandoned. Then he went to rest and certainly slept, for as he was a stout man his breathing was rather loud and heavy and could be heard by people coming and going outside his door. By this time the courtyard giving access to his room was full of ashes mixed with pumice-stones; so that its level had risen, and if he had stayed in the room any longer he would never have got out. He was wakened, came out and joined Pomponianus and the rest of the household who had sat up all night. They debated whether to stay indoors or take their chance in the open, for the buildings were now shaking with violent shocks, and seemed to be swaying to and fro as if they were torn from their foundations. Outside on the other hand, there was the danger of falling pumice-stones, even though these were light and porous; however, after comparing the risks they chose the latter. In my uncle's case one reason outweighed the other, but for the others it was a choice of fears. As a protection against falling objects they put pillows on their heads tied down with cloths.

Elsewhere there was daylight by this time, but they were still in darkness, blacker and denser than any ordinary night, which they relieved by lighting torches and various kinds of lamp. My uncle decided to go down to the shore and investigate on the spot the possibility of any escape by sea, but he found the waves still wild and dangerous. A sheet was spread on the ground for him to lie down, and he repeatedly asked for cold water to drink. Then the flames and smell of sulphur which gave warning of the approaching fire drove the others to take flight and roused him to stand up. He stood leaning on two slaves and then suddenly collapsed, I imagine because the dense fumes choked his breathing by blocking his windpipe which was constitutionally weak and narrow and often inflamed. When daylight returned on the 26th – two days after the last day he had seen – his body was found intact and uninjured, still fully clothed and looking more like sleep than death.

Meanwhile my mother and I were at Misenum . . . After my uncle's departure I spent the rest of the day with my books, as this was my reason for staying behind. Then I took a bath, dined, and then dozed fitfully for a while. For several days past there had been earth tremors which were not particularly alarming because they are frequent in Campania: but that night the shocks were so violent that everything felt as if it were not only shaken but overturned. My mother hurried into my room and found me already getting up to wake her if she were still asleep. We sat down in the forecourt of the house, between the buildings and the sea close by. I don't know whether I should call this courage or folly on my part (I was only 17 at the time) but I called for a volume of Livy and went on reading as if I had nothing else to do. I even went on with the extracts I had been making. Up came a friend of my uncle's who had just come from Spain to join him. When he saw us sitting there and me actually reading, he scolded us both – me for my foolhardiness and my mother for allowing it. Nevertheless, I remained absorbed in my book.

By now it was dawn, but the light was still dim and faint. The buildings round us were already tottering, and the open space we were in was too small for us not to be in real and imminent danger if the house collapsed. This finally decided us to leave the town. We were followed by a panic-stricken mob of people wanting to act on someone else's decision in preference to their

own (a point in which fear looks like prudence), who hurried us
on our way by pressing hard behind in a dense crowd. Once
beyond the buildings we stopped, and there we had some
extraordinary experiences which thoroughly alarmed us. The
carriages we had ordered to be brought out began to run in
different directions though the ground was quite level, and
would not remain stationary even when wedged with stones.
We also saw the sea sucked away and apparently forced back by
the earthquake: at any rate it receded from the shore so that
quantities of sea creatures were left stranded on dry sand. On
the landward side a fearful black cloud was rent by forked and
quivering bursts of flame, and parted to reveal great tongues of
fire, like flashes of lighting magnified in size.

At this point my uncle's friend from Spain spoke up still more
urgently: "If your brother, if your uncle is still alive, he will
want you both to be saved; if he is dead, he would want you to
survive him – why put off your escape?" We replied that we
would not think of considering our own safety as long as we
were uncertain of his. Without waiting any longer, our friend
rushed off and hurried out of danger as fast as he could.

Soon afterwards the cloud sank down to earth and covered the
sea; it had already blotted out Capri and hidden the promontory
of Misenum from sight. Then my mother implored, entreated
and commanded me to escape as best I could – a young man
might escape, whereas she was old and slow and could die in
peace as long as she had not been the cause of my death too. I
refused to save myself without her, and grasping her hand forced
her to quicken her pace. She gave in reluctantly, blaming herself
for delaying me. Ashes were already falling, not as yet very
thickly. I looked round: a dense black cloud was coming up
behind us, spreading over the earth like a flood. "Let us leave the
road while we can still see," I said, "or we shall be knocked down
and trampled underfoot in the dark by the crowd behind." We
had scarcely sat down to rest when darkness fell, not the dark of a
moonless or cloudy night, but as if the lamp had been put out in a
closed room. You could hear the shrieks of women, the wailing of
infants, and the shouting of men; some were calling their parents,
others their children or their wives, trying to recognize them by
their voices. People bewailed their own fate or that of their

relatives, and there were some who prayed for death in their terror of dying. Many besought the aid of the gods, but still more imagined there were no gods left, and that the universe was plunged into eternal darkness for evermore. There were people, too, who added to the real perils by inventing fictitious dangers: some reported that part of Misenum had collapsed or another part was on fire, and though their tales were false they found others to believe them. A gleam of light returned, but we took this to be a warning of the approaching flames rather than daylight. However, the flames remained some distance off; then darkness came on once more and ashes began to fall again, this time in heavy showers. We rose from time to time and shook them off, otherwise we should have been buried and crushed beneath their weight. I could boast that not a groan or cry of fear escaped me in these perils, had I not derived some poor consolation in my mortal lot from the belief that the whole world was dying with me and I with it.

At last the darkness thinned and dispersed into smoke or cloud; then there was genuine daylight, and the sun actually shone out, but yellowish as it is during an eclipse. We were terrified to see everything changed, buried deep in ashes like snowdrifts. We returned to Misenum where we attended to our physical needs as best we could, and then spent an anxious night alternating between hope and fear. Fear predominated, for the earthquakes went on, and several hysterical individuals made their own and other people's calamities seem ludicrous in comparison with their frightful predictions.

TYRANNY, BED-WRESTLING AND ENTERTAINMENTS FOR THE PEOPLE: THE REIGN OF DOMITIAN, AD 81–96

Suetonius

Domitian succeeded Titus as emperor. His reign augured well and then declined into violence.

I

Domitian was born upon the ninth of the kalends of November, when his father was consul-elect and was to enter upon his office

the month following. His birth took place in the sixth region of
the city at the Pomegranate, in the house which he afterwards
converted into a temple of the Flavian family. His childhood
and youth, so the report goes, were spent in so much poverty
and infamy, that he owned not so much as one piece of plate;
and it is well known that Clodius Pollio, a man of praetorian
rank, against whom there is a poem of Nero's extant entitled
Luscio, kept a note in his handwriting which he sometimes
produced, in which Domitian promised him the use of his body
for one night. Some likewise have said that he had similar
relations with Nerva, who succeeded him. In the war with
Vitellius he fled into the Capitol with his uncle Sabinus and a
part of the troops they had in the city. But the enemy breaking
in and the temple being set on fire, he hid himself all night with
the sacristan; and early the next morning, disguised as a priest
of Isis, and mixing with the worshippers belonging to that vain
superstition, he passed over the Tiber, with only one attendant,
to the house of a woman who was the mother of one of his
schoolfellows, and lurked there so close that, though the enemy,
who were at his heels, searched very strictly after him, they
could not discover him. At last, after the victory of his party, he
showed himself, and being generally saluted by the name of
Caesar, he assumed the office of praetor of the City, with
consular authority, but in fact had nothing but the name;
for the jurisdiction he transferred to his next colleague. But
he used his absolute power so licentiously that even then he
showed what kind of prince he was likely to prove. And not to
recite every particular, after he had brought dishonour to the
wives of many men of distinction, he took Domitia Longina
from her husband, Aelias Lamia, and married her; and in one
day disposed of above twenty offices in the city and the
provinces; upon which Vespasian said several times, that "he
marvelled that he did not send him a successor too".

2

He likewise designed an expedition into Gaul and Germany,
notwithstanding that none was necessary, and his father's
friends advised him against it; and this he did only because
he yearned to equal his brother in achievements and reputa-

tion. But for this he was sharply rebuked, and that he might the more effectually be reminded of his age and position, was made to live with his father, and his litter had to follow his father's and brother's carriage, as often as they went abroad; but he attended them in their triumph for the conquest of Judaea, mounted on a white horse. Of the six consulships which he held, only one was ordinary; and that he obtained by the cession and interest of his brother. He greatly affected a modest behaviour and, above all, a taste for poetry; insomuch, that he rehearsed his performances in public, though it was an art he had formerly little cultivated, and which he afterwards despised and abandoned. Yet, devoted as he was at this time to poetical pursuits, when Vologaesus, king of the Parthians, desired succours against the Alani, with one of Vespasian's sons to command them, he laboured with might and main to procure for himself that appointment. But the scheme proving abortive, he endeavoured by presents and promises to engage other kings of the East to make a similar request. After his father's death, he was for some time in doubt whether he should not offer the soldiers a donative double to that of his brother, and made no scruple of saying frequently, "that he had been left his partner in the empire, but that his father's will had been treacherously laid aside". From that time forward, he was constantly engaged in plots against his brother, both publicly and privately; until, his brother falling dangerously ill, he ordered all his attendants to leave him, under pretence of his being dead, before the breath had really left his body; and, at his decease, paid him no other honour than that of enrolling him among the gods; and he often carped at his memory, in sneering fashion, both in speeches and in edicts.

3

In the beginning of his reign, he used to retire into a secret place for one hour every day, and there do nothing else but catch flies, and stick them through the body with a sharp pin. When someone, therefore, enquired whether anybody was with Caesar, Vibius Crispus made answer, not impertinently, "No, not so much as a fly." Soon after his advancement, his wife Domitia, by whom he had a son in his second consulship, and whom the year following he complimented with the title of Augusta, falling madly in love with Paris, the actor, he put her away; but within a short time afterwards, being unable to bear the separation he took her home again, pretending that the people had called upon him to do so. In the administration of the empire, he conducted himself for a good while in a variable manner, as one composed of an equal mixture of vices and virtues, until at length he turned his virtues also into vices: being (so far as we may conjecture), over and above his natural inclination, made covetous by want, and cruel by fear.

4

He exhibited, at frequent intervals, magnificent and costly shows, not only in the amphitheatre, but also in the circus; in which, beside the usual races with chariots drawn by two or four horses abreast, he represented a battle between both horse and foot, and a sea fight in the amphitheatre. The people were also entertained with the chase of wild beasts and the combat of gladiators, even in the night time, by torchlight; nor did men only take part in these spectacles, but women also. He regularly attended the games given by the quaestors, which had been disused for some time, but were revived by him; and upon those occasions, always gave the people the liberty of demanding two pairs of gladiators out of his own school, who appeared last in court uniforms. At all the shows of gladiators, there always stood at his feet a little boy dressed in scarlet, with a prodigiously small head, with whom he used to confer often, and sometimes on serious matters. Certain it is, he was overheard asking him "what he thought of the last appointment in the provinces, namely that of making Mettius Rufus governor of Egypt".

He exhibited naval fights, performed by fleets almost as numerous as those usually employed in real engagements; making a vast lake near the Tiber and building seats around it; and these he would witness himself during the greatest storms and showers that might rage. He set forth also the Secular games, computing not from the year in which they had been exhibited by Claudius, but from the time of Augustus' celebration of them. In these, upon the day of the Circensian sports, in order to have a hundred races performed, he reduced each course from seven rounds to five. He likewise instituted, in honour of Jupiter Capitolinus, a solemn contest in music to be performed every five years; besides horse racing and gymnastic exercises, with more prizes than are at present allowed. Herein the concurrents strove also for the prize in elocution, both Greek and Latin; and besides single harpers, there were others who played concerted pieces or solos, without vocal accompaniment. Young girls also ran races in the stadium, at which he presided in his sandals, dressed in a purple robe, made after the Grecian fashion, and wearing upon his head a golden crown bearing the images of Jupiter, Juno, and Minerva; with the flamen of Jupiter, and the college of priests sitting by his side in the same dress, excepting only that their crowns had also his own image on them.

He likewise celebrated every year upon the Alban mount the festival of Minerva, for whom he had appointed a college of priests, out of which were chosen by lot persons to preside as governors over the college; these were obliged to entertain the people with extraordinary chases of wild beasts, and stage-plays, beside contests for prizes in oratory and poetry. At the festival of the Seven Hills, he distributed large hampers of provisions to the senatorian and equestrian orders, and small baskets to the common people, encouraging them to eat by falling to himself. The day after, he scattered among the people a variety of cakes and other delicacies to be scrambled for; and upon the greater part of them falling amidst the seats of the crowd, he ordered five hundred tickets to be thrown into each range of benches belonging to the senatorian and equestrian orders.

5

Many noble and stately buildings which had been consumed by fire, he rebuilt; and among them the Capitol, which had been burned down a second time; but all the inscriptions were in his own name, without any credit being given to the original founders. He likewise erected a new temple in the Capitol to Jupiter Custos, and a Forum, which is now called Nerva's, as also the temple of the Flavian family, a stadium, for races both of men and horses, an odeum, for musical performances, and a naumachia, for naval battles; out of the stone dug from which, the sides of the Circus Maximus, which had been burnt down, were rebuilt.

6

He undertook several expeditions, some voluntarily, and some from necessity. That against the Catti was unprovoked, but that against the Carmatians was necessary; an entire legion, with its commander, having been cut off by them. He sent two expeditions against the Dacians; the first upon the defeat of Oppius Sabinus, a man of consular rank; and the other, upon that of Cornelius Fuscus, prefect of the praetorian cohorts, to whom he had entrusted the conduct of the war. After several battles with the Catti and Dacians, he celebrated a double triumph. But for his victories over the Sarmatians, he only bore in procession the laurel crown to Jupiter Capitolinus. The civil war stirred up by Lucius Antonius, governor of Upper Germany, he dispatched, without being personally present at it, with wonderful good fortune; for, at the very moment of joining battle, the Rhine suddenly thawing, the troops of the barbarians which were ready to join L. Antonius, were prevented from crossing the river. Of this victory he had intelligence by presages, before the messengers arrived with the news. For upon the very day the battle was fought, a splendid eagle spread its wings round his statue at Rome, and made a great flapping noise in token of much joy. And shortly after a rumour became common that Antonius was slain; nay, many avouched confidently that they saw his head brought to the city.

7

He introduced many innovations in matters of common practice. The dole of viands distributed in little baskets in lieu of a public supper, he abolished, and revived the old custom of regular and complete suppers. To the four former parties in the Circensian games, he added two new ones who wore gold and scarlet. He prohibited the players from acting in the theatre, but permitted them the free and lawful exercise of their art in private houses. He gave order that no males should be gelded;

and reduced the price of the eunuchs who were still left in the hands of the dealers in slaves. On the occasion of a great plenitude of wine, and as much scarcity of corn, supposing that the tillage of the ground was neglected for the sake of attending too much to the cultivation of vineyards, he published a proclamation forbidding the planting of any new vines in Italy, and ordering the vines in the provinces to be cut down, nowhere permitting more than one half of them to remain. However, he did not persist in the full execution of this act. Some of the greatest offices he conferred upon his freedmen and soldiers. He forbad two legions to be quartered in the same camp, and more than a thousand sesterces to be deposited by any soldier with the standards; because it was thought that Lucius Antonius had been stimulated in his late project by the large sum deposited in the military chest by the two legions which he had in the same winter quarters. He made an addition to the soldiers' stipend, of three gold pieces a year.

8

In the administration of justice he was precise and energetic. Many a time, sitting out of course in the Forum, he reversed the definitive sentences of the One Hundred, given through favour or selfish interest. He occasionally cautioned the judges of the Court of Recovery to beware of being too ready to admit claims for freedom brought before them. He set a mark of infamy upon judges who were convicted of taking bribes, as well as upon their assessors. He likewise persuaded the tribunes of the people to prosecute a corrupt aedile for extortion, and to desire the senate to appoint judges for his trial. He likewise took such effectual care in punishing magistrates of the city and governors of provinces, guilty of malversation, that they never were at any time more moderate or more just. Most of these, since his reign, we have seen prosecuted for crimes of various kinds. Having taken upon himself the reformation of the public manners, he restrained the licence of the populace in sitting promiscuously with the knights in the theatre. Defamatory libels, published to injure persons of rank, of either sex, he suppressed, and not without visiting shame and ignominy upon the authors. He expelled a man of quaestorian rank from the senate for practising mimicry and dancing. From women of dishonest life, he took away the privilege and use of their litters; as also the right of receiving legacies or inheriting estates. He struck out of the list of judges a Roman knight for taking back his wife whom he had divorced and prosecuted for adultery. He condemned several men of the senatorian and equestrian orders, upon the ancient Scantinian law against pederasty or sodomy. The loose crimes of the Vestal Virgins, which had been overlooked by his father and brother, he punished severely, but in different ways: namely, offences committed before his reign, with death, and those since its commencement, according to the ancient custom, that is, to be let down into some underground place, and there starved to death; for, having given liberty to the two sisters called Ocellatae, to choose the mode of death which they preferred, and banished those who had deflowered them, he afterwards commanded that Cornelia Maximilla, the president of the vestals, who had formerly been acquitted upon a charge of incontinence, and a long time after was again prosecuted and condemned, should be buried alive; and those who had been guilty with her, beaten to death with rods in the Comitium; excepting only a man of praetorian rank, to whom, because he confessed the fact while the case was dubious, and it was not established against him, though the witnesses had been put to the torture, he granted the favour of exile. And to preserve pure and undefiled the reverence due to the gods, he ordered the soldiers to demolish a tomb which one of his freedmen had erected for his son out of the stones designed for the temple of Jupiter Capitolinus, and to sink in the sea the bones and relics buried there.

9

At first he abhorred bloodshed and slaughter so much that, before his father's arrival in Rome, calling to mind the verse of Virgil,

Impia quam caesis gens est epulata juvencis,

Ere impious man, restrained from blood in vain,
Began to feast on flesh of bullocks slain,

he designed to have published a proclamation, "to forbid the sacrifice of oxen". Before his accession to the imperial authority, and during some time afterwards, he scarcely ever gave the least grounds for being suspected of covetousness or avarice; but, on the contrary, he often afforded proofs, not only of his justice, but his liberality. To all about him he was generous even to profusion, and recommended nothing more earnestly to them than to avoid doing anything base or beggarly. He would not accept the property left him by those who had children. He also set aside a legacy bequeathed by the will of Ruscus Caepio, who had ordered his heir "to make a present yearly to each of the senators upon their first assembling". He exonerated all those who had been under prosecution from the treasury for above five years before; and would not suffer a suit to be renewed, unless it was done within a year, and on condition that the prosecutor should be banished if he could not make good his cause. The secretaries of the quaestors having engaged in trade, according to custom, but contrary to the Clodian law, he pardoned them for what was past. Such portions of land as had been left when it was divided among the veteran soldiers, he granted to the ancient possessors, as belonging to them by prescription. He put a stop to false prosecutions in the exchequer, by severely punishing the prosecutors and this saying of his was much quoted: "A prince who does not punish informers, encourages them."

10

But he did not long continue in this course of clemency and justice, although he sooner fell into cruelty than into avarice. He put to death a scholar of Paris, the pantomimic, though but a child and ill at the time, only because, both in person and the practice of his art, he resembled his master, and he did likewise Hermogenes of Tarsus for some oblique reflections in his History; besides crucifying the scribes who had copied the work. One who was master of a band of gladiators happening to say, "that a Thrax was a match for a Murmillo, but not so for the exhibitor of the games", he ordered him be dragged from the benches into the arena, and exposed to the dogs, with this label upon him, "a Parmularian (one who favoured the Thrax party) guilty of talking impiously". He put to death many senators, and among them several men of consular rank. In this number were Civica Cerealis, when he was proconsul in Africa, Salvidienus Orfitus, and Acilius Glabrio in exile, under the pretence of their planning to revolt again him. The rest he punished upon very trivial occasions; Aelius Lamia for some jocular expressions, which were of old date and perfectly innocent; because, upon Domitian's commending his voice, after he had taken his wife from him, he replied, "Alas! I hold my tongue." And when Titus advised him to take another wife, he answered him thus: "What! have you a mind to marry again?"

Salvius Cocceianus was condemned to death for keeping the birthday of his uncle Otho, the emperor; Mettius Pompusianus, because he was commonly reported to have an imperial nativity, and to carry about with him a map of the world upon vellum, with the speeches of kings and generals extracted out of Titus Livius, and for giving his slaves the names of Mago and Hannibal; Sallustius Lucullus, lieutenant in Britain, for suffering some lances of a new invention to be called "Lucullean", and Junius Rusticus, for publishing a treatise in praise of Paetus Thrasea and Helvidius Priscus, and calling them both "most upright men". Upon this occasion, he likewise banished all the philosophers from the city and Italy. He put to death the younger Helvidius for writing a farce, in which, under the character of Paris and Oenone, he reflected upon his having divorced his wife; and also Flavius Sabinus, one of his cousins, because, upon his being chosen at the consular election to that office, the public crier had, by a blunder, proclaimed him to the people not consul, but emperor.

Becoming still more cruel after his victory in the civil war, he employed the utmost industry to discover those of the adverse party who absconded: many of them he racked with a newly devised torture, inserting fire through their private parts; and some he dismembered by cutting off their hands. Certain it is, that only two of any note were pardoned, namely a tribune who wore the narrow stripe, and a centurion; who, to clear themselves from the charge of being concerned in any rebellious project, proved themselves to have been guilty of prostitution, and consequently incapable of exercising any influence either over the general or the soldiers.

11

Now in his cruelties he was not only excessive, but also subtle and crafty, pouncing upon his victims when they least expected it. He sent for a certain collector of his rents the very day before he crucified him, and invited him to come into his own bed-chamber, where he made him sit down upon the bed beside him; and dismissed him in a very merry, light-hearted manner, deigning him also the favour of a plate of meat from his own table. When he was on the point of condemning to death Aretinus Clemens, a man of consular rank, and one of his friends and emissaries, he retained him about his person the same or greater favour than ever, until at last, as they were riding together in the same litter, upon seeing the man who had informed against him, he said, "What sayest thou, Clemens, shall we hear tomorrow what this base slave shall have to say?" Treating with disdain and contempt the patience of men, he never pronounced a heavy sentence without some preface that promised clemency; so that there was not a surer sign of some horrible end than a mild and gentle beginning. Some person who stood accused of treason, he brought into the senate, and when he had declared that "he should prove that day how dear he was to the senate", he so influenced them, that they condemned the accused to be punished according to the ancient custom; that is, to have their necks locked in pillory, and so be beaten to death with rods. Then, as if horrified by the cruelty of the punishment, he would intercede in these words (for it is not impertinent to give them just as he delivered them), "Permit me, Conscript Fathers, so far to prevail upon your affection for me, however extraordinary the request may seem, as to grant the condemned criminals the favour of dying in the manner they choose; for by this you shall spare your own eyes, and all the world shall know that I was present in the senate."

12

Having emptied his coffers by the expense of his buildings and public spectacles, and the increased stipend granted to the soldiers, he made an attempt at the reduction of the army, in order to lessen the military charges. But perceiving that he would thereby expose himself to the insults of the barbarians and still be unrelieved of his burdens, he plunged into every manner of robbery and extortion to raise money. The estates of the living and the dead were sequestered upon any charge, by whomsoever preferred. It was sufficient, if any word or deed whatsoever were charged against a man, to make it high treason against the prince. Inheritances, were they never so far off, and no matter to whom they belonged, were confiscated, in case but one person should come forth and say, "that he had made the emperor his heir". Besides these exactions, the poll tax on the Jews was levied with extreme rigour, both on those who lived after the manner of Jews in the city, without publicly professing themselves to be such, and on those who, concealing their origin, avoided paying the tribute imposed upon that people. I remember, when I was a youth, to have been present when an old man, 90 years of age, was stripped naked by the procurator, in a very crowded court, that it might be determined whether he was circumcised or not.

From his very youth Domitian was neither civil nor kind, but of a forward, audacious bent, and excessive both in word and deed. When Caenis, his father's concubine, upon her return from Istria, offered him her lips to kiss, as she had been used to do, he presented his hand. Being indignant that his brother's son-in-law should be attended by servants clad in white, he cried out, as if they aped the imperial livery:

Too many princes are not good.

13

But once he mounted the imperial seat, he had the impudence to boast in the senate, "that it was he who had given the empire to his father and brother both, and they had but delivered it back to him". And upon taking his wife again, after divorcing her, he gave out by proclamation, "that he had recalled her to his couch", as if his bed were consecrated, like that on which the images of the gods reposed. He was not a little pleased, too, at hearing the acclamations of the people in the amphitheatre on a day of festival, "All happiness to our lord and lady." But when, during the celebration of the Capitoline trial of skill, the whole concourse of people entreated him with one voice to restore

Palfurius Sura to his place in the senate from which he had been long before expelled (he having then carried away the prize of eloquence from all the orators who had contended for it), he did not vouchsafe to give them an answer, but only commanded silence, by the voice of the crier. With equal arrogance, when he dictated the form of a letter to be used by his procurators, he began it thus: "Our lord and god commands so and so"; when it became a rule that no one should style him otherwise either in writing or speaking. He suffered no statues to be erected for him in the Capitol, unless they were of gold and silver, and of a stated weight. He built so many fine gates and arches, surmounted by representations of chariots drawn by four horses and other triumphal ornaments, in different quarters of the city, that a wit inscribed on one of the arches the Greek word meaning "it is enough", thus making a play on its similar sound to the word for "an arch".

He filled the office of consul 17 times, more than any man had ever assumed before him, and for the seven middle occasions in successive years; but in scarcely any of them had he more than the title; for he never continued in office beyond the kalends of May, and for the most part only till the ides of January. After his two triumphs, when he assumed the cognomen of Germanicus, he called the months of September and October, Germanicus and Domitian, after his own names, because he commenced his reign in the one and was born in the other.

14

By this course of life, becoming both hated and feared by all men, he was surprised in the end, and murdered by his friend and favourite freedmen who, together with his wife, conspired his death. He had long before suspected the very year and day, as well as the manner, of his death; for when he was but a youth the Chaldaean astrologers had told him all. His father once laughed at him, sitting at supper, for refusing to eat some mushrooms, saying that if he knew his fate, he would be afraid of the sword instead. Being, therefore, always stricken with fear and lowness of spirits at the least suspicion of danger, he was moved, it is credibly reported, to withdraw the edict ordering the destruction of the vines, chiefly because the copies of it which were dispersed had the following lines written upon them:

> Gnaw thou my root, yet shall my juice suffice
> To pour on Caesar's head in sacrifice.

It was from the same apprehension and fear, that he refused a new honour, one that had never been devised before, offered to him by the senate, though he was ordinarily greedy of all such compliments. What they decreed was this: that as often as he held the consulship, Roman knights, chosen by lot, should walk before him, clad in the Trabea, with lances in their hands, among his lictors and apparitors. As the time of the danger which he dreaded drew near, he became daily more and more perplexed; insomuch that he lined the walls of the porticos in which he used to walk with the stone called Phengites, brought from Cappadocia, which was as hard as marble, white and translucent; by the reflection of which he could see every object behind him. He seldom gave an audience to persons in custody, unless in private, being alone, and he himself holding their chains in his hand. He condemned to death Epaphroditus, his secretary, because it was believed that he had assisted Nero, when utterly forsaken, to kill himself; and by this means he hoped to persuade his servants that the life of a master was not to be attempted, in any emergency.

15

To conclude, his last victim was Flavius Clemens, his cousin-german, who is thought by some to have been a convert to the Christian religion, a man most contemptible for his slothfulness and negligence, whose sons, then of very tender age, he had openly avowed would be his successors; and, discarding their former names, had ordered one to be called Vespasian, and the other Domitian. Nevertheless, he suddenly killed him, upon a very slender suspicion (of Jewish manners), when he was scarcely out of his consulship. By this deed, more than anything else, he hastened his own destruction. For the space of eight months, there was so much lightning at Rome, seen and reported to him, that at last he cried out, "Let him now strike whom he will," meaning God or Jupiter. The Capitol was struck, as were also the temple of the Flavian family, with the Palatine house, and his own bedchamber. The tablet also, inscribed upon the base of his triumphal statue was carried away by the fury of the tempest, and fell upon a neighbouring monument. The tree which just before the advancement of Vespasian had been prostrated and rose again, suddenly fell a second time. The goddess Fortune of Praeneste, to whom it was his custom on New Year's Day to commend the empire for the ensuing year, and who had always given him a favourable reply, now in this last year delivered a most woeful one, and not without mention of blood. He dreamt that Minerva, whom he worshipped even to a superstitious excess, was withdrawing from her sanctuary, saying that she could not protect him any longer, because she was disarmed by Jupiter.

But nothing so much disquieted him as an answer given by Ascletario, the astrologer, and the accident that happened to him. This Ascletario had been informed against, and did not deny his having predicted that which by his art and learning he foresaw. Domitian asked him what end he thought he should come to himself. And when he made answer, that his destiny was to be torn to pieces by dogs, he ordered him immediately to be slain, and in order to prove the rashness and uncertainty of his art, caused him to be very carefully buried. But in the execution of this order, it chanced that the funeral pile was blown down by a sudden tempest, and the body, half burned, was rent piecemeal by dogs; which, being observed by Latinus, the comic actor, as he chanced to pass that way, he told it, among the other news of the day, to the emperor at supper.

16

The day before his death, he ordered some dates, served up at table, to be kept till the next day, adding, "if I have the luck to use them". And turning to those who were nearest him, he said, "Tomorrow the moon in Aquarius will be bloody instead of watery, and an event will happen which will be much talked of all the world over." About midnight, he was so terrified that he leaped out of bed. That morning he tried and passed sentence on a soothsayer sent from Germany, who being consulted about the lightning, foretold from it a change in the government. And as he scratched an ulcerous tumour on his forehead, seeing the blood run down his face, he said, "Would this were all that is to befall me!" Then, upon his asking the time of the day, instead of telling him the fifth hour, which was the one he feared, false word was brought to him that it was the sixth. Overjoyed at this information, as if all danger were now passed, and hastening to cherish his body and make much of himself, he was stopped by Parthenius, his chamberlain, who told him that a person was come to wait upon him about a matter of great consequence, which would admit of no delay. Ordering all persons to leave him, therefore, he retired into his chamber, and was there murdered.

17

Touching the manner and means of his death, this much is of common report: the conspirators being in some doubt when and where they should attack him, whether while he was in the bath, or at supper, Stephanus, a steward of Domitilla's, then under prosecution for defrauding his mistress, offered them his counsel and help; and wrapping up his left arm, as if it was hurt, in wool and bandages for some days, to prevent suspicion, at the hour appointed he secreted a dagger in them. Pretending then to make a discovery of a conspiracy, and being for that reason admitted, he presented to the emperor a memorial, and while he was reading it in great astonishment, stabbed him in the groin. But Domitian, though wounded, making resistance, Clodianus, one of his guards, Maximus, a freedman of Parthenius', Saturius, his principal chamberlain, with some gladiators, fell upon him, and stabbed him in seven places. A boy who had the charge of the lares in his bedchamber, and was then in attendance as usual, gave these further particulars: that he was ordered by Domitian, upon receiving his first wound, to reach him a dagger which lay under his pillow, and call in his domestics; but that he found nothing at the head of the bed, excepting the hilt of a poniard, and that all the doors were fastened: that the emperor in the meantime got hold of Stephanus, and throwing him upon the ground, struggled a long time with him; one while endeavouring to wrench the dagger from him, another while, though his fingers were hurt and mangled, to pluck out his eyes.

He was killed upon the fourteenth of the kalends of October, in the forty-fifth year of his age, and the fifteenth of his reign. His corpse was carried out upon a common bier by the public bearers, and buried by his nurse Phyllis, at his suburban villa on the Latin Way. But she afterwards privately conveyed his remains to the temple of the Flavian family and mingled them with the ashes of Julia, the daughter of Titus, whom she had also nursed.

18

He was tall in stature, his countenance modest, and inclined to ruddiness, with large eyes, though his sight was dim. His presence was graceful and comely, especially in his youth, excepting only that his toes were bent somewhat inward. In course of time, he became disfigured by baldness, corpulence, and the slenderness of his legs, which were reduced by a long illness. He was so sensible of how much the modesty of his countenance recommended him, that he once made boast to the senate, "Thus far you have approved both of my disposition and my countenance." His baldness irked him so much, that he considered it an affront to himself if any other person was twitted with it, either in jest or in earnest; though in a small tract he published, addressed to a friend, "concerning the preservation of the hair", he uses for their mutual consolation the words following:

"Seest thou my graceful mien, my stately form?

and yet the fate of my hair awaits me; yet with a stout heart I endure that the bush of my head disappears in my fresh youth. And this would I have you know, that nothing is more pleasing, and nothing more fleeting, than beauty."

19

He so disliked exertion and fatigue, that he scarcely ever walked through the city on foot. In his expeditions and on a march, he seldom rode on horseback, but was generally carried in a litter.

He had no disposition toward the exercise of arms, but delighted in the use of the bow and arrow. Many persons have seen him often kill a hundred wild animals, of various kinds, at his Alban retreat, and fix his arrows in their heads with such dexterity, that he could, in two shots, plant them, like a pair of horns, in front. He would sometimes direct his arrows against the hand of a boy standing at a distance, with his fingers apart; and such was his precision that they all passed through the void spaces between the fingers, doing the boy no harm at all.

20

In the beginning of his empire, he neglected the study of all liberal sciences, though he took care to restore, at a huge expense, the libraries which had been burned down; collecting manuscripts from all parts, and sending scribes to Alexandria, either to copy or correct them. Yet he never gave himself the trouble of reading history or poetry, or of employing his pen even for private purposes. Except for the commentaries and acts of Tiberius Caesar, he never read anything. His letters, speeches, and edicts, were all drawn up for him by others; though he could converse with elegance, and sometimes voiced memorable original sentiments. As for example: "Would that I were as fair and well favoured as Maecius fancies himself to be." And of the head of someone whose hair was reddish and sprinkled with grey, he said, "that it was snow mixed with mead". It was his saying that the lot of princes was very miserable, for they were never credited with the discovery of a conspiracy, unless they were slain first.

21

When he had leisure, he amused himself with dice, even on days that were not festivals, and in the morning. He went to the bath early, and made a plentiful dinner, insomuch that he seldom ate more at supper than a Matian apple, to which he added a draught of wine, out of a small flask. He gave frequent and sumptuous banquets, but they were short, for he never prolonged them after sunset, and held no revel afterwards. For, till bed time, he did nothing else but walk by himself in his own chamber.

22

In fleshly lust he was excessive; and the ordinary use of Venus, as if it was a kind of exercise, he called Clinopale, or bed-wrestling. It was commonly reported that he himself used, with pincers, to depilate his concubines, and to swim about in company with the lowest prostitutes. His brother's daughter, Julia, was offered him in marriage when she was a virgin; but being at that time enamoured of Domitia, he resolutely refused her. Yet not long afterwards, when she was given to another, he was ready enough to solicit her favours, and that even while Titus was living. But after she was bereft of father and husband both, he loved her with most ardent affection, and that openly; insomuch that he was the occasion of her death, by forcing her to miscarry when she was with child by him.

23

The people took his death very indifferently, but the soldiers felt it to the very heart; and immediately endeavoured to have him ranked among the gods. They were also ready to revenge his loss, if there had been any to take the lead. However, they soon after effected it, by resolutely demanding the punishment of all those who had been concerned in his assassination. On the contrary, the senate was so overjoyed, that they met in all haste, and in a full assembly reviled his memory in the most bitter terms; ordering ladders to be brought in, and his shields and images to be pulled down before their eyes and dashed in pieces upon the floor of the senate house; passing at the same time a decree to obliterate his titles everywhere, and abolish all memory of him. A few months before his death, a raven on the Capitol uttered these words: "All will be well." Some person gave this interpretation of the prodigy:

Nuper Tarpeio quae sedit culmine comix,
"Est bene," non potuit dicere; dixit, "Erit."

Late croaked a raven from Tarpeia's height,
"All is not yet, but shortly will be, right."

It is reported likewise that Domitian dreamed that a golden excrescence grew out of the back of his neck, which he con-

sidered as a certain sign of happy days for the empire after him.
And so it fell out shortly after: such was the just and moderate
conduct of the emperors succeeding him.

AGRICOLA IN ACTION AT MONS GRAUPIUS, BRITAIN, AD 84

Tacitus

*Agricola was appointed governor of Britain in AD 77, where he conquered
Anglesey and consolidated the Forth-Clyde line. An excursion to the Moray
Firth in AD 84 saw his crushing defeat of the Caledonians at Mons Graupius.*

Even while Agricola was still speaking the troops showed
intense eagerness, and the end of his speech was greeted with
a wild burst of enthusiasm. Without delay they went off to arm
themselves. The men were so thrilled that they were ready to
rush straight into action; but Agricola marshalled them with
care. The auxiliary infantry, 8,000 in number, formed a strong
centre, while 3,000 cavalry were distributed on the flanks. The
legions were stationed in front of the camp rampart: victory
would be vastly more glorious if it cost no Roman blood, while if
the auxiliaries should be repulsed the legions could come to
their rescue. The British army was posted on higher ground in a
manner calculated to impress and intimidate its enemy. Their
front line was on the plain, but the other ranks seemed to mount
up the sloping hillside in close-packed tiers. The flat space
between the two armies was taken up by the noisy manoeuvring
of the charioteers. Agricola now saw that he was greatly outnumbered, and fearing that the enemy might fall simultaneously on his front and flanks, he opened out his ranks.
The line now looked like being dangerously thin, and many
urged him to bring up the legions. But he was always an
optimist and resolute in the face of difficulties. He sent away
his horse and took up his position on foot in front of the colours.

The fighting began with exchanges of missiles, and the
Britons showed both steadiness and skill in parrying our spears
with their huge swords or catching them on their little shields,
while they themselves rained volleys on us. At last Agricola
called upon four cohorts of Batavians and two of Tungrians to

close and fight it out at the sword's point. These old soldiers had been well drilled in sword-fighting, while the enemy were awkward at it, with their small shields and unwieldy swords, especially as the latter, having no points, were quite unsuitable for a cut-and-thrust struggle at close quarters. The Batavians, raining blow after blow, striking them with the bosses of their shields, and stabbing them in the face, felled the Britons posted on the plain and pushed on up the hillsides. This provoked the other cohorts to attack with vigour and kill the nearest of the enemy. Many Britons were left behind half dead or even unwounded, owing to the very speed of our victory. Our cavalry squadrons, meanwhile, had routed the war chariots, and now plunged into the infantry battle. Their first onslaught was terrifying, but the solid ranks of the enemy and the roughness of the ground soon brought them to a standstill and made the battle quite unlike a cavalry action. Our infantry had only a precarious foothold and were being jostled by the horses' flanks; and often a runaway chariot, or riderless horses careering about wildly in their terror, came plunging into the ranks from the side or in head-on collision.

The Britons on the hilltops had so far taken no part in the action and had leisure to note with contempt the smallness of our numbers. They were now starting to descend gradually and envelop our victorious rear. But Agricola, who had expected just such a move, threw in their path four squadrons of cavalry which he was keeping in hand for emergencies and turned their spirited charge into a disorderly rout. The tactics of the Britons now recoiled on themselves. Our squadrons, obedient to orders, rode round from the front of the battle and fell upon the enemy in the rear. The open plain now presented a grim, awe-inspiring spectacle. Our horsemen kept pursuing them, wounding some, making prisoners of others, and then killing them as new enemies appeared. On the British side, each man now behaved according to his character. Whole groups, though they had weapons in their hands, fled before inferior numbers; elsewhere, unarmed men deliberately charged to face certain death.

Equipment, bodies, and mangled limbs lay all around on the bloodstained earth; and even the vanquished now and then recovered their fury and their courage. When they reached the woods, they rallied and profited by their local knowledge to ambush the first rash pursuers. Our men's over-confidence might even have led to serious disaster. But Agricola was everywhere at once. He ordered strong cohorts of light infantry to ring the woods like hunters. Where the thickets were denser, dismounted troopers went in to scour them; where they thinned out, the cavalry did the work. At length, when they saw our troops, re-formed and steady, renewing the pursuit, the Britons turned and ran. They no longer kept formation or looked to see where their comrades were, but scattering and deliberately keeping apart from each other they penetrated far into trackless wilds. The pursuit went on till night fell and our soldiers were tired of killing. Of the enemy some 10,000 fell; on our side, 360 men – among them Aulus Atticus, the prefect of a cohort, whose youthful impetuosity and mettlesome horse carried him deep into the ranks of the enemy.

For the victors it was a night of rejoicing over their triumph and their booty. The Britons dispersed, men and women wailing together, as they carried away their wounded or called to the survivors. Many left their homes and in their rage actually set fire to them, or chose hiding-places, only to abandon them at once. At one moment they would try to concert plans, then suddenly break off their conference. Sometimes the sight of their dear ones broke their hearts; more often it goaded them to fury; and we had proof that some of them laid violent hands on their wives and children in a kind of pity. The next day revealed the effects of our victory more fully. An awful silence reigned on every hand; the hills were deserted, houses smoking in the distance, and our scouts did not meet a soul.

DOMITIAN AND THE YES-MEN, c. AD 90

Juvenal

An attack on the imperial practice of promoting cronies to privy councillors. Domitian was not alone in this sin – almost all emperors did it, at the cost of sage advice.

Look here, once again Crispinus!
    I'll often have to call

Him onto my stage, this monster of
    evil without one small
Redeeming virtue, this low debauchee,
    diseased and dread

Strong only in lust that scorns no
    one except the unwed.
What does it matter, then, how big
    are the colonnades
That tire his horses, how broad the
    woods where he drives in shade,
How many lots near the forum, how many
    mansions, he's bought?
No bad man is happy, least of all a
    seducer who's brought
To incest, with whom a filleted
    priestess lately has lain,
To be, for that, interred while blood
    still pulsed in her veins.
But to lighter matters. Although if
    another had done the same,
He'd fall in the censor's grasp; for
    what would be called a shame
In Tom, Dick, or Harry became in
    Crispinus simply a grace.
What can you do when any charge you
    can bring him to face
Is less dreadful and foul than the
    man himself? He bought a mullet
For three hundred dollars – something
    like fifty a pound, as they would put it
Who want to exaggerate and make up
    a real fish tale.
I'd praise the cunning of his schemes
    if he prevailed
By any such costly gift upon a
    childless old man
To name him first in his will, or
    for better reasons, planned

To send it to some fine doxy who
   shuns the public glance
Behind shades of a litter with
   picture windows. Not a chance:
He bought it all for himself. We see
   a lot of things done
Today that the frugal glutton Apicius
   would have shunned.
Crispinus, did you, who formerly
   wore a G-string supplied
By your native papyrus, pay that price
   for a fish? You might
Have purchased the fisherman himself
   perhaps for less
Than the fish; and for the same amount
   you could possess
A farm in the provinces or a bigger
   estate like those
Down in Apulia. What sort of feasts
   must we suppose
The emperor himself gobbled up
   when by a parasite duke
In purple of palace pomp those hundreds
   of bucks were puked –
A mere appetizer, that fish, hors-d'oeuvre
   in a modest feast.
This man's now chief of the knights,
   who once was only too pleased
To sell his Egyptian brothers, yelling,
   "Mudcats for sale!"
Begin, Calliope! Here's no lyric for
   song; a tale
That's true is to be the subject.
   Now let's take our seats.

Pierian maidens, recount the story.
   And in that I treat
You to the name of maiden, may I be
   profited.

When the last of the Flavians was flaying
  a world half dead,
And Rome was slave to a baldheaded
  Nero, there appeared
In a net in the Adriatic, before the
  shrine that's reared
To Venus high over Greek Ancona, a
  turbot whose size
Was gigantic. It bulged at the
  meshes – a fish as much a prize
As those the Sea of Azov hides under
  ice till the sun
Cracks open the crust, and sluggish
  but fat from cold, they run
To the rushing Black Sea's mouth.
  The skipper means this whale
Of a fish for the chief pontiff – for
  who'd dare put on sale
Or buy so big a fish when even the
  beaches were thick
With informers? Customs men, inspecting
  seaweed, would be quick
To dash off and charge the helpless
  fisher, with no qualms
At swearing the fish long fattened in
  Caesar's ponds, therefrom
Escaped, and must be returned to its
  former lord. If we come
To believe what's held by Armillatus
  or Palfurius,

Everything that swims, is delicious,
  rare, or curious,
In any ocean whatever, belongs to the
  royal purse.
So, lest it go to waste, it shall be
  a gift he confers.
By now unwholesome autumn was yielding
  to frost at last,

Malarial patients hoped for relief,
   and cold winter's blast
Kept the fish quite fresh. And yet
   he hurried as if the hot
South Wind were dogging his heels.
   And when he'd gone somewhat
Past the lake where Alba, though ruined,
   tends the Trojan flame
And prays in the smaller temple of
   Vesta, a crowd that came
In wonder blocked his passage a while;
   and as it withdrew,
The gates on easy hinges swung out;
   and the senators who
Were excluded stared at the fish that
   got in. And it was sped
To this son of Atreus. Then the man
   of Picenum said:
"Accept a fish far too big for a
   mortal's kitchen. Declare
This a festival day. Make haste to
   vomit all that rich fare
In your stomach and eat a turbot
   preserved for your own reign.
The fish itself desired to be caught."
   What could be more inane,

More barefaced? And yet King Rooster's
   comb began to rise
With delight; when his power's
   praised as equal to that in the skies,
There's nothing a godlike emperor can't
   believe of himself.
But no dish big enough for the fish
   could be found on any shelf!
So the chief advisers were called
   into council – men he hated,
Upon whose faces was spread the ashen
   fear created

By his great and dangerous friendship.
    The first to rush
At the steward's call, "Hurry up, he's
    waiting!" was Pegasus,
Pulling on a snatched-up robe; for
    recently he'd been
Appointed as bailiff over the stunned
    city. Back then,
What else would a prefect be? But
    he was the best of the lot,
The most just interpreter of the law,
    although he thought,
In even those vicious times, that
    justice should not be dealt
By swords. Then came delightful old
    Crispus, whose unexcelled
And gentle spirit was equalled by
    his eloquent speech.
What better adviser for the monarch
    of the whole reach
Of oceans, lands, and nations if
    only he had been free,

Under that scourge and plague, to
    condemn his brutality
And give good moral advice? But what's
    more dangerous to men
Than the ear of a tyrant, upon whose
    whim the fate of a friend
Who spoke of showers, the heat, the
    rainy spring, depends?
So he never swam against the tide,
    nor was he such
A citizen as could utter the freeborn
    thoughts that touched
His heart, or risk his life for truth.
    He lived in this way
Through many winters and on to his
    eightieth birthday,

Protected in even that court by weapons
   like these from harm.
Behind him hurried Acilius, a man the
   same age, at his arm
The son who did not deserve the cruel
   death in store,
So quickly rushed upon him by his
   ruler's swords.
But to be both old and noble has become
   long since
The same as being a prodigy; it follows,
   hence,
That I'd rather be a clod, baby
   brother of giants, than those.
It was no help, therefore, to his
   wretched son that in close
Combat, as a naked huntsman, he speared
   Numidian bears

In the Alban arena. For who would
   not nowadays be aware
Of patrician tricks? Who'd think that
   old-fashioned ruse you achieved,
Brutus, was wonderful? Kings wearing
   beards are easily deceived.
With no happier face, though of ignoble
   bloodlines, Rubrius came –
Condemned long ago of crime no one
   mentions, yet deeper in shame
Than a satire-writing pervert. Then
   appeared the gluttonous belly
Of Montanus, and slightly later
   Montanus himself; and smelly
Crispinus, exuding at early daybreak
   enough strong scent
To outsmell two funerals. More
   vicious than he, next went
Pompeius, who had a tender whisper
   that slit men's throats;

And Fuscus, who, planning wars in his
   marble halls, would devote
His guts to Romanian vultures.
   Cautious Veiento in turn
Arrived with lethal Catullus, who with
   passion burned
For a girl he'd never seen – in even
   our time a great
And notable marvel, a blind sycophant,
   a dread courtier straight
From the beggars' bridges, worthy to
   beg at chariot wheels
And blow soft kisses to those descending
   the Arician hill.

No one was more amazed at the fish,
   for he said a great deal
About it, turning left. But the
   creature lay to his right.
In the same way, he'd praise a Cilician
   gladiator's fight
Or the hoist that snatches boy actors
   up into the flies.
But Veiento will not be outdone. Like
   a seer who prophesies
When nipped, O Bellona, by your gadfly,
   in frenzy he cries:
"An omen divine you have here, of a
   brilliant, great victory!
You'll capture some barbarous king,
   or Prince Arviragus will be
Knocked out of his British car and die.
   This beast, I opine,
Is of foreign birth. For see you not
   along the spine
Those spearlike fins?" There was nothing
   left for Fabricius, then,
Except to mention the turbot's age
   and its origin.

"Then what's your advice?" the emperor
  asked. "Cut it in two?"
"Heaven forfend," said Montanus; "such
  indignity will not do!
Command a deep vessel to be molded,
  of size so immense
Its thin walls can fitly embrace his
  gigantic circumference.
For the dish a great and instant
  Prometheus must come!

Make haste with clay, with wheel!
  But henceforth, O Caesar, let some
Good potters always attend your camp."
  This proposal, suited
Well to the man, won out. The old
  dissipations rooted
Deep in the royal court he knew, and
  Nero's soirées
That lasted beyond midnight, till a
  second hunger was raised
Inside them, when the blood by Falernian
  wine was heated.
No one in my time had greater knowledge
  of eating than he did.
He knew at the first bite if an oyster
  was born on a bed
In the Lucrine Bay, on Campania's
  rocks, or had been sped
From Kent; a glance revealed the coast
  where a sea urchin was bred.
The session's adjourned and the
  councillors are sent outside
Whom the mighty monarch had dragged
  posthaste and terrified
To his Alban palace as though he'd
  give them news of fierce
Germanic tribes on the warpath, or
  there had come to his ears,

With the speed of carrier pigeons flown
    from the faraway
Outposts of the empire, some quite
    alarming communiqué.
Even so, if only he had devoted to
    trifling nonsense

Like this all those days of cruelty
    and violence
When he robbed the city of its most
    noble and brilliant souls,
Unpunished, with none to avenge!
    But once he began to hold
Great terror for men in the lower
    classes, he was killed,
Soaked in the noble Lamian blood
    that he had spilled.

COLLAPSING HOUSES, ROME, c. AD 90

Strabo

The mass of Roman people lived in tenements or insulae. *As Strabo records, these were often flimsily built and prone to fire.*

In Rome there is continual need of wood and stone for ceaseless building caused by the frequent falling down of houses, and on account of conflagrations and of sales which seem never to cease. These sales are a kind of voluntary falling down of houses, each owner knocking down and rebuilding according to his individual taste. For these purposes the numerous quarries, forests, and rivers in the region which convey the materials, offer wonderful facilities.

Augustus Cæsar endeavoured to avert from the city the dangers alluded to, and instituted a company of freedmen, who should be ready to lend their assistance in the case of conflagration, while as a preventive against falling houses he decreed that all new buildings should not be carried to the same height as formerly, and those erected along the public ways should not exceed 70 feet in height. But these improvements must have ceased except for the facilities afforded to Rome by the quarries, the forests, and the ease of transport.

IMMIGRANTS, ROME, C. AD 90

Martial

What race is so distant from us, what race is so barbarous, O Caesar, that from it no spectator is present in your city! The cultivator of Rhodope [in Thrace] is here from Haemus, sacred to Orpheus. The Scythian who drinks the blood of his horses is here; he, too, who quaffs the waters of the Nile nearest their springing; and he also whose shore is laved by the most distant ocean. The Arabian has hastened hither; the Sabaeans have hastened; and here the Cilicians have anointed themselves with their own native perfume. Here come the Sicambrians with their hair all twisted into a knot, and here the frizzled Ethiopians. Yet though their speech is all so different, they all speak together hailing you, O Emperor, as the true father of your country.

WINDOW SHOPPING, ROME, C. AD 90

Martial

Mamurra is a fictitious character of assumed gentility. The experience described was real enough, however. The main shopping area in Rome centred on the streets around the Forum. From Martial's Epigrams.

Mamurra, after having walked long and anxiously in the bazaars where golden Rome proudly displayed her riches, examined the handsome young slaves, yes devoured them with his eyes – not those slaves exposed in the open shops, but those kept for sale to select people in private rooms, and are not exhibited to common folk, such as I. Tired of this inspection he uncovers various tables, square ones and round; next asks to see some rich ivory ornaments displayed on the upper shelves. Then, after four times measuring a dinner couch for six guests, all adorned as it was with tortoise shell, he regretted sorrowfully "that it was not big enough for his citron wood table." He consulted his nose to find out if the bronzes had the true Corinthian aroma, and criticized some statues by Polycletus! Next, complaining that some crystal vases had been spoiled by mixing in glass, he marked and had set aside ten myrrhine cups. He weighed ancient bowls, and inquired for goblets that had been ennobled by the hand of Mentor. He counted emeralds set in chased gold, and examined the largest pearl ear-pendants. He sought on every counter for real sardonyxes, and cheapened some large jaspers. At last, when forced by fatigue to retire, at the eleventh hour he bought two small cups for one small coin and bore them home himself.

ADVICE TO FATHERS ON EDUCATION, C. AD 95

Quintilian

I would, therefore, have a father conceive the highest hopes of his son from the moment of his birth. If he does so, he will be more careful about the ground work of his education. For there is absolutely no foundation for the complaint that but few men have the power to take in the knowledge that is imparted to them, and that the majority are so slow of understanding that education is a waste of time and labour. On the contrary you will find that most are quick to reason and ready to learn. Reasoning comes as naturally to man as flying to birds, speed to horses and ferocity to beasts of prey: our minds are endowed by nature with such activity and sagacity that the soul is believed to proceed from heaven. Those who are dull and unteachable are as abnormal as prodigious births and monstrosities, and are but few in number. A proof of what I say is to be found in the fact that boys commonly show promise of many accomplishments, and when such promise dies away as they grow up, this is plainly due not to the failure of natural gifts, but to lack of the requisite care. But, it will be urged, there are degrees of talent. Undoubtedly, I reply, and there will be a corresponding variation in actual accomplishment: but that there are many who gain nothing from education, I absolutely deny. The man who shares this conviction, must, as soon as he becomes a father, devote the utmost care to fostering the promise shown by the son whom he destines to become an orator.

Above all see that the child's nurse speaks correctly. The ideal, according to Chrysippus, would be that she should be a philosopher: failing that he desired that the best should be chosen, as far as possible. No doubt the most important point is that they should be of good character: but they should speak correctly as well. It is the nurse that the child first hears, and her words that he will first attempt to imitate. And we are by nature most tenacious of childish impressions, just as the flavour first absorbed by vessels when new persists, and the colour imparted by dyes to the primitive whiteness of wool is indelible. Further it is the worst impressions that are most durable. For, while what is good readily deteriorates, you will never turn vice into virtue. Do not therefore allow the boy to become accustomed even in infancy to a style of speech which he will subsequently have to unlearn.

As regards parents, I should like to see them as highly educated as possibly, and I do not restrict this remark to fathers alone. We are told that the eloquence of the Gracchi owed much to their mother Cornelia, whose letters even today testify to the cultivation of her style. Laelia, the daughter of Gaius Laelius, is said to have reproduced the elegance of her father's language in her own speech, while the oration delivered before the triumvirs by Hortensia, the daughter of Quintus Hortensius, is still read and not merely as a compliment to her sex. And even those who have not had the fortune to receive a good education should not for that reason devote less care to their son's education; but should on the contrary show all the greater diligence in other matters where they can be of service to their children.

"A FINE CROP OF POETS": PUBLIC READINGS OF LITERATURE, ROME, c. AD 97

Pliny

This year has raised a fine crop of poets; there was scarcely a day throughout the month of April when someone was not giving a public reading. I am glad to see that literature flourishes and there is a show of budding talent, in spite of the fact that people are slow to form an audience. Most of them sit about in public places, gossiping and wasting their time when they could be giving their attention, and give orders that they are to be told at intervals whether the reader has come in and has read the preface, or is coming to the end of the book. It is not till that moment – and even then very reluctantly – that they come dawdling in. Nor do they stay very long, but leave before the end, some of them trying to slip out unobserved and other marching boldly out. And yet people tell how in our father's time the Emperor Claudius was walking on the Palatine when he heard voices and asked what was happening; on learning that Nonianus was giving a reading he surprised the audience by joining it unannounced. Today the man with any amount of leisure, invited well in advance and given many a reminder, either never comes at all, or, if he does, complains that he has wasted a day – just because he has not wasted it. The more praise and honour then is due to those whose interest in writing and reading aloud is not damped by the idleness and conceit of their listeners.

Personally I have failed scarcely anyone, though I admit that most of the invitations came from my friends; for there are very few people who care for literature without caring for me too. That is why I stayed in town longer than I intended, but now I can return to my country retreat and write something myself. I shall not read it to my friends, for I don't want it to seem that I went to hear them with the intention of putting them in my debt. Here as elsewhere a duty performed deserves no gratitude if a return is expected.

SOME LAWS OF THE ROAD, c. AD 100

Anon

VI The width of a road is 2 metres on the straight and 4 on a bend.

VII Roads must be kept in good repair. If the road is not laid with stones, anyone may drive his beasts where he likes.

THE MANNERS AND CUSTOMS OF THE GERMANS, c. AD 100

Tacitus

The Germans morbidly fascinated Roman intellectuals, for they were the only people to throw off imperial rule at its strongest. Tacitus' Germania was a warning-blast against the corrupt effeminacy of the empire, when contrasted with the pure warrior lifestyle of the Germanic tribes.

On the field of battle it is a disgrace to a chief to be surpassed in courage by his followers, and to the followers not to equal the courage of their chief. And to leave a battle alive after their chief has fallen means lifelong infamy and shame. To defend and protect him, and to let him get the credit for their own acts of heroism, are the most solemn obligations of their allegiance. The chiefs fight for victory, the followers for their chief. Many noble youths, if the land of their birth is stagnating in a long period of peace and inactivity, deliberately seek out other tribes which have some war in hand. For the Germans have no taste for peace; renown is more easily won among perils, and a large body of retainers cannot be kept together except by means of violence and war. They are always making demands on the generosity of their chief, asking for a coveted war-horse or a spear stained with the blood of a defeated enemy. Their meals, for which plentiful if homely fare is provided, count in lieu of pay. The wherewithal for this openhandedness comes from war and plunder. A German is not so easily prevailed upon to plough the land and wait patiently for harvest as to challenge a foe and earn wounds for his reward. He thinks it tame and spiritless to accumulate slowly by the sweat of his brow what can be got quickly by the loss of a little blood.

When not engaged in warfare they spend a certain amount of time in hunting, but much more in idleness, thinking of nothing else but sleeping and eating. For the boldest and most warlike men have no regular employment, the care of house, home, and fields being left to the women, old men, and weaklings of the family. In thus dawdling away their time they show a strange inconsistency – at one and the same time loving indolence and hating peace.

It is a national custom for gifts of cattle or agricultural produce to be made to the chiefs, individual citizens making voluntary contributions for this purpose. These are accepted as tokens of honour, but serve also to supply their wants. They take particular pleasure in gifts received from neighbouring states, such as are sent not only by individuals but by communities as well – choice horses, splendid arms, metal discs, and collars. And we have now taught them to accept presents of money also.

It is a well-known fact that the peoples of Germany never live in cities and will not even have their houses adjoin one another. They dwell apart, dotted about here and there, wherever a spring, plain, or grove takes their fancy. Their villages are not laid out in the Roman style, with buildings adjacent and connected. Every man leaves an open space round his house, perhaps as a precaution against the risk of fire, perhaps because they are inexpert builders. They do not even make use of stones or wall-tiles; for all purposes they employ rough-hewn timber, ugly and unattractive-looking. Some parts, however, they carefully smear over with a clay of such purity and brilliance that it looks like painting or coloured design. They also have the habit of hollowing out underground caves, which they cover with masses of manure and use both as refuges from the winter and as storehouses for produce. Such shelters temper the keenness of the frosts; and if an invader comes, he ravages the open country, while these hidden excavations are either not known to exist, or else escape detection simply because they cannot be found without a search.

The universal dress in Germany is a cloak fastened with a brooch or, failing that, a thorn. They pass whole days by the fireside wearing no garment but this. It is a mark of great wealth to wear undergarments, which are not loose like those of the Sarmatians and Parthians, but fit tightly and follow the contour of every limb. They also wear the skins of wild animals – the tribes near the river frontiers without any regard to appearance, the more distant tribes with some refinement of taste, since in their part of the country there is no finery to be bought. These latter people select animals with care, and after stripping off the hides decorate them with patches of the skin of creatures that live in the unknown seas of the outer ocean. The dress of the women differs from that of the men in two respects only: women often wear outer garments of linen ornamented with a purple pattern; and as the upper part of these is sleeveless, the whole of their arms, and indeed the parts of their breasts nearest the shoulders, are exposed.

Their marriage code, however, is strict, and no feature of their morality deserves higher praise. They are almost unique among barbarians in being content with one wife apiece – all of them, that is, except a very few who take more than one wife not to satisfy their desires but because their exalted rank brings them many pressing offers of matrimonial alliances. The dowry is brought by husband to wife, not by wife to husband. Parents and kinsmen attend and approve the gifts – not gifts chosen to please a woman's fancy or gaily deck a young bride, but oxen, a horse with its bridle, or a shield, spear, and sword. In consideration of such gifts a man gets his wife, and she in her turn brings a present of arms to her husband. This interchange of gifts typifies for them the most sacred bond of union, sanctified by mystic rites under the favour of the presiding deities of wedlock. The woman must not think that she is excluded from aspirations to manly virtues or exempt from the hazards of warfare. That is why she is reminded, in the very ceremonies which bless her marriage at its outset, that she enters her husband's home to be the partner of his toils and perils, that both in peace and in war she is to share his sufferings and adventures. That is the meaning of the team of oxen, the horse ready for its rider, and the gift of arms. On these terms she must live her life and bear her children. She is receiving something that she must hand over intact and undepreciated to her children, something for her sons' wives to receive in their turn and pass on to her grandchildren.

By such means is the virtue of their women protected, and they live uncorrupted by the temptations of public shows or the excitements of banquets. Clandestine love-letters are unknown to men and women alike. Adultery is extremely rare, considering the size of the population. A guilty wife is summarily punished by her husband. He cuts off her hair, strips her naked, and in the presence of kinsmen turns her out of his house and flogs her all through the village. They have in fact no mercy on a wife who prostitutes her chastity. Neither beauty, youth, nor wealth can find her another husband. No one in Germany finds vice amusing, or calls it "up-to-date" to seduce and be seduced. Even better is the practice of those states in which only virgins may marry, so that a woman who has once been a bride has finished with all such hopes and aspirations. She takes one husband, just as she has one body and one life. Her thoughts must not stray beyond him or her desires survive him. And even that husband she must love not for himself, but as an embodiment of the married state. To restrict the number of children, or to kill any of those born after the heir, is considered wicked. Good morality is more effective in Germany than good laws are elsewhere.

In every home the children go naked and dirty, and develop that strength of limb and tall stature which excite our admiration. Every mother feeds her child at the breast and does not depute the task to maids or nurses. The young master is not distinguished from the slave by any pampering in his upbringing. They live together among the same flocks and on the same earthen floor, until maturity sets apart the free and the spirit of valour claims them as her own. The young men are slow to mate, and thus they reach manhood with vigour unimpaired. The girls, too, are not hurried into marriage. As old and full-grown as the men, they match their mates in age and strength, and the children inherit the robustness of their parents. The sons of sisters are as highly honoured by their uncles as by their own fathers. Some tribes even consider the former tie the closer and more sacred of the two, and in demanding hostages prefer nephews to sons, thinking that this gives them a firmer grip on men's hearts and a wider hold on the family. However, a man's heirs and successors are his own children, and there is no such thing as a will. When there is no issue, the first in order of succession are brothers, and then uncles, first on the father's, then on the mother's side. The more relatives and connections by marriage a man has, the greater authority he commands in old age. There is nothing to be gained by childlessness in Germany.

ROLL CALL OF THE FIRST COHORT OF TUNGRIANS, VINDOLANDA, BRITAIN, c. AD 100

Anon

To defend the empire, Rome was obliged to use the martial services of numerous non-Italian peoples. The Tungrians were Romanized Gauls from the Meuse region.

18 May, net number of the First Cohort of Tungrians, of which the commander is Iulius Verecundus the prefect, 752, including 6 centurions.

Of whom there are absent:

guards of the governor	46
at the office of Ferox	
at Coria	337
	including (?) 2 centurions
at London	(?) a centurion
. . .	6
	including 1 centurion
. . .	9
	including 1 centurion
. . .	11
at (?) . . .	(?) 1
	45
total absentees	456
	including 5 centurions
remainder, present	296
	including 1 centurion
from these:	
sick	15
wounded	6
suffering from inflammation of the eyes	10
total of these	31
remainder, fit for active service	265
	including 1 centurion.

AN APPEAL FOR BEER, VINDOLANDA, BRITAIN, C. AD 100

Masclus

Masclus, a decurion, writes to Flavius Cerialis, prefect of the Ninth Cohort of Batavians. (The Batavians, like the Tungrians, were Gauls in Roman employ.)

Masclus to Cerialis his king,[1] greeting. Please, my lord, give instructions (?) as to what you want us to have done tomorrow. Are we all to return with the standard or only half of us? . . . most fortunate and be well-disposed towards me. My fellow-soldiers have no beer. Please order some to be sent. (Back) To Flavius Cerialis, prefect, from Masclus, decurion.

A BIRTHDAY INVITATION, BRITAIN, C. AD 100

Claudia Severa

The recipient of this birthday invitation was Sulpicia Lepidina, the wife of a Roman praefectus stationed at Vindolanda on the north frontier of England. The sender was another officer's wife, presumably stationed nearby.

Claudia Severa to her Lepidina greetings. On the third day before the Ides of September, sister, for the day of the celebration of my birthday, I give you a warm invitation to make sure that you come to us, to make the day more enjoyable for me by your arrival, if you are present (?). Give my greetings to your Cerialis. My Aelius and my little son send him (?) their greetings. (2nd hand) I shall expect you, sister. Farewell, sister, my dearest soul, as I hope to prosper, and hail. (Back, 1st hand) To Sulpicia Lepidina, (wife) of Cerialis, from Severa.

[1] i.e. patron

SLAVES MURDER THEIR MASTER, MOLI DI GAETA, c. AD 100

Pliny the Younger

From a letter to Acilius.

This horrible affair demands more publicity than a letter –
Larcius Macedo, a senator and ex-praetor, has fallen a victim
to his own slaves. Admittedly he was a cruel and overbearing
master, too ready to forget that his father had been a slave, or
perhaps too keenly conscious of it. He was taking a bath in his
house at Formiae when suddenly he found himself surrounded;
one slave seized him by the throat while the others struck his face
and hit him in the chest and stomach and – shocking to say – in his
private parts. When they thought he was dead they threw him on
to the hot pavement, to make sure he was not still alive. Whether
unconscious or feigning to be so, he lay there motionless, thus
making them believe that he was quite dead. Only then was he
carried out, as if he had fainted with the heat, and received by his
slaves who had remained faithful, while his concubines ran up,
screaming frantically. Roused by their cries and revived by the
cooler air he opened his eyes and made some movement to show
that he was alive, it being now safe to do so. The guilty slaves fled,
but most of them have been arrested and a search is being made
for the others. Macedo was brought back to life with difficulty,
but only for a few days; at least he died with the satisfaction of
having revenged himself, for he lived to see the same punishment
meted out as for murder. There you see the dangers, outrages,
and insults to which we are exposed. No master can feel safe
because he is kind and considerate; for it is their brutality, not
their reasoning capacity, which leads slaves to murder masters.

CHARIOT-RACING, ROME, c. AD 100

Pliny the Younger

*The horse-and-chariot never appealed to the Romans as a weapon of war
(they preferred to conquer on foot), but they did adopt the combination as
mass entertainment, particularly in the early days of the empire. Nero*

reputedly enlarged the Circus Maximus to seat 200,0000 chariot-racing spectators. Followers were divided into "Blues" and "Greens", after the colours worn by the drivers, a fan rivalry which would eventually permeate the empire and even lead to serious civil disturbances.

I have been spending all the last few days amongst my notes and papers in most welcome peace. How could I – in the city? The Races were on, a type of spectacle which has never had the slightest attraction for me. I can find nothing new or different in them: once seen is enough, so it surprises me all the more that so many thousands of adult men should have such a childish passion for watching galloping horses and drivers standing in chariots, over and over again. If they were attracted by the speed of the horses or the drivers' skill one could account for it, but in fact it is the racing-colours they really support and care about, and if the colours were to be exchanged in mid-course during a race, they would transfer their favour and enthusiasm and rapidly desert the famous drivers and horses whose names they shout as they recognize them from afar. Such is the popularity and importance of a worthless shirt – I don't mean with the crowd, which is worth less than the shirt, but with certain serious individuals. When I think how this futile, tedious, monotonous business can keep them sitting endlessly in their seats, I take pleasure in the fact that their pleasure is not mine. And I have been very glad to fill my idle hours with literary work during these days which others have wasted in the idlest of occupations.

THE LIFE OF A ROMAN GENTLEMAN, AD 100

Pliny the Younger

I do not think I have ever spent a more delightful time than during my recent visit to Spurinna's house; indeed I enjoyed myself so much that if it is my fortune to grow old, there is no one whom I should prefer to take as my model in old age, as there is nothing more methodical than that time of life. Personally I like to see men map out their lives with the regularity of the fixed courses of the stars, and especially old men. For while one is young a little disorder and rush – so to speak – is not unbecoming; but for old folks, whose days of exertion are past, and in whom personal ambition is disgraceful, a placid and well-ordered life is highly suitable. That is the principle upon which Spurinna acts most religiously; even trifles, or what would be trifles were they not of daily occurrence, he goes through in fixed order, and, as it were, orbit.

In the morning he keeps his couch; at the second hour he calls for his shoes and walks three miles, exercising mind as well as body. If he has friends with him, the time is passed in conversation on the noblest of themes, otherwise a book is read aloud, and sometimes this is done even when his friends are present, but never in such a way as to bore them. Then he sits down, and there is more talk for preference; afterward he enters his carriage, taking with him either his wife – who is a pattern lady – or one of his friends, a distinction I recently enjoyed. How delightful, how charming that privacy is! What glimpses of old times one gets! What noble deeds and noble men he tells you of! What lessons you drink in! Yet at the same time it is his wont to so blend his learning with modesty, that he never seems to be playing the schoolmaster.

After riding seven miles he walks another mile, then resumes his seat, or betakes himself to his room and his pen; for he composes, both in Latin and Greek, the most scholarly lyrics. They have a wonderful grace, wonderful sweetness and wonderful humour, and the chastity of the writer enhances its charm. When he is told that the bathing hour has come – which is the ninth hour in winter and the eighth in summer – he takes a walk naked in the sun, if there is no wind. Then he plays at ball for a long spell, throwing himself heartily into the game, for it is by means of this kind of active exercise that he battles with old age.

After his bath he lies down and waits a little while ere taking food, listening in the meantime to the reading of some light and pleasant book. All this time his friends are at perfect liberty to imitate his example or do anything else they prefer. Then dinner is served, the table being as bright as it is modest, and the silver plain and old-fashioned: he has also some Corinthian vases in use, for which he has a taste but not a mania. The dinner is often relieved by actors of comedy, so that the pleasures of the table may have a seasoning of letters. Even in the summer the meal lasts well into the night, but no one finds it long, for it has kept up with such good humour and charm. The consequence is that, though he has passed his seventy-seventh year, his hearing and eyesight are as good as ever, his body is still active and alert, and the only symptom of his age is his wisdom.

This is the sort of life that I [Pliny] have vowed and determined to forestall, and I shall enter upon it with zest, as soon as my age justifies me in beating a retreat.

PETTY CRIMES, ROMAN EGYPT, C. AD 100

Various

Aurelius Nilus

To Flavius Thennyras, logistes of the Oxyrhynchite district, from Aurelius Nilus, son of Didymus, of the illustrious and most illustrious city of Oxyrhynchos, an egg seller by trade. I hereby agree on the august, divine oath by our lord the Emperor and the Cæsars to offer my eggs in the market place publicly for sale, and to supply to the said city, every day without intermission; and I acknowledge that it shall be unlawful for me in the future to sell secretly or in my house. If I am detected in so doing, I shall be liable to penalty.

Syrus

I married a woman of my own tribe . . . a free-born woman, of free parents, and have children by her. Now Tabes, daughter of Ammonios and her husband Laloi, and Psenesis and Straton their sons, have committed an act that disgraces all the chiefs of the town, and shows their recklessness; they carried off my wife and children to their own house, calling them their slaves, although they were free, and my wife has brothers living who are free. When I remonstrated, they seized me and beat me shamefully.

Tarmouthis

On the fourth of this month, Taorsenouphis, wife of Ammonios Phimon, an elder of the village of Bacchias although she had no occasion against me, came to my house, and made herself most unpleasant to me. Besides tearing my tunic and cloak, she carried off 16 drachmæ that I had put by, the price of vegetables I had sold. And on the fifth her husband, Ammonios Phimon, came to my house, pretending he was looking for my husband, and took my lamp and went up into the house. And he went off with a pair of silver armlets, weighing forty drachmæ, while my husband was away from home.

PILFERING WATER, ROME, c. AD 100

Frontinus

A former governor of Britain, Frontinus was appointed commissioner of water in Rome in AD 97. The post was not a sinecure; the population of the capital had reached a million and the supply of water (much of which came via towering aqueducts) was acute. More so, as Frontinus discovered, because it was being illegally syphoned off.

The New Anio is drawn from the river in the district of Sinbrinum, at about the forty-second milestone along the Via Sublacensis. On either side of the river at this point are fields of rich soil which make the banks less firm, so that the water in the aqueduct is discoloured and muddy even without the damage done by storms. So a little way along from the inlet a cleansing basin was built where the water could settle and be purified between the river and the conduit. Even so, in the event of rain, the water reaches the city in a muddy state. The length of the New Anio is about 47 miles, of which over 39 are underground and more than 7 carried on structures above the ground. In the upper reaches a distance of about two miles in various sections is carried on low structures or arches. Nearer the city, from the seventh Roman mile-stone, is half a mile on substructures and five miles on arches. These arches are very high, rising in certain places to a height of 109 feet.

. . . All the aqueducts reach the city at different levels. So some serve the higher districts and some cannot reach loftier ground. For the hills of Rome have gradually increased in height because of the rubble from frequent fires. There are five aqueducts high enough at entrance to reach all the city, but they supply water at different pressures . . .

Anyone who wants to tap water for private consumption must send in an application and take it, duly signed by the Emperor, to the Commissioner. The latter must take immediate action on Caesar's grant, and enrol one of the Imperial freedmen to help him in the business . . . The right to water once granted cannot be inherited or bought, and does not go with the property, though long ago a privilege was extended to the public baths that their right should last in perpetuity . . . When grants lapse, notice is given and record made in the ledgers, which are consulted so that future applicants can be given vacant supplies. The previous custom was to cut off these lapsed supplies at once, to make some profit by a temporary sale to the landowners or even to outsiders. Our Emperor felt that property should not suddenly be left without water, and that it would be fairer to give thirty days' notice for other arrangements to be made by the interested party . . .

Now that I have explained the situation with regard to private supply, it will be pertinent to give some examples of the ways in which men have broken these very sound arrangements and have been caught red-handed. In some reservoirs I have found larger valves in position than had been granted, and some have not even had the official stamp on them. When a stamped valve exceeds the legal dimensions, then the private advantage of the controller who stamped it is uncovered. When a valve is not even stamped, then both parties are clearly liable, chiefly the purchaser, but also the controller. Sometimes stamped valves of the correct dimensions open into pipes of a larger cross-section. The result is that the water is not kept in for the legal distance, but forced through a short, narrow pipe and easily fills the larger one which is joined to it. So care must be taken that, when a valve is stamped, the pipes connected to it should be stamped as of the correct length ordered by Senatorial decree. For then and only then will the controller be fully liable when he knows that only stamped pipes must be positioned.

When valves are sited, good care must be taken to see that they are placed in a horizontal line, not one above the other. A lower inlet gets a greater pressure of water, the upper one less, because the supply of water is taken by the lower. In some pipes no valves are positioned at all. These are called "free" pipes, and are opened and closed to suit the watermen.

Another of the watermen's intolerable practices is to make a new outlet from the cistern when a water-grant is transferred to a new owner, leaving the old one for themselves to get water from for sale. I would say that it was one of the Commissioner's chief duties to put a stop to this. For it affects not only the proper protection of the supply, but also the upkeep of the reservoir which would be ruined if needlessly filled with outlets.

Another financial scheme of the watermen, which they call "puncturing", must also be abolished. There are long separate stretches all over the city through which the pipes pass hidden under the pavement. I found out that these pipes were being tapped everywhere by the "puncturers", from which water was supplied by private pipe to all the business premises in the area, with the result that only a meagre amount reached the public utilities. I can estimate the volume of water stolen in this way from the amount of lead piping which was removed when these branch pipes were dug up.

SUMMER IN TUSCANY, C. AD 104

Pliny the Younger

A letter to Domitius Apollinaris.

I am touched by your kind concern when you try to dissuade me from my intention of staying in Tuscany in summer. You think the place is unhealthy, but while it is perfectly true that the Tuscan strip of sea-coast is relaxing and dangerous to the health, my property is some distance away from the sea, and is in fact at the very foot of the Apennines, which are considered the healthiest of mountains. So to rid you of all your fears on my account, let me tell you about the climate, the countryside, and the lovely situation of my house, which will be a pleasure alike for me to tell and you to hear.

The climate in winter is cold and frosty, and so quite impossible for myrtles and olives and any other trees which will only flourish in a continuous mild temperature, but the laurel can grow and does very well; it is sometimes killed off by the cold, but not oftener than in the neighbourhood of Rome. The summer is wonderfully temperate, for there is always some movement of the air, more often a breeze than a real wind. Hence the number of elderly people living there – you can see the grandfathers and great-grandfathers of people who have reached their own manhood, and hear old stories and tales of the past, so that a visit here is like a return to another age.

The countryside is very beautiful. Picture to yourself a vast amphitheatre such as could only be a work of nature; the great spreading plain is ringed round by mountains, their summits crowned by ancient woods of tall trees, where there is a good deal of mixed hunting to be had. Down the mountain slopes are timber woods interspersed with small hills of soil so rich that there is scarcely a rocky outcrop to be found; these hills are fully as fertile as the level plain and yield quite as rich a harvest, though it ripens rather later in the season. Below them the vineyards spreading down every slope weave their uniform pattern far and wide, their lower limit bordered by a belt of shrubs. Then come the meadows and cornfields, where the land can be broken up only by heavy oxen and the strongest ploughs, for the soil is so stiff that it is thrown up in great clods at the first ploughing and is not thoroughly broken until it has been gone over nine times. The meadows are bright with flowers, covered with trefoil and other delicate plants which always seem soft and fresh, for everything is fed by streams which never run dry; though the ground is not marshy where the water collects, because of its downward slope, so that any surplus water it cannot absorb is drained off into the river Tiber flowing through the fields. The river is navigable, so that all produce is conveyed to Rome by boat, but only in winter and spring – in summer its level falls and its dry bed has to give up its claim to the title of a great river until the following autumn. It is a great pleasure to look down on the countryside from the mountain, for the view seems to be a painted scene of unusual beauty rather than a real landscape, and the harmony to be found in this variety refreshes the eye wherever it turns.

My house is on the lower slopes of a hill but commands as good a view as if it were higher up, for the ground rises so gradually that the slope is imperceptible, and you find yourself at the top without noticing the climb. Behind it is the Apennine range, though some way off, so that even on a still and cloudless day there is a breeze from the mountains, but one which has had its force broken by the distance so that it is never cutting nor boisterous. It faces mainly south, and so from midday onwards in summer (a little earlier in winter) it seems to invite the sun into the colonnade. This is broad, and long in proportion, with several rooms opening out of it as well as the old-fashioned type of entrance hall.

In front of the colonnade is a terrace laid out with box hedges clipped into different shapes, from which a bank slopes down, also with figures of animals cut out of box facing each other on either side. On the level below there waves – or I might have said ripples – a bed of acanthus. All round is a path hedged by bushes which are trained and cut into different shapes, and then a drive, oval like a racecourse, inside which are various box figures and clipped dwarf shrubs. The whole garden is enclosed by a dry-stone wall which is hidden from sight by a box hedge planted in tiers; outside is a meadow, as well worth seeing for its natural beauty as the formal garden I have described; then fields and many more meadows and woods.

From the end of the colonnade projects a dining-room: through its folding doors it looks on to the end of the terrace, the adjacent meadow, and the stretch of open country beyond, while from its windows on one side can be seen part of the terrace and the projecting wing of the house, on the other the tree-tops in the enclosure of the adjoining riding-ground. Almost opposite the middle of the colonnade is a suite of rooms set slightly back and round a small court shaded by four plane trees. In the centre a fountain plays in a marble basin, watering the plane trees round it and the ground beneath them with its light spray. In this suite is a bedroom which no daylight, voice, nor sound can penetrate, and next to it an informal dining-room where I entertain my personal friends; it looks on to the small courtyard, the colonnade, and the view from the colonnade. There is also another room, green and shady from the nearest plane tree, which has walls decorated with marble up to the ceiling and a fresco (which is no less attractive) of birds perched on the branches of trees. Here is a small fountain with a bowl surrounded by tiny jets which together make a lovely murmuring sound. At the corner of the colonnade is a large bedroom facing the dining-room; some windows look out on to the terrace, others on to the meadow, while just below the windows in front is an ornamental pool, a pleasure both to see and to hear, with its water falling from a height and foaming white when it strikes the marble. This room is very warm in winter when it is bathed in sunshine, and on a cloudy day hot steam from the adjacent furnace-room serves instead. Then you pass through a large and cheerful dressing-room, belonging to the bath, to the cooling-room, which contains a good-sized shady swimming-bath. If you want more space to swim or warmer water, there is a pool in the courtyard and a well near it to tone you up with cold water when you have had enough of the warm. Next to the cooling-room is a temperate one which enjoys the sun's kindly warmth, though not as much as the hot room which is built out in a bay. This contains three plunging-baths, two full in the sun and one in the shade, though still in the light. Over the dressing-room is built the ball court, and this is large enough for several sets of players to take different kinds of exercise. Not far from the bath is a staircase leading to three rooms and then to a covered arcade. One room looks on to the small court with the four plane trees, another on to the meadow, and the third faces the vineyard and has an uninterrupted view across the sky. The head of the arcade is divided off as a room, from which can be seen the riding-ground, the vineyard, and the mountains. Next to it is another room which has plenty of sun, especially in winter, and then comes a suite which connects the riding-ground with the house.

That is the appearance and lay-out of the front of the house. Down the side is a covered arcade for summer use which is built on higher ground and seems not to look down on but be actually touching the vineyard below; half-way along is a dining-room which receives the fresh breezes blowing down the Apennine valleys. Its broad windows at the back look on to the vineyard, and so do its folding doors, but through the arcade between, and along the side where there are no windows, there is a private staircase which is used for serving at dinner parties. At the far end is a bedroom with a view of the arcade as pleasant as that of the vineyard. Underneath runs a semi-underground arcade which never loses its icy temperature in summer and is airy enough not to need to admit the outside air. Next to both these arcades begins an open one where the dining-room ends, which is cool before noon but hot during the later part of the day. It leads to two suites, one of four and the other of three rooms, which are alternately sunny or shady as the sun moves round.

The design and beauty of the buildings are greatly surpassed by the riding-ground. The centre is quite open so that the whole extent of the course can be seen as one enters. It is planted round with ivy-clad plane trees, green with their own leaves above, and below with the ivy which climbs over trunk and branch and links tree to tree as it spreads across them. Box shrubs grow between the plane trees, and outside there is a ring of laurel bushes which add their shade to that of the planes. Here the straight part of the course ends, curves round in a semicircle, and changes its appearance, becoming darker and more densely shaded by the cypress trees planted round to shelter it, whereas the inner circuits – for there are several – are in open sunshine; roses grow there and the cool shadow alternates with the pleasant warmth of the sun. At the end of the winding alleys of the rounded end of the course you return to the straight path, or rather paths, for there are several separated by intervening box hedges. Between the grass lawns here there are box shrubs clipped into innumerable shapes, some being letters which spell the gardener's name or his master's; small obelisks of box alternate with fruit trees, and then suddenly in the midst of this ornamental scene is what looks like a piece of rural country planted there. The open space in the middle is set off by low plane trees planted on each side; farther off are acanthuses with their flexible glossy leaves, then more box figures and names.

At the upper end of the course is a curved dining-seat of white marble, shaded by a vine trained over four slender pillars of Carystian marble. Water gushes out through pipes from under the seat as if pressed out by the weight of people sitting there, is caught in a stone cistern and then held in a polished marble basin which is regulated by a hidden device so as to remain full without overflowing. The preliminaries and main dishes for dinner are placed on the edge of the basin, while the lighter ones float about in vessels shaped like birds or little boats. A fountain opposite plays and catches its water, throwing it high into the air so that it falls back into the basin, where it is played again at once through a jet connected with the inlet. Facing the seat is a bedroom which contributes as much beauty to the scene as it gains from its position. It is built of shining white marble, extended by folding doors which open straight out among the trees; its upper and lower windows all look out into the greenery above and below. A small alcove which is part of the room but separated from it contains a bed, and although it has windows in all its walls, the light inside is dimmed by the dense shade of a flourishing vine which climbs over the whole building up to the roof. There you can lie and imagine you are in a wood, but without the risk of rain. Here too a fountain rises and disappears underground, while here and there are marble chairs which anyone tired with walking appreciates as much as the building itself. By every chair is a tiny fountain, and throughout the riding-ground can be heard the sound of the streams directed into it, the flow of which can be controlled by hand to water one part of the garden or another or sometimes the whole at once.

I should have been trying long ago not to say too much, had I not suggested that this letter should take you into every corner of the place. I don't imagine you will find it tiresome to read about a spot which could hardly tire you on a visit, especially as you have more opportunities if you want an occasional rest, and can take a seat, so to speak, by putting down the letter. Besides, I have been indulging the love I have for all the places I have largely laid out myself or where I have perfected an earlier design. In short (for why should I not state my opinion, right or wrong?) I think a writer's first duty is to read his title, to keep on asking himself what he set out to say, and to realize that he will not say too much if he sticks to his theme, though he certainly will if he brings in extraneous matter. You know the number of lines Homer and Virgil devote to their descriptions of the arms of Achilles and Aeneas: yet neither passage seems long because both poets are carrying out their original intention. You see too how Aratus traces and tabulates the smallest stars, but because this is his main subject and not a digression his work does not lack proportion. It is the same with me, if I may "compare small things with great". I am trying to set my entire house before your eyes, so, if I introduce nothing irrelevant, it is the house I describe which is extensive, not the letter describing it.

But to return to my starting-point – for I shall justly be censured under my own law if I pursue this digression further – these are my reasons for preferring my home in Tuscany to one in Tusculum, Tibur, or Praeneste.[A] And I can add another reason: I can enjoy a profounder peace there, more comfort, and fewer cares; I need never wear a formal toga and there are no neighbours to disturb me; everywhere there is peace and quiet, which adds as much to the healthiness of the place as the clear sky and pure air. There I enjoy the best of health, both mental and physical, for I keep my mind in training with work and my body with hunting. My servants too are healthier here than anywhere else; up to the present I have not lost a single one of those I brought here with me – may I be forgiven for saying so, and may the gods continue to make this the pride of the place and a joy to me.

"ONE PROLONGS HIS EYEBROWS WITH SOME DAMP SOOT STAINING THE EDGE OF A NEEDLE": HOMOSEXUALS IN ROME, c. AD 105

Juvenal

The poet Juvenal (c. AD 55-c. 140) was not politically correct. His Second Satire, *in which he satirizes homosexuals, is below.*

I would fain flee to Sarmatia and the frozen Sea when people who ape the Curii[1] and live like Bacchanals dare talk about morals. In the first place, they are unlearned persons, though you may find their houses crammed with plaster casts of Chrysippus;[2] for their greatest hero is the man who has brought a likeness of Aristotle or Pittacus,[3] or bids his shelves preserve an original portrait of Cleanthes.[4] Men's faces are not to be

---

[A] In Latium (Frascati, Tivoli, and Palestrina). These are popular places for a country seat; Pliny does not own property there himself.

trusted; does not every street abound in gloomy-visaged debauchees? And do you rebuke foul practices, when you are yourself the most notorious delving-ground among Socratic reprobates? A hairy body, and arms stiff with bristles, give promise of a manly soul: but sleek are your buttocks when the grinning doctor cuts into the swollen piles. Men of your kidney talk little; they glory in taciturnity, and cut their hair shorter than their eyebrows. Peribomius[5] himself is more open and more honest; his face, his walk, betray his distemper, and I charge Destiny with his failings. Such men excite your pity by their frankness; the very fury of their passions wins them pardon. Far worse are those who denounce evil ways in the language of a Hercules; and after discoursing upon virtue, prepare to practise vice. "Am I to respect you, Sextus," quoth the ill-famed Varillus, "when you do as I do? How am I worse than yourself?" Let the straight-legged man laugh at the club-footed, the white man at the blackamoor: but who could endure the Gracchi railing at sedition? Who will not confound heaven with earth, and sea with sky, if Verres denounce thieves, or Milo[6] cut-throats? If Clodius condemn adulterers, or Catiline upbraid Cethegus;[7] or if Sulla's three disciples[8] inveigh against proscriptions? Such a man was that adulterer[9] who, after lately defiling himself by a union of the tragic style, revived the stern laws that were to be a terror to all men – ay, even to Mars and Venus – at the moment when Julia was relieving her fertile womb and giving birth to abortions that displayed the similitude of her uncle. Is it not then right and proper that the very worst of sinners should despise your pretended Scauri,[10] and bite back when bitten?

Laronia could not contain herself when one of these sourfaced worthies cried out, "What of you, Julian Law?[11] What, gone to sleep?" To which she answered smilingly, "O happy times to have you for a censor of our morals! Once more may Rome regain her modesty; a third Cato has come down to us from the skies! But tell me, where did you buy that balsam juice that exhales from your hairy neck? Don't be ashamed to point out to me the shopman! If laws and statutes are to be raked up, you should cite first of all the Scantinian;[12] enquire first into the things that are done by men; men do more wicked things than we do, but they are protected by their numbers, and the tight-locked shields of their phalanx. Male effeminates agree won-drously well among themselves; never in our sex will you find such loathsome examples of evil . . .

"Do we women ever plead in the courts? Are we learned in the Law? Do your court-houses ever ring with our bawling? Some few of us are wrestlers; some of us eat meat-rations: you men spin wool and bring back your tale of work in full baskets when it is done; you twirl round the spindle big with fine thread more deftly than Penelope, more delicately than Arachne,[13] doing work such as an unkempt drab squatting on a log would do. Everybody knows why Hister left all his property to his freed-man, why in his life-time he gave so many presents to his young wife; the woman who sleeps third in a big bed will want for nothing. So when you take a husband, keep your mouth shut; precious stones[14] will be the reward of a well-kept secret. After this, what condemnation can be pronounced on us women? Our censor absolves the raven and passes judgment on the pigeon!"

While Laronia was uttering these plain truths, the would-be Stoics made off in confusion; for what word of untruth had she spoken? Yet what will not other men do when you, Creticus, dress yourself in garments of gauze, and while everyone is marvelling at your attire, launch out against the Proculae and the Pollittae? Fabulla is an adulteress; condemn Carfinia of the same crime if you please; but however guilty, they would never wear such a gown as yours. "O but," you say, "these July days are so sweltering!" Then why not plead without clothes? Such madness would be less disgraceful. A pretty garb yours in which to propose or expound laws to our countrymen flushed with victory, and with their wounds yet unhealed; and to those mountain rustics who had laid down their ploughs to listen to you! What would you not exclaim if you saw a judge dressed like that? Would a robe of gauze sit becomingly on a witness? You, Creticus, you, the keen, unbending champion of human liberty, to be clothed in a transparency! This plague has come upon us by infection, and it will spread still further, just as in the fields the scab of one sheep, or the mange of one pig, destroys an entire herd; just as one bunch of grapes takes on its sickly colour from the aspect of its neighbour.

Some day you will venture on something more shameful than this dress; no one reaches the depths of turpitude all at once. By degrees you will be welcomed by those who in their homes put long fillets round their brows, swathe themselves with necklaces, and propitiate the Bona Dea with the stomach of a porker and a huge bowl of wine, though by an evil usage the Goddess warns off all women from entering the door; none but males may approach her altar.[15] "Away with you! profane women" is the cry; "no booming horn, no she-minstrels here!" Such were the secret torchlight orgies with which the Baptae[16] wearied the Cecropian[17] Cotytto. One prolongs his eyebrows with some damp soot staining the edge of a needle, and lifts up his blinking eyes to be painted; another drinks out of an obscenely shaped glass, and ties up his long locks in a gilded net; he is clothed in blue checks, or smooth-faced green; the attendant swears by Juno like his master. Another holds in his hand a mirror like that carried by the effeminate Otho: a trophy of the Auruncan Actor,[18] in which he gazed at his own image in full armour when he was just ready to give the order to advance – a thing notable and novel in the annals of our time, a mirror among the kit of Civil War! It needed, in truth, a mighty general to slay Galba, and keep his own skin sleek; it needed a citizen of highest courage to ape the splendours of the Palace on the field of Bebriacum,[19] and plaster his face with dough! Never did the quiver-bearing Samiramis[20] the like in her Assyrian realm, nor the despairing Cleopatra on board her ship at Actium. No decency of language is there here: no regard for the manners of the table. You will hear all the foul talk and squeaking tones of Cybele; a grey-haired frenzied old man presides over the rites; he is a rare and notable master of mighty gluttony, and should be hired to teach it. But why wait any longer when it were time in Phrygian fashion to lop off the superfluous flesh?

Gracchus has presented to a cornet player – or perhaps it was a player on the straight horn – a dowry of 400,000 sesterces. The

17 *i.e.* Athenian, Cecrops being the first monarch of Athens.
18 The words *Actoris Aurunci spolium* are a quotation from Virg. *Aen.* xii 94.
19 The engagement in which Otho was defeated by Vitellius.
20 Mythical founder of the Assyrian empire with her spouse Ninus.
21 Gracchus was one of the Salii, priests of Mars.
22 *i.e.* the Campus Martius.
23 The Luperci were a priesthood who, on certain appointed days, dressed in goatskin and struck women to improve fertility.
24 The *podium* was a balustrade set all round the amphitheatre, from which VIPs witnessed the performance.
25 The battle in which 300 Fabii were killed.
26 Ireland.

A LOVE LETTER, C. AD 108

Pliny the Younger

Pliny writes to his third wife, Calpurnia. He was approximately 47 at the time.

You cannot believe how much I miss you. I love you so much, and we are not used to separations. So I stay awake most of the night thinking of you, and by day I find my feet carrying me (a true word, carrying) to your room at the times I usually visited you; then finding it empty I depart, as sick and sorrowful as a lover locked out. The only time I am free from this misery is when I am in court and wearing myself out with my friends' lawsuits. You can judge then what a life I am leading, when I find my rest in work and distraction in troubles and anxiety.

SHOULD I FOUND A FIRE-BRIGADE?, BITHYNIA, AD 112

Pliny the Younger

In AD 111 Pliny the Younger was sent as Imperial representative to the province of Bithynia and Pontus, on the south coast of the Black Sea. The extracts below are from Pliny's correspondence with the Emperor Trajan.

While I was making a progress in a different part of the province, a prodigious fire broke out at Nicomedia, which not only consumed several private houses, but also two public buildings: the old men's hospice and the Temple of Isis, though they stood on opposite sides of the street. The occasion of its spreading thus far was partly owing to the violence of the wind, and partly to the indolence of the people, who, I am well assured, stood fixed and idle spectators of this terrible calamity. The truth is, the city was not provided with engines, buckets, or any one single instrument proper to extinguish fires; these I have now, however, given directions to have prepared. Pray determine, Sir, whether it may not be advisable to institute a company of firemen, consisting of not more than 150 members. I will take care that none but those whose calling it is shall be admitted into it, and that the privileges granted them shall not be extended to any other purpose. As this incorporated body will consist of so small a number, it will be easy enough to keep them under proper regulation.

The Emperor Trajan to Pliny, in reply to the above.
You are of opinion that it would be proper to constitute a company of firemen in Nicomedia, agreeably to what has been practised in other cities. But it is to be remembered that these sort of societies have greatly disturbed the peace of that province in general, and of those cities in particular. Whatever name we give them, and for whatever purposes they may be founded, those who are bound together for a purpose will not fail to form themselves into political associations before long. It will therefore be safer to provide such machines as are of service for extinguishing fires, enjoining the owners of house property to employ these themselves, and if it should be necessary, to call in the help of the populace.

THE PERSECUTION OF THE CHRISTIANS, BITHYNIA, AD 112

Pliny the Younger

A more irretractile problem than fire-brigades awaited Pliny in Bithynia. This was the quiet expansion of the Christian religion. Again he seeks his master's opinion.

Pliny to the Emperor Trajan.
It is a rule, Sir, which I inviolably observe, to refer myself to you in all my doubts; for who is more capable of removing my scruples, or of guiding my uncertainty? Having never been

present at any trials of the Christians, I am unacquainted as to the method and limits to be observed in examining and punishing them. Whether, therefore, any difference is to be made with respect to age, or no distinction is to be observed between the young and the adult; whether repentance admits to a pardon; or if a man has been once a Christian, it avails him nothing to recant; whether the mere profession of Christianity, albeit without any criminal act, or only the crimes associated therewith are punishable; in all these points I am greatly doubtful.

In the meanwhile the method I have observed towards those who have been denounced to me as Christians, is this: I interrogated them whether they were Christians; if they confessed I repeated the question twice again, adding a threat of capital punishment; if they still persevered, I ordered them to be executed. For I was persuaded, that whatever the nature of their creed, a contumacious and inflexible obstinacy certainly deserved chastisement. There were others also brought before me possessed with the same infatuation: but being citizens of Rome, I directed them to be carried thither.

These accusations, from the mere fact that the matter was being investigated, began to spread, and several forms of the mischief came to light. A placard was posted up without any signature, accusing a number of people by name. Those who denied that they were Christians, or had ever been so, who repeated after me an invocation to the gods, and offered religious rites with wine and frankincense to your statue (which I had ordered to be brought for the purpose, together with those of the gods), and finally cursed the name of Christ (none of which, it is said, those who are really Christians can be forced into performing), I thought proper to discharge. Others who were named by the informer at first confessed themselves Christians, and then denied it; true, they had been of that persuasion formerly, but had now quitted it (some three years, others many years, and a few as much as twenty-five years ago). They all worshipped your statue, and the images of the gods, and cursed the name of Christ.

They affirmed, however, that the whole of their guilt or their error was, that they met on a certain fixed day before it was light and sang an antiphonal chant to Christ, as to a god, binding themselves by a solemn oath, not to any wicked deeds, but never to commit any fraud, theft or adultery, never to falsify their word, nor deny a trust when they should be called upon to deliver it up; after which it was their custom to separate, and then reassemble to partake of food – food of an ordinary innocent kind.[1] Even this practice, however, they had abandoned after the publication of my edict, by which, according to your orders, I had forbidden political associations. I judged it so much the more necessary to extract the real truth, with the assistance of torture, from two female slaves, called deaconesses. But I could discover nothing but depraved and excessive superstition.

I therefore thought it proper to adjourn all further proceedings in this affair, in order to consult with you. For the matter is well worth referring to you, especially considering the numbers endangered: persons of all ranks and ages, and of both sexes, are and will be involved in the prosecution. For this contagious superstition is not confined to the cities only, but has spread through the villages and the countryside. Nevertheless it seems still possible to check and cure it. The temples, at least, which were once almost deserted, begin now to be frequented, and the sacred solemnities, after a long intermission, are again revived; while there is a general demand for sacrificial animals which for some time past have met with but few purchasers. From hence it is easy to imagine, what numbers might be reclaimed from this error if the door is left open to repentance.

The Emperor Trajan to Pliny, in reply to the above.
The method you have pursued, my dear Pliny, in the proceedings against those who were denounced to you as Christians is extremely proper. It is not possible to lay down any general rule to be applied in all cases of this nature. But no search is to be made for these people. When they are denounced, and found guilty, they must be punished, with the restriction, however, that where the party denies himself to be a Christian, and shall

---

[1] It was a common accusation, as against the Jews in the Middle Ages, that they were in the habit of eating children.

give proof that he is not, by invoking our gods, let him (notwith-standing any former suspicion) be pardoned upon his repentance. Informations without the accuser's name subscribed must not be admitted in evidence against anyone, as it is introducing a very dangerous precedent, and out of accord with the spirit of our times.

ON THE CITY OF ROME, c. AD 118

Juvenal

From Juvenal's Satire III. *The speaker is Umbriscus, who has decided to quit hot, overcrowded, venal, class-ridden Rome for the country delights of Cumae.*

"But why, my friend, should I at Rome remain?
I cannot teach my stubborn lips to feign;
Nor, when I hear a great man's verses, smile
And beg a copy, if I think them vile.
I'm no astrologer, I have no skill
To read the stars; I neither can nor will
Promise a father's death; I never pried
In toads for poison, nor in aught beside.
Others may aid the adulterer's vile design
And bear the insidious gift, the melting line.
Straightforwardly with all I ever deal:
I'm honest, and I'll help no man to steal.
In no proconsul's train I therefore quit,
A palsied limb for every use unfit.
Who now finds favour? He whose conscious breast
Swells with dark deeds always to be suppressed.
He pays, he owes, thee nothing (strictly just!)
Who gives an honest secret to thy trust;
The man whom Verres loves must have the power
Verres to prosecute from hour to hour.
But let not all the sand that Tagus pours
In Ocean's lap, not all his glittering stores,
Be deemed a bribe sufficient to requite
The loss of peace by day, of sleep by night.
Oh, take not, take not, what thy soul rejects,
Nor sell the faith which he who buys suspects.
"That nation by the 'great' admired, caressed

(But hated, shunned by *me* above the rest),
No longer now restrained by wounded pride,
I haste to show. Nor thou my warmth deride:
I cannot rule my spleen and calmly see
A Grecian capital in Italy.
Grecian? Oh, no! with this vast sewer compared,
The dregs of Greece are scarcely worth regard.
Long since, the stream that wanton Syria laves[1]
Has disembogued its filth in Tiber's waves:
Its lingo, manners, arts, and all the scum
Of Antioch's streets, its minstrel, harp, and drum.
Hie to the Circus, ye who pant to prove
A barbarous mistress, an outlandish love!
Hie to the Circus! there in crowds they stand,
Tires on their head and timbrels in their hand.
Your country clown the *trechedipna* wears,
And round his *ceromatic* neck he bears
A *niceterian*[2] prize; while every land,
Sicyon and Amydon, Alaband,
Tralles and Samos, and a thousand more
Thrive on his indolence and daily pour
Their starving myriads forth. Hither they come
And batten on the genial soil of Rome,
Minions, then lords, of every princely dome:
A flattering, cringing, treacherous, artful race
Of torrent tongue and never-blushing face;
A Protean tribe, one knows not what to call,
That shifts to every form and shines in all:
Grammarian, painter, augur, rhetorician,
Rope-dancer, conjurer, fiddler, and physician –
All trades his own your hungry Greekling counts;
And bid him mount the sky, the sky he mounts!
Was't a Sarmatian, Moor, or Thracian flew?[3]
No, 'twas a Greek, and an Athenian too!
    "Shall I not fly their purple pomp? Shall he
Sign, and recline at table, before me,
Who wafted was to Rome by those same winds
Which bring us damsons, figs, and tamarinds?
That on the Aventine I first drew air

And from the womb was nursed on Sabine fare
Avails me not: our birthright now is lost,
And all our privilege an empty boast.

   "For lo! where, versed in every soothing art,
The wily Greek assails his patron's heart;
Finds in each dull harangue an air, a grace,
And all Adonis in a Gorgon face;
Admires the voice that grates upon the ear
Like the shrill scream of amorous chanticleer;
Compares the scraggy neck and weedy girth
To Hercules's brawn, when from the earth
He raised Antaeus,[4] and his every vein
Swelled with the toil and more than mortal pain.
We too can cringe as low and praise as warm,
But flattery from the Greeks alone can charm.
See, they step forth and portray to the life
The naked nymph, the mistress, or the wife.
So well, you view the very woman there
And fancy all beneath the girdle bare.
In Greece, no more the favourites of the stage[5]
Boast an exclusive power to charm the age:
The happy art with them a nation shares,
Greece is a theatre where *all* are players.
If you, his patron, smile – he bursts with mirth;
You weep – he droops, the saddest soul on earth;
You call for fire – he courts the mantle's heat;
"'Tis warm,' you cry – and he dissolves in sweat.
We are not on a level, he and I,
He's bound to win, and here's the reason why:
Ready at every moment to change face,
He'll smile or frown as others set the pace,
And, throwing up his hands, to applaud he'll start,
Should but his friend get taken short or fart,
Or turn his golden winecup upside-down
And make a gurgling noise to amuse the clown.

   "Besides, no shame his furious lust restrains;
All ties he breaks, all sanctity profanes:
Wife, daughter, son and future son-in-law,
And when these fail – debauch the grandam hoar!

He'll notice every word, haunt every ear,
Your secrets learn, and thus be held in fear.
Turn to their schools. Yon grey professor see,
Smeared with the sanguine stains of perfidy.
That tutor most accursed his pupil sold,[6]
That Stoic sacrificed his friend for gold;
A true-born Grecian! littered on the coast[7]
When the Gorgonian hack[8] a pinion lost.
No place for any Roman here remains,
Where Diphilus, where Erymanthus reigns,
Miscreants who, faithful to their native art,
Admit no rival in a patron's heart.
For let them fasten on his easy ear,
And drop one hint, one secret slander there,
Sucked from their country's venom or their own,
That instant they possess the man alone;
While I am spurned, contemptuous, from the door,
My long, long service thought upon no more.
'Tis but a client lost; and that, I find,
Sits wondrous lightly on a patron's mind.
    "And (not to flatter our poor pride, my friend)
What merit with the great can we pretend?
Though; in our duty, we prevent the day
And, darkling, run our humble court to pay;
When the brisk praetor long before is gone,
And hastens with stern voice his lictors on,
Lest his colleagues o'erpass him in the street
And first the rich and childless matrons greet,
Alba and Modia, who impatient wait
And think the morning homage comes too late.
Here free-born youths wait the rich servant's call
And, if they walk beside him, yield the wall.
Wherefore? The slave, forsooth, can fling away
On one voluptuous night a colonel's pay;
But when Calvina, as you hurry by,
Inflames the fancy, check your roving eye,
And, frugal of your scanty means, forbear
To invite the harlot from her lofty chair.
Produce at Rome a witness: let him boast

The sanctity of Berecyntia's host,[9]
Of Numa, or of him whose zeal divine[10]
Snatched pale Minerva from her blazing shrine.
To search his rent-roll first the bench prepares,
His honesty employs their latest cares:
What table does he keep, what slaves maintain,
And what, they ask, and where, is his domain?
These weighty matters known, his faith they rate,
And square his probity to his estate.
The poor may swear by all the immortal Powers,
By the Great Gods of Samothrace[11] and ours:
'His oaths are false!' they cry, 'he scoffs at Heaven
And all its thunders; scoffs – and is forgiven!'

   "Add, that the wretch is still a theme of scorn
If the soiled cloak be patched, the gown o'erworn;
If, through the bursting shoe, the foot is seen
Or the rough stitch tell where the rent has been.
O Poverty, thy thousand ills combined
Sink not so deep into the generous mind
As the contempt and laughter of mankind.
'Up! Up! These cushioned stalls,' the marshal cries,
'Are for the Knights alone. For shame! arise.'
'For shame'? Aye, you say well: the pander's heir,
The spawn of hulks and stews, is seated there.
The auctioneer's spruce son, the trainer's boy,
The swordsman's offspring, clap their hands for joy:
Leading the loud applause that greets the play,
They're arbiters of taste in Rome today.
So Otho fixed it, whose preposterous pride
First dared to chase us from their Honours' side.[12]
In these cursed walls, where girls are wed for gain,
When do the poor a wealthy wife obtain?
When are they named in Wills? When called to share
The aediles council and assist the chair?
Long since should they have risen, thus slighted, spurned,
And left their home, but *not* to have returned.

   "Depressed by indigence, the good and wise
In every clime by painful efforts rise;
Here by more painful still, where scanty cheer,

Poor lodging, mean attendance, all is dear.
Off earthenware you scorn at Rome to eat;
But, called abruptly to the Marsian's seat,
From such well pleased you'ld take your simple food,
Nor blush to wear the cheap Venetian hood.

  "There's many a part of Italy, 'tis said,
Where none assume the toga but the dead.
There, when the toil forgone and annual play
Mark from the rest some high and solemn day,
To theatres of turf the rustics throng,
Charmed with the farce that charmed their sires so long;
And baby, of the pallid mask in dread,
Hides in his mother's breast his little head.
No modes of dress high birth distinguish there:
All ranks, all orders, the same habit wear,
And the dread aedile's dignity is known
(Oh, sacred badge!) by his white vest alone.
But here, beyond our means arrayed we go
In all the gay varieties of show;
And when our purse supplies the charge no more,
Borrow unblushing from our neighbour's store.
Such is the reigning vice; and so we flaunt,
Proud in distress and prodigal in want.
Briefly, my friend, here all are slaves to gold,
And words, and smiles, and everything, are sold.
What will you give for Cossus' nod? How high
The silent notice of Veiento buy?
'His Lordship's shaving.' 'Master's out just now
Off'ring his favourite's hair: you know – a vow.'
The house is full of cakes, for which you'll pay;
So 'Take your cash and keep your cake,' you'll say,
Angry that you must swell a servant's hoard
And bribe the slave for leave to bribe his lord.

  "Who fears the crash of houses in retreat
At simple Gabii, cool Praeneste's seat,
Volsinium's craggy heights embowered in wood,
Or Tibur sloping to sweet Anio's flood?
But half the city here by shores is stayed,
And feeble cramps that lend a treacherous aid;

For thus the bailiffs patch the riven wall,
Thus prop the mansion tottering to its fall,
Then bid the tenant court secure repose
While the pile nods to every blast that blows.
Oh, may I live where no such fears molest,
No midnight fires burst on my hour of rest!
Hark! Hark! Ucalegon begins to call
For water, and removes his little all
In frantic haste. Meantime, the flames aspire
And the third floor is wrapt in smoke and fire
While you unconscious doze. Up, ho! and know
The impetuous blaze, which spreads dismay below,
By swift degrees will reach the aerial cell
Where, crouching, underneath the roof you dwell,
Where only tiles protect you from the rain
And gentle doves a nesting-place obtain.
Codrus had but one bed and that too short
For Procula. His goods of every sort
Were else but few: six little pipkins graced
His cupboard head, a little jar was placed
On a snug shelf beneath, and near it lay
A Chiron of the same cheap marble – clay.
And was this all? Oh, no, he yet possessed
A few Greek books shrined in an ancient chest,
Where barbarous mice through many an inlet crept
And fed on heavenly verses while he slept.
Codrus, in fact, had nothing. It is true;
And yet poor Codrus lost that nothing too.
One final curse is added to complete
His woes; for cold and hungry through the street
The wretch must beg, and in the hour of need
Find none to lodge, to clothe him, or to feed.
  "But should the raging flames on grandeur prey
And low in dust Asturicus' palace lay,
The dishevelled matron sighs, the Senate mourns,
The pleaders cease, the judge his court adjourns.
All join to wail the city's hapless fate,
And rail at fire with more than common hate.
Lo, while it burns the obsequious courtiers haste

With rich materials to repair the waste.
One brings him marble; one, a splendid piece
By Euphranor or Polyclete[13] of Greece;
One, ornaments which graced of old the fane
Of Asia's gods; one, figured plate and plain;
One, cases, books, and busts the shelves to grace,
And piles of coin his specie to replace.
So much the childless Persicus swells his store
(Though deemed the richest of the rich before),
That all ascribe the flames to thirst of pelf
And swear he must have fired the house himself.

   "Oh, had you from the Circus power to fly,
In many a halcyon village[14] you might buy
Some elegant retreat for what will here
Scarce hire a gloomy garret through the year.
There shallow wells, by Nature formed, which need
No rope, no labouring arm, shall ever feed
Your garden, and provide an easy shower
To cheer the weakling plant, the opening flower.
There live, delighted with the rustic's lot,
And till with your own hands the little spot.
The little spot shall make you large amends,
And feed a host of vegetarian friends.
Forsooth, in any corner we can get,
To call one lizard ours is something yet.

   "Flushed with a mass of half-digested food,
Which clogs the stomach and inflames the blood,
What crowds, with watching wearied and o'erpressed,
Curse the slow hours and die for want of rest!
Nay, who can hope his languid lids to close
When lodging-houses banish all repose?
Sleep to the rich alone his visit pays:
There lies the root of all this dire disease.
The carts' loud rumbling through the narrow way,
The drovers' clamour at each casual stay,
From drowsy Drusus[15] would his slumber take
And keep the calves of Proteus[16] awake.
If business call, the obsequious crowds divide,
As o'er their heads the millionaire will ride

In a Liburnian car,[17] and read or write
Or (if the early hour to rest invite)
Curtain the window and enjoy the night.
He's first to reach the goal, while, by the throng
Elbowed and jostled, scarce we creep along.
Sedan-poles, tubs, beams in my ribs I feel;
I'm plastered o'er with mud from head to heel;
While huge feet trample on me as I go,
And soldiers plant their hobnails on my toe.

   "See, from the dole a vast tumultuous throng,
Each followed by his kitchen, pours along:[18]
Huge pans, which Corbulo[19] could scarce uprear,
With steady neck a puny slave must bear,
And, lest amid the way the flames expire,
Glide nimbly on, and, gliding, fan the fire;
Through the close press with sinuous efforts wind
And, piece by piece, leave his botched rags behind.
Look! groaning on, the unwieldy wagon spreads
Some cumbrous log, tremendous, o'er our heads.
Here comes a dray with pine-tree raised on high,
That threatens death to every passer-by.
Lord! should the axle crack that bears the weight
Of huge Ligurian stone, and pour the freight
On the pale crowd beneath, what would remain,
What joint, what bone, what atom of the slain?
The body with the soul would vanish quite,
Invisible as air to mortal sight.
Meanwhile, unconscious of the fellow's fate,
At home they heat the water, scour the plate,
Arrange the strigils, fill the cruse with oil,
And ply their several tasks with fruitless toil.
The master of the house, poor mangled ghost,
Sits pale and trembling on the Stygian coast,
Scared at the horrors of the unwonted scene,
At Charon's threatening voice and scowling mien;
Nor hopes a passage, thus abruptly hurled,
Without his farthing, to the nether world.

   "Pass we these different dangers and survey
What other evils threat our nightly way.

And first behold the mansion's towering size,
Where floors on floors to the top storey rise,
Whence heedless garreteers their potsherds throw,
And wound the unwary wretch that walks below:
Clattering, the storm descends from heights unknown,
Ploughs up the street, and dents the flinty stone.
'Tis madness, dire improvidence of ill,
To sup abroad before you sign your Will,
Since Fate in ambush lies and marks his prey
From every wakeful window in the way.
Pray, then; and count your humble prayer well sped
If only pots be emptied on your head.
    "The drunken bully, who has thrashed tonight
No victim, sleepless lies until daylight;
And, while the thirst of blood his bosom burns,
From side to side in restless anguish turns
Like Peleus' son[20] when, quelled by Hector's thrust,
His loved Patroclus bit the Phrygian dust.
There are who murder as an opiate take,
And only when no brawls await them wake;
Yet even these heroes, flushed with youth and wine,
All contest with the purple robe decline,
Securely give the lengthened train to pass,
The sun-bright flambeaus and the lamps of brass.
Me, whom the moon or candle's paler gleam,
Whose wick I husband to the last extreme,
Guides through the gloom, he braves devoid of fear.
The prelude to our doughty quarrel hear,
If that be deemed a quarrel, where, heaven knows,
He only gives and I receive the blows!
Across my path he strides and bids me 'Stand!'
I bow, obedient to the dread command:
What else remains when madness, rage, combine
With youth and strength superior far to mine?
'Whence come you, rogue?' he cries; 'Whose beans tonight
Have stuffed you thus? What cobbler clubbed his mite
For leeks and sheep's-head porridge? Dumb! quite dumb!
Speak, or be kicked: yet once again, your home?
Where shall I find you, at what beggar's stand,

What prayer-shop, whimpering with outstretched hand?'
Whether I strive some humble plea to frame,
Or steal in silence by, 'tis just the same:
I'm beaten first, then dragged in rage away,[21]
Bound over or else punished for the fray.
Mark here the boasted freedom of the poor:
Beaten and bruised, that goodness to adore
Which, at their humble prayer, suspends its ire
And sends them home with yet a tooth entire!
   "Nor this the worst; for when deep midnight reigns
And bolts secure your doors, and massy chains;
When noisy inns a transient silence keep
And harassed Nature woos the balm of sleep,
Then thieves and murderers ply their dreadful trade,
With stealthy steps your secret couch invade:
Roused from the treacherous calm, aghast you start,
And the cold steel is buried in your heart.
Hither from bogs and rocks and caves pursued
(The Pontine Marsh and Gallinarian wood),
The dark assassins flock as to their home,
And fill with dire alarm the streets of Rome,
Such countless multitudes our peace annoy,
That bolts and shackles every forge employ,
And cause so wide a waste, the country fears
A want of ore for mattocks, rakes, and shares.
Oh, happy were our sires, estranged from crimes,
And happy, happy were the good old times
Which saw, beneath their kings', their tribunes' reign,
One jail the nation's criminals contain.
   "Much could I add, more reasons could I cite,
If time were ours, to justify my flight.
But see, the impatient team is moving on,
The sun declining, and I must be gone:
Long since the driver murmured at my stay,
And jerked his whip to beckon me away.
Farewell, my friend; with this embrace we part:
Cherish my memory ever in your heart;
And when from crowds and business you repair
To breathe at your Aquinum freer air,

Fail not to draw me from my loved retreat
To Helvine Ceres[22] and Diana's seat.
For your bleak hills my Cumae I'll resign,
And (if you welcome interest such as mine)
Come in stout shoes to hear your angry rhymes
Directed at man's follies and his crimes."

Notes

1 The Orontes.

2 *Trechedipna*, a "run-to-dinner coat"; *ceromaticus*, from *ceroma*, an oil used by wrestlers: *niceterium*, a prize of victory – all used to ridicule the use of Greek forms.

3 i.e. was Daedalus a Sarmatian, etc.?

4 A giant of Libya, son of Poseidon and Gaea. He was invincible while in contact with the ground, but Hercules lifted him up and crushed him to death.

5 Juvenal mentions four of these Greek actors by name: Antiochus, Stratocles, Demetrius, and Haemus.

6 Publius Egnatius Celer, a Stoic, accused Barea Soranus who was convicted and put to death. See Tacitus, *Ann.* xvi. 23, 30–2, 33; *Hist.*. iv. 20 and 40.

7 Near Tarsus in Cilicia.

8 Pegasus, the winged horse of the fountain which sprang from the blood of Medusa.

9 P. Cornelius Scipio received the image of Cybele (Berecyntia) when brought from Phrygia to Rome, 204 BC

10 L. Caecilius Metellus, who lost his sight when rescuing the Palladium from a fire in the temple of Vesta, 241 BC

11 The Cabiri, fertility gods of Phrygian origin, identified with the Curetes and Corybantes, and later with the Dioscuri. They were called by the Greeks the "Great Gods".

12 By a law of Otho the first fourteen rows in the theatre behind the *orchestra* were reserved for knights, the wealthy middle class, each of whom had to possess a capital of 400,000 sesterces.

13 Euphranor (*fl.* 336 BC) and Polycletus (*fl.* 452–412 BC), two celebrated Greek sculptors.

14 Juvenal names Sora, Fabrateria, and Frusino.

15 Probably the Emperor Claudius, super veterem segnitiae notam (Suetonius, *Claudius*, v).

16 i.e. seals, which are proverbially sluggish. Cf. Pliny, *Hist. Nat.* ix. 13; Virgil, *Georg.* iv. 432.

17 A huge litter.

18 Each client is followed by a slave bearing on his head a kitchener to keep the dole hot.

19 Cn. Domitius Corbulo, who distinguished himself against the Parthians under Claudius and Nero, was famed for his great strength.

20 Achilles.

21 i.e. before a magistrate.

22 The meaning of "Helvine" is unknown, but the inscription found at Aquinum was no doubt part of an altar erected to the goddess under this title.

FEMALE ATHLETES AND GLADIATORS, AD 116

Juvenal

And what about female athletes, with their purple
Track-suits, and wrestling in mud? Not to mention our
  lady-fencers –
We've all seen *them* stabbing the stump with a foil,
Shield well advanced going through the proper
  motions:
Just the right training needed to blow a matronly horn
At the Floral Festival – unless they have higher
  ambitions,
And the goal of all their practice is the real arena.
But then, what modesty can be looked for in some
Helmeted hoyden, a renegade from her sex,
Who thrives on masculine violence – yet would not
  prefer
To *be* a man, since the pleasure is so much less?
What a fine sight for some husband – *it might be you* – his
  wife's
Equipment put up at auction, baldric, armlet, plumes
And one odd shinguard! Or if the other style
Of fighting takes her fancy, imagine your delight when
The dear girl sells off her greaves! (And yet these same
  women
Have such delicate skins that even sheer silk chafes
  them;
They sweat in the finest chiffon.) Hark how she snorts
At each practice thrust, bowed down by the weight of
  her helmet;
See the big coarse puttees wrapped round her ample
  hams – Then
wait for the laugh, when she lays her weapons aside
And squats on the potty! Tell me, you noble ladies,
Scions of our great statesmen – Lepidus, blind Metellus,
Fabius the Guzzler – what gladiator's woman
Ever rigged herself out like this, or sweated at fencing-
  drill?

TWO DAYS IN THE LIFE OF AN EMPEROR'S SON, c. AD 139

Marcus Aurelius

Aurelius (AD 121–80) was adopted as the son of Emperor Antoninus Pius when he was 17. The letters below are to his tutor in Latin Literature, Fronto.

Hail, most revered master.

We are well. By a satisfactory arrangement of meals I worked from three o'clock a.m. till eight. For the next hour I paced about in slippers most contentedly before my bedroom. Then putting on my boots and my cloak – for we had been told to come in that dress – I went off to pay my respects to my Lord.[1]

We set out for the chase and did doughty deeds. We did hear say that boars had been bagged, for we were not lucky enough to see any. However, we climbed quite a steep hill; then in the afternoon we came home. I to my books: so taking off my boots and doffing my dress I passed nearly two hours on my couch, reading Cato's speech on the property of Pulchra, and another in which he impeached a Tribune. Ho, you cried to your boy, go as fast as you can and fetch me those speeches from the libraries of Apollo! It is no use your sending, for those volumes among others have followed me here. So you must get round the librarian of Tiberius' library: a little *douceur* will be necessary in which he and I can go shares when I come back to town. Well, these speeches read, I wrote a little wretched stuff, fit to be dedicated to the deities of water and fire; truly, today I have been unlucky in my writing, the lucubration of a sportsman or a vintager, such as those whose catches ring through my bedroom, a noise every whit as hateful and wearisome as that of the law-courts. What is this I have said? Nay, 'tis true, for my master is an *orator*.

I think I must have taken a chill, whether from walking about in my slippers in the early morning, or from writing badly, I know not. I only know that, rheumy enough at all times, I seem to be more drivelling than ever today. So I will

---

[1] His father by adoption; the Emperor Antoninus Pius.

pour the oil on my head and go to sleep, for not a drop of it do I intend to pour into my lamp today, so tired am I with riding and sneezing. Farewell for my sake, dearest and sweetest of masters, whom I would make bold to say I long to see more than Rome itself.

Hail, my sweetest of masters.

We are well. I slept somewhat late owing to my slight cold, which seems now to have subsided. So from five a.m. till nine I spent the time partly in reading some of Cato's *Agriculture* and partly in writing not quite such wretched stuff, by heavens, as yesterday. Then after paying my respects to my father, I relieved my throat, I will not say by *gargling* – though the word is, I believe, found in Novius and elsewhere – but by swallowing honey-water as far as the gullet and ejecting it again. After easing my throat I went off to my father and attended him at sacrifice. Then we went to luncheon. What do you think I ate? A wee bit of bread, though I saw the others devouring beans, onions, and herrings full of roe. We then worked hard at grape-gathering, and had a good sweat, and were merry and, as the poet says, "still left some clusters hanging high as gleanings of the vintage". After six o'clock we came home.

I did but little work and that to no purpose. Then I had a long chat with my little mother as she sat upon the bed. My talk was this: What do you think my Fronto is now doing? Then she: What do you think my Gratia is doing? Then I: And what do you think our little sparrow, the wee Gratia, is doing? Whilst we were chattering in this way and disputing which of us two loved the one or the other of you two the better, the gong sounded, an intimation that my father had gone to his bath. So we had supper, after we had bathed in the oil-press room; I do not mean bathed in the oil-press room, but when we had bathed, had supper there, and we enjoyed hearing the yokels chaffing one another. After coming back, before I turn over and snore, I get my task done and give my dearest of masters an account of the day's doings, and if I could miss him more I would not grudge wasting away a little more. Farewell, my Fronto, wherever you are, most honey-sweet, my love, my delight. How is it between you and me? I love you and you are away.

THE GOLDEN AGE: AN ORATION TO ROME, c. AD 150

Aelius Aristides

The reign of the Antoninus Pius (AD 138–151) saw the empire in unparalleled peace and prosperity. One cause of this was the extension of Roman citizenship which erased some of the divisions between the high and low, between provincial and Roman. Another was extension of commerce to the ends of the empire. Aristides' Oration to Rome is literary gratitude for the blessings of the empire.

10. [. . .] Your possession is equal to what the sun can pass, and the sun passes over your land. Neither the Chelidonean nor the Cyanean promontories limit your empire, nor does the distance from which a horseman can reach the sea in one day, nor do you reign within fixed boundaries, nor does another dictate to what point your control reaches; but the sea like a girdle lies extended, at once in the middle of the civilized world and of your hegemony.

11. Around it lie the great continents greatly sloping, ever offering to you in full measure something of their own. Whatever the seasons make grow and whatever countries and rivers and lakes and arts of Hellenes and non-Hellenes produce are brought from every land and sea, so that if one would look at all these things, he must needs behold them either by visiting the entire civilized world or by coming to this city. For whatever is grown and made among each people cannot fail to be here at all times and in abundance. And here the merchant vessels come carrying these many products from all regions in every season and even at every equinox, so that the city appears a kind of common emporium of the world.

12. Cargoes from India and, if you will, even from Arabia the Blest one can see in such numbers as to surmise that in those lands the trees will have been stripped bare and that the inhabitants of these lands, if they need anything, must come here and beg for a share of their own. Again one can see Babylonian garments and ornaments from the barbarian country beyond arriving in greater quantity and with more ease than if shippers from Naxos or from Cythnos, bearing some-

thing from those islands, had but to enter the port of Athens. Your farms are Egypt, Sicily and the civilized part of Africa.

13. Arrivals and departures by sea never cease, so that the wonder is, not that the harbour has insufficient space for merchant vessels, but that even the sea has enough, [if] it really does.

And just as Hesiod said about the ends of the Ocean, that there is a common channel where all waters have one source and destination, so there is a common channel to Rome and all meet here, trade, shipping, agriculture, metallurgy, all the arts and crafts that are or ever have been, all the things that are engendered or grow from the earth. And whatever one does not see here neither did nor does exist. And so it is not easy to decide which is greater, the superiority of this city in respect to the cities that now are or the superiority of this empire in respect to the empires that ever were.

34. But that which deserves as much wonder and admiration as all the rest together, and constant expression of gratitude both in word and action, shall now be mentioned. You who hold so vast an empire and rule it with such a firm hand and with so much unlimited power have very decidedly won a great success, which is completely your own.

36. For of all who have ever gained empire you alone rule over men who are free. Caria has not been given to Tissaphernes, nor Phrygia to Pharnabazus, nor Egypt to someone else; nor is the country said to be enslaved, as household of so-and-so, to whomsoever it has been turned over, a man himself not free. But just as those in states of one city appoint the magistrates to protect and care for the governed, so you, who conduct public business in the whole civilized world exactly as if it were one city state, appoint the governors, as is natural after elections, to protect and care for the governed, not to be slave masters over them. Therefore governor makes way for governor unobtrusively, when his time is up, and far from staying too long and disputing the land with his successor, he might easily not stay long enough even to meet him.

37. Appeals to a higher court are made with the ease of an appeal from deme to dicastery, with no greater menace for those who make them than for those who have accepted the local

verdict. Therefore one might say that the men of today are ruled by the governors who are sent out, only in so far as they are content to be ruled.

38. Are not these advantages beyond the old "Free Republic" of every people? For under Government by the People it is not possible to go outside after the verdict has been given in the city's court nor even to other jurors, but, except in a city so small that it has to have jurors from out of town, one must ever be content with the local verdict . . . [deprived] undeservedly, or, as plaintiff, not getting possession even after a favourable verdict.

But now in the last instance there is another judge, a mighty one, whose comprehension no just claim ever escapes.

39. There is an abundant and beautiful equality of the humble with the great and of the obscure with the illustrious, and, above all, of the poor man with the rich and of the commoner with the noble, and the word of Hesiod comes to pass, "For he easily exalts, and the exalted he easily checks," namely this judge and princeps as the justice of the claim may lead, like a breeze in the sails of a ship, favouring and accompanying, not the rich man more, the poor man less, but benefitting equally whomsover it meets.

59. But there is that which very decidedly deserves as much attention and admiration now as all the rest together. I mean your magnificent citizenship with its grand conception, because there is nothing like it in the records of all mankind. Dividing into two groups all those in your empire – and with this word I have indicated the entire civilized world – you have everywhere appointed to your citizenship, or even to kinship with you, the better part of the world's talent, courage, and leadership, while the rest you recognized as a league under your hegemony.

60. Neither sea nor intervening continent are bars to citizenship, nor are Asia and Europe divided in their treatment here. In your empire all paths are open to all. No one worthy of rule or trust remains an alien, but a civil community of the World has been established as a Free Republic under one, the best, ruler and teacher of order; and all come together as into a common civic center, in order to receive each man his due.

61. What another city is to its own boundaries and territory, this city is to the boundaries and territory of the entire civilized world, as if the latter were a country district and she had been appointed common town. It might be said that this one citadel is the refuge and assembly place of all perioeci or of all who dwell in outside demes.

62. She has never failed them, but like the soil of the earth, she supports all men; and as the sea, which receives with its gulfs all the many rivers, hides them and holds them all and still, with what goes in and out, is and seems ever the same, so actually this city receives those who flow in from all the earth and has even sameness in common with the sea. The latter is not made greater by the influx of rivers, for it has been ordained by fate that with the waters flowing in, the sea maintain its volume; here no change is visible because the city is so great.

63. Let this passing comment, which the subject suggested, suffice. As we were saying, you who are "great greatly" distributed your citizenship. It was not because you stood off and refused to give a share in it to any of the others that you made your citizenship an object of wonder. On the contrary, you sought its expansion as a worthy aim, and you have caused the word Roman to be the label, not of membership in a city, but of some common nationality, and this not just one among all, but one balancing all the rest. For the categories into which you now divide the world are not Hellenes and Barbarians, and it is not absurd, the distinction which you made, because you show them a citizenry more numerous, so to speak, than the entire Hellenic race. The division which you substituted is one into Romans and non-Romans. To such a degree have you expanded the name of your city.

64. Since these are the lines along which the distinction has been made, many in every city are fellow-citizens of yours no less than of their own kinsmen, though some of them have not yet seen this city. There is no need of garrisons to hold their citadels, but the men of greatest standing and influence in every city guard their own fatherlands for you. And you have a double hold upon the cities, both from here and from your fellow citizens in each.

65. No envy sets foot in the empire, for you yourselves were the first to disown envy, when you placed all opportunities in

view of all and offered those who were able a chance to be not
governed more than they governed in turn. Nor does hatred
either steal in from those who are not chosen. For since the
constitution is a universal one and, as it were, of one state,
naturally your governors rule not as over the property of others
but as over their own. Besides, all the masses have as a share in it
the permission to take refuge with you from the power of the
local magnates, but there is the indignation and punishment
from you which will come upon them immediately, if they
themselves dare to make any unlawful change.

66. Thus the present regime naturally suits and serves both
rich and poor. No other way of life is left. There has developed
in your constitution a single harmonious, all embracing union;
and what formerly seemed to be impossible has come to pass in
your time: [maintenance] of control over an empire, over a vast
one at that, and at the same time firmness of rule [without]
unkindness.

74. Thus a courage like that of Hellenes and Egyptians and any
others one might mention is surpassed by yours, and all, far as
they are behind you in actual arms, trail still further in the
conception. On the one hand you deemed it unworthy of your
rule for those from this city to be subject to the levy and to the
hardships and to enjoy no advantage from the present felicity;
on the other hand you did not put your faith in alien mercenaries. Still you needed soldiers before the hour of crisis. So what
did you do? You found an army of your own for which the
citizens were undisturbed. This possibility was provided for you
by that plan for all the empire, according to which you count no
one an alien when you accept him for any employment where
he can do well and is then needed.

75. Who then have been assembled and how? Going over the
entire league, you looked about carefully for those who would
perform this liturgy, and when you found them, you released
them from the fatherland and gave them your own city, so that
they became reluctant henceforth to call themselves by their
original ethnics. Having made them fellow-citizens, you made
them also soldiers, so that the men from this city would not be
subject to the levy, and those performing military service would

none the less be citizens, who together with their enrolment in the army had lost their own cities but from that very day had become your fellow-citizens and defenders.

90. It appears to me that in this state you have established a constitution not at all like any of those among the rest of mankind. Formerly there seemed to be three constitutions in human society. Two were tyranny and oligarchy, or kingship and aristocracy, since they were known under two names each according to the view one took in interpreting the character of the men in control. A third category was known as democracy whether the leadership was good or bad. The cities had received one or the other constitution as choice or chance prevailed for each. Your state, on the other hand, is quite dissimilar; it is such a form of government as if it were a mixture of all the constitutions without the bad aspects of any one. That is why precisely this form of constitution has prevailed. So when one looks at the strength of the People and sees how easily they get all that they want and ask, he will deem it a complete democracy except for the faults of democracy. When he looks at the Senate sitting as a council and keeping the magistracies, he will think that there is no aristocracy more perfect than this. When he looks at the Ephor and Prytanis, who presides over all of these, him from whom it is possible for the People to get what they want and for the Few to have the magistracies and power, he will see in this one, the One who holds the most perfect monarchic rule, One without a share in the vices of a tyrant and One elevated above even kingly dignity.

91. It is not strange that you alone made these distinctions and discoveries how to govern both in the world and in the city itself. For you alone are rulers, so to speak, according to nature. Those others who preceded you established an arbitrary, tyrannical rule. They became masters and slaves of each other in turn, and as rulers they were a spurious crew. They succeeded each other as if advancing to the position in a ball game. Macedonians had a period of enslavement to Persians, Persians to Medes, Medes to Assyrians, but as long as men have known you, all have known you as rulers. Since you were free right from the start and had begun the game as it were in the rulers'

position, you equipped yourselves with all that was helpful for the position of rulers, and you invented a new constitution such as no one ever had before, and you prescribed for all things fixed rules and fixed periods.

99. Cities gleam with radiance and charm, and the whole earth has been beautified like a garden. Smoke rising from plains and fire signals for friend and foe have disappeared, as if a breath had blown them away, beyond land and sea. Every charming spectacle and an infinite number of festal games have been introduced instead. Thus like an ever-burning sacred fire the celebration never ends, but moves around from time to time and people to people, always somewhere, a demonstration justified by the way all men have fared. Thus it is right to pity only those outside your hegemony, if indeed there are any, because they lose such blessings.

A BOY COMPLAINS, ROMAN EGYPT, AD 2ND CENTURY

Theon

Theon to his father Theon, greeting. It was a fine thing of you not to take me with you to the city! If you won't take me with you to Alexandria I won't write to you, or speak to you, or say good-bye to you, and if you go to Alexandria I won't take your hand nor ever greet you again. That is what will happen if you won't take me. Mother said to Achelaus: "It quite upsets him to be left behind". It was good of you to send me presents . . . on the 12th, the day you sailed. Send me a lyre, I implore you. If you won't, I won't eat, I won't drink; there, now!

THE MARTYRDOM OF POLYCARP, SMYRNA, C. AD 155

Anon

Polycarp was the Bishop of Smyrna. For the Roman authorities, Emperor worship was a constitutional necessity; thus the Christian Polycarp, in refusing a pinch of incense for Caesar, became guilty of treason. His martyrdom was recorded in this anonymous letter from the Church at Smyrna to the Church at Philomelium.

Now the glorious Polycarp at the first, when he heard it, so far from being dismayed, was desirous of remaining in town; but the greater part persuaded him to withdraw. So he withdrew to a farm not far distant from the city; and there he stayed with a few companions, doing nothing else night and day but praying for all men and for the churches throughout the world; for this was his constant habit. And while praying he falleth into a trance three days before his apprehension; and he saw his pillow burning with fire. And he turned and said unto those that were with him: "It must needs be that I shall be burned alive".

And as those that were in search of him persisted, he departed to another farm; and forthwith they that were in search of him came up; and not finding him, they seized two slave lads, one of whom confessed under torture; for it was impossible for him to lie concealed, seeing that the very persons who betrayed him were people of his own household. And the captain of the police, who chanced to have the very name, being called Herod, was eager to bring him into the stadium, that he himself might fulfil his appointed lot, being made a partaker with Christ, while they – his betrayers – underwent the punishment of Judas himself.

So taking the lad with them, on the Friday about the supper hour, the gendarmes and horsemen went forth with their accustomed arms, hastening *as against a robber*. And coming up in a body late in the evening, they found the man himself in bed in an upper chamber in a certain cottage; and though he might have departed thence to another place, he would not, saying, *The will of God be done.* So when he heard that they were come, he went down and conversed with them, the bystanders marvelling at his age and his constancy, and wondering how there should be so much eagerness for the apprehension of an old man like him. Thereupon forthwith he gave orders that a table should be spread for them to eat and drink at that hour, as much as they desired. And he persuaded them to grant him an hour that he might pray unmolested; and on their consenting, he stood up and prayed, being so full of the grace of God, that for two hours he could not hold his peace, and those that heard were amazed, and many repented that they had come against such a venerable old man.

But when at length he brought his prayer to an end, after remembering all who at any time had come in his way, small and great, high and low, and all the universal Church throughout the world, the hour of departure being come, they seated him on an ass and brought him into the city, it being a high sabbath. And he was met by Herod the captain of police and his father Nicetes, who also removed him to their carriage and tried to prevail upon him, seating themselves by his side and saying, "Why, what harm is there in saying, Caesar is Lord, and offering incense", with more to this effect, "and saving thyself?" But he at first gave them no answer. When however they persisted, he said, "I am not going to do what ye counsel me". Then they, failing to persuade him, uttered threatening words and made him dismount with speed, so that he bruised his shin, as he got down from the carriage. And without even turning round, he went on his way promptly and with speed, as if nothing had happened to him, being taken to the stadium; there being such a tumult in the stadium that no man's voice could be so much as heard.

But as Polycarp entered into the stadium, a voice came to him from heaven: "Be strong, Polycarp, and play the man" And no one saw the speaker, but those of our people who were present heard the voice. And at length, when he was brought up, there was a great tumult, for they heard that Polycarp had been apprehended. When then he was brought before him, the proconsul inquired whether he were the man. And on his confessing that he was, he tried to persuade him to a denial saying, "Have respect to thine age", and other things in accordance therewith, as it is their wont to say; "Swear by the genius of Caesar; repent and say, Away with the atheists". Then Polycarp with solemn countenance looked upon the whole multitude of lawless heathen that were in the stadium, and waved his hand to them; and groaning and looking up to heaven he said, "Away with the atheists". But when the magistrate pressed him hard and said, "Swear the oath, and I will release thee; revile the Christ," Polycarp said, "Fourscore and six years have I been His servant, and He hath done me no wrong. How then can I blaspheme my King who saved me?" . . .

Saying these things and more besides, he was inspired with courage and joy, and his countenance was filled with grace, so that not only did it not drop in dismay at the things which were said to him, but on the contrary the proconsul was astounded and sent his own herald to proclaim three times in the midst of the stadium, "Polycarp hath confessed himself to be a Christian". When this was proclaimed by the herald, the whole multitude both of Gentiles and of Jews who dwelt in Smyrna cried out with ungovernable wrath and with a loud shout, "This is the teacher of Asia, the father of the Christians, the puller down of our gods, who teacheth numbers not to sacrifice nor worship". Saying these things, they shouted aloud and asked the Asiarch Philip to let a lion loose upon Polycarp. But he said that it was not lawful for him, since he had brought the sports to a close. Then they thought fit to shout out with one accord that Polycarp should be burned alive. For it must needs be that the matter of the vision should be fulfilled, which was shown him concerning his pillow, when he saw it on fire while praying, and turning round he said prophetically to the faithful who were with him, "I must needs be burned alive".

These things then happened with so great speed, quicker than words could tell, the crowds forthwith collecting from the workshops and baths timber and faggots, and the Jews more especially assisting in this with zeal, as is their wont. But when the pile was made ready, divesting himself of all his upper garments and loosing his girdle, he endeavoured also to take off his shoes, though not in the habit of doing this before, because all the faithful at all times vied eagerly who should soonest touch his flesh. For he had been treated with all honour for his holy life even before his grey hairs came. Forthwith then the instruments that were prepared for the pile were placed about him; and as they were going likewise to nail him to the stake, he said, "Leave me as I am; for He that hath granted me to endure the fire will grant me also to remain at the pile unmoved, even without the security which ye seek from nails".

In spite of the efforts of the Romans, Christianity thrived in the Empire. (Ironically enough, the Roman genius for building roads, and the establishment of civil order, positively aided Christian proselytizers.) Eventually, in the fourth century, it was adopted by Constantine, as the Empire's official religion.

THE VIRTUES OF ANTONINUS PIUS, C. AD 170

Marcus Aurelius

As described by his adopted son.

"In my father [Antoninus Pius] I observed his meekness; his constancy without wavering in those things which after due examination . . . he had determined. How free from all vanity he carried himself in matters of honour and dignity (as they are esteemed); his laboriousness and assiduity, his readiness to hear any man that had aught to say tending to any common good! how generally and impartially he would give every man his due: his skill and knowledge when rigor or extremity, when indulgence or moderation were in season. His moderate condescending to other men's occasions as an ordinary man, neither absolutely requiring his friends that they should wait on him at his ordinary meals, nor that they should of necessity accompany him in his journeys. His sociability, his gracious and delightful conversation never reached satiety, his care of his body was within bounds and measures, not as one who did not wish to live long, or overstudious of neatness and elegancy; yet not as one that did not regard it, so that through his own [care of his health] he seldom needed any medicine.

"He was not easily moved and tossed up and down, but loved to be constant, both in the same places and businesses; and after his great fits of headache he would return fresh and vigorous to his wonted affairs. He was very discreet and moderate in exhibiting public sights and shows for the pleasure and pastime of the people; in public buildings, congiaria [*i.e.* distribution of money or corn doles], and the like. He did not use the baths at unseasonable hours. He was never curious or anxious about his food, or about the style or colour of his clothes, or about any mere matter of external beauty. In all his conversation, he was far from all inhumanity, boldness, incivility, greediness, or impetuosity; never doing anything with such earnestness and intention that a man could say of him, that he flew into a heat about it, but contrariwise, all things distinctly, as at leisure, without trouble, orderly, soundly, and agreeably . . .

"Remember Antoninus Pius's constancy in things that were done by him in accordance with reason, his equability in all things; how he would never give over a matter until he understood the whole state of it fully and plainly; and how patiently and without any resentment he would bear with them that did unjustly condemn him; how he would never be overhasty in anything, nor give ear to slanders or false accusations, but examine and observe with the best diligence the several actions and dispositions of men. He would easily be content with a few things – mere lodgings, bedding, the ordinary food and attendance. He bore with those who opposed his opinions and even rejoiced if any man could better advise him, and finally he was exceedingly religious without superstition."

MARCUS AURELIUS MEDITATES, THE DANUBE, C. AD 170

Marcus Aurelius

Aurelius succeeded to the throne (at the age of 40) on Antoninus Pius's death in AD 161. His reign was marked by plague, incessant Germanic incursions and uprisings in the East (see p311). He triumphed over all. Matthew Arnold once called Aurelius "the most beautiful figure in history"; certainly he was amongst the most dutiful of Emperors. A Stoic by inclination and education, his Meditations, *composed whilst defending the Danube, show both the high ideals which guided him and the melancholic thoughts which dogged him.*

1. Injustice is a sin. Nature has constituted rational beings for their own mutual benefit, each to help his fellows according to their worth, and in no wise to do them hurt; and to contravene her will is plainly to sin against this eldest of all the deities. Untruthfulness, too, is a sin, and against the same goddess. For Nature is the nature of Existence itself; and existence connotes the kinship of all created beings. Truth is but another name for

this Nature, the original creator of all true things. So, where a wilful lie is a sin because the deception is an act of injustice, an involuntary lie is also a sin because it is a discordant note in Nature's harmony, and creates mutinous disorder in an orderly universe. For mutinous indeed it is, when a man lets himself be carried, even involuntarily, into a position contrary to truth; seeing that he has so neglected the faculties Nature gave him that he is no longer able to distinguish the false from the true.

Again, it is a sin to pursue pleasure as a good and to avoid pain as an evil. It is bound to result in complaints that Nature is unfair in her rewarding of vice and virtue; since it is the bad who are so often in enjoyment of pleasures and the means to obtain them, while pains and events that occasion pains descend upon the heads of the good. Besides, if a man is afraid of pain, he is afraid of something happening which will be part of the appointed order of things, and this is itself a sin; if he is bent on the pursuit of pleasure, he will not stop at acts of injustice, which again is manifestly sinful. No; when Nature herself makes no distinction and if she did, she would not have brought pains and pleasures into existence side by side – it behoves those who would follow in her footsteps to be like-minded and exhibit the same indifference. He therefore who does not view with equal unconcern pain or pleasure, death or life, fame or dishonour – all of them employed by Nature without any partiality – clearly commits a sin. And in saying that nature employs them without partiality, I mean that every successive generation of created things equally passes through the same experiences in turn; for this is the outcome of the original impulse which in the beginning moved Providence – by taking certain germs of future existences, and endowing them with productive powers of self-realization, of mutation, and of succession – to progress from the inception of the universe to its present orderly system.

2. A man of finer feelings would have taken leave of the world before ever sampling its falsehood, double-dealing, luxury, and pride; but now that all these have been tasted to satiety, the next best course would be to end your life forthwith. Or are you really resolved to go on dwelling in the midst of iniquity and has experience not yet persuaded you to flee from the pestilence? For infection of the mind is a far more dangerous pestilence

than any unwholesomeness or disorder in the atmosphere around us. Insofar as we are animals, the one attacks our lives; but as men, the other attacks our manhood.

3. Despise not death; smile, rather, at its coming; it is among the things that Nature wills. Like youth and age, like growth and maturity, like the advent of teeth, beard, and grey hairs, like begetting, pregnancy, and childbirth, like every other natural process that life's seasons bring us, so is our dissolution. Never, then, will a thinking man view death lightly, impatiently, or scornfully; he will wait for it as but one more of Nature's processes. Even as you await the baby's emergence from the womb of your wife, so await the hour when the little soul shall glide forth from its sheath.

But if your heart would have comfort of a simpler sort, then there is no better solace in the face of death than to think on the nature of the surroundings you are leaving, and the characters you will no longer have to mix with. Not that you must find these offensive; rather, your duty is to care for them and bear with them mildly; yet never forget that you are parting from men of far other principles than your own. One thing, if any, might have held you back and bound you to life; the chance of fellowship with kindred minds. But when you contemplate the weariness of an existence in company so discordant, you cry, "Come quickly, Death, lest I too become forgetful of myself."

4. The sinner sins against himself; the wrongdoer wrongs himself, becoming the worse by his own action.

5. A man does not sin by commission only, but often by omission.

6. Enough if your present opinion be grounded in conviction, your present action grounded in unselfishness, and your present disposition contented with whatever befalls you from without.

7. Erase fancy; curb impulse; quench desire; let sovereign reason have the mastery.

8. A single life-principle is divided amongst all irrational creatures, and a single mind-principle distributed among the rational; just as this one earth gives form to all things earthy, and just as all of us who have sight and breath see by the self-same light and breathe of the self-same air.

9. All things that share the same element tend to seek their own kind. Things earthy gravitate towards earth, things aqu-

eous flow towards one another, things aerial likewise – whence the need for the barriers which keep them forcibly apart. The tendency of flames is to mount skyward, because of the elemental fire; even here below, they are so eager for the company of their own kind that any sort of material, if it be reasonably dry, will ignite with ease, since there is only a minority of its ingredients which is resistant to fire. In the same way, therefore, all portions of the universal Mind are drawn towards one another. More strongly, indeed; since, being higher in the scale of creation, their eagerness to blend and combine with their affinities is proportionately keener. This instinct for reunion shows itself in its first stage among the creatures without reason, when we see bees swarming, cattle herding, birds nesting in colonies, and couples mating; because in them soul has already emerged, and in such relatively higher forms of life as theirs the desire for union is found at a level of intensity which is not present in stones or sticks. When we come to beings with reason, there are political associations, comradeships, family life, public meetings, and in times of war treaties and armistices; and among the still higher orders, a measure of unity even exists between bodies far separated from one another – as for example with the stars. Thus ascent in the ranks of creation can induce fellow-feeling even where there is no proximity.

Yet now see what happens. It is we – we, intelligent beings – who alone have forgotten this mutual zeal for unity; among us alone the currents are not seen to converge. Nevertheless, though man may flee as he will, he is still caught and held fast; Nature is too strong for him. Observe with care, and you will see: you will sooner find a fragment of earth unrelated to the rest of earth than a man who is utterly without some link with his fellows.

10. Everything bears fruit; man, God, the whole universe, each in its proper season. No matter that the phrase is restricted in common use to vines and such like. Reason, too, yields fruit, both for itself and for the world; since from it comes a harvest of other good things, themselves all bearing the stamp of reason.

11. Teach them better, if you can; if not, remember that kindliness has been given you for moments like these. The gods themselves show kindness to such men; and at times, so in-

dulgent are they, will even aid them in their endeavours to secure health, wealth, or reputation. This you too could do; who is there to hinder you?

12. Work yourself hard, but not as if you were being made a victim, and not with any desire for sympathy or admiration. Desire one thing alone: that your actions or inactions alike should be worthy of a reasoning citizen.

13. Today I have got myself out of all my perplexities; or rather, I have got the perplexities out of myself – for they were not without, but within; they lay in my own outlook.

14. Everything is banal in experience, fleeting in duration, sordid in content; in all respects the same today as generations now dead and buried have found it to be.

15. Facts stand wholly outside our gates; they are what they are, and no more; they know nothing about themselves, and they pass no judgment upon themselves. What is it, then, that pronounces the judgment? Our own guide and ruler, Reason.

16. A rational and social being is not affected in himself for either better or worse by his feelings, but by his will; just as his outward behaviour, good or bad, is the product of will, not of feelings.

17. For the thrown stone there is no more evil in falling than there is good in rising.

18. Penetrate into their inmost minds, and you will see what manner of critics you are afraid of, and how capable they are of criticizing themselves.

19. All things are in process of change. You yourself are ceaselessly undergoing transformation, and the decay of some of your parts, and so is the whole universe.

20. Leave another's wrongdoing where it lies.

21. In the interruption of an activity, or the discontinuance and, as it were, death of an impulse, or an opinion, there is no evil. Look back at the phases of your own growth: childhood, boyhood, youth, age: each change itself a kind of death. Was this so frightening? Or take the lives you lived under your grandfather and then under your mother and then your father; trace the numerous differences and changes and discontinuances there were in those days, and ask yourself, "Were they so frightening?" No more so, then, is the cessation, the interruption, the change from life itself.

22. Your own mind, the Mind of the universe, your neighbour's mind – be prompt to explore them all. Your own, so that you may shape it to justice; the universe's, that you may recollect what it is you are a part of; your neighbour's, that you may understand whether it is informed by ignorance or knowledge, and also may recognize that it is kin to your own.

23. As a unit yourself, you help to complete the social whole; and similarly, therefore, your every action should help to complete the social life. Any action which is not related either directly or remotely to this social end disjoints that life, and destroys its unity. It is as much the act of a schismatic as when some citizen in a community does his utmost to dissociate himself from the general accord.

24. Childish squabbles, childish games, "petty breaths supporting corpses" – why, the ghosts in Homer have more evident reality!

25. First get at the nature and quality of the original cause, separate it from the material to which it has given shape, and study it; then determine the possible duration of its effects.

26. The woes you have had to bear are numberless because you were not content to let Reason, your guide and master, do its natural work. Come now, no more of this!

27. When those about you are venting their censure or malice upon you, or raising any other sort of injurious clamour, approach and penetrate into their souls, and see what manner of men they are. You will find little enough reason for all your painstaking efforts to win their good opinion. All the same, it still remains your duty to think kindly of them; for Nature has made them to be your friends, and even the gods themselves lend them every sort of help, by dreams and by oracles, to gain the ends on which their hearts are set.

28. Upwards and downwards, from age to age, the cycles of the universe follow their unchanging round. It may be that the World-Mind wills each separate happening in succession; and if so, then accept the consequences. Or, it may be, there was but one primal act of will, of which all else is the sequel; every event being thus the germ of another. To put it another way, things are either isolated units, or they form one inseparable whole. If

that whole be God, then all is well; but if aimless chance, at least you need not be aimless also.

Soon earth will cover us all. Then in time earth, too, will change; later, what issues from this change will itself in turn incessantly change, and so again will all that then takes its place, even unto the world's end. To let the mind dwell on these swiftly rolling billows of change and transformation is to know a contempt for all things mortal.

A GOVERNOR PLOTS INSURRECTION, SYRIA, AD 175

Avidius Cassius

Cassius was governor of Syria. His rebellion against Emperor Marcus Aurelius was put down by his own soldiers.

Unhappy state, unhappy, which suffers under the rule of pluto-crats and men whose sole ambition is wealth. Marcus[1] is an admirable man, but in his desire for a reputation for mercy, he permits men to live whose lives he cannot himself approve. Where is Cassius, whose name I bear in vain? Where is that other Marcus, Cato the Censor? Where is our ancestral discipline? Long ago it perished, now it is not even missed. Marcus Antoninus spends his time on philosophy, on speculating about first principles, the soul, virtue and justice, but gives no thought to the state. This is a task for the sword, for common sense unstinted, to restore the state to its ancient condition. As for these governors of provinces, can I call these men proconsuls and governors who consider their provinces entrusted to them by the Senate solely as a means to indulgence and to wealth? You have heard how our philosopher's prefect of the guard was a beggar and a pauper only three days before his appointment, and then suddenly became rich? How, I ask, except from the vitals of the state, and the coffers of the provincials. Well, let them enrich themselves, let them be millionaires, in time they will be obliged to replenish the Treasury. Let but the gods favour the right, and Cassius' men restore good government to the state.

[1] Marcus Aurelius Antoninus.

PART THREE

FALL

Rome AD 181–476

INTRODUCTION

The warlike states of antiquity, Greece, Macedonia and Rome, educated a race of soldiers; exercised their bodies, disciplined their courage, multiplied their forces by regular evolutions, and converted the iron which they possessed into strong and servicable weapons. But this superiority insensibly declined with their laws and manners; and the feeble policy of Constantine and his successors armed and instructed, for the ruin of the empire, the rude valour of the Barbarian mercenaries.

Edward Gibbon, *History of the Decline and Fall of the Roman Empire*, 1777–88

The eminent historian of Ancient Rome Edward Gibbon set the date of its Fall as AD 476, and there it has stayed. In that year, the Germanic soldier Odoacer pensioned off the boy emperor Romulus Augustulus and turned Italy into a personal kingdom. The Eastern Empire, based at Constantinople (Byzantium) continued, but the unfortunate – if grandly titled – Romulus Augustulus was the last emperor to rule from the West. There was a kind of revival under Justinian, who briefly reconquered Italy (from his base at Constantinople) in the 550s, but the "classic" Roman Empire tumbled to ruins in AD 476.

The significance of AD 476 was probably lost on those who lived through it; Odoacer's *coup* was but one more incident in a long dark line of upheavals and tragedies. For Rome was three centuries in Decline before it Fell absolutely.

The Romans themselves had little doubt that their geopolitical misfortunes stemmed from their own decadence – and the contrasting warrior manliness of the "Barbarians" who cease-lessly slashed at the imperial frontier until they definitively cut through, on the Danube in AD 230, on the Rhine in AD 406. Even as long before as c. AD 100 Tacitus, in his *Germania*, had been moved to warn that the moral virtues of the German tribes and their simple rustic lifestyle (where "In every home the children go naked and dirty, and develop that strength of limb and tall stature which excites our admiration", see pp251–255) was creating a warrior enemy that pampered, licentious, effete Romans would be unable to resist. Ammianus Marcellinus sounded a similar warning in his portrait of Roman decadence in c. AD 370 (pp345–351), a mere forty years before Alaric the Visigoth sacked Rome.

That much of the Roman population, the upper classes in particular, had slipped into delinquency is unquestionable. Certainly this delinquency also had an effect on political morale, largely because the aristocracy increasingly withdrew from public life and offered no dutiful example. Yet the Romans had not entirely been strangers to orgiastic vice in the heyday of the Empire. There was more to Rome's lingering death than turpitude.

In truth, the Roman Empire was a victim of its own success. The sheer extent of the Empire produced a frontier tens of thousands of miles in length, much of which needed to be garrisoned. With the westwards migration, from the second century onwards, of the Goths, Vandals and other Germanic tribes (and behind these, coming out of Russia, the Huns), the Rhinish and Danubian frontiers of the Empire were the scene of bloody battle after bloody battle. There were other flashpoints in the Empire too, such as Britain and Persia. The maintenance and preservation of the Empire was thus a massive military exercise, which had mortal political and economic ramifications.

Politically, the army as the guarantor of the Empire believed itself, even more than hitherto, the rightful maker of emperors – and that these should indeed be drawn from its own ranks. After the murder of Commodus in AD 180, most of those to don the imperial purple were generals, often from the Danubian frontier. It was a sign of the times when Maximinus I, a Danubian peasant, took the throne in AD 235. If some of these "barracks emperors" were successful in temporarily stemming the Germanic invader – and they were, particularly Gallienus (killing 50,000 Goth warriors at Naissus in AD 268), Aurelian, and Valentinian I – they were unable to achieve a total, decisive victory. Not the least reason for this was that "barracks emperors" themselves always had one eye on attempted and actual usurpations by rival generals. As Ammianus commented, "What fury of foreign peoples, what barbarian cruelty, can be compared with the harm done by civil wars?" Moreover, the soldiery commanded by the "barracks emperors" was not the Roman soldiery of yore. Successive failures of conscription obliged emperors to recuit whomsoever they could. Much of the "Roman" army was actually composed of the very barbarians it fought – save these Germans were hired, for money.

Undoubtedly, the most dramatic solution to the problem of the military defence of the Empire came in AD 330 when Constantine founded a new capital, Constantinople, on the site of Byzantium on the Bosphorus. (The solution was anticipated by Diocletian, who had effected a division of the empire into eastern and western halves, ruling from Nicomedia in the east.) The relocation made for better supervision of the defences of the Danube and Euphrates but politically split the Empire into two. Under later rulers, the splitting of the Empire into two was formalized, with an Emperor apiece. Unsurprisingly, the internecine intrigues between the two thrones were frequent. Indeed, it is fair to say that when Alaric achieved his earth-shattering sack of Rome in AD 410 he did so because the regent in the West, Stilicho, was more concerned with plotting against the Eastern throne than defending the Western one.

Economically, the burden of imperial defence was intolerable. To pay for the army, emperors resorted to a standard measure: taxing the populace. "No man shall possess any property that is exempt from taxes," declared Emperor Theodosius in AD 383. Actually, the burden of taxes tended to fall on the agricultural poor, a happenstance which increasingly alienated them from the state (and caused them to refuse conscription). When inflation – which rose to 1000 per cent – wiped out soldiers' wages, emperors pacified the military with "donatives" (cash gifts) which caused higher taxes still. Taxation was by no means the sole financial problem of the Empire. There was the trade deficit, there was bullion hoarding, there was the collapse of the imperial currency which followed the lightening of the weight of silver and gold coins . . .

The later Roman Empire, in other words, was a bankrupt militarized state with an ineffective army, a parasitic inverted aristocracy and a hostile peasantry. Large parts of it ceased to be "Roman" at all, as barbarian tribes settled under official imperial approval and then with no approval at all. The career of Gaiseric the Vandal was the exemplar. After moving from Germany, through Gaul, through Spain, the Vandals ended up in Roman North Africa in AD 429. Faced with such a strong foe as Gaiseric, the authorities granted him federate status in what is now Morocco and western Algeria. Four years later, however, Gaiseric seized Tunisia and Carthage and openly ruled as a sovereign outside Rome's suzerainty.

One other factor in Rome's fall might be mentioned: Christianity. The ineluctable growth of the religion of Jesus caused numerous persecutions (particularly under Diocletian and Galerius), although most Emperors tended to adopt a policy of "live-and-let-live". Then, in AD 311, by the Edict of Serdica (Sofia), Constantine I granted freedom of worship to Christians. Reputedly, Constantine granted this tolerance because he saw a vision of the cross before his successful battle at Milvian Bridge, but there was a political judgment involved. Christianity alone had the potential to unite the various peoples of the Empire, with their different skins, different cultures, different classes. Constantine's official approval of Christianity gave it a boost from which it never faltered during the Empire, despite the odd attempted revival of paganism such as that by "Julian the Apostate".

Constantine was largely correct in his estimation of the dynamic of Christianity. In AD 476 when the last remnant of Empire in the West crashed, Christianity emerged from the ruins remarkably unscathed. The Medieval future belonged to it.

DIDIUS JULIANUS BUYS THE ROMAN EMPIRE AT AUCTION, AD 193

Herodian

After the reign of Marcus Aurelius, the Empire slipped ineluctably into blood and chaos. His natural son, Commodus, ruled with increasing megalomania (and fondness for bizarre religions), until he was assassinated. A city official, Pertinax, was then elevated to the throne, but the Praetorian Guards dispatched him after a mere three months because of his parsimony. The successor to Pertinax was Didius Julianus, a rich senator who purchased the throne at auction.

When the report of the murder of the Emperor [Pertinax] spread among the people, consternation and grief seized all minds, and men ran about beside themselves. An undirected effort possessed the people, – they strove to hunt out the doers of the deed, yet could neither find nor punish them. But the Senators were the worst disturbed, for it seemed a public calamity that they had lost a kindly father and a righteous ruler. Also a reign of violence was dreaded, for one could guess that the soldiery would find that much to their liking.

When the first and the ensuing days had passed, the people dispersed, each man fearing for himself; men of rank, however, fled to their estates outside the city, in order not to risk themselves in the dangers of a change on the throne. But at last when the soldiers were aware that the people were quiet, and that no one would try to avenge the blood of the Emperor, they nevertheless remained inside their barracks and barred the gates; yet they set such of their comrades as had the loudest voices upon the walls, and had them declare that the Empire was for sale at auction, and promise to him who bid highest that they would give him the power, and set him with the armed hand in the imperial palace.

When this proclamation was known, the more honourable and weighty Senators, and all persons of noble origin and property, would not approach the barracks to offer money in so vile a manner for a besmirched sovranty. However, a certain Julianus – who had held the consulship, and was counted rich – was holding a drinking bout late that evening, at the time the news came of what the soldiers proposed. He was a man

notorious for his evil living; and now it was that his wife and
daughter and fellow feasters urged him to rise from his ban-
queting couch and hasten to the barracks, in order to find out
what was going on. But on the way they pressed it on him that
he might get the sovranty for himself, and that he ought not to
spare the money to outbid any competitors with great gifts to
the soldiers.

When he came to the wall of the camp, he called out to the troops
and promised to give them just as much as they desired, for he had
ready money and a treasure room full of gold and silver. About the
same time too came Sulpicianus, who had also been consul and was
præfect of Rome and father-in-law of Pertinax, to try to buy the
power also. But the soldiers did not receive him, because they feared
lest his connection with Pertinax might lead him to avenge him by
some treachery. So they lowered a ladder and brought Julianus
into the fortified camp; for they would not open the gates, until they
had made sure of the amount of the bounty they expected. When he
was admitted he promised first to bring the memory of Commodus
again into honour and restore his images in the Senate house, where
they had been cast down; and to give the soldiers the same lax
discipline they had enjoyed under Commodus. Also he promised
the troops as large a sum of money as they could ever expect to
require or receive. The payment should be immediate, and he
would at once have the cash brought over from his residence.

Captivated by such speeches, and with such vast hopes
awakened, the soldiers hailed Julianus as Emperor, and demanded that along with his own name he should take that of
Commodus. Next they took their standards, adorned them
again with the likeness of Commodus and made ready to go
with Julianus in procession.

The latter offered the customary imperial sacrifices in the
camp; and then went out with a great escort of the guards. For
it was against the will and intention of the populace, and with a
shameful and unworthy stain upon the public honour that he
had bought the Empire, and not without reason did he fear the
people might overthrow him. The guards therefore in full
panoply surrounded him for protection. They were formed
in a phalanx around him, ready to fight; they had "their
Emperor" in their midst; while they swung their shields and

lances over his head, so that no missile could hurt him during
the march. Thus they brought him to the palace, with no man
of the multitude daring to resist; but just as little was there any
cheer of welcome, as was usual at the induction of a new
Emperor. On the contrary the people stood at a distance
and hooted and reviled him as having bought the throne with
lucre at an auction.

*Didius Julianus held power only from 28 March, AD 193 to 1 June of
the same year, being deposed and slain when Septimius Severus and the
Danube legions marched on Rome to avenge Pertinax. The ringleaders of
the Prætorians were executed; the rest of the guardsmen dishonourably
discharged and banished from Italy.*

A PROTOTYPE JET ENGINE, ALEXANDRIA,
C. AD 200

Hero of Alexandria

*Hero invented the first steam-engine on the reaction-turbine (jet) principle.
The poor materials to his hand would have ensured, through leakage and
friction, that it could not have powered anything.*

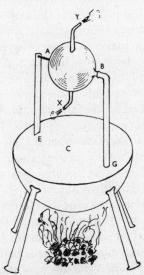

A hollow globe rotates on two bearings A and B, which is hollow, and through the pipe GB rises steam from a boiler C.

In escaping through the nozzles X and Y, which are bent at right angles to the axis of the globe, it causes the globe to spin round merrily.

EMPEROR SEPTIMIUS SEVERUS IS MADE A GOD, ROME, AD 211

Herodian

Severus, who ruled the Empire from AD 193 to 211, was an energetic military reformer. He raised the legions to thirty-three in number (Trajan had maintained thirty) and upped their pay. With his new army he took Byzantium, bested the Parthians, and in AD 208 marched to Britain, where he restored Hadrian's Wall as an effective frontier after its breaching by the Caledonian tribes. Severus died at York, reputedly advising his sons with his last breath: "Be on good terms with one another, be generous to the soldiers, and don't care about anyone else!"?

It is the Roman custom to give divine status to those of their emperors who die with heirs to succeed them. This ceremony is called deification. Public mourning, with a mixture of festive and religious ritual, is proclaimed throughout the city, and the body of the dead man is buried in the normal way with a costly funeral. Then they make an exact wax replica of the man, which they put on a huge ivory bed, strewn with gold-threaded coverings, raised high up in the entrance to the palace. This image, deathly pale, rests there like a sick man. Either side of the bed is attended for most of the day, the whole Senate sitting on the left, dressed in black, while on the right are all the women who can claim special honours from the position of their husbands or fathers. Not one of these can be seen wearing gold or adorned with necklaces, but they are all dressed in plain white garments, giving the appearance of mourners.

This continues for seven days, during each of which doctors come and approach the bed, take a look at the supposed invalid and announce a daily deterioration in his condition. When at last the news is given that he is dead, the bed or bier is raised on the shoulders of the noblest members of the Equestrian Order and chosen young Senators, carried along the Sacred Way, and placed in the Forum Romanum, where the Roman magistrates usually lay down their office. Tiers of seats rise up on either side, and on one flank a chorus of children from the noblest and most respected families stands facing a body of women selected on merit. Each group sings hymns and songs of thanksgiving in honour of the dead emperor, composed in a solemn and mournful key.

After this the bier is raised and carried outside the city walls to the Campus Martius, where on the widest part of the plain a square structure is erected, looking like a house, made from only the largest timbers jointed together. The whole inside is filled with firewood, and the outside is covered with golden garments, ivory decorations and rich pictures. On top of this rests another structure, similar in design and finish but smaller, with doors and open panels. Third and fourth storeys, decreasing in size, are topped by a fifth, the smallest of all. The shape of the whole might be compared with a lighthouse at the entrance to a harbour which guides ships on safe courses at night by its light. (Such a lighthouse is commonly called a *Pharos*.) When the bier has been taken to the second storey and put inside, aromatic herbs and incense of every kind produced on earth, together with flowers, grasses and juices collected for their smell, are brought and poured in in heaps. Every nation and city, every person without distinction of rank or position competes in bringing these last gifts in honour of their emperor. When the pile of aromatic material is very high and the whole space filled, a mounted display is held around the structure. The whole Equestrian Order rides round, wheeling in well-disciplined circles in the Pyrrhic style. Chariots also circle in the same formations, the charioteers dressed in purple and carrying images with the masks of famous Roman generals and emperors.

The display over, the heir to the throne takes a brand and sets it to the building. All the spectators crowd in and add to the flame. Everything is very easily and readily consumed by the fire because of the mass of firewood and incense inside. From the highest and smallest storey, as from some battlement, an eagle is released and carried up into the sky with the flames. The

Romans believe that this bird bears the soul of the emperor from earth to heaven. Thereafter the dead emperor is worshipped with the rest of the gods.

A CUCKOLD LAMENTS, ROMAN EGYPT, AD 2ND CENTURY

Serenus

Serenus to his beloved sister Isidora, many greetings. Before all else I pray for your health, and every day and evening I perform the act of veneration on your behalf to Thoeris[1] who loves you. I assure you that ever since you left me I have been in mourning, weeping by night and lamenting by day. Since we bathed together on Phaophi 12th, I never bathed nor anointed myself till Athur 12th.[2] You sent me letters which would have shaken a stone, so much did your words move me. Instantly I answered you and gave the letter sealed to the messenger on the 12th, together with letters for you. Apart from your saying and writing: "Colobus has made me a prostitute", he (Colobus) said to me: "Your wife sent me a message saying 'He himself (Serenus) has sold the chain, and himself put me in the boat'". You say this to prevent my being believed any longer with regard to my embarkation. See how many things I have sent to you! Whether you are coming or not, let me know.

Deliver to Isidora from Serenus.

A SOLDIER WRITES HOME, ITALY, AD 2ND CENTURY

Apion

The writer was a Romanized Egyptian stationed in Italy; he writes to his father.

Apion to Epimachus, his father and lord, heartiest greetings. First of all I pray that you are in health and continually prosper and fare well, with my sister and her daughter and my brother.

1 The hippopotamus goddess, benevolent to mothers and young infants.
2 A whole month.

I thank the lord Serapis that when I was in danger at sea he saved me. Straightway upon entering Misenum I received my travelling money from Caesar, three gold pieces. And I am well. I beg you, therefore, honoured father, write me a few lines, first regarding your health, secondly regarding that of my brother and sister, thirdly that I may kiss your hand, because you have brought me up so well, and on this account I hope for early promotion, if the gods will. Greetings to Capito, to my brother and sister, to Serenilla and to my friends. I send you by Euctemon a little portrait of myself. My military name is Antonius Maximus. I pray for your good health.

Athenonike company.

P.S. – Greetings from Serenus, son of Agathus Daemon, and from Turbo, son of Gallonius.

To Philadelphia for Epimachus from his son Apion.

To be handed to the office of the first cohort of the Apamaeans to Julianus, paymaster, from Apion, to be forwarded to Epimachus his father.

MOB INSURRECTION, ROME, AD 235

Herodian

A mutiny against Emperor Alexander Severus (a distant descendant of Septimius) in AD 235 left a Danubian peasant by the name of Maximinus on the imperial throne. Although he survived the revolt below, he fell to the assassin in AD 238 – a year which saw no less than seven caesars, as military usurper upon military usurper tried their luck on the throne.

About the same time a calamitous event occurred at Rome, which owed its origin and cause to the daring and rashness of two Senators. It was the general practice for citizens to go to the Senate House to find out the news. The troops left behind by Maximinus in the Praetorian Camp, who were near the end of their period of service and had remained at home because of their age, heard of this habit, and came as far as the entrance to the Senate wishing to find out what was happening. They were standing with the rest of the crowd, unarmed and in plain clothes and cloaks. Most of them stayed at the doors, but two or three wanted especially to hear the debate, and went into the chamber just past the base of the statue of Victory. As the soldiers stood completely off their guard with their hands in the folds of their cloaks, two members of the Senate, one an ex-consul Gallinicus, Carthaginian by birth, and the other an ex-praetor called Maecenas, attacked and struck them with the swords which they carried in their garments, wounding them in the chest. All Senators went about armed in the present state of unrest and disorder, some quite blatantly, to have some means of defending themselves against sudden attacks from their opponents. The wounded soldiers were unable to hit back because of the surprise nature of the blows, and fell in front of the base of the statue. The rest of the troops were staggered to see what had happened to their comrades, and fled in fear of the size of the mob, since they were unarmed.

Gallinicus ran from the Senate into the middle of the crowd, showing his hands and sword covered in blood, and urged them to chase and kill those whom he called the enemies of the Senate and of Rome, men who were the friends and allies of Max-iminus. The people were easily duped into heaping praises on Gallinicus, and followed after the soldiers as best they could, pelting them with stones. But the latter, though few in number and wounded, managed to escape into their camp, and were able to shut the gates. Seizing their arms, they guarded the walls of the camp.

Gallinicus, once having ventured on such a course, did his best to stir up civil war and destruction in the city. He persuaded, the mob to break into the public arsenals to get the weapons from them, which were more suitable for cere-monies than for fighting, so that each man would have some-thing to protect himself with. He threw open the compounds and led out the gladiators with their own specialized weapons. Any pikes, swords or axes in private possession or in the shops were all seized. The people in their frenzy fashioned into weapons any tool of any battleworthy material that came to hand. Then they advanced on the camp in a body and, as if conducting a regular siege, attacked the gates and walls. But the soldiers had the advantage of long training and were protected by the battlements and their shields. They fired arrows at them and succeeded in keeping them at a distance with long spears, eventually forcing them back from the wall. As the mob tired and the wounded gladiators were keen to withdraw now that evening was coming on, the soldiers noticed them turning away and presenting their backs, walking carelessly off without a thought that a few men would dare to attack such large numbers. So, quickly opening the gates, they ran upon the crowd, and cut down the gladiators, many of the citizens dying in the crush. The soldiers only chased them for a short distance from the camp, and on their return stayed within their wall.

This failure increased the temper of the mob and of the Senate. Generals were chosen, picked from the whole of Italy; all the young men were assembled and armed with improvized weapons; then most of these were taken off by Maximus to make war on Maximinus. The rest stayed behind to guard and defend the city. There were repeated ineffectual attacks on the walls of the camp. The troops were fighting from higher positions, and the attackers, frequently wounded, retired in disorder. Balbinus, who had remained in Rome, issued a proclamation in which he begged the people to come to terms, promised amnesty to the soldiers and pardon for all their crimes. But neither side would listen to him. Indeed the trouble increased, for the large crowd thought it a disgrace to be thwarted by such a few men, while the soldiers were furious at suffering the same sort of treatment from the citizens of Rome as they had from the barbarians.

Finally, when all their attacks on the wall proved unavailing, the generals decided to cut all the water-conduits that flowed into the camp, and so overcome them by depriving them of water and anything to drink. So they started work, and channelled off all the camp water into other runnels, cutting or blocking up the ones which led into the camp. When they realized their danger, the soldiers had no alternative in this predicament but to open the gates and to go out on attack. A fierce fight ensued, and the mob fled pursued by the advancing soldiers for a long distance through the city. Defeated in the hand-to-hand struggle, they quickly climbed onto the roofs, from where they attacked the soldiers by throwing tiles, stones and pieces of pot at them, causing great distress because the soldiers were not daring enough to climb up after them in their ignorance of the buildings. Houses and shops were bolted, but the soldiers set fire to the doors and to any wooden balconies, of which there were many in the city. The fire consumed the greater part of the city very easily because the houses were so close together and mostly made of wood. Many rich citizens were impoverished, losing wonderful costly possessions, valuable both from the incomes derived from them and for the expensive finery contained in them. In addition a large number of men who could not escape because their exits were cut off by the fire perished in the flames. The rich had all their property looted when the lawless, worthless elements among the population joined the troops in ransacking the houses. In this way an area of the city was destroyed equal to the whole area of any other city in the world.

CERTIFICATE OF HAVING SACRIFICED TO THE PAGAN GODS, EGYPT, 26 JUNE, AD 250

Issued during Decius' persecution of the Christians, AD 249–51. The so-called "Restorer of the Cults" demanded that every Christian suspect in the Empire perform a single sacrifice to the traditional gods; those who did so were issued with a "Certificate of Sacrifice". Those who did not, were put to death.

To the Commissioners of Sacrifice of the Village of Alexander's Island: from Aurelius Diogenes, the son of Satabus, of the Village of Alexander's Island, aged 72 years: – scar on his right eyebrow.

I have always sacrificed regularly to the gods, and now, in your presence, in accordance with the edict, I have done sacrifice, and poured the drink offering, and tasted of the Sacrifices, and I request you to certify the same, Farewell.

                        Handed in by me, *Aurelius Diogenes*.

I certify that I saw him sacrificing . . .[1]

Done in the first year of the Emperor, Cæsar Gaius Messius Quintus Trajanus Decius, Pius, Felix, Augustus: the second of the month Epith.

---

[1] The magistrate's signature is obliterated.

THE DEFEAT OF THE GOTHS: THE EMPEROR REPORTS, MACEDONIA, AD 269

Claudius II

Claudius' victories against the Goths earned him the title of Gothicus. A year after this missive he fell to the plague epidemic which ravaged the Empire in the late third century.

We have destroyed 320,000 of the Goths; we have sunk 2,000 of their ships. The rivers are bridged over with shields, the shores are covered with lances and with swords. The fields are hidden under the superincumbent bones, no road is free from them. We have taken so many women that each soldier can have two or three allotted to him.

AURELIAN CONQUERS ZENOBIA, SYRIA, AD 273

Vopiscus

Zenobia was queen of Palmyra, a city-state in Syria, which sought to break Roman power in the East and Egypt. That she failed was due to the military brilliance of Emperor Aurelian, popularly known as manu ad ferrum ("hand on hilt"). Aurelian later paraded her through Rome in golden chains.

After taking Tyana and winning a small battle near Daphne, Aurelian took possession of Antioch, having promised to grant pardon to all the inhabitants, and – acting on the counsel of the venerable Apollonius – he showed himself most humane and merciful. Next, close by Emessa, he gave battle to Zenobia and to her ally Zaba, – a great battle in which the very fate of the Empire hung in the issue. Already the cavalry of Aurelian were weary, wavering, and about to take flight, when, by divine assistance, a kind of celestial apparition renewed their courage, and the infantry coming to the aid of the cavalry, they rallied stoutly. Zenobia and Zaba were defeated, and the victory of Aurelian was complete. Aurelian, thus made master of the East, entered Emessa as conqueror. First of all he presented himself in the temple of Elagabalus, as if to discharge himself of an ordinary vow, – but there he beheld the same divine figure which he had seen come to succour him during the battle. Therefore in that same place he consecrated some temples, with splendid presents; he also erected in Rome a temple to the Sun, and consecrated it with great pomp.

Afterward he marched on Palmyra, to end his labours by the taking of that city. The robber bands of Syria, however, made constant attacks while his army was on the march; and during the siege he was in great danger by being wounded by an arrow.

Finally wearied and discouraged by his losses, Aurelian undertook to write to Zenobia, pledging her – if she would surrender, to preserve her life, – in the following letter.

"*Aurelian, Emperor of Rome and 'Restorer of the Orient' to Zenobia and those waging war on her side.* You should have done what I commanded you in my former letter. I promise you life if you surrender. You, O Zenobia, can live with your family in the place which I will assign you upon the advice of the venerable Senate. You must deliver to the treasury of Rome your jewels, your silver, your gold, your robes of silk, your horses and your camels. The Palmyrenes, however, shall preserve their local rights."

Zenobia replied to this letter with a pride and boldness, not at all in accord with her fortune. For she imagined that she could intimidate him.

"*Zenobia, Queen of the East, to Aurelian Augustus.* No one, saving you, has ever required of me what you have in your letter. One ought in war to hearken only to the voice of courage. You demand that I surrender myself, as if you did not know that the Queen Cleopatra preferred to die rather than to live in any other save her royal station. The Persians do not abandon us, and we will wait their succours. The Saracens and the Armenians are on our side. The brigands of Syria have defeated your army, O Aurelian; – what will it be when we have received the reenforcements which come to us from all sides. You will lower then that tone with which you, – as if already full conqueror, – now bid me to surrender."

On the reading of this letter the Emperor did not blush, yet he was angered, and at once assembling his army with his generals, and surrounding Palmyra on all sides, the great Emperor devoted his attention to everything; for he cut off the succours from the Persians, and corrupted the hordes of Saracens and Armenians, winning them over sometimes by his severity, sometimes by his adroitness; in brief, after many attacks, the valiant Queen was vanquished. Although she fled on camels by which she strove to reach the Persians, the cavalrymen sent in pursuit captured her, and brought her to Aurelian.

The tumult of the soldiers – requiring that Zenobia be given up for punishment – was very violent; but Aurelian conceived that it would be shameful to put to death a woman; so he contented himself with executing most of those men who had fomented, prepared, and conducted this war, reserving Zenobia to adorn his triumph and to feast the eyes of the Roman People. It is grievous that he must needs place in the number of those massacred the philosopher Longinus, who was, – it is said, – the master of Zenobia in the Greek tongue. It is alleged that Aurelian consented to his death because there was attributed to him that aforenamed letter so full of offensive pride.

It is seldom and even difficult that Syrians remain faithful. The Palmyrenes, who had been defeated and conquered, seeing that Aurelian had gone away and was busy with the affairs of Europe, wished to give the power to one Achilleus, a kinsman of Zenobia, and stirred up a great revolt. They slew 600 archers and Sandrion, whom Aurelian had left as governor in their region; but the Emperor, ever in arms, hastened back from Europe, and destroyed Palmyra, even as it deserved.

In his magnificent triumph, celebrated in Rome after Aurelian had conquered Tetricius, the usurping "Emperor of Gaul," and other enemies, Zenobia was led in procession, exposed to public view, adorned with jewels, and loaded with chains of gold so heavy that some of her guards had to hold them up for her. Later, however, she was treated with great humanity, granted a palace near Rome, and spent her last days in peace and luxury.

DIOCLETIAN SEIZES THE CHRISTIANS' BOOKS, CIRTA, NUMIDIA, c. AD 303

Anon

The revival of the Roman state under Diocletian (reigned AD 284–305) entailed severe repression of the Christians, whose religion was adjudged unpatriotic (requiring, as it did, adherence to a supranational faith). The Great Persecution, which began in AD 303, forbade all assemblies of Christians, ordered the destruction of their churches, and their sacred books. Below is an account of a state search for Christian books in Cirta, Roman North Africa.

When the magistrates and a policeman, guided by the apostatizing secretaries of the bishop, came to the house of Felix the tailor, he brought out five books, and when they came to the house of Proiectus he brought out five big and two little books. Victor the schoolmaster brought out two books, and four books of five volumes each. Felix the "Perpetual Flamen" said to him: "Bring your scriptures out: you have more." Victor the schoolmaster said, "If I had had more I should have brought them out."

When they came to the house of Eutychia who was a Caesarian [*i.e.*, in the government service], the flamen said, "Bring out your books that you may obey the law." "I have none," he replied. "Your answer," said Felix the flamen, "is taken down."

At the house of Coddeo, Coddeo's wife brought out six books. Felix said, "Look and see if you have not got some more." The woman said, "I have no more." Felix said to Bos, the policeman, "Go in and see if she has any more." The policeman reported, "I have looked and found none."

CONSTANTINE THE GREAT OVERTHROWS MAXENTIUS, AD 312

Eusebius

Born in c. AD 274, Constantine was the proclaimed successor of his father, Emperor Constantius Chlorus. Political intrigues on the death of the latter, however, meant that there were no less than five other emperors by 308. Eventually, Roman rule in the west became a straight struggle between Constantine and Maxentius. (The eastern half of the Roman Empire fell to Licinius.) As Eusebius relates below, Constantine – a pagan – reputedly had a vision of a blazing cross inscribed "By this, Conquer" before his decisive battle with Maxentius at Milvian Bridge outside Rome. On becoming sole emperor in the west, Constantine accorded civil rights and toleration to his

Christian subjects. Later in his reign, having become master of the East as well the West, he founded "Constantinople" (see p336–338) and declared Christianity the state religion. Yet it was only shortly before his death (AD 337) that Constantine himself was baptized.

God the Supreme Governor of the world appointed Constantine to be prince and sovran . . . so that while others have been raised to this eminence by the election of their fellow men, he is the only one to whose elevation no mortal may boast to have contributed.

As soon as he was established on the throne, he began to care for the interests of his paternal inheritance [especially Gaul and Britain], and visited with much considerate kindness all those provinces which had previously been under his father's government.

Having subdued various barbarian neighbours of his part of the Empire, he beheld Rome the imperial city oppressed by the tyranny of Maxentius, emperor of Italy and Africa, and Constantine speedily resolved to deliver her. Being convinced however that he needed some more powerful aid than his military forces could afford him, on account of the wicked and magical enchantments which were so diligently practiced by the tyrant, he began to seek for Divine assistance, as more important even than weapons, and a huge army. He considered how divers emperors had invoked the heathen gods yet had come to destruction. On the other hand he recollected that his father, who had pursued an entirely opposite course, who had condemned their error and honoured one supreme God during his whole life, had found Him to be the Savior and Protector of his Empire, and the Giver of every good thing.

Accordingly he called on Him with earnest prayer and supplications that He would reveal to him who He was, and stretch forth His right hand to help him in his present difficulties. And while Constantine was thus praying with fervent entreaty, a most marvellous sight appeared to him in heaven, the account of which might have been difficult to receive with credit had it been related by any other person. But since the victorious emperor himself not long afterwards declared it to the writer of this history, when he was honoured with his acquaintance and society, and confirmed this statement with an oath, who could refuse to accredit the relation, since the testimony of after times has established its truth? He said that about midday, when the sun was beginning to decline, he saw with his own eyes the trophy of a cross of light in the heavens, above the sun, and bearing the inscription "BY THIS, CONQUER." At this sight he himself was struck with amazement, and his whole army also, which happened to be following him on some expedition and witnessed the miracle.

He said, also, that he doubted within himself what this apparition could mean. Presently he fell asleep and in his sleep the Christ of God appeared to him with the same sign which he had seen in the heavens, and commanded him to procure a standard made in the likeness of that sign, and to use it as a safeguard in all engagements with his enemies.

At dawn of day he arose and told his friends his secret, then he called together his goldsmiths and jewellers, and sat in their midst, and described to them the figure of the sign which he had seen, bidding them copy it in gold and precious stones. It was made in the following manner. A long spear overlaid with gold formed the figure of the cross by means of a piece transversely laid over it. On the top of the whole was fixed a crown, formed by the intertexture of gold and precious stones; and thereon were two letters indicating the name of Christ, . . . the Greek letter P [Latin R] being intersected by X [Latin CH] exactly in its center; and these letters the Emperor was in the habit of wearing on his helmet at a later period. From the traverse piece which crossed the spear was a purple streamer, embroidered with jewels and gold; and on the staff hung a square banner bearing a golden portrait, half length, of the pious Emperor and of his children.

Constantine now devoted himself to the study of Christianity and the Bible, and he made the priests of God his councilors and deemed it incumbent upon him to honour the God who appeared to him with all devotion. After this, being fortified by well-grounded hopes in Him, he undertook to quench the fury of the fire of tyranny.

Meantime Maxentius at Rome was giving himself utterly over to deeds of cruelty and lust, and on one occasion caused his guards to massacre a great multitude of the Roman populace.

In short it is impossible to describe the manifold acts of oppression by which this tyrant of Rome oppressed all his subjects; so that by this time they were reduced to the most extreme penury and want of necessary food, a scarcity such as our contemporaries do not remember ever to have existed before at Rome.

Constantine, however, filled with compassion on account of all these miseries, began to arm himself with all warlike preparations against the tyranny, and marched with his forces eager to reinstate the Romans in the freedom they had inherited from their ancestors. . . . The Emperor, accordingly, confiding in the help of God, advanced against the first, second, and third divisions of the tyrant's forces, defeated them all with ease at the first assault, and made his way into the very interior of Italy.

Already he was close to Rome, when to save him from the need of fighting with all the Romans for the tyrant's sake, God Himself drew the tyrant, as it were by secret cords, a long way outside the gates. For once, as in the days of Moses and the Hebrew nation, who were worshippers of God, He cast Pharaoh's chariots and his host into the waves of the Red-Sea, so at this time did Maxentius, and the soldiers and guards with him, sink to the bottom as a stone, when in his flight before the divinely aided forces of Constantine, he essayed to cross the river [Tiber] which lay in his way, over which he had made a strong bridge of boats, and had framed an engine of destruction – really against himself, but in hope of ensnaring thereby him who was beloved by God. But God brought this engine to be Maxentius's undoing: for the machine, erected on the bridge with the ambuscade concealed therein, giving way unexpectedly before the appointed time, the passage began to sink down, and the boats with the men in them went bodily to the bottom. And first the wretch himself, then his armed attendants and guards, even as the sacred oracles had before described "sank as lead in the mighty waters." So Constantine and his men might well have rejoiced, even as did Moses and the Israelites over the fate of Pharaoh's host in the Red Sea.

Then Constantine entered the imperial city in triumph. And here the whole body of the Senate, and others of rank and distinction in the city – freed as it were from the restraint of a prison, along with the whole Roman populace, their faces expressing the gladness in their hearts, received him with acclamations and excess of joy – men, women, and children, with countless multitudes of servants, greeting him as "Deliverer, Preserver, and Benefactor" with incessant plaudits.

A FLUTE-PLAYER'S CONTRACT, ROMAN EGYPT, AD 322

Aurelius Psenymis

In the consulship of our lords Licinius Augustus (6th time) and Licinius Caesar (2nd time). To Aurelius Eugenius, gymnasiarch and senator of Hermopolis, greetings from Aurelius Psenymis, son of Kollouthos and Melitene, a fluteplayer from Hermopolis. I agree that I have contracted and pledged myself to you, the squire, to present myself at the village at the vintage-time in the vineyards with the appointed grape-treaders. There I will serve, without fail, the grape-treaders and others with my flute-playing. I promise not to leave the grape-treaders till the end of the vintage in the coming prosperous 10th special fiscal year. For the flute-playing and the pleasure I give, I shall receive the agreed sum from the contracting party.

Signed, the 24th of Choiak in the above-named consulship,
Aurelius Psenymis.

I will fulfil the conditions as stated.

I, Aurelius Pinoution, his assistant, have written for Anicetus, since he is illiterate.

CONSTANTINE FOUNDS CONSTANTINOPLE, AD 324–330

Sozomen

Military needs decided Constantine on the founding of a new capital for the Empire. The site chosen was Byzantium on the Bosphorus – a position which enabled closer supervision of the all-important Danube and Euphrates defences. To mark its capital status the city was renamed Constantinople. Today it is the site of Istanbul.

The Emperor [Constantine] always intent on the advancement of religion erected splendid [Christian] temples to God in every place – especially in great cities such as Nicomedia in Bithynia, Antioch on the Orontes, and Byzantium. He greatly improved this latter city, and made it equal to Rome in power and influence; for when he had settled his empire as he was minded, and had freed himself from foreign foes, he resolved on founding a city which should be called by his own name, and should equal in fame even Rome. With this intent he went to the plain at the foot of Troy on the Hellespont . . . and here he laid out the plan of a large and beautiful city, and built gates on a high spot of ground, whence they are still visible from the sea to sailors. But when he had proceeded thus far, God appeared to him by night and bade him seek another site for his city.

Led by the divine hand, he came to Byzantium in Thrace beyond Chalcedon in Bithynia, and here he desired to build his city, and render it worthy of the name of Constantine. In obedience to the command of God, he therefore enlarged the city formerly called Byzantium, and surrounded it with high walls; likewise he built splendid dwelling houses; and being aware that the former population was not enough for so great a city, he peopled it with men of rank and their families, whom he summoned from Rome and from other countries. He imposed special taxes to cover the expenses of building and adorning the city, and of supplying the inhabitants with food. He erected all the needed edifices for a great capital – a hippodrome, fountains, porticoes and other beautiful adornments. He named it *Constantinople* and *New Rome*, – and established it as the Roman capital for all the inhabitants of the North, the South, the East, and the shores of the Mediterranean, from the cities on the Danube and from Epidamnus and the Ionian Gulf to Cyrene and Libya.

He created another Senate which he endowed with the same honours and privileges as that of Rome, and he strove to render the city of his name equal in every way to Rome in Italy; nor were his wishes in vain, for by the favour of God, it became the most populous and wealthy of cities. As this city became the capital of the Empire during the period of Christian religious prosperity, it was not polluted by altars, Grecian temples, nor pagan sacrifices. Constantine also honoured this new city of Christ by adorning it with many and splendid houses of prayer, in which the Deity vouchsafed to bless the efforts of the Emperor by giving sensible manifestations of his presence.

CONSTANTINE ORDERS THE BUILDING OF THE CHURCH OF THE HOLY SEPULCHRE, JERUSALEM, AD 325

Constantine

A letter to Macarius, Bishop of Jerusalem.

Such is the Grace of our Saviour, that no words of mine can fitly unfold the tale of its latest manifestation. For it is beyond all wonder that the Sepulchre, the evidence of His most sacred Passion, should have lain hid in the earth through so many years, now at last by the destruction of our common foe[1] to be revealed to his slaves whom we now set free. It seems to me that if the wise men of the whole earth were brought together in one place, and were to endeavour to speak words meet for such a subject, they could not touch even the fringe of the matter. For the miracle as much outruns human comprehension as divine things are above human. Wherefore I have ever and especially this one aim, that inasmuch as the true Faith is daily illumined by fresh miracles, so should all our minds be urged to follow the Divine Law in all reverence and concord. So, though I conceive that everyone must acknowledge it, I wish in the first place to convince you that nothing is more important to me than by God's command to have set free that Holy Place, which had been, as it were, the vile pedestal of an idol, and to have relieved it from a heavy load that crushed it. For that place which from the first was holy in God's eyes, later was made yet more holy, in that it brought the evidence of our Lord's Passion to light. This place, I say, it is our duty to adorn with the beauty of the builder's art. So it becomes your discretion to dispose and arrange everything needful for the work, so that not only the Basilica itself may be superior to all others, but that everything

[1] Licinianus, the former Emperor of the East, defeated by Constantine in AD 326.

about it may easily surpass the most beautiful edifices in all other cities.

The fabric and adornment of the walls I have already entrusted to my friend Dracilianus, deputy of the praetorian prefects, and to the Governor of the province. Our Piety commands that craftsmen and labourers and whatever else they have decided, with your approval, to be required for the work, shall be provided forthwith under their immediate care. As for the columns, however, and the marbles, or whatever you consider, on a general survey, to be yet more precious or ornamental, make haste to write to me personally in the matter. And when I have seen from your letter what sort of materials and what quantities are needed, they shall be brought together from all parts.

For the hall of the Basilica, I should like your opinion whether the ceiling should be panelled, or adorned with some other type of work. If it is panelled, it can be finished with gilding. It remains for your Reverence forthwith to notify the magistrates mentioned above of the cost of the craftsmen, labourers, and the other expenses, and to inform me immediately of your opinion not only about the marbles and the columns, but about the ceiling, whether you think panelling will have the best appearance.

May God keep you, beloved brother.

THE EMPEROR AS PILGRIM: CONSTANTIUS II VISITS ROME, AD 357

Ammianus Marcellinus

Constantius II was Eastern Roman Emperor AD 337–361.

As he went on, having entered Rome, that home of sovereignty and of all virtues, when he arrived at the rostra, he gazed with amazed awe on the Forum, the most renowned monument of ancient power; and, being bewildered with the number of wonders on every side to which he turned his eyes, having addressed the nobles in the senate-house, and harangued the populace from the tribune, he retired, with the goodwill of all, into his palace, where he enjoyed the luxury he had wished for.

And often, when celebrating the equestrian games, was he delighted with the talkativeness of the common people, who were neither proud, nor, on the other hand, inclined to become rebellious from too much liberty, while he himself also reverently observed a proper moderation. For he did not, as was usually done in other cities, allow the length of the gladiatorial contests to depend on his caprice; but left it to be decided by various occurrences. Then, traversing the summits of the seven hills, and the different quarters of the city, whether placed on the slopes of the hills or on the level ground, and visiting, too, the suburban divisions, he was so delighted that whatever he saw first he thought the most excellent of all. Admiring the temple of the Tarpeian Jupiter, which is as much superior to other temples as divine things are superior to those of men; and the baths of the size of provinces; and the vast mass of the amphitheatre, so solidly erected of Tibertine stone, to the top of which human vision can scarcely reach; and the Pantheon with its vast extent, its imposing height, and the solid magnificence of its arches, and the lofty niches rising one above another like stairs, adorned with the images of former emperors; and the temple of the city, and the forum of peace, and the theatre of Pompey, and the odeum, and the racecourse, and the other ornaments of the Eternal City.

But when he came to the Forum of Trajan, the most exquisite structure, in my opinion, under the canopy of heaven, and admired even by the deities themselves, he stood transfixed with wonder, casting his mind over the gigantic proportions of the place, beyond the power of mortal to describe, and beyond the reasonable desire of mortals to rival. Therefore giving up all hopes of attempting anything of this kind, he contented himself with saying that he should wish to imitate, and could imitate, the horse of Trajan, which stands by itself in the middle of the hall, bearing the emperor himself on his back.

And the royal prince Hormisda, whose departure from Persia we have already mentioned, standing by answered, with the refinement of his nature. "But first, O Emperor, command such a stable to be built for him, if you can, that the horse on which you purpose to make may have as fair a domain as this which we see." And when he was asked what he thought of Rome, he said that "he was particularly delighted with it because he had learned that men died also there."

Now after he had beheld all these various objects with awful admiration, the emperor complained of fame, as either deficient in power, or else spiteful, because, though it usually exaggerates everything, it fell very short in its praises of the things which are at Rome; and having deliberated for some time what he should do, he determined to add to the ornaments of the city by erecting an obelisk in the Circus Maximus, the origin and form of which I will describe when I come to the proper place.

JULIAN IS PROCLAIMED AUGUSTUS, PARIS, AD 360

Julian

The accession of Constantine's sons in AD 337 saw a massacre of the males belonging to the younger line of the Flavian dynasty. Julian (too young, it was considered, to be a threat) was almost the sole survivor. He came to the imperial throne via an outstandingly successful career as soldier, particularly in the Rhineland; in AD 360 his troops proclaimed him Augustus. Below is his letter to his cousin, Constantius II, concerning the proclamation. The opportune death of Constantius II in the following year gave Julian the government of the empire. He died in AD 363 fighting the Persians.

As far as concerns my projects, I have kept faith to the uttermost extent no less with the spirit than with the terms of our compact, with sentiments constant and unchanged, as substantial evidence can testify. When I was but newly created Caesar, you hurled me into the dreadful turmoil of battle. I was content with the power delegated to me, and like a faithful steward filled your ears with repeated news of the successes which rewarded our hopes. Nothing did I attribute to the risks taken by myself, though there is abundant proof that when the Germans were routed and in retreat, I was ever the first in the fray, the last to seek repose from toil. But (if I may have your indulgence in speaking) if, as you suppose, there has been a revolution, it was the soldiery, who seeing themselves wearing their lives away unprofitably in many severe struggles, suddenly accomplished what they had long been meditating, in dissatisfaction and impatience with a commander who was himself but a subordinate, with a Caesar who was powerless to recompense their prolonged exertions and incessant victories. And this anger of the soldiers was met, not with promotions or even the annual pay to which they were entitled, but with something quite unlooked-for, namely, the order to leave the icy climate to which they are accustomed, to march into the most distant parts of the East, to be separated from their wives and children, and to go in poverty and rags.

Exasperated beyond their wont, they gathered together by night and besieged the palace, acclaiming Julian Augustus with loud and repeated shouts. I was terrified, I admit it, and withdrew out of sight; as long as I could I remained apart, seeking safety in silence and concealment. But since they gave me no respite, I came forth, and stood in the sight of all, behind the sole fortification of my defenceless breast, thinking to calm the tumult by my authority, or by soothing words. They flared up then in extraordinary fashion, and went to such lengths that when I tried to overcome their obstinacy with my entreaties, they pressed menacingly upon me and threatened me with death. Conquered at last, and reflecting that if I were struck down some other perhaps would gladly see himself proclaimed Emperor in my stead, I yielded, in the hope of appeasing their violence.

This is the tale of events, which I beg you will receive with equanimity. Do not imagine that anything else took place, nor heed the evil whisperings of the malicious, who, for their own profit, are wont to sow discord among princes. Ignore flattery, the mother of wrongs, give heed to justice, the most excellent of all virtues, and accept in good faith the equitable conditions which I propose, with the reflection that they are the best both for the Roman state and for ourselves, linked as we are by the kind tie of blood, and by the lofty eminence of our fortune. Pardon me, for what I reasonably propose, I wish not so much to see carried out, as approved by you for utility and justice. With eagerness I await your commands.

I will set down in brief the measures which I consider necessary. I shall furnish teams of Spanish horses, and I shall mingle with the slaves and the guards a contingent of young foreign bondmen, barbarians from this side of the Rhine, or at least deserters who surrendered to us. Your Clemency will assign to us praetorian prefects of ascertained equity and merit; the remaining ordinary magistrates, and the promotions of military commanders, must be left to my judgment, as also the appointment of my personal guard. For it would be senseless, when it can be avoided, to surround the person of the Emperor with men whose characters are as unfamiliar as their sentiments.

One thing I will affirm without hesitation of any kind, that neither of their own free will nor under compulsion will the Gauls consent to send their recruits to foreign or distant parts, for they have been harassed with long-drawn disturbances and severe disasters; their youth is almost entirely wiped out, so that remembering past afflictions they will encounter fresh burdens with despair. Nor would it be opportune to send assistance from this province against the Parthians, for the inroads of the barbarians here have scarcely been stayed, and if you will suffer me to speak the truth, this province, after the continual blows it has received, is actually in need of powerful assistance from without.

If, as I think, I have written in a vein of salutary exhortation, actually, I entreat and beseech you. For I know (if I am not presuming on my position) what difficult affairs, situations almost abandoned and lost, have been saved and re-established by the agreements of princes, who have made mutual concessions. The example of our ancestors shows that rulers who are of this mind find a means to live in prosperity and happiness, and leave a cheerful remembrance of themselves to posterity for all time.

AN EMPEROR'S GIFT, C. AD 360

Julian

A letter addressed to Evagrius, a professor of rhetoric.

For your kindness to me I am making you a present of a small property of four fields which my grandmother gave me in Bithynia. It is too small to bring a man riches or raise him to affluence, at the same time it has a certain charm, as you will see when I describe it in detail. In writing to you there is no reason for not using a thoroughly affected style, loaded with Muses and Graces.

This property is not more than two and a half miles from the sea; it is not, therefore, pestered with people selling things, nor with sailors and their tiresome chatter; on the other hand it is not devoid of the gifts of Nereus, for you get fresh fish there, so fresh that it is actually gasping, and if you leave the house and mount a little rise, you will see the Propontis with its islands, and the city called after the great Emperor.[1] Then you need not walk on seaweed or slime, nor are you incommoded by the unpleasing and nameless refuse which the sea casts up on the sands; you tread upon herbs and thyme, and sweet-smelling turf. There is peace profound on the place, whether you want to lie at ease with a book, or to rest your eyes by gazing on that loveliest of sights, the sea with its ships. When I was a youngster I thought this the most delightful of summer retreats, for there is plenty of running water, and a charming bath, a garden and trees. When I grew up I used to long for it, and often went there, and my visits there were never without literary occupation.

There is a modest record there of my husbandry, a small vineyard producing a sweet wine with a fine bouquet, which does not require to be long matured before it can harbour Dionysus and the Graces. On the contrary, the grape hanging on the vine, or just crushed in the press, exhales the scent of roses, and the new must in the jars is already "extract of nectar", if Homer is to be believed. Why, then, did I not extend the vineyard, why not a number of *clos* of such a wonderful vine? Perhaps I was not a sufficiently industrious cultivator, but since I am a small drinker myself, and as far as I am concerned, Dionysus must keep company with the water-nymphs, I only raised what was sufficient for myself and my friends, and men of that sort are few. So then, dear friend, the gift I am making you, small though it be, is a gracious one between friends, a gift "from home to home", to borrow a word of the wise poet Pindar.

[1] Constantinople.

I have written this in a hurry by lamplight, so if there are mistakes, do not criticise them severely, like one professor judging another.

I was one man's field, then another's, to a third and fourth I passed,
Each thought that he owned me but I was Fortune's, first and last.

DELINQUENCY IN ROME: THE RICH, C. AD 370

Ammianus Marcellinus

There were numerous Christian complainants concerning the delinquency of the Romans; Ammianus Marcellinus was unusual in being a committed pagan. He served in the armies of Rome in Gaul, the East and Germany before settling in Rome as an historian.

Some men, distinguished (as they think) by famous forenames, pride themselves beyond measure in being called Reburri, Flavonii, Pagonii, Gereones, and Dalii, along with Tarracii and Pherrasii, and many other equally fine-sounding indications of eminent ancestry.

Others, resplendent in silken garments, as though they were to be led to death, or as if (to speak without any evil omen) they were bringing up the rear preceded by an army, are followed by a throng of slaves drawn up in troops, amid noise and confusion.

When such men, each attended by fifty servants, have entered the vaulted rooms of a bath, they shout in threatening tones: "Where on earth are our attendants?" If they have learned that an unknown courtesan has suddenly appeared, some woman who has been a common prostitute of the crowd of our city, some old strumpet, they all strive to be the first to reach her, and caressing the newcomer, extol her with such disgraceful flattery as the Parthians do Samiramis, the Egyptians their Cleopatras, the Carians Artemisia, or the people of Palmyra Zenobia. And those who stoop to do such things are men in the time of whose forefathers a senator was punished with the censor's brand of infamy, if he had dared, while this was still considered unseemly, to kiss his wife in the presence of their own daughter.

Some of these men, when one begins to salute them breast to breast, like menacing bulls turn to one side their heads, where they should be kissed, and offer their flatterers their knees to kiss or their hands, thinking that quite enough to ensure them a happy life; and they believe that a stranger is given an abundance of all the duties of courtesy, even though the great men may perhaps be under obligation to him, if he is asked what hot baths or waters he uses, or at what house he has been put up.

And although they are so important and, in their own opinion, such cultivators of the virtues, if they learn that someone has announced that horses or chariots are coming from anywhere whatever, they hover over this same man and ask him questions as anxiously as their ancestors looked up to the two sons of Tyndareus, when they filled everything with joy by announcing those famous victories of olden days.

Their houses are frequented by idle chatterboxes, who with various pretences of approval applaud every word of the man of loftier fortune, emulating the witty flatteries of the parasites in the comedies. For just as the parasites puff up boastful soldiers by attributing to them the sieges and battles against thousands of enemies, comparing them with the heroes of old, so these also, admiring the rows of columns hanging in the air with lofty façade, and the walls gleaming with the remarkable colours of precious stones, raise these noble men to the gods.

Sometimes at their banquets the scales are even called for, in order to weigh the fish, birds, and dormice that are served, whose great size they commend again and again, as hitherto unexampled, often repeating it to the weariness of those present, especially when thirty secretaries stand near by, with pen-cases and small tablets, recording these same items, so that the only thing lacking seems to be a schoolmaster.

Some of them hate learning as they do poison, and read with attentive care only Juvenal and Marius Maximus, in their boundless idleness handling no other books than these, for what reason it is not for my humble mind to judge.

Whereas, considering the greatness of their fame and of their parentage, they ought to pore over many and varied works; they ought to learn that Socrates, when condemned to death and thrown into prison, asked a musician, who was skilfully rendering a song of the lyric poet Stesichorus, that he might be taught to do this while there was still time. And when the musician asked of what use that could be to him, since he was to die on the following day, Socrates replied: "In order that I may know something more before I depart from life."

But a few among them are so strict in punishing offences, that if a slave is slow in bringing the hot water, they condemn him to suffer three hundred lashes; if he has intentionally killed a man, although many people insist that he be condemned to death, his master will merely cry out: "What should a worthless fellow do, notorious for wicked deeds? But if he dares to do anything else like that hereafter, he shall be punished."

But the height of refinement with these men at present is, that it is better for a stranger to kill any man's brother than to decline his invitation to dinner. For a senator thinks that he is suffering the loss of a rich property, if the man whom he has, after considerable weighing of pros and cons, invited once, fails to appear at his table.

Some of them, if they make a longish journey to visit their estates, or to hunt by the labours of others, think that they have equalled the marches of Alexander the Great or of Caesar; or if they have sailed in their gaily painted boats from the Lake of Avernus to Puteoli, it is the adventure of the golden fleece, especially if they should dare it in the hot season. And if amid the gilded fans flies have lighted on the silken fringes, or through a rent in the hanging curtain a little ray of sun has broken in, they lament that they were not born in the land of the Cimmerians.

Then when they come from the bath of Silvanus or from the healing waters of Mamaea, as any one of them emerges he has himself dried with the finest linens, opens the presses and carefully searches amongst garments shimmering with shifting light, of which he brings enough with him to clothe eleven men. At length, some are chosen and he puts them on; then he takes back his rings, which, in order that the dampness may not injure them, he has handed to a servant, and after his fingers have been as good as measured to receive them, he departs.

And, indeed, if any veteran has recently retired because of his years from service with the emperor, such a company of admirers attend him that . . . is considered to be the leader of the old song; the others quietly listen to what he says. He alone, like the father of a family, tells irrelevant stories and entertaining tales, and in most of them cleverly deceiving his hearers.

Some of these, though few in number, shrink from the name of gamblers, and therefore desire to be called rather *tesserarii*, persons who differ from each other only as much as thieves do from brigands. But this must be admitted, that while the friendships at Rome are lukewarm, those alone which are formed at the gambling table, as if they were gained by glorious toil, have a bond of union and are united by complete firmness of exceeding affection; whence some members of these companies are found to be so harmonious that you would take them for the brothers Quintilius. And so you may see a man of low station, who is skilled in the secrets of diceplaying, walking abroad like Porcius Cato after his unexpected and unlooked for defeat for the praetorship, with a set expression of dignity and sorrow because at some great banquet or assemblage a former proconsul was given a higher place of honour.

Some lie in wait for men of wealth, old or young, childless or unmarried, or even for those who have wives or children – for no distinction is observed in this respect – enticing them by wonderful trickeries to make their wills; and when they have set their last decisions in order and left some things to these men, to humour whom they have made their wills in their favour, they forthwith die; so that you would not think that the death was brought about by the working of the allotment of destiny, nor could an illness easily be proved by the testimony of witnesses; nor is the funeral of these men attended by any mourners.

Another, who attained some rank, moderate though it be, walking with neck puffed up, looks askance at his former acquaintances, so that you might think that a Marcellus was returning after the taking of Syracuse.

Many of them, who deny that there are higher powers in heaven, neither appear in public nor eat a meal nor think they can with due caution take a bath, until they have critically examined the calendar and learned where, for example, the planet Mercury is, or what degree of the constellation of the Crab the moon occupies in its course through the heavens.

Another, if he finds a creditor of his demanding his due with too great urgency, resorts to a charioteer who is all too ready to dare any enterprise, and causes the creditor to be charged with being a poisoner; and he is not let off until he has surrendered the bill of indebtedness and paid heavy costs. And besides, the accuser has the voluntary debtor put in prison as if he were his property, and does not set him free until he acknowledges the debt.

In another, place a wife by hammering day and night on the same anvil – as the old proverb has it – drives her husband to make a will, and the husband insistently urges his wife to do the same. Skilled jurists are brought in on both sides, one in a bedroom, the other, his rival, in the dining-room to discuss disputed points. These are joined by opposing interpreters of horoscopes, on the one side making profuse promises of prefectures and the burial of rich matrons, on the other telling women that for their husbands' funerals now quietly approaching they must make the necessary preparations. And a maid-servant bears witness, by nature some-what pale, . . . As Cicero says: "They know of nothing on earth that is good unless it brings gain. Of their friends, as of their cattle, they love those best from whom they hope to get the greatest profit."

When these people seek any loan, you will see them in slippers like a Micon or a Laches; when they are urged to pay, they wear such lofty buskins and are so arrogant that you would think them Cresphontes and Temenus, the famous Heraclidae. So much for the senate.

DELINQUENCY IN ROME: THE COMMON PEOPLE, C. AD 370

Ammianus Marcellinus

Let us now turn to the idle and slothful commons. Among them some who have no shoes are conspicuous as though they had cultured names, such as the Messores, Statarii, Semicupae and Serapini, and Cicymbricus, with Gluturinus and Trulla, and Lucanicus with Porclaca and Salsula, and countless others.

These spend all their life with wine and dice, in low haunts, pleasures, and the games. Their temple, their dwelling, their assembly, and the height of all their hopes is the Circus Maximus. You may see many groups of them gathered in the fora, the cross-roads, the streets, and their other meeting-places, engaged in quarrelsome arguments with one another, some (as usual) defending this, others that.

Among them those who have enjoyed a surfeit of life, influential through long experience, often swear by their hoary hair and wrinkles that the state cannot exist if in the coming race the charioteer whom each favours is not first to rush forth from the barriers, and fails to round the turning-point closely with his ill-omened horses.

And when there is such a dry rot of thoughtlessness, as soon as the longed-for day of the chariot-races begins to dawn, before the sun is yet shining clearly they all hasten in crowds to the spot at top speed, as if they would outstrip the very chariots that are to take part in the contest; and torn by their conflicting hopes about the result of the race, the greater number of them in their anxiety pass sleepless nights.

If from there they come to worthless theatrical pieces, any actor is hissed off the boards who has not won the favour of the low rabble with money. And if this noisy form of demonstration is lacking, they cry in imitation of the Tauric race that all strangers – on whose aid they have always depended and stood upright – ought to be driven from the city. All this in foul and absurd terms, very different from the expressions of their interests and desires made by your commons of old, of whose many witty and happy sayings tradition tells us.

And it has now come to this, that in place of the lively sound of approval from men appointed to applaud, at every public show an actor of afterpieces, a beast-baiter, a charioteer, every kind of player, and the magistrates of higher and lower rank, nay even matrons, are constantly greeted with the shout, "You should be these fellows' teachers!"; but what they ought to learn no one is able to explain.

The greater number of these gentry, given over to over-stuffing themselves with food, led by the charm of the odour of cooking and by the shrill voices of the women, like a flock of peacocks screaming with hunger, stand even from cockcrow beside the pots on tip-toe and gnaw the ends of their fingers as they wait for the dishes to cool. Others hang over the nauseous mass of half-raw meat, while it is cooking, watching it so intently that one would think that Democritus with other dissectors was examining the internal organs of dismembered animals and showing by what means future generations might be cured of internal pains.

THE HUNS, C. AD 370

Ammianus Marcellinus

The Huns were the most feared of the barbarian nomads who eventually engulfed the Roman Empire in the West.

The Huns have been but lightly touched on in old records. They live beyond the Sea of Azov, by the frozen Ocean, and their barbarity passes all bounds. From their earliest childhood, babies' faces are deeply scored with steel and these puckered scars slow down the growth of hair that comes with adolescence. So they grow up beardless, but without any charm, like eunuchs. All have strong, well-knit limbs and sturdy necks, and are so appallingly misshapen and deformed that you would take them for animals standing on two legs, or for the posts crudely fashioned into images which are used for the balustrades of bridges.

They may be horribly ugly as men, but they are so tough in their way of life that they have no need of fire or of good-tasting food. Their diet consists of the roots of wild plants and half-raw meat from some animal or other. They warm this meat up a little by putting it between their thighs and the backs of their horses. They never live in houses, which they avoid like tombs set apart from common use. You cannot even find among them a hut roofed over with reeds, but they wander and roam through the mountains and woods, and from their cradles have grown accustomed to bearing with frost, hunger and thirst. They never enter strangers' houses, unless forced by dire necessity, for they feel no safety in being under a roof.

They wear clothes made of linen or the skins of wood-mice, and the same dress serves them inside and outside the home. Once a tunic of some dull colour has been put over their necks, it is not taken off or changed until it is in tatters and has shredded into rags from the constant use. They cover their heads with round caps, and their hairy legs in goat-skins. Their shoes are not fashioned on lasts, and this prevents them from walking freely. This means that they are not very adept at infantry battles.

They are almost glued to their horses, which are sturdy but ugly creatures. They sometimes sit on them side-saddle to perform their usual tasks. It is on horseback that all Huns remain day and night, to buy and sell, to eat and drink, and, leaning forward on the narrow necks of their mounts, they collapse into a sleep deep enough to allow all manner of dreams. It is on horseback too that they all consult together when any discussion arises about some important matter.

They are disciplined by no king, but are content with the wild leadership of chiefs under whom they burst through any obstacle. When provoked to battle they enter the fight in wedge formation with horrible discordant yells. They are lightly armed for speed and surprise, and so they suddenly disperse on purpose for the assault. Charging in no definite ranks, they rush around dealing out widespread slaughter. You will never catch them attacking earthworks or hurling their javelins at enemy camps because of their preoccupation with speed. They easily earn the reputation thereby of being the fiercest warriors on earth. Their missiles are hurled from a distance and instead of arrow tips have sharpened bones fastened on most cleverly. Then they gallop over the intervening ground, and, reckless of their own lives, use their swords in hand-to-hand combat. While their opponents are on their guard against sword-thrusts, they lasso them with twisted nooses and by enmeshing their limbs make them totally incapable of riding or walking.

No one ever ploughs or touches a plough among them, for the whole people wanders about without fixed abode, with no homestead, no laws, no habitual diet. They always look like fugitives, as they travel with the wagons in which they live. In these wagons, their wives weave their coarse garments, have intercourse with their husbands, and give birth to their children whom they bring up to puberty. None of them, if asked, can tell you where he comes from, for he was conceived in one place, born in another far away, and brought up in a third yet more distant spot.

They are faithless and inconstant in observing truce, wafted on the faintest breeze of any new hope, and give their all to utter violence and madness. Like senseless animals, they are completely ignorant of the distinction between right and wrong, and in parleys they are ambiguous and deceitful, bound by no reverence for religion or superstition. Gold enflames their desires inordinately. They are so changeable and easily angered that they are often estranged from friends more than once on the same day, although there is no cause for annoyance, and are reconciled again, although no one brings them together.

"SO DESTRUCTIVE A SLAUGHTER": THE BATTLE OF ADRIANOPLE, 9 AUGUST AD 378

Ammianus Marcellinus

The westwards expansion of the Huns pushed the Visigoths across the Danube into the eastern Roman empire, where the authorities permitted them to settle. Pernickety imperial interference, however, caused the Visigoths to revolt and in AD 378 Emperor Valens met them in battle at Adrianople (Hadrianopolis) in Thrace. There ensued one of the worst defeats of Roman arms.

When the day broke which the annals mark as the fifth of the Ides of August, the Roman standards were advanced with haste. The baggage had been placed close to the walls of Adrianople, under a sufficient guard of soldiers of the legions. The treasures and the chief insignia of the Emperor's rank were within the walls, with the prefect and the principal members of the council.

Then, having traversed the broken ground which divided the two armies, as the burning day was progressing towards noon, at last, after marching eight miles, our men came in sight of the wagons of the enemy, which had been reported by the scouts to be all arranged in a circle. According to their custom, the barbarian host raised a fierce and hideous yell, while the Roman generals marshalled their line of battle.

While arms and missiles of all kinds were meeting in fierce conflict . . . our men began to retreat; but presently, aroused by the reproaches of their officers, they made a fresh stand, and the battle increased like a conflagration, terrifying our soldiers, numbers of whom were pierced by strokes of javelins hurled at them, and by arrows.

Then the two lines of battle dashed one against the other, like the prows of ships. Thrusting mightily, they were tossed to and fro like waves of the sea. Our left wing had advanced actually up to the wagons, intending to push on still farther if properly supported. But they were deserted by the rest of the cavalry. They were so much pressed by the superior numbers of the enemy that they were overwhelmed and beaten down like the ruins of a great rampart.

Soon our infantry too was left unsupported. The companies and regiments were shoved together so closely that a soldier could scarcely draw his sword, or even withdraw his hand after he had once stretched it out.

By this time such great clouds of dust arose that it was hardly possible to see the sky. The air resounded with terrible cries. The darts, which brought death on every side, reached their mark and fell with deadly effect, for no one could see them quickly enough to place himself on guard. The barbarians, rushing on with their enormous army, beat down our horses and men and gave us no open spaces where we could fall back to operate. They were so closely packed that it became impossible for us to escape by forcing a path through them. Our men finally began to despise the thought of death and, again taking their swords, slew all they encountered. Helmets and breatplates were smashed in pieces by mutual blows of battle-axes.

Then you might see the barbarian, towering in his fierceness, hissing or shouting, fall with his legs pierced through, or his right hand cut off, sword and all, or his side transfixed, and still, in the last gasp of life, casting around his defiant glances.

The plain was covered with corpses, showing the mutual ruin of the combatants. The groans of the dying, or of men horribly wounded, were intense and caused much dismay on all sides. Amidst all this great tumult and confusion, our infantry were exhausted by toil and danger, until at last they had neither the strength left to fight nor the spirit to plan anything. Their spears were broken by the frequent collisions, so that they were forced to content themselves with their drawn swords, which they thrust into the dense battalions of the enemy, disregarding their own safety, and seeing that every possibility of escape was cut off.

The sun, now high in the heavens, scorched the Romans, who were emaciated by hunger, worn out with battle, and scarcely able to bear the weight of their own weapons. At last our columns were entirely beaten back by the overpowering weight of the barbarians. They took to disorderly flight – the only resource under the circumstances – each man seeking to save himself as best he could.

Scarcely one third of the entire army escaped. Never, except in the battle of Cannae, had there been so destructive a slaughter recorded in our annals.

THE CONVERSION OF AUGUSTINE, AD 386

St Augustine

Augustine of Hippo was the greatest of the early church fathers. After a dissolute young manhood in Carthage (he was born in Numidia, modern-day Tunisia), he became at teacher in Rome, then Milan. Following a spiritual crisis he converted to Christianity. This personal spiritual struggle is the subject of the autobiographical Confessions *(AD 400).*

BOOK THREE CHAPTER I

1: I came to Carthage, where a caldron of unholy loves was seething and bubbling all around me. I was not in love as yet, but I was in love with love; and, from a hidden hunger, I hated myself for not feeling more intensely a sense of hunger. I was looking for something to love, for I was in love with loving, and I hated security and a smooth way, free from snares. Within me I had a dearth of that inner food which is thyself, my God – although that dearth caused me no hunger. And I remained without any appetite for incorruptible food – not because I was already filled with it, but because the emptier I became the more I loathed it. Because of this my soul was unhealthy; and, full of sores, it exuded itself forth, itching to be scratched by scraping on the things of the senses. Yet, had these things no soul, they would certainly not inspire our love. To love and to be loved was sweet to me, and all the more when I gained the enjoyment of the body of the person I loved. Thus I polluted the spring of friendship with the filth of concupiscence and I dimmed its luster with the slime of lust. Yet, foul and unclean as I was, I still craved, in excessive vanity, to be thought elegant and urbane. And I did fall precipitately into the love I was longing for. My God, my mercy, with how much bitterness didst thou, out of thy infinite goodness, flavour that sweetness for me! For I was not only beloved but also I secretly reached the climax of enjoyment; and yet I was joyfully bound with troublesome tics, so that I could be scourged with the burning iron rods of jealousy, suspicion, fear, anger, and strife.

CHAPTER IV

Among such as these, in that unstable period of my life, I studied the books of eloquence, for it was in eloquence that I was eager to be eminent, though from a reprehensible and vainglorious motive, and a delight in human vanity. In the ordinary course of study I came upon a certain book of Cicero's, whose language almost all admire, though not his heart. This particular book of his contains an exhortation to philosophy and was called *Hortensius*. Now it was this book which quite definitely changed my whole attitude and turned my prayers toward, thee, O Lord, and gave me new hope and new desires. Suddenly every vain hope became worthless to me, and with an incredible warmth of heart I yearned for an immortality of wisdom and began now to arise that I might return to thee. It was not to sharpen my tongue further that I made use of that book. I was now nineteen; my father had been dead two years, and my mother was providing the money for my study of rhetoric. What won me in it [i.e., the *Hortensius*] was not its style but its substance.

8. How ardent was I then, my God, how ardent to fly from earthly things to thee! Nor did I know how thou wast even then dealing with me. For with thee is wisdom. In Greek the love of wisdom is called "philosophy", and it was with this love that that book inflamed me. There are some who seduce through

philosophy, under a great, alluring, and honourable name, using it to colour and adorn their own errors. And almost all who did this, in Cicero's own time and earlier, are censored and pointed out in his book.

BOOK V CHAPTER XIII

23. And to Milan I came, to Ambrose the bishop, famed through the whole world as one of the best of men, thy devoted servant. His eloquent discourse in those times abundantly provided thy people with the flour of thy wheat, the gladness of thy oil, and the sober intoxication of thy wine. To him I was led by thee without my knowledge, that by him I might be led to thee in full knowledge. That man of God received me as a father would, and welcomed my coming as a good bishop should. And I began to love him, of course, not at the first as a teacher of the truth, for I had entirely despaired of finding that in thy Church – but as a friendly man. And I studiously listened to him – though not with the right motive – as he preached to the people. I was trying to discover whether his eloquence came up to his reputation, and whether it flowed fuller or thinner than others said it did. And thus I hung on his words intently, but, as to his subject matter, I was only a careless and contemptuous listener. I was delighted with the charm of his speech, which was more erudite, though less cheerful and soothing, than Faustus' style. As for subject matter, however, there could be no comparison, for the latter was wandering around in Manichean deceptions, while the former was teaching salvation most soundly. But "salvation is far from the wicked", such as I was then when I stood before him. Yet I was drawing nearer, gradually and unconsciously.

BOOK VIII CHAPTER XII

28. Now when deep reflection had drawn up out of the secret depths of my soul all my misery and had heaped it up before the sight of my heart, there arose a mighty storm, accompanied by a mighty rain of tears. That I might give way fully to my tears and lamentations, I stole away from Alypius, for it seemed to me that solitude was more appropriate for the business of weeping. I went far enough away that I could feel that even

his presence was no restraint upon me. This was the way I felt at the time, and he realized it. I suppose I had said something before I started up and he noticed that the sound of my voice was choked with weeping. And so he stayed alone, where we had been sitting together, greatly astonished. I flung myself down under a fig tree – how I know not – and gave free course to my tears. The streams of my eyes gushed out an acceptable sacrifice to thee. And, not indeed in these words, but to this effect, I cried to thee: "And thou, O Lord, how long? How long, O Lord? Wilt thou be angry forever? Oh, remember not against us our former iniquities." For I felt that I was still enthralled by them. I sent up these sorrowful cries: "How long, how long? Tomorrow and tomorrow? Why not now? Why not this very hour make an end to my uncleanness?"

29. I was saying these things and weeping in the most bitter contrition of my heart, when suddenly I heard the voice of a boy or a girl I know not which – coming from the neighbouring house, chanting over and over again, "Pick it up, read it; pick it up, read it." ["tolle lege, tolle lege"] Immediately I ceased weeping and began most earnestly to think whether it was usual for children in some kind of game to sing such a song, but I could not remember ever having heard the like. So, damming the torrent of my tears, I got to my feet, for I could not but think that this was a divine command to open the Bible and read the first passage I should light upon. For I had heard how Anthony, accidentally coming into church while the gospel was being read, received the admonition as if what was read had been addressed to him: "Go and sell what you have and give it to the poor, and you shall have treasure in heaven; and come and follow me." By such an oracle he was forthwith converted to thee.

So I quickly returned to the bench where Alypius was sitting, for there I had put down the apostle's book when I had left there. I snatched it up, opened it, and in silence read the paragraph on which my eyes first fell: "Not in rioting and drunkenness, not in chambering and wantonness, not in strife and envying, but put on the Lord Jesus Christ, and make no provision for the flesh to fulfill the lusts thereof." I wanted to read no further, nor did I need to. For instantly, as the sentence ended, there was infused in my heart something like the light of full certainty and all the gloom of doubt vanished away.

THE HAZARDS OF SEA TRAVEL, THE MEDITERRANEAN, c. AD 400

Synesius

Synesius was Bishop of Ptolemais in Roman Egypt.

Although we started from Bendideum at early dawn, we had scarcely passed Pharius Myrmex by noonday, for our ship went aground two or three times in the bed of the harbour. This mishap at the very outset seemed a bad omen, and it might have been wiser to desert a vessel which had been unlucky from the very start . . . Hear my story then, that you may have no further leisure for your mocking wit, and I will tell you first of all how our crew made up. Our skipper was fain of death owing to his bankrupt condition; then besides him we had twelve sailors, thirteen in all! More than half of them, including the skipper, were Jews – a graceless race and fully convinced of the piety of sending to Hades as many Greeks as possible. The remainder were a collection of peasants who even as late as last year had never gripped an oar, but the one batch and the other were alike in this, that every man of them had some personal defect . . . We had embarked to the number of more than fifty, about a third of us being women, most of them young and comely. Do not, however, be too quick to envy us, for a screen separated us from them and a stout one at that, the suspended fragment of a recently torn sail, to virtuous men the very wall of Semiramis. Nay, Priapus himself might well have been temperate had he taken passage with Amarantus, for there was never a moment when this fellow allowed us to be free from fear of the uttermost danger . . . as the hours passed the seas increased continually in volume. Now it so happened that this was the day on which the Jews make what they term the "Preparation", and they reckon the night, together with the day following this, as a time during which it is not lawful to work with one's hands. They keep this day holy and apart from the others, and they pass it in rest from labour of all kinds. Our skipper accordingly let go the rudder from his hands the moment he guessed that the sun's rays had left the earth, and throwing himself prostrate, "Allowed to trample on him what sailor so desired" [Sophocles, *Ajax*].

We who at first could not understand why he was thus lying down, imagined that despair was the cause of it all. We rushed to his assistance and implored him not to give up the last hope yet. Indeed the hugest waves were actually menacing the vessel, and the very deep was at war with itself. Now it frequently happens that when the wind has suddenly relaxed its violence, the billows already set in motion do not immediately subside; they are still under the influence of the wind's force, to which they yield and with which they battle at the same time, and the oncoming waves fight against those subsiding. I have every need of my store of flaming language, so that in recounting such immense dangers I may not fall into the trivial. To people who are at sea in such a crisis, life may be said to hang by a thread only, for if our skipper proved at such a moment to be an orthodox observer of the Mosaic law, what was life worth in the future? Indeed we soon understood why he had abandoned the helm, for when we begged him to do his best to save the ship, he stolidly continued reading his roll. Despairing of persuasion, we finally attempted force, and one staunch soldier – for many Arabs of the cavalry were of our company – one staunch soldier, I say, drew his sword and threatened to behead the fellow on the spot if he did not resume control of the vessel. But the Maccabean in very deed was determined to persist in his observances. However, in the middle of the night he voluntarily returned to the helm. "For now," he said, "we are clearly in danger of death, and the law commands." On this the tumult sprang up afresh, groaning of men and shrieking of women. All called upon the gods, and cried aloud; all called to mind those they loved . . . Then someone loudly proclaimed that every one possessing gold should suspend it about the neck, and those who possessed it did so, as well as those who had anything of the value of gold. The women themselves put on their jewellery, and distributed cords to those who needed them: such is the time-honoured custom. Now this is the reason for it. It is a matter of necessity that the corpse from a shipwreck should carry with it the fee for burial, inasmuch as whosoever comes across the dead body and profits by it, will fear the laws of Adrastia [Nemesis], and will scarcely grudge sprinkling a little sand on the one who has given to him so much more in value . . .

But day broke before all this had time to occur, and never, I know, did we behold the sun with greater joy. The wind grew more moderate as the temperature became milder, and thus, as the moisture evaporated, we were able to work the rigging and handle the sails. We were unable, it is true, to replace our sail by a new one, for this was already in the hands of the pawnbroker, but we took it in like the swelling folds of a garment, and lo, in four hours' time we who had imagined ourselves already in the jaws of death, were disembarking in a remote desert place, possessing neither town nor farm near it, only an expanse of open country of one hundred and thirty stadia. Our ship was riding in the open sea, for the spot was not a harbour, and it was riding on a single anchor. The second anchor had been sold, and a third. Amarantus did not possess. When now we touched the dearly Beloved land, we embraced the earth as a real living mother. We sent up hymns of gratitude to Providence, as in our custom, and to all this we added a mention of the present good fortune by which we had been saved contrary to all expectation. Thus we waited two days until the sea should have abated its fury. When, however, we were unable to discover any way out by land, for we could find no one in the country, we decided to try our fortune again at sea.

[. . . *a further storm causes their ship to run aground again* . . .]

Now provisions began to run short. So little accustomed were we to such accidents and so little had we anticipated a voyage of such length, that we had not brought a sufficient stock and, what is more, we had not husbanded what he had on board . . . Everyone kept avariciously whatever he could get hold of, and no one gave a present to his neighbour, but now we have abundance, and this is how it all happened. The Libyan women would have offered even bird's milk to the women of our party. They bestowed upon them all the products of earth and air alike; to wit, cheeses, flour, barley cakes, lamb, poultry and eggs; one of them even made a present of a bustard, a bird of very delicious flavour. A yokel would call it at first sight a peacock. They bring these presents to the ship, and our women accept them and share them with those who wish it. At present they who go fishing have become generous – a man, a child, comes to me one after another, and makes me a present, now a fish caught on the line, invariably some dainty that the rocks produce. To please you I take nothing from the women, that there may be no truce between them and me, and that I may be in no difficulty about denial, when I have to abjure all connexion with them. And yet what was to hinder me from rejoicing in necessities? So much comes in from all sides. The kindness of the inhabitants of the country towards their women guests you probably attribute to their virtue alone. Such is not the case; and it is worth while to explain all this to you, particularly as I have so much leisure. The wrath of Aphrodite, it would seem, lies heavy on the land; the women are as unlucky as the Lemnians; their breasts are overfull and they have disproportionately large chests, so that the infants obtain nourishment held not by the mother's arm, but by her shoulder, the nipple being turned upwards. One might of course maintain that Ammon and the country of Ammon is as good a nurse of children as of sheep, and that nature has there endowed cattle and humanity alike with fuller and more abundant fountains of milk, and so to that end are ampler breasts or reservoirs needed. Now, when these women hear from men who have had commerce with others beyond the frontier, that all women are not like this, they are incredulous. So when they fall in with a foreign woman, they make up to her in every way until they have gained their object, which is to examine her bosom, and then the woman who has examined the stranger tells another, and they call one another like the Cicones, they flock together to the spectacle and bring presents with them. We happened to have with us a young female slave who came from Pontus. Art and nature had combined to make her more highly chiselled than an ant. All the stir was about this one, and she made much gain from the women, and for the last three days the richest in the neighbourhood have been sending for her, and have passed her on from one to the other. She was so little embarrassed that she readily exhibited herself in undress.

So much for my story. The divinity has shaped it for you in mingling the comic with the tragic element. I have done likewise in the account I have given you. I know this letter is too long, but as when with you face to face, so in writing to you I am insatiable, and as it is by no means certain that I shall be able to talk with you again. I take all possible pleasure in writing to you now. Moreover, by fitting the letter into my diary, about which I take great pains, I shall have the reminiscences of many days . . . As for you, may you never trust yourself to the sea. Or at least, if you really must do so, let it not be at the end of the month.

BUYING SUMMER CLOTHES, c. AD 400

Synesius

They say that a fellow who sells boots has come from Athens. It is the same person, I think, from whom you bought for me last year some laced shoes. Now, according to my information, he has extended the area of his trade; he has robes in the Attic style, he has light summer clothes which will become you, and mantles such as I like for the summer season. Before he sells all these goods, or, at least, the finest of them, invite the stranger here, for you must remember that the first purchaser will choose the best of everything, without troubling himself about those who come to buy after him, and buy for me three or four of these mantles. In any case, whatever you pay, I will repay you ten times over.

EMBARRASSING RELATIVES, c. AD 400

Synesius

Aeschines had already been interred three days when his niece came to visit his tomb for the first time. Custom, you know, does not permit girls to attend funerals once they are engaged to be married. However, even then she was dressed in purple, with a diaphanous veil over her hair, and she had decked herself with gold and precious stones that she might not be a sign of evil omen to her betrothed. Seated upon a chair with double cushions and silver feet, so they say, she railed against the untimeliness of the misfortune, on the ground that Aeschines should have died either before her wedding or after it, and she was angry with us because we were in grief. Scarcely waiting for the seventh day, on which we had met for the funeral banquet, she mounted her mule cart, in company with that talkative old nurse of hers, and when the forum was thronged, set out on her stately course for Teucheira with all her adornments.

Next week she is preparing to display herself crowned with fillets, and with a towering head-dress like Cybele.

We are in no way wronged by this, except in the fact, patent to the whole world, that we have relations with very bad taste. The one who has been wronged is Harmonius, the father of her janitor, as Sappho might say, a man who although wise and moderate in all respects in his own life, vied with Cecrops himself on the ground of noble birth. The granddaughter of this man, himself greater than Cecrops, her uncle and janitor, Herodes has now given away to the Sosii and Tibii. Perchance they are right who extol the bridegroom elect to us because of his mother, pointing to his descent from the famous Laïs. Now Laïs was a slave bought from Sicily, according to one historian; whence this mother of fair offspring who bore the famous man. She of old lived an irregular life with a shipmaster for her owner – afterwards with an orator, who also owned her, and after these in the third instance with a fellow-slave, at first secretly in the town, then conspicuously, and was a mistress of her art. When by reason of oncoming wrinkles she gave up the practice of her art, she trained in her calling young persons whom she palmed off on strangers. Her son, the orator, asserts that he is dispensed by law from the duty of supporting a mother who is beyond the pale. Out upon such a law! The mother has been clearly revealed to those thus born; it is only the other parent who is doubtful. All the care that is due to parents from those born in wedlock should be bestowed by the fatherless on the mother alone.

ALARIC THE VISIGOTH SACKS ROME, AD 410

Jordanes

After their initial settlement in the eastern Empire (see pp353–355), the Visigoths made a series of incursive thrusts into the western Empire, reaching

Italy in AD 401. When his demands for Roman gold and lands were not
satisfied, he eventually marched upto the outskirts of Rome itself and, in AD
410, was treacherously allowed through the gates. The Visigoths only stayed
for three days, and did minimal physical damage, but the psychological
shockwaves were imense: For the first time in nigh on 800 years Rome had
been taken by an enemy. Roman invincibility had been dealt a blow from
which it would never arise.

But after [Emperor] Theodosius, the lover of peace and of the
Gothic race, had passed from human cares, his sons began to
ruin both empires by their luxurious living and to deprive their
Allies, that is to say the Goths, of the customary gifts. The
contempt of the Goths for the Romans soon increased, and for
fear their valour would be destroyed by long peace, they
appointed Alaric king over them. He was of a famous stock,
and his nobility was second only to that of the Amali, for he
came from the family of the Balthi, who because of their daring
valour had long ago received among their race the name *Baltha*,
that is, The Bold. Now when this Alaric was made king, he took
counsel with his men and persuaded them to seek a kingdom by
their own exertions rather than serve others in idleness. In the
consulship of Stilicho and Aurelian he raised an army and
entered Italy, which seemed to be bare of defenders, and came
through Pannonia and Sirmium along the right side. Without
meeting any resistance, he reached the bridge of the river
Candidianus at the third milestone from the royal city of
Ravenna.

This city lies amid the streams of the Po between swamps and
the sea, and is accessible only on one side. Its ancient inhabitants, as our ancestors relate, were called *Ainetoi*, that is,
"Laudable". Situated in a corner of the Roman Empire above
the Ionian Sea, it is hemmed in like an island by a flood of
rushing waters. On the east it has the sea, and one who sails
straight to it from the region of Corcyra and those parts of
Hellas sweeps with his oars along the right hand coast, first
touching Epirus, then Dalmatia, Liburnia and Histria and at
last the Venetian Isles. But on the west it has swamps through
which a sort of door has been left by a very narrow entrance. To
the north is an arm of the Po, called the Fossa Asconis. On the

south likewise is the Po itself, which they call the King of the rivers of Italy; and it has also the name Eridanus . . .

But as I was saying, when the army of the Visigoths had come into the neighbourhood of this city, they sent an embassy to the Emperor Honorius, who dwelt within. They said that if he would permit the Goths to settle peaceably in Italy, they would so live with the Roman people that men might believe them both to be of one race; but if not, whoever prevailed in war should drive out the other, and the victor should henceforth rule unmolested. But the Emperor Honorius feared to make either promise. So he took counsel with his Senate and considered how he might drive them from the Italian borders. He finally decided that Alaric and his race, if they were able to do so, should be allowed to seize for their own home the provinces farthest away, namely, Gaul and Spain. For at this time he had almost lost them, and moreover they had been devastated by the invasion of Gaiseric, king of the Vandals. The grant was confirmed by an imperial rescript, and the Goths, consenting to the arrangement, set out for the country given them.

When they had gone away without doing any harm in Italy, Stilicho, the Patrician and father-in-law of the Emperor Honorius, – for the Emperor had married both his daughters, Maria and Thermantia, in succession, but God called both from this world in their virgin purity – this Stilicho, I say, treacherously hurried to Pollentia, a city in the Cottian Alps. There he fell upon the unsuspecting Goths in battle, to the ruin of all Italy and his own disgrace. When the Goths suddenly beheld him, at first they were terrified. Soon regaining their courage and arousing each other by brave shouting, as is their custom, they turned to flight the entire army of Stilicho and almost exterminated it. Then forsaking the journey they had undertaken, the Goths with hearts full of rage returned again to Liguria whence they had set out. When they had plundered and spoiled it, they also laid waste Aemilia, and then hastened towards the city of Rome along the Flaminian Way, which runs between Picenum and Tuscia, taking as booty whatever they found on either hand. When they finally entered Rome, by Alaric's express command they merely sacked it and did not set the city on fire, as wild peoples usually do, nor did they permit serious damage to be done to the holy places. Thence they departed to bring like ruin upon Campània and Lucania, and then came to Bruttii. Here they remained a long time and planned to go to Sicily and thence to the countries of Africa.

Now the land of the Bruttii is at the extreme southern bound of Italy, and a corner of it marks the beginning of the Apennine mountains. It stretches out like a tongue into the Adriatic Sea and separates it from the Tyrrhenian waters. It chanced to receive its name in ancient times from a Queen Bruttia. To this place came Alaric, king of the Visigoths, with the wealth of all Italy which he had taken as spoil, and from there, as we have said, he intended to cross over by way of Sicily to the quiet land of Africa. But since man is not free to do anything he wishes without the will of God, that dread strait sunk several of his ships and threw all into confusion. Alaric was cast down by his reverse and, while deliberating what he should do, was suddenly overtaken by an untimely death and departed from human cares. His people mourned for him with the utmost affection. Then turning from its course the river Busentus near the city of Consentia – for this stream flows with its wholesome waters from the foot of a mountain near that city – they led a band of captives into the midst of its bed to dig out a place for his grave. In the depths of this pit they buried Alaric, together with many treasures, and then turned the waters back into their channel. And that none might ever know the place, they put to death all the diggers. They bestowed the kingdom of the Visigoths on Athavulf his kinsman, a man of imposing beauty and great spirit; for though not tall of stature, he was distinguished for beauty of face and form.

When Athavulf became king, he returned again to Rome, and whatever had escaped the first sack his Goths stripped bare like locusts, not merely despoiling Italy of its private wealth, but even of its public resources. The Emperor Honorius was powerless to resist even when his sister Placidia, the daughter of the Emperor Theodosius by his second wife, was led away captive from the city. But Athavulf was attracted by her nobility, beauty and chaste purity, and so he took her to wife in lawful marriage at Forum Julii, a city of Aemilia. When the barbarians learned of this alliance, they were the more effectually terrified, since the Empire and the Goths now seemed to be made one.

A CHURCHMAN LAMENTS THE SACK OF ROME, BETHLEHEM, AD 410

St Jerome

Jerome was born in Dalmatia and educated at Rome. In the year AD 410, he was in Bethlehem, engaged in his monumental translation of the Bible from Hebrew into Latin.

I shudder when I think of the calamities of our time. For twenty years the blood of Romans has been shed daily between Constantinople and the Alps. Scythia, Thrace, Macedon, Thessaly, Dacia, Achaia, Epirus – all these regions have been sacked and pillaged by Goths and Alans, Huns and Vandals. How many noble and virtuous women have been made the sport of these beasts! Churches have been overthrown, horses stalled in the holy places, the bones of the saints dug up and scattered.

Indeed, the Roman world is falling; yet we still hold up our heads instead of bowing them. The East, indeed, seemed to be free from these perils; but now, in the year just past, the wolves of the North have been let loose from their remotest fastnesses, and have overrun great provinces. They have laid siege to Antioch, and invested cities that were once the capitals of no mean states.

> Had I a hundred tongues, a hundred mouths,
> A voice of iron, I could not compass all
> Their crimes, nor tell their penalties by name.[1]

Well may we be unhappy, for it is our sins that have made the barbarians strong; as in the days of Hezekiah, so to day is God using the fury of the barbarian to execute His fierce anger. Rome's army, once the lord of the world, trembles to-day at sight of the foe.

---

[1] Virgil, *The Aeneid*

Who will hereafter believe that Rome has to fight now within her own borders, not for glory but for life? and, as the poet Lucan says, "if Rome be weak, where shall strength be found?"

And now a dreadful rumour has come to hand. Rome has been besieged, and its citizens have been forced to buy off their lives with gold. My voice cleaves to my throat; sobs choke my utterance. The city which had taken the whole world captive is itself taken. Famine too has done its awful work.

The world sinks into ruin; all things are perishing save our sins; these alone flourish. The great city is swallowed up in one vast conflagration; everywhere Romans are in exile.

Who could believe it? Who could believe that Rome, built up through the ages by the conquest of the world, had fallen; that the mother of nations had become their tomb? Who could imagine that the proud city, with its careless security and its boundless wealth, is brought so low that her children are outcasts and beggars? We cannot indeed help them; all we can do is to sympathize with them, and mingle our tears with theirs.

PRISCUS AT THE COURT OF ATTILA THE HUN, C. AD 450

Priscus

The author was an envoy sent from the Eastern Roman Empire at Constantinople to make peace with Attila, King of the Huns.

We set out with the barbarians, and arrived at Sardica, which is thirteen days for a fast traveller from Constantinople. Halting there we considered it advisable to invite Edecon and the barbarians with him to dinner. The inhabitants of the place sold us sheep and oxen, which we slaughtered, and we prepared a meal. In the course of the feast, as the barbarians lauded Attila and we lauded the Emperor, Bigilas remarked that it was not fair to compare a man and a god, meaning Attila by the man and Theodosius by the god. The Huns grew excited and hot at this remark. But we turned the conversation in another direction, and soothed their wounded feelings; and after dinner, when we separated, Maximin presented Edecon and Orestes with silk garments and Indian gems . . .

When we arrived at Naissus we found the city deserted, as though it had been sacked; only a few sick persons lay in the churches. We halted at a short distance from the river, in an open space, for all the ground adjacent to the bank was full of the bones of men slain in war. On the morrow we came to the station of Agintheus, the commander-in-chief of the Illyrian armies (*magister militum per Illyricum*), who was posted not far from Naissus, to announce to him the Imperial commands, and to receive five of those seventeen deserters, about whom Attila had written to the Emperor. We had an interview with him, and having treated the deserters with kindness, he committed them to us. The next day we proceeded from the district of Naissus towards the Danube; we entered a covered valley with many bends and windings and circuitous paths. We thought we were travelling due west, but when the day dawned the sun rose in front; and some of us unacquainted with the topography cried out that the sun was going the wrong way, and portending unusual events. The fact was that that part of the road faced the east, owing to the irregularity of the ground. Having passed these rough places we arrived at a plain which was also well wooded. At the river we were received by barbarian ferrymen, who rowed us across the river in boats made by themselves out of single trees hewn and hollowed. These preparations had not been made for our sake, but to convey across a company of Huns; for Attila pretended that he wished to hunt in Roman territory, but his intent was really hostile, because all the deserters had not been given up to him. Having crossed the Danube, and proceeded with the barbarians about seventy stadia, we were compelled to wait in a certain plain, that Edecon and his party might go on in front and inform Attila of our arrival. As we were dining in the evening we heard the sound of horses approaching, and two Scythians arrived with directions that we were to set out to Attila. We asked them first to partake of our meal, and they dismounted and made good cheer. On the next day, under their guidance, we arrived at the tents of Attila, which were numerous, about three o'clock, and when we wished to pitch our tent on a hill the barbarians who met us prevented us, because the tent of Attila was on low ground, so we halted where the Scythians desired . . . (Then a

message is received from Attila, who was aware of the nature of
their embassy, saying that if they had nothing further to
communicate to him he would not receive them, so they
reluctantly prepared to return.) When the baggage had been
packed on the beasts of burden, and we were perforce preparing
to start in the night time, messengers came from Attila bidding
us wait on account of the late hour. Then men arrived with an
ox and river fish, sent to us by Attila, and when we had dined
we retired to sleep. When it was day we expected a gentle and
courteous message from the barbarian, but he again bade us
depart if we had no further mandates beyond what he already
knew. We made no reply, and prepared to set out, though
Bigilas insisted that we should feign to have some other com-
munication to make. When I saw that Maximin was very
dejected, I went to Scottas (one of the Hun nobles, brother
of Onegesius), taking with me Rusticius, who understood the
Hun language. He had come with us to Scythia, not as a
member of the embassy, but on business with Constantius,
an Italian whom Aetius had sent to Attila to be that monarch's
private secretary. I informed Scottas, Rusticius acting as interpreter, that Maximin would give him many presents if he would
procure him an interview with Attila; and, moreover, that the
embassy would not only conduce to the public interests of the
two powers, but to the private interest of Onegesius, for the
Emperor desired that he should be sent as an ambassador to
Byzantium, to arrange the disputes of the Huns and Romans,
and that there he would receive splendid gifts. As Onegesius was
not present it was for Scottas, I said, to help us, or rather help
his brother, and at the same time prove that the report was true
which ascribed to him an influence with Attila equal to that
possessed by his brother. Scottas mounted his horse and rode to
Attila's tent, while I returned to Maximin and found him in a
state of perplexity and anxiety, lying on the grass with Bigilas. I
described my interview with Scottas, and bade him make
preparations for an audience of Attila. They both jumped
up, approving of what I had done, and recalled the men
who had started with the beasts of burden. As we were considering what to say to Attila, and how to present the Emperor's
gifts, Scottas came to fetch us, and we entered Attila's tent,

which was surrounded by a multitude of barbarians. We found Attila sitting on a wooden chair. We stood at a little distance and Maximin advanced and saluted the barbarian, to whom he gave the Emperor's letter, saying that the Emperor prayed for the safety of him and his. The king replied, "It shall be unto the Romans as they wish it to be unto me," and immediately addressed Bigilas, calling him a shameless beast, and asking him why he ventured to come when all the deserters had not been given up . . .

After the departure of Bigilas, who returned to the Empire (nominally to find the deserters whose restoration Attila demanded, but really to get the money for his fellow-conspirator Edecon), we remained one day in that place, and then set out with Attila for the northern parts of the country. We accompanied the barbarian for a time, but when we reached a certain point took another route by the command of the Scythians who conducted us, as Attila was proceeding to a village where he intended to marry the daughter of Eskam, though he had many other wives, for the Scythians practise polygamy. We proceeded along a level road in a plain and met with navigable rivers – of which the greatest, next to the Danube, are the Drecon, Tigas, and Tiphesas – which we crossed in the Monoxyles, boats made of one piece, used by the dwellers on the banks: the smaller rivers we traversed on rafts which the barbarians carry about with them on carts, for the purpose of crossing morasses. In the villages we were supplied with food – millet instead of corn, and mead, as the natives call it, instead of wine. The attendants who followed us received millet, and a drink made of barley, which the barbarians call kam. Late in the evening, having travelled a long distance, we pitched our tents on the banks of a fresh-water lake, used for water by the inhabitants of the neighbouring village. But a wind and storm, accompanied by thunder and lightning and heavy rain, arose, and almost threw down our tents; all our utensils were rolled into the waters of the lake. Terrified by the mishap and the atmospherical disturbance, we left the place and lost one another in the dark and the rain, each following the road that seemed most easy. But we all reached the village by different ways, and raised an alarm to obtain what we lacked. The Scythians of the village sprang out of their huts at the noise, and, lighting the reeds which they use for kindling fires, asked what we wanted. Our conductors replied that the storm had alarmed us; so they invited us to their huts and provided warmth for us by lighting large fires of reeds. The lady who governed the village – she had been one of Bleda's wives – sent us provisions and good-looking girls to console us (this is a Scythian compliment). We treated the young women to a share in the eatables, but declined to take any further advantage of their presence. We remained in the huts till day dawned and then went to look for our lost utensils, which we found partly in the place where we had pitched the tent, partly on the bank of the lake, and partly in the water. We spent that day in the village drying our things; for the storm had ceased and the sun was bright. Having looked after our horses and cattle, we directed our steps to the princess, to whom we paid our respects and presented gifts in return for her courtesy. The gifts consisted of things which are esteemed by the barbarians as not produced in the country – three silver phials, red skins, Indian pepper, palm fruit, and other delicacies.

Having advanced a distance of seven days farther, we halted at a village; for as the rest of the route was the same for us and Attila, it behoved us to wait, so that he might go in front. Here we met with some of the "western Romans", who had also come on an embassy to Attila – the count Romulus, Promotus governor of Noricum, and Romanus a military captain. With them was Constantius whom Aetius had sent to Attila to be his secretary, and Tatulus, the father of Orestes; these two were not connected with the embassy, but were friends of the ambassadors. Constantius had known them of old in the Italies, and Orestes had married the daughter of Romulus. The object of the embassy was to soften the soul of Attila, who demanded the surrender of one Silvanus, a dealer in silver plate in Rome, because he had received golden vessels from a certain Constantius. This Constantius, a native of Gaul, had preceded his namesake in the office of secretary to Attila. When Sirmium in Pannonia was besieged by the Scythians, the bishop of the place consigned the vessels to his (Constantius') care, that if the city were taken and he survived they might be used to ransom him; and in case he were slain, to ransom the citizens who were led into captivity. But when the city was enslaved, Constantius violated his engagement, and, as he happened to be at Rome on business, pawned the vessels to Silvanus for a sum of money, on condition that if he gave back the money within a prescribed period the dishes should be returned, but otherwise should become the property of Silvanus. Constantius, suspected of treachery, was crucified by Attila and Bleda; and afterwards, when the affair of the vessels became known to Attila, he demanded the surrender of Silvanus on the ground that he had stolen his property. Accordingly Aetius and the Emperor of the Western Romans sent to explain that Silvanus was the creditor of Constantius, the vessels having been pawned and not stolen, and that he had sold them to priests and others for sacred purposes. If, however, Attila refused to desist from his demand, he, the Emperor, would send him the value of the vessels, but would not surrender the innocent Silvanus.

Having waited for some time until Attila advanced in front of us, we proceeded, and having crossed some rivers we arrived at a large village, where Attila's house was said to be more splendid than his residences in other places. It was made of polished boards, and surrounded with a wooden enclosure, designed, not for protection, but for appearance. The house of Onegesius was second to the king's in splendour, and was also encircled with a wooden enclosure, but it was not adorned with towers like that of the king. Not far from the enclosure was a large bath which Onegesius – who was the second in power among the Scythians – built, having transported the stones from Pannonia; for the barbarians in this district had no stones or trees, but used imported material. The builder of the bath was a captive from Sirmium, who expected to win his freedom as payment for making the bath. But he was disappointed, and greater trouble befell him than mere captivity among the Scythians, for Onegesius appointed him bathman, and he used to minister to him and his family when they bathed.

When Attila entered the village he was met by girls advancing in rows, under thin white canopies of linen, which were held up by the outside women who stood under them, and were so large that seven or more girls walked beneath each. There were many lines of damsels thus canopied, and they sang

Scythian songs. When he came near the house of Onegesius, which lay on his way, the wife of Onegesius issued from the door, with a number of servants, bearing meat and wine, and saluted him and begged him to partake of her hospitality. This is the highest honour that can be shown among the Scythians. To gratify the wife of his friend, he ate, just as he sat on his horse, his attendants raising the tray to his saddlebow; and having tasted the wine, he went on to the palace, which was higher than the other houses and built on an elevated site. But we remained in the house of Onegesius, at his invitation, for he had returned from his expedition with Attila's son. His wife and kinsfolk entertained us to dinner, for he had no leisure himself, as he had to relate to Attila the result of his expedition, and explain the accident which had happened to the young prince, who had slipped and broken his right arm. After dinner we left the house of Onegesius, and took up our quarters nearer the palace, so that Maximin might be at a convenient distance for visiting Attila or holding intercourse with his court. The next morning, at dawn of day, Maximin sent me to Onegesius, with presents offered by himself as well as those which the Emperor had sent, and I was to find out whether he would have an interview with Maximin and at what time. When I arrived at the house, along with the attendants who carried the gifts, I found the doors closed, and had to wait until some one should come out and announce our arrival. As I waited and walked up and down in front of the enclosure which surrounded the house, a man, whom from his Scythian dress I took for a barbarian, came up and addressed me in Greek, with the word *Xaire*, "Hail!" I was surprised at a Scythian speaking Greek. For the subjects of the Huns, swept together from various lands, speak, besides their own barbarous tongues, either Hunnic or Gothic, or – as many as have commercial dealings with the western Romans – Latin; but none of them easily speak Greek, except captives from the Thracian or Illyrian sea-coast; and these last are easily known to any stranger by their torn garments and the squalor of their heads, as men who have met with a reverse. This man, on the contrary, resembled a well-to-do Scythian, being well dressed, and having his hair cut in a circle after Scythian fashion. Having returned his salutation, I asked him who he was and whence he had come into a foreign land and adopted Scythian life. When he asked me why I wanted to know, I told him that his Hellenic speech had prompted my curiosity. Then he smiled and said that he was born a Greek and had gone as a merchant to Viminacium, on the Danube, where he had stayed a long time, and married a very rich wife. But the city fell a prey to the barbarians, and he was stript of his prosperity, and on account of his riches was allotted to Onegesius in the division of the spoil, as it was the custom among the Scythians for the chiefs to reserve for themselves the rich prisoners. Having fought bravely against the Romans and the Acatiri, he had paid the spoils he won to his master, and so obtained freedom. He then married a barbarian wife and had children, and had the privilege of eating at the table of Onegesius. He considered his new life among the Scythians better than his old life among the Romans, and the reasons he gave were as follows: "After war the Scythians live in inactivity, enjoying what they have got, and not at all, or very little, harassed. The Romans, on the other hand, are in the first place very liable to perish in war, as they have to rest their hopes of safety on others, and are not allowed, on account of their tyrants to use arms. And those who use them are injured by the cowardice of their generals, who cannot support the conduct of war. But the condition of the subjects in time of peace is far more grievous than the evils of war, for the exaction of the taxes is very severe, and unprincipled men inflict injuries on others, because the laws are practically not valid against all classes. A transgressor who belongs to the wealthy classes is not punished for his injustice, while a poor man, who does not understand business, undergoes the legal penalty, that is if he does not depart this life before the trial, so long is the course of lawsuits protracted, and so much money is expended on them. The climax of the misery is to have to pay in order to obtain justice. For no one will give a court to the injured man unless he pay a sum of money to the judge and the judge's clerks."

In reply to this attack on the Empire, I asked him to be good enough to listen with patience to the other side of the question. "The creators of the Roman republic," I said, "who were wise and good men, in order to prevent things from being done at haphazard made one class of men guardians of the laws, and appointed another class to the profession of arms, who were to have no other object than to be always ready for battle, and to go forth to war without dread, as though to their ordinary exercise having by practice exhausted all their fear beforehand. Others again were assigned to attend to the cultivation of the ground, to support both themselves and those who fight in their defence, by contributing the military corn-supply . . . To those who protect the interests of the litigants a sum of money is paid by the latter, just as a payment is made by the farmers to the soldiers. Is it not fair to support him who assists and requite him for his kindness? The support of the horse benefits the horseman . . . Those who spend money on a suit and lose it in the end cannot fairly put it down to anything but the injustice of their case. And as to the long time spent on lawsuits, that is due to concern for justice, that judges may not fail in passing correct judgments, by having to give sentence offhand; it is better that they should reflect, and conclude the case more tardily, than that by judging in a hurry they should both injure man and transgress against the Deity the institutor of justice . . . The Romans treat their servants better than the king of the Scythians treats his subjects. They deal with them as fathers or teachers, admonishing them to abstain from evil and follow the lines of conduct whey they have esteemed honourable; they reprove them for their errors like their own children. They are not allowed, like the Scythians, to inflict death on them. They have numerous ways of conferring freedom; they can manumit not only during life, but also by their wills, and the testamentary wishes of a Roman in regard to his property are law."

My interlocutor shed tears, and confessed that the laws and constitution of the Romans were fair, but deplored that the governors, not possessing the spirit of former generations, were ruining the State.

As we were engaged in this discussion a servant came out and opened the door of the enclosure. I hurried up, and enquired how Onegesius was engaged, for I desired to give him a message from the Roman ambassador. He replied that I should meet him if I waited a little, as he was about to go forth. And after a short time I saw him coming out, and addressed him, saying,

"The Roman ambassador salutes you, and I have come with gifts from him, and with the gold which the Emperor sent you. The ambassador is anxious to meet you, and begs you to appoint a time and place." Onegesius bade his servants receive the gold and the gifts, and told me to announce to Maximin that he would go to him immediately. I delivered the message, and Onegesius appeared in the tent without delay. He expressed his thanks to Maximin and the Emperor for the presents, and asked why he sent for him. Maximin said that the time had come for Onegesius to have greater renown among men, if he would go to the Emperor, and by his wisdom arrange the objects of dispute between the Romans and Huns, and establish concord between them; thereby he will procure many advantages for his own family, as he all his children will always be friends of the Emperor and the Imperial family. Onegesius inquired what measures would gratify the Emperor and how he could arrange the disputes. Maximin replied: "If you cross into the lands of the Roman Empire you will lay the Emperor under an obligation, and you will arrange the matters at issue by investigating their causes and deciding them on the basis of the peace." Onegesius said he would inform the Emperor and his ministers of Attila's wishes, but the Romans need not think they could ever prevail with him to betray his master or neglect his Scythian training and his wives and children, or to prefer wealth among the Romans to bondage with Attila. He added that he would be of more service to the Romans by remaining in his own land and softening the anger of his master, if he were indignant for aught with the Romans, than by visiting them and subjecting himself to blame if he made arrangements that Attila did not approve of. He then retired, having consented that I should act as an intermediary in conveying messages from Maximin to himself, for it would not have been consistent with Maximin's dignity as ambassador to visit him constantly.

The next day I entered the enclosure of Attila's palace, bearing gifts to his wife, whose name was Kreka. She had three sons, of whom the eldest governed the Acatiri and the other nations who dwell in Pontic Scythia. Within the enclosure were numerous buildings, some of carved boards beautifully fitted together, others of straight, fastened on round wooden blocks which rose to a moderate height from the ground. Attila's wife lived here, and, having been admitted by the barbarians at the door, I found her reclining on a soft couch. The floor of the room was covered with woollen mats for walking on. A number of servants stood round her, and maids sitting on the floor in front of her embroidered with colours linen cloths intended to be placed over the Scythian dress for ornament. Having approached, saluted, and presented the gifts, I went out, and walked to another house, where Attila was, and waited for Onegesius, who, as I knew, was with Attila. I stood in the middle of a great crowd – the guards of Attila and his attendants knew me, and so no one hindered me. I saw a number of people advancing, and a great commotion and noise, Attila's egress being expected. And he came forth from the house with a dignified gait, looking round on this side and on that. He was accompanied by Onegesius, and stood in front of the house; and many persons who had lawsuits with one another came up and received his judgment. Then he returned into the house, and received ambassadors of barbarous peoples.

As I was waiting for Onegesius, I was accosted by Romulus and Promotus and Romanus, the ambassadors who had come from Italy about the golden vessels; they were accompanied by Rusticius and by Constantiolus, a man from the Pannonian territory, which was subject to Attila. They asked me whether we had been dismissed or are constrained to remain, and I replied that it was just to learn this from Onegesius that I was waiting outside the palace. When I enquired in my turn whether Attila had vouchsafed them a kind reply, they told me that his decision could not be moved, and that he threatened war unless either Silvanus or the drinking-vessels were given up . . .

As we were talking about the state of the world, Onegesius came out; we went up to him and asked him about our concerns. Having first spoken with some barbarians, he bade me inquire of Maximin what consular the Romans are sending as an ambassador to Attila. When I came to our tent I delivered the message to Maximin, and deliberated with him what answer we should make to the question of the barbarian. Returning to Onegesius, I said that the Romans desired him to come to them and adjust the matters of dispute, otherwise the Emperor will send whatever ambassador he chooses. He then bade me fetch Maximin, whom he conducted to the presence of Attila. Soon after Maximin came out, and told me that the barbarian wished Nomus or Anatolius or Senator to be the ambassador, and that he would not receive any other than one of these three; when he (Maximin) replied that it was not meet to mention men by name and so render them suspected in the eyes of the Emperor, Attila said that if they do not choose to comply with his wishes the differences will be adjusted by arms.

When we returned to our tent the father of Orestes came with an invitation from Attila for both of us to a banquet at three o'clock. When the hour arrived we went to the palace, along with the embassy from the western Romans, and stood on the threshold of the hall in the presence of Attila. The cup-bearers gave us a cup, according to the national custom, that we might pray before we sat down. Having tasted the cup, we proceeded to take our seats; all the chairs were ranged along the walls of the room on either side. Attila sat in the middle on a couch; a second couch was set behind him, and from it steps led up to his bed, which was covered with linen sheets and wrought coverlets for ornament, such as Greeks and Romans use to deck bridal beds. The places on the right of Attila were held chief in honour, those on the left, where we sat, were only second. Berichus, a noble among the Scythians, sat on our side, but had the precedence of us. Onegesius sat on a chair on the right of Attila's couch, and over against Onegesius on a chair sat two of Attila's sons; his eldest son sat on his couch, not near him, but at the extreme end, with his eyes fixed on the ground, in shy respect for his father. When all were arranged, a cup-bearer came and handed Attila a wooden cup of wine. He took it, and saluted the first in precedence, who, honoured by the saluta-tion, stood up, and might not sit down until the king, having tasted or drained the wine, returned the cup to the attendant. All the guests then honoured Attila in the same way, saluting him, and then tasting the cups; but he did not stand up. Each of us had a special cupbearer, who would come forward in order to present the wine, when the cup-bearer of Attila retired. When the second in precedence and those next to him had been honoured in like manner, Attila toasted us in the same way according to the order of the seats. When this ceremony was over the cup-bearers retired, and tables, large enough for three or four, or even more, to sit at, were placed next the table of Attila, so that each could take of the food on the dishes without leaving his seat. The attendant of Attila first entered with a dish full of meat, and behind him came the other attendants with bread and viands, which they laid on the tables. A luxurious meal, served on silver plate, had been made ready for us and the barbarian guests, but Attila ate nothing but meat on a wooden trencher. In everything else, too, he showed himself temperate; his cup was of wood, while to the guests were given goblets of gold and silver. His dress, too, was quite simple, affecting only to be clean. The sword he carried at his side, the latchets of his Scythian shoes, the bridle of his horse were not adorned, like those of the other Scythians, with gold or gems or anything costly. When the viands of the first course had been consumed we all stood up, and did not resume our seats until each one, in the order before observed, drank to the health of Attila in the goblet of wine presented to him. We then sat down, and a second dish was placed on each table with eatables of another kind. After this course the same ceremony was observed as after the first. When evening fell torches were lit, and two barbarians coming forward in front of Attila sang songs they had composed, celebrating his victories and deeds of valour in war. And of the guests, as they looked at the singers, some were pleased with the verses, others reminded of wars were excited in their souls, while yet others, whose bodies were feeble with age and their spirits compelled to rest, shed tears. After the songs a Scythian, whose mind was deranged, appeared, and by uttering outlandish and senseless words forced the company to laugh. After him Zerkon, the Moorish dwarf, entered. He had been sent by Attila as a gift to Aetius, and Edecon had persuaded him to come to Attila in order to recover his wife, whom he had left behind him in Scythia; the lady was a Scythian whom he had obtained in marriage through the influence of his patron Bleda. He did not succeed in recovering her, for Attila was angry with him for returning. On the occasion of the banquet he made his appearance, and threw all except Attila into fits of unquenchable laughter by his appearance, his dress, his voice, and his words, which were a confused jumble of Latin, Hunnic, and Gothic. Attila, however, remained immovable and of unchanging countenance nor by word or act did he betray anything approaching to a smile of merriment except at the entry of Ernas, his youngest son, whom he pulled by the cheek, and gazed on with a calm look of satisfaction. I was surprised that he made so much of this son, and neglected his other children but a barbarian who sat beside me and knew Latin, bidding me not reveal what he told, gave me to understand that prophets had forewarned Attila that his race would fall, but would be restored by this boy. When the night had advanced we retired from the banquet, not wishing to assist further at the potations.

THE BATTLE OF THE CATALAUNIAN PLAINS, AD 451

Jordanes

Already the ruler of a dominion that stretched from north of the Caspian sea to the Danube, from the Rhine to the frontier of China, Attila the Hun attacked the Roman western empire in AD 451. The official cause of the invasion was a plea to Attila from a sister of Valentinian III to rescue her from an unwanted wedding. Attila proposed himself as bridegroom instead, and demanded a dowry consisting of half the western empire. When his "offer" was turned down, he marched on Gaul. Near Chalons-sur-Marne Attila was confronted by a combined Roman and "federated" German army. And lost the one battle of his life.

The armies met in the Catalaunian Plains. The battlefield was a plain rising by a sharp slope to a ridge which both armies sought to gain; for advantage of position is a great help. The Huns with their forces seized the right side, the Romans, the Visigoths and their allies the left, and then began a struggle for the yet untaken crest. Now Theodorid with his Visigoths held the right wing, and Aetius with the Romans the left [of the line against Attila]. On the other side, the battle line of the Huns was so arranged that Attila and his bravest followers were stationed in the centre. In arranging them thus the king had chiefly his own safety in view, since by his position in the very midst of his race, he would be kept out of the way of threatened danger. The innumerable peoples of divers tribes, which he had subjected to his sway, formed the wings. Now the crowd of kings – if we may call them so – and the leaders of various nations hung upon Attila's nod like slaves, and when he gave a sign even by a glance, without a murmur each stood forth in fear and trembling, or at all events did as he was bid. Attila alone was king of kings over all and concerned for all.

So then the struggle began for the advantage of position we have mentioned. Attila sent his men to take the summit of the mountain, but was outstripped by Thorismud [crown prince of the Visigoths] and Aetius, who in their effort to gain the top of the hill reached higher ground, and through this advantage easily routed the Huns as they came up.

When Attila saw his army was thrown into confusion by the event he urged them on with a fiery harangue and . . . inflamed by his words they all dashed into the battle.

And although the situation was itself fearful, yet the presence of the king dispelled anxiety and hesitation. Hand to hand they clashed in battle, and the fight grew fierce, confused, monstrous, unrelenting – *a fight whose like no ancient time has ever recorded*. There were such deeds done that a brave man who missed this marvellous spectacle could not hope to see anything so wonderful all his life long. For if we may believe our elders a brook flowing between low banks through the plain was greatly increased by blood from the wounds of the slain. Those whose wounds drove them to slake their parching thirst drank water mingled with gore. In their wretched plight they were forced to drink what they thought was the blood they had poured out from their own wounds.

Here King Theodorid [the Visigoth] while riding by to encourage his army, was thrown from his horse and trampled under foot by his own men, thus ending his days at a ripe old age. But others say he was slain by the spear of Andag of the host of the Ostrogoths who were then under the sway of Attila. Then the Visigoths fell on the horde of the Huns and nearly slew Attila. But he prudently took flight and straightway shut himself and his companions within the barriers of the camp which he had fortified with wagons. [The battle now became confused: chieftains became separated from their forces: night fell with the Roman-Gothic army holding the field of combat.]

At dawn on the next day the Romans saw that the fields were piled high with corpses, and that the Huns did not venture forth; they thought that the victory was theirs, but knew that Attila would not flee from battle unless overwhelmed by a great disaster. Yet he did nothing cowardly, like one that is overcome, but with clash of arms sounded the trumpets and threatened an attack. His enemies determined to wear him out by a siege. It is said that the king remained supremely brave even in this extremity and had heaped up a funeral pyre of horse trappings, so that if the enemy should attack him he was determined to cast himself into the flames, that none might have the joy of wounding him, and that the lord of so many races might not fall into the hands of his foes.

However, owing to dissensions between the Romans and Goths he was allowed to escape to his home land, and in this most famous war of the bravest tribes, 160,000 men are said to have been slain on both sides.

A PORTRAIT OF THEODORIC THE VISIGOTH, TOULOUSE, AD 454

Sidonius Apollinaris

Apollinaris was a Gallo-Roman aristocrat (indeed, he was briefly the son-in-law of an Emperor, the hapless Eparchius Avitus). He favoured cooperation, not war, with the Visigoths who were besieging the Empire. Here Apollinaris records a visit to Theodoric's court at Toulouse.

You have often begged a description of Theodoric the Gothic king, whose gentle breeding fame commends to every nation; you want him in his quantity and quality, in his person, and the manner of his existence. I gladly accede, as far as the limits of my page allow, and highly approve so fine and ingenuous a curiosity.

Well, he is a man worth knowing, even by those who cannot enjoy his close acquaintance, so happily have Providence and Nature joined to endow him with the perfect gifts of fortune; his way of life is such that not even the envy which lies in wait for a king can rob him of his proper praise. And first as to his person. He is well set up, in height above the average man, but below the giant. His head is round, with curled hair retreating somewhat from brow to crown. His nervous neck is free from disfiguring knots. The eyebrows are bushy and arched; when the lids droop, the lashes reach almost half-way down the cheeks. The upper ears are buried under overlying locks, after the fashion of his race. The nose is finely aquiline; the lips are thin and not enlarged by undue distention of the mouth. Every day the hair springing from his nostrils is cut back; that on the face springs thick from the hollow of the temples, but the razor has not yet come upon his cheek, and his barber is assiduous in eradicating the rich growth on the lower part of the face. Chin, throat, and neck are full, but not fat, and all of fair complexion; seen close, their colour is fresh as that of youth; they often flush, but from modesty, and not from anger. His shoulders are smooth, the upper- and forearms strong and hard; hands broad, breast prominent; waist receding. The spine dividing the broad expanse of back does not project, and you can see the spring of the ribs; the sides swell with salient muscle, the well-girt flanks are full of vigour. His thighs are like hard horn; the knee-joints firm and masculine; the knees themselves the comeliest and least wrinkled in the world. A full ankle supports the leg, and the foot is small to bear such mighty limbs.

Now for the routine of his public life. Before daybreak he goes with a very small suite to attend the service of his priests. He prays with assiduity, but, if I may speak in confidence, one may suspect more of habit than conviction in this piety. Administrative duties of the kingdom take up the rest of the morning. Armed nobles stand about the royal seat; the mass of guards in their garb of skins are admitted that they may be within call, but kept at the threshold for quiet's sake; only a murmur of them comes in from their post at the doors, between the curtain and the outer barrier. And now the foreign envoys are introduced. The king hears them out, and says little; if a thing needs more discussion he puts it off, but accelerates matters ripe for dispatch. The second hour arrives; he rises from the throne to inspect his treasure-chamber or stable. If the chase is the order of the day, he joins it, but never carries his bow at his side, considering this derogatory to royal state. When a bird or beast is marked for him, or happens to cross his path, he puts his hand behind his back and takes the bow from a page with the string all hanging loose; for as he deems it a boy's trick to bear it in a quiver, so he holds it effeminate to receive the weapon ready strung. When it is given him, he sometimes holds it in both hands and bends the extremities towards each other; at others he sets it, knot-end downward, against his lifted heel, and runs his finger up the slack and wavering string. After that, he takes his arrows, adjusts, and lets fly. He will ask you beforehand what you would like him to transfix; you choose, and he hits. If there is a miss through either's error, your vision will mostly be at fault, and not the archer's skill.

On ordinary days, his table resembles that of a private person. The board does not groan beneath a mass of dull and unpolished silver set on by panting servitors; the weight lies rather in the conversation than in the plate; there is either sensible talk or none. The hangings and draperies used on these occasions are sometimes of purple silk, sometimes only of linen; art, not costliness, commends the fare, as spotlessness rather than bulk the silver. Toasts are few, and you will oftener see a thirsty guest impatient, than a full one refusing cup or bowl. In short, you will find elegance of Greece, good cheer of Gaul, Italian nimbleness, the state of public banquets with the attentive service of a private table, and everywhere the discipline of a king's house. What need for me to describe the pomp of his feast days? No man is so unknown as not to know of them. But to my theme again. The siesta after dinner is always slight and sometimes intermitted. When inclined for the board-game, he is quick to gather up the dice, examines them with care, shakes the box with expert hand, throws rapidly, humorously apostrophizes them, and patiently waits the issue. Silent at a good throw, he makes merry over a bad, annoyed by neither fortune, and always the philosopher. He is too proud to ask or to refuse a revenge; he disdains to avail himself of one if offered; and if it is opposed will quietly go on playing. You effect recovery of your man without obstruction on his side; he recovers his without collusion upon yours. You see the strategist when he moves the pieces; his one thought is victory. Yet at play he puts off a little of his kingly rigour, inciting all to good fellowship and the freedom of the game: I think he is afraid of being feared. Vexation in the man whom he beats delights him; he will never believe that his opponents have not let him win unless their annoyance proves him really victor. You would be surprised how often the pleasure born of these little happenings may favour the march of great affairs . . . I myself am gladly beaten by him when I have a favour to ask, since the loss of my game may mean the gaining of my cause. About the ninth hour, the burden of government begins again. Back come the importunates, back the ushers to remove them; on all sides buzz the voices of petitioners, a sound which lasts till evening, and does not diminish till interrupted by the royal repast; even then they disperse to attend their various patrons among the courtiers, and are astir till bedtime. Sometimes, though this is rare, supper is enlivened by sallies of mimes, but no guest is ever exposed to the wound of a biting tongue. Withal there is no noise of hydraulic organ, or choir with its conductor intoning a set piece; you will hear no players of lyre of flute, no master of the music, no girls with cithara or tabor; the king cares for no strains but those which no less charm the mind with virtue than the ear with melody. When he rises to withdraw, the treasury watch begins its vigil; armed sentries stand on guard during the first hours of slumber. But I am wandering from my subject. I never promised a whole chapter on the kingdom, but a few words about the king. I must stay my pen; you asked for nothing more than one or two facts about the person and the tastes of Theodoric and my own aim was to write a letter, not a history.

LEO AND MAJORIAN DEMAND THE PRESERVATION OF ROME'S BUILDINGS, AD 458

Leo and Majorian

The Visigoths were not the only destroyers of Rome. The city's inhabitants, from rich to poor, routinely plundered its great buildings for materials. The imperial edict below condemning the practice was no more successful than those which preceded or succeeded it. Rome was largely ruined by its own inhabitants.

Emperors Leo and Majorian, the August, to Emilian, Prefect of The City of Rome:

In our governance of the state, we wish to correct the fact,
which we have long condemned, that people are able to change
the appearance of a venerable city. For it is clearly evident that
the public buildings which form the entire adornment of the
city of Rome are being gradually destroyed in response to the
punishable suggestion of the Offices of the City. Citing the
fallacious pretext of an urgent need for freestone for the construction of a public building, the admirable structures of
ancient buildings are dismantled. For the restoration of some
small building, large ones are being destroyed. This provides
opportunities for anyone putting up a private building, by the
grace of the appointed magistrates of the city, to take the
necessary materials from public sites and to transport them
to some other place, when in fact they form part of the city's
splendour and one should therefore preserve them out of civic
conscience, even where the buildings are in need of repair.

That is why we decree by this general law that nobody shall
destroy or damage the whole set of buildings, that is to say, the
temples and monuments founded by our forefathers, which
were built for the public's use or enjoyment; this is to be
enforced so that a magistrate who decides to make such an
act shall have to pay a fine of fifty pounds of gold. As for
employees and bookkeepers obeying his orders and not daring
to resist him on their own initiative, they expose themselves to
punishment by beating, and they shall also have their hands
amputated – those hands with which they profane the monuments of the ancestors, when they should be preserved.

As for the places that until now individuals have claimed for
themselves – a piece of mischief that must be abolished – we
forbid that anything be removed from them, since, in fact, they
continue to form part of the public property, and we desire that
they be repaired and have restored to them those parts that
have been removed, the authorization to make a claim to them
having henceforth been suspended.

If urgent and overwhelming reasons make it necessary to
dismantle any section, either because of the building of another
public work or in order that vital repair work be undertaken,
we prescribe that the issue be submitted, with all applicable
information, to the venerable Senate. If after due deliberation it

should consider that such action needs to be taken, the case is to be referred to our own benevolence in order that whatever we find to be beyond repair, we may order that it, at least, be transferred and made to adorn another public building, O Emilian, very dear and very affectionate father.

For these reasons, Your Illustrious Highness, please be so kind as to publish, by displaying edicts, this very salutary constitution, in order that decisions that we have taken with forethought in the interest of the Eternal City be observed with the appropriate submission and devotion.

Signed at Ravenna,
11 July AD 458

A COUNTRY HOUSE PARTY, NÎMES, c. AD 460

Sidonius Apollinaris

To your question why, having got as far as Nîmes, I still leave your hospitality expectant, I reply by giving the reason for my delayed return. I will even dilate upon the causes of my dilatoriness, for I know that what I enjoy is your enjoyment too. The fact is, I have passed the most delightful time in the most beautiful country in the company of Tonantius Ferreolus and Apollinaris. The most charming hosts in the world. Their estates march together; their houses are not far apart; and the extent of intervening ground is just too far for a walk and just too short to make the ride worth while. The hills above the houses are under vines and olives; they might be Nysa and Aracynthus, famed in song. The view from one villa is over a wide flat country, that from the other over woodland; yet different though their situations are, the eye derives equal pleasure from both. But enough of sites; I have now to unfold the order of my entertainment.

Sharp scouts were posted to look out for our return; and not only were the roads patrolled by men from each estate, but even winding short-cuts and sheep-tracks were under observation, to make it quite impossible for us to elude the friendly ambush. Into this, of course, we fell, no unwilling prisoners; and our captors instantly made us swear to dismiss every idea of continuing our journey until a whole week had elapsed. And so every morning began with a flattering rivalry between the two hosts, as to which of their kitchens should first smoke for the refreshment of their guest; nor though I am personally related to one, and connected through my relatives with another, could I manage by alternation to give them quite equal measure, since age and dignity of praetorian rank gave Ferreolus a prior right of invitation over and above his other claims.

From the first moment we were hurried from one pleasure to another. Hardly had we entered the vestibule of either house when we saw two opposite pairs of partners in the ball game, repeating each other's movements as they turned in wheeling circles; in another place one heard the rattle of dice-boxes and the shouts of contending players; in yet another, were books in abundance ready to your hand; you might have imagined yourself among the shelves of some grammarian, or the tiers of the Athenaeum, or a bookseller's towering cases. They were so arranged that the devotional works were near the ladies' seats; where the master sat were those ennobled by the great style of Roman eloquence. The arrangement had this defect, that it separated certain books by certain authors in manner as near to each other as in matter they are far apart. Thus, Augustine writes like Varro, and Horace like Prudentius; but you had to consult them on different sides of the room. Turrianus Rufinus' interpretation of Adamantius-Origen was eagerly examined by the readers of theology among us; according to our different points of view we had different reasons to give for the censure of this Father by certain of the clergy as too trenchant a controversialist and best avoided by the prudent. But the translation is so literal and yet renders the spirit of the work so well that neither Apuleius' version of Plato's *Phaedo* nor Cicero's of the *Ctesiphon* of Demosthenes is more admirably adapted to the use and rule of our Latin tongue.

While we were engaged in these discussions as fancy prompted each, appears an envoy from the cook to warn us that the hour of bodily refreshment is at hand. And, in fact, the fifth hour had just elapsed, proving that the man was punctual, and had properly marked the advance of the hours upon the water-clock. The dinner was short, but abundant, served in the fashion affected in senatorial houses where inveterate usage prescribes numerous courses of very few dishes, though, to afford variety, roast alternated with stew. Amusing and instructive anecdotes accompanied our potations; wit went with the one sort, learning with the other. To be brief, we were entertained with decorum, refinement and good cheer. After dinner, if we were at Vorocingus (the name of one estate), we walked over to our quarters and our own belongings. If at Prusianum, as the other is called, (the young) Tonantius and his brother turned out of their beds for us because we could not be always dragging our gear about: they are surely the elect among the nobles of our own age.

The siesta over, we took a short ride to sharpen our jaded appetites for supper. Both of our hosts had baths in their houses, but in neither did they happen to be available; so I set my servants to work in the rare sober intervals which the convivial bowl, too often filled, allowed their sodden brains. I made them dig a pit at their best speed near a spring, or by the river; into this a heap of red-hot stones was thrown, and the glowing cavity covered over with an arched roof of wattled hazel. This still left interstices, and to exclude the light and keep in the steam given off when water was thrown on the hot stones, we laid coverings of Cilician goats' hair over all. In these vapour baths we passed whole hours with lively talk and repartee; all the time the cloud of hissing steam enveloping us induced the healthiest perspiration.

When we had perspired enough we were bathed in hot water; the treatment removed the feeling of repletion, but left us languid; we therefore finished off with a bracing douche from fountain, well or river. For the River Gardon runs between the two properties; except in time of flood, when the stream is swollen and clouded with melted snow, it looks red through its tawny gravels, and flows still and pellucid over its pebbly bed, teeming none the less with the most delicate fish. I could tell you of suppers fit for a king; it is not my sense of shame, but simply want of space which sets a limit to my revelations. You would have a great story if I turned the page and continued on the other side; but I am always ashamed to disfigure the back of a letter with an inky pen. Besides, I am on the point of leaving here, and hope, by Christ's grace, that we shall meet very shortly; the story of my friends' banquets will be better told at my own table or at yours – provided only that a good week's interval elapses to restore me the healthy appetite I long for. There is nothing like thin living to give tone to a system disordered by excess. Farewell.

THE MAGNIFICENCE OF THE BARBARIAN PRINCE SIGISMER, BURGUNDY, c. AD 470

Sidonius

Sigismer was a Frank. The newly enriched barbarians became as fond of lavish adornment as the Romans.

You take such pleasure in the sight of arms and those who wear them, that I can imagine your delight if you could have seen the young prince Sigismer on his way to the palace of his father-in-law in the guise of a bridegroom or suitor in all the pomp and bravery of the tribal fashion. His own steed with its caparisons, other steeds laden with flashing gems, paced before and after; but the conspicuous interest in the procession centred in the prince himself, as with a charming modesty he went afoot amid his bodyguard and footmen, in flame-red mantle, with much glint of ruddy gold, and gleam of snowy silken tunic, his fair hair, red cheeks and white skin according with the three hues of his equipment. But the chiefs and allies who bore him company were dread of aspect, even thus on peace intent. Their feet were laced in boots of bristly hide reaching to the heels; ankles and legs were exposed. They wore high tight tunics of varied colour hardly descending to their bare knees, the sleeves covering only the upper arm. Green mantles they had with crimson borders; baldrics supported swords hung from their shoulders, and pressed on sides covered with cloaks of skin secured by brooches. No small part of their adornment consisted of their arms; in their hands they grasped barbed spears and missile axes; their left sides were guarded by shields, which flashed with tawny golden bosses and snowy silver borders, betraying at once their wealth and their good taste. Though the business in hand was wedlock, Mars was no whit less prominent in all this pomp than

Venus. Why need I say more? Only your presence was wanting to the full enjoyment of so fine a spectacle. For when I saw that you had missed the things you love to see, I longed to have you with me in all the impatience of your longing soul.

PART FOUR

EPILOGUE

The Roman Empire in the East, AD 477–565

INTRODUCTION

When the Roman empire in the West fell in AD 476, the empire in the East, based at Constantinople, carried on business much as usual. And did so for another thousand years. For the city-empire, renamed Byzantium, had several blessings not allowed its deceased western counterpart. Founded by Constantine as an explicitly Christian city, its people had long been binded and bonded by one faith, and they remained so. Social divisions also tended to be smaller in Byzantium; there was no overweening aristocracy, for instance, but there was a large middle class. The military, meanwhile, were subservient to political and religious leadership. Fortuitously situated on the Bosphorus, Byzantium was the trading crossroads between Eastern Europe and Asia and, charging 10 per cent on all goods in and out of the city, was splendidly wealthy. In comparision with the fallen western empire, Byzantium enoyed remarkable internal stability.

The Byzantine empire had its fair quotient of enemies without. Some – like Attila the Hun – were paid off in tons of gold, others were met with arms. Unlike the old joint empire, the eastern empire had a short land frontier to defend. After garrisoning the lower Danube, it could turn its attentions to Asia. Any seaborne invasion of the city itself was nigh impossible and to foil any land attack Theodosius II (AD 408–50) erected new walls.

Byzantium, however, ceased to be meaningfully Roman after the reign of Justinian I, whose 38-year reign saw three major accomplishments. Firstly, aided by the outstanding general Belisarius, Justinian reconquered much of the old Roman empire. In AD 534 North Africa was retaken. From Africa, Belisarius crossed to Italy and after five years' fighting took Rome. Secondly, Justinian oversaw a massive church-building programme, which included the domed Hagia Sophia, the Church of Holy Wisdom, in Byzantium. Thirdly, he created another sort of monument: a codification of Roman law. Ten experts were engaged to rationalize and precis the entire legal experience of Rome, and their labour was published in AD 534 in a series of books, the *Corpus of Civil Law*. According to Justinian, one volume of the series, the *Digest*, reduced 3,000,000 lines of Roman law to just 150,000.

The reign of Justinian was not entirely glorious. In AD 532 the two citizens' societies, the Greens and the Blues, united in the Nika revolt and Justinian almost fled the city but was stiffened by the courage of his wife and joint-ruler Theodora (a former prostitute). A decade later, Byzantium was visited by the bubonic plague. And if Procopius, a former secretary to Belisarius, is to be believed, Justinian himself was a blood-thirsty, spendthrift despot, "the devil incarnate".

On Justinian's death, the reconquered territories soon passed to other masters. The Lombards took northern Italy. The Avars took Pannonia and Dacia to found a Bulgar–Slav kingdom. The Persians overran the eastern provinces. However, his churches and consolidation of Roman law endured. The Hagia Sophia still stands today. The *Corpus of Civil Law* has influenced the legal structures of most of the nations of the Western world.

It was a swan-song for the Roman Empire. For Justinian was absolutely the last truly decent Roman emperor. The reason was simple: Justinian, like all the emperors before him, spoke Latin. All those who occupied the throne in Byzantium after him spoke another language. They spoke Greek.

THE SECRET HISTORY OF EMPRESS THEODORA, C. AD 500–525

Procopius

The daughter of a Byzantine bear-tamer, Theodora married Justinian in AD 525. Before wedding the emperor-apparent she was infamous for her dissolution. Procopius was an advocate who wrote The Secret History *of Justinian's reign; as secretary to Justinian's most able general, Belisarius, he also penned the regime's official war history, Wars of Justinian.*

In Byzantium there was a man called Acacius, a keeper of the circus animals, belonging to the Green faction and entitled the Bearward. This man died of sickness while Anastasius occupied the imperial throne, leaving three daughters, Comito, Theodora, and Anastasia, of whom the eldest had not yet completed her seventh year. The widow married again, hoping that her new husband would from then on share with her the management of her house and the care of the animals. But the Greens' Dancing-master, a man called Asterius, was offered a bribe to remove these two from their office, in which he installed his Paymaster without any difficulty, for the Dancing-masters were allowed to arrange such matters just as they chose. But when the wife saw the whole populace congregated in the circus, she put wreaths on the heads of the little girls and in both their hands, and made them sit down as suppliants. The Greens refused absolutely to admit the supplication; but the Blues gave them a similar office, as their Bearward too had died.

When the children were old enough, they were at once put on the stage there by their mother, as their appearance was very attractive; not all at the same time, however, but as each one seemed to her to be mature enough for this profession. The eldest one, Comito, was already one of the most popular harlots of the day. Theodora, who came next, clad in a little tunic with long sleeves, the usual dress of a slave girl, used to assist her in various ways, following her about and invariably carrying on her shoulders the bench on which her sister habitually sat at public meetings. For the time being Theodora was still too undeveloped to be capable of sharing a man's bed or having intercourse like a woman; but she acted as a sort of male prostitute to satisfy customers of the lowest type, and slaves at that, who when accompanying their owners to the theatre seized their opportunity to divert themselves in this revolting manner; and for some considerable time she remained in a brothel, given up to this unnatural bodily commerce. But as soon as she was old enough and fully developed, she joined the women on the stage and promptly became a courtesan, of the type our ancestors called "the dregs of the army". For she was not a flautist or harpist; she was not even qualified to join the corps of dancers; but she merely sold her attractions to anyone who came along, putting her whole body at his disposal.

Later she joined the actors in all the business of the theatre and played a regular part in their stage performances, making herself the butt of their ribald buffoonery. She was extremely clever and had a biting wit, and quickly became popular as a result. There was not a particle of modesty in the little hussy, and no one ever saw her taken aback: she complied with the most outrageous demands without the slightest hesitation, and she was the sort of girl who if somebody walloped her or boxed her ears would make a jest of it and roar with laughter; and she would throw off her clothes and exhibit naked to all and sundry those regions, both in front and behind, which the rules of decency require to be kept veiled and hidden from masculine eyes.

She used to tease her lovers by keeping them waiting, and by constantly playing about with novel methods of intercourse she could always bring the lascivious to her feet; so far from waiting to be invited by anyone she encountered, she herself by cracking dirty jokes and wiggling her hips suggestively would invite all who came her way, especially if they were still in their teens. Never was anyone so completely given up to unlimited self-indulgence. Often she would go to a bring-your-own-food dinner-party with ten young men or more, all at the peak of their physical powers and with fornication as their chief object in life, and would lie with all her fellow-diners in turn the whole night long: when she had reduced them all to a state of exhaustion she would go to their menials, as many as thirty on occasions, and copulate with every one of them; but not even so could she satisfy her lust.

One night she went into the house of a distinguished citizen during the drinking, and, it is said, before the eyes of all the guests she stood up on the end of the couch near their feet, pulled up her dress in the most disgusting manner as she stood there, and brazenly displayed her lasciviousness. And though she brought three openings into service, she often found fault with Nature, grumbling because Nature had not made the openings in her nipples wider than is normal, so that she could devise another variety of intercourse in that region. Naturally she was frequently pregnant, but by using pretty well all the tricks of the trade she was able to induce immediate abortion.

Often in the theatre, too, in full view of all the people she would throw off her clothes and stand naked in their midst, having only a girdle about her private parts and her groins – not, however, because she was ashamed to expose these also to the public, but because no one is allowed to appear there absolutely naked: a girdle round the groins is compulsory. With this minimum covering she would spread herself out and lie face upwards on the floor. Servants on whom this task had been imposed would sprinkle barley grains over her private parts, and geese trained for the purpose used to pick them off one by one with their bills and swallow them. Theodora, so far from blushing when she stood up again, actually seemed to be proud of this performance. For she was not only shameless herself, but did more than anyone else to encourage shamelessness.

Many times she threw off her clothes and stood in the middle of the actors on the stage, leaning over backwards or pushing out her behind to invite both those who had already enjoyed her and those who had not been intimate as yet, parading her own special brand of gymnastics. With such lasciviousness did she misuse her own body that she appeared to have her private parts not like other women in the place intended by nature, but in her face! And again, those who were intimate with her showed by so doing that they were not having intercourse in accordance with the laws of nature; and every person of any decency who happened to meet her in the forum would swing round and beat a hasty retreat, for fear he might come in contact with any of the hussy's garments and so appear tainted with this pollution. For to those who saw her, especially in the early hours of the day, she was a bird of ill omen. As for her fellow-actresses, she habitually and constantly stormed at them like a fury; for she was malicious in the extreme.

Later she accompanied Hecebolus, a Tyrian who had taken over the government of Pentapolis,[1] in order to serve him in the

---

[1] A group of five cities in Libya

most revolting capacity, but she got into bad odour with him and was shot out without more ado; as a result she found herself without even the necessities of life, which from then on she provided in her customary fashion by making her body the tool of her lawless trade. First she came to Alexandria; then after making a tour round the whole East she returned to Byzantium, in every city following an occupation which a man had better not name, I think, if he hopes ever to enjoy the favour of God. It was as if the unseen powers could not allow any spot on earth to be unaware of Theodora's depravity.

JUSTINIAN SUPRESSES THE NIKA REVOLT, BYZANTIUM, AD 532

Procopius

The most serious internal threat to the rule of Justinian.

At this time [1 January] an insurrection broke out unexpectedly in Byzantium among the populace, and, contrary to expectation, it proved to be a very serious affair, and ended in great harm to the people and to the senate, as the following account will show.

In every city the population has been divided for a long time past into the Blue and the Green factions; but within comparatively recent times it has come about that, for the sake of these names and the seats which the rival factions occupy in watching the games, they spend their money and abandon their bodies to the most cruel tortures, and even do not think it unworthy to die a most shameful death. And they fight against their opponents knowing not for what end they imperil themselves, but knowing well that, even if they overcome their enemy the fight, the conclusion of the matter for them will be to be carried off straight away to the prison, and finally, after suffering extreme torture, to be destroyed. So there grows up in them against their fellow men a hostility which has no cause, and at no time does it cease or disappear, for it gives place neither to the ties of marriage nor of relationship nor of friendship, and the case is the same even though those who differ with respect to these colours be brothers or any other kin . . . I, for my part, am unable to call this anything except a disease of the soul . . .

At this time the officers of the city administration in Byzantium were leading away to death some of the rioters. But the members of the two factions, conspiring together and declaring a truce with each other, seized the prisoners and then straightway entered the prison and released all those who were in confinement there . . . Fire was applied to the city as if it had fallen under the hand of an enemy . . . The emperor and his consort, with a few members of the senate shut themselves up in the palace and remained quietly there. Now the watch-word which the populace passed to one another was Nika ["Conquer"] . . .

. . . On the fifth day of the insurrection in the late afternoon the Emperor Justinian gave orders to Hypatius and Pompeius, nephews of the late emperor, Anastasius, to go home as quickly as possible, either because he suspected that some plot was being matured by them against his own person, or, it may be, because destiny brought them to this. But they feared that the people would force them to the throne (as in fact occurred), and they said that they would be doing wrong if they should abandon their sovereign when he found himself in such danger. When the Emperor Justinian heard this, he inclined still more to his suspicion, and he bade them quit the palace instantly . . .

On the following day at sunrise it became known to the people that both men had quit the palace where they had been staying. So the whole population ran to them, and they declared Hypatius emperor and prepared to lead him to the market place to assume the power. But the wife of Hypatius, Mary, a discreet woman, who had the greatest reputation for prudence, laid hold of her husband and would not let go, but cried out with loud lamentation and with entreaties to all her kinsmen that the people were leading him on the road to death. But since the throng overpowered her, she unwillingly released her husband, and he by no will of his own came to the Forum of Constantine, where they summoned him to the throne . . .

The emperor and his court were deliberating as to whether it would be better for them if they remained or if they took to flight in the ships. And many opinions were expressed favouring either course. And the Empress Theodora also spoke to the following effect: "My opinion then is that the present time, above all others, is inopportune for flight, even though it bring safety . . . For one who has been an emperor it is unendurable to be a fugitive. May I never be separated from this purple, and may I not live that day on which those who meet me shall not address me as mistress. If, now, it is your wish to save yourself, O Emperor, there is no difficulty. For we have much money, and there is the sea, here the boats. However consider whether it will not come about after you have been saved that you would gladly exchange that safety for death. For as for myself, I approve a certain ancient saying that royalty is a good burial-shroud." When the queen had spoken thus, all were filled with boldness, and, turning their thoughts towards resistance, they began to consider how they might be able to defend themselves if any hostile force should come against them . . . All the hopes of the emperor were centred upon Belisarius and Mundus, of whom the former, Belisarius, had recently returned from the Persian war bringing with him a following which was both powerful and imposing, and in particular he had a great number of spearmen and guards who had received their training in battles and the perils of warfare . . .

When Hypatius reached the hippodrome, he went up immediately to where the emperor is accustomed to take his place and seated himself on the royal throne from which the emperor was always accustomed to view the equestrian and athletic contests. And from the palace Mundus went out through the gate which, from the circling descent, has been given the name of the Snail . . . Belisarius, with difficulty and not without danger and great exertion, made his way over ground covered by ruins and half-burned buildings, and ascended to the stadium . . . Concluding that he must go against the populace who had taken their stand in the hippodrome – a vast multitude crowding each other in great disorder – he drew his sword from its sheath and, commanding the others to do likewise, with a shout he advanced upon them at a run. But the populace, who were standing in a mass and not in order, at the sight of armoured soldiers who had a great reputation for bravery and experience in war, and seeing that they struck out with their swords unsparingly, beat a hasty retreat . . . Mundus straightway made a sally into the hippodrome through the entrance which they call the Gate of Death. Then indeed from both sides the partisans of Hypatius were assailed with might and main and destroyed . . . There perished among the populace on that day more than thirty thousand . . . The soldiers killed both Hypatius and Pompeius on the following day and threw bodies into the sea . . . This was the end of the insurrection in Byzantium.

BELISARIUS RECONQUERS AFRICA, AD 534

Procopius

Procopius recounts Belisarius' quashing of the Vandal kingdom in North Africa, the first step in Justinian's restoration of the Roman empire to its ancient limits.

Belisarius, upon reaching Byzantium with Gelimer [king of the Vandals, captured by Belisarius] and the Vandals, was counted worthy to receive such honours, as in former times were assigned to those generals of the Romans who had won the greatest and most noteworthy victories. And a period of about 600 years had now passed since anyone had attained these honours, except, indeed, Titus and Trajan, and such other emperors as had led armies against some barbarian nation and had been victorious. For he displayed the spoils and slaves from the war in the midst of the city and led a procession which the Romans call a "triumph", not, however, in the ancient manner, but going on foot from his own house to the hippodrome and then again from the barriers [the starting line for the racers at the Hippodrome] until he reached the place where the imperial throne is. And there was booty – first of all, whatever articles are wont to be set apart for the royal service, – thrones of gold and carriages in which it is customary for a king's consort to ride, and much jewellery made of precious stones, and golden drinking cups, and all the other things which are useful for the royal table. And there was also silver weighing many thousands of talents and all the royal treasure amounting to an exceedingly great sum (for Gizeric [leader of the Vandals' sack of Rome of 455] had despoiled the Palatium in Rome) and among these were the treasures of the Jews, which Titus, the son of Vespasian, together with certain others, had brought to Rome after the capture of Jerusalem. And one of the Jews, seeing these things, approached one of those known to the emperor and said: "These treasures I think it inexpedient to carry into the palace in Byzantium. Indeed, it is not possible for them to be elsewhere than in the place where Solomon, the king of the Jews, formerly placed them. For it is because of these that Gizeric captured the palace of the Romans, and that now the Roman army has captured that of the Vandals." When this had been brought to the ears of the Emperor, he became afraid and quickly sent everything to the sanctuaries of the Christians in Jerusalem. And there were slaves in the triumph, among whom was Gelimer himself, wearing some sort of a purple garment upon his shoulders, and all his family, and as many of the Vandals as were very tall and fair of body. And when Gelimer reached the hippodrome and saw the emperor sitting upon a lofty seat and the people standing on either side and realized as he looked about in what an evil plight he was, he neither wept nor cried out, but ceased not saying over in the words of the Hebrew scripture: "Vanity of vanities, all is vanity." And when he came before the emperor's seat, they stripped off the purple garment, and compelled him to fall prone on the ground and do obeisance to the Emperor Justinian. This also Belisarius did, as being a suppliant of the emperor along with him. And the Emperor Justinian and the Empress Theodora presented the children of Ilderic [sometime king of the Vandals] and his offspring and all those of the family of the Emperor Valentinian with sufficient sums of money, and to Gelimer they gave lands not to be despised in Galatia and permitted him to live there together with his family. However, Gelimer was by no means enrolled among the patricians, since he was unwilling to change from the faith of Arius.

A little later the triumph [to honour his consulship] was celebrated by Belisarius in the ancient manner also. For he had the fortune to be advanced to the office of consul, and therefore was borne aloft by the captives, and as he was thus carried in his curule chair, he threw to the populace those very spoils of the Vandalic war. For the people carried off the silver plate and golden girdles and a vast amount of the Vandals' wealth of other sorts as a result of Belisarius' consulship, and it seemed that after a long interval of disuse an old custom was being revived . . .

THE PLAGUE, BYZANTIUM, AD 542

Procopius

The "pestilence" which gripped Byzantium in AD 542 was one of the severest outbreaks of bubonic plague in recorded history.

During these times there was a pestilence, by which the whole human race came near to being annihilated. Now in the case of all other scourges sent from heaven some explanation of a cause might be given by daring men, such as the many theories propounded by those who are clever in these matters; for they love to conjure up causes which are absolutely incomprehensible to man, and to fabricate outlandish theories of natural philosophy knowing well that they are saying nothing sound but considering it sufficient for them, if they completely deceive by their argument some of those whom they meet and persuade them to their view. But for this calamity it is quite impossible either to express in words or to conceive in thought any explanation, except indeed to refer it to God. For it did not come in a part of the world nor upon certain men, nor did it confine itself to any season of the year, so that from such circumstances it might be possible to find subtle explanations of a cause, but it embraced the entire world, and blighted the lives of all men, though differing from one another in the most marked degree, respecting neither sex nor age.

For much as men differ with regard to places in which they live, or in the law of their daily life, or in natural bent, or in active pursuits, or in whatever else man differs from man, in the case of this disease alone the difference availed naught. And it attacked some in the summer season, others in the winter, and still others at the other times of the year. Now let each one express his own judgment concerning the matter, both sophist and astrologer, but as for me, I shall proceed to tell where this disease originated and the manner in which it destroyed men. It started from the Egyptians who dwell in Pelusium. Then it divided and moved in one direction towards Alexandria and the rest of Egypt, and in the other direction it came to Palestine on the borders of Egypt; and from there it spread over the whole world, always moving forward and travelling at times favorable to it. For it seemed to move by fixed arrangement, and to tarry for a specified time in each country, casting its blight slightingly upon none, but spreading in either direction right out to the ends of the world, as if fearing least some corner of the earth might escape it. For it left neither island nor cave nor mountain ridge which had human inhabitants; and if it had passed by any land, either not affecting the men there or touching them in indifferent fashion, still at a later time it came back; then those who dwelt round about this land, whom formerly it had afflicted most sorely, it did not touch at all, but it did not remove from the place in question until it had given up its just and proper tale of dead, so as to correspond exactly to the number destroyed at the earlier time among those who dwelt round about. And this disease always took its start from the coast, and from there went up to the interior.

And in the second year it reached Byzantium in the middle of spring, where it happened that I was staying at that time. And it came as follows. Apparitions of supernatural beings in human guise of every description were seen by many persons, and those who encountered them thought that they were struck by the man they had met in this or that part of the body, as it havened, and immediately upon seeing this apparition they were seized also by the disease. Now at first those who met these creatures tried to turn them aside by uttering the holiest of names and exorcizing them in other ways as well as each one could, but they accomplished absolutely nothing, for even in the sanctuaries where the most of them fled for refuge they were dying constantly. But later on they were unwilling even to give heed to their friends when they called to them, and they shut themselves up in their rooms and pretended that they did not hear, although their doors were being beaten down, fearing, obviously, that he who was calling was one of those demons. But in the case of some the pestilence did not come on in this way, but they saw a vision in a dream and seemed to suffer the very same thing at the hands of the creature who stood over them, or else to hear a voice foretelling to them that they were written down in the number of those who were to die. But with the majority it came about that they were seized by the disease without becoming aware of what was coming either through a waking vision or a dream. And they were taken in the following manner. They had a sudden fever, some when just roused from sleep, others while walking about, and others while otherwise engaged, without any regard to what they were doing. And the body showed no change from its previous colour, nor was it hot as might be expected when attacked by a fever, nor indeed did any inflammation set in, but the fever was of such a languid sort from its commencement and up till evening that neither to the sick themselves nor to a physician who touched them would it afford any suspicion of danger. It was natural, therefore, that not one of those who had contracted the disease expected to die from it. But on the same day in some cases, in others on the following day, and in the rest not many days later, a bubonic swelling developed; and this took place not only in the particular part of the body which is called *boubon*, that is, "below the abdomen", but also inside the armpit, and in some cases also beside the ears, and at different points on the thighs.

Up to this point, then, everything went in about the same way with all who had taken the disease. But from then on very marked differences developed; and I am unable to say whether the cause of this diversity of symptoms was to be found in the difference in bodies, or in the fact that it followed the wish of Him who brought the disease into the world. For there ensued with some a deep coma, with others a violent delirium, and in either case they suffered the characteristic symptoms of the disease. For those who were under the spell of the coma forgot all those who were familiar to them and seemed to lie sleeping constantly. And if anyone cared for them, they would eat without waking, but some also were neglected, and these would die directly through lack of sustenance. But those who were seized with delirium suffered from insomnia and were victims of a distorted imagination; for they suspected that men were coming upon them to destroy them, and they would become excited and rush off in flight, crying out at the top of their voices. And those who were attending them were in a state of constant exhaustion and had a most difficult time of it throughout. For this reason everybody pitied them no less than the sufferers, not because they were threatened by the pestilence in going near it (for neither physicians nor other persons were found to contract this malady through contact with the sick or with the dead, for many who were constantly engaged either in burying or in attending those in no way connected with them held out in the performance of this service beyond all expectation, while with many others the disease came on without warning and they died straightway); but they pitied them because of the great hardships which they were undergoing. For when the patients fell from their beds and lay rolling upon the floor, they kept putting them back in place, and when they were struggling to rush headlong out of their houses, they would force them back by shoving and pulling against them. And when water chanced to be near, they wished to fall into it, not so much because of a desire for drink (for the most of them rushed into the sea), but the cause was to be found chiefly in the diseased state of their minds. They had also great difficulty in the matter of eating, for they could not easily take food. And many perished through lack of any man to care for them, for they were either overcome by hunger, or threw themselves down from a height. And in those cases where neither coma nor delirium came on, the bubonic swelling became mortified and the sufferer, no longer able to endure the pain, died. And one would suppose that in all cases the same thing would have been true, but since they were not at all in their senses, some were quite unable to feel the pain; for owing to the troubled condition of their minds they lost all sense of feeling.

Now some of the physicians who were at a loss because the symptoms were not understood, supposing that the disease centred in the bubonic swellings, decided to investigate the bodies of the dead. And upon opening some of the swellings, they found a strange sort of carbuncle that had grown inside them. Death came in some cases immediately, in others after many days; and with some the body broke out with black pustules about as large as a lentil and these did not survive even one day, but all succumbed immediately. With many also a vomiting of blood ensued without visible cause and straightway brought death. Moreover I am able to declare this, that the most illustrious physicians predicted that many would die, who unexpectedly escaped entirely from suffering shortly afterwards, and that they declared that many would be saved, who were destined to be carried off almost immediately. So it was that in this disease there was no cause which came within the province of human reasoning; for in all cases the issue tended to be something unaccountable. For example, while some were helped by bathing, others were harmed in no less degree. And of those who received no care many died, but others, contrary to reason, were saved. And again, methods of treatment showed different results with different patients. Indeed the whole matter may be stated thus, that no device was discovered by man to save himself, so that either by taking precautions he should not suffer, or that when the malady had assailed him he should get the better of it; but suffering came without warning and recovery was due to no external cause. And in the case of women who were pregnant death could be certainly foreseen if they were taken with the disease. For some died through miscarriage, but others perished immediately at the time of birth with the infants they bore. However, they say that three women in confinement survived though their children perished, and that one woman died at the very time of childbirth but that the child was born and survived.

Now in those cases where the swelling rose to an unusual size and a discharge of pus had set in, it came about that they escaped from the disease and survived, for clearly the acute condition of the carbuncle had found relief in this direction, and this proved to be in general an indication of returning health; but in cases where the swelling preserved its former appearance there ensued those troubles which I have just mentioned. And with some of them it came about that the thigh was withered, in which case, though the swelling was there, it did not develop the least suppuration. With others who survived the tongue did not remain unaffected, and they lived on either lisping or speaking incoherently and with difficulty.

Now the disease in Byzantium ran a course of four months, and its greatest virulence lasted about three. And at first the deaths were a little more than the normal, then the mortality rose still higher, and afterwards the tale of dead reached 5,000 each day, and again it even came to 10,000 and still more than that. Now in the beginning each man attended to the burial of the dead of his own house, and these they threw even into the tombs of others, either escaping detection or using violence; but afterwards confusion and disorder everywhere became complete. For slaves remained destitute of masters, and men who in former times were very prosperous were deprived of the service of their domestics who were either sick or dead, and many houses became completely destitute of human inhabitants. For this reason it came about that some of the notable men of the city because of the universal destitution remained unburied for many days.

And it fell to the lot of the emperor, as was natural, to make provision for the trouble. He therefore detailed soldiers from the palace and distributed money, commanding Theodorus to take charge of this work; this man held the position of announcer of imperial messages, always announcing to the emperor the petitions of his clients, and declaring to them in turn whatever his wish was. In the Latin tongue the Romans designate this office by the term *Referendarius*. So those who had not as yet fallen into complete destitution in their domestic affairs attended individually to the burial of those connected with them. But Theodorus, by giving out the emperor's money and by making further expenditures from his own purse, kept burying the bodies which were not cared for. And when it came about that all the tombs which had existed previously were filled with the dead, then they dug up all the places about the city one after the other, laid the dead there, each one as he could, and departed; but later on those who were making these trenches, no longer able to keep up with the number of the dying, mounted the towers of the fortifications in Sycae, and tearing off the roofs threw the bodies there in complete disorder; and they piled them up just as each one happened to fall, and filled practically all the towers with corpses, and then covered them again with their roofs. As a result of this an evil stench pervaded the city and distressed the inhabitants still more, and especially whenever the wind blew fresh from that quarter.

At that time all the customary rites of burial were overlooked. For the dead were not carried out escorted by a procession in the customary manner, nor were the usual chants sung over them, but it was sufficient if one carried on his shoulders the body of one of the dead to the parts of the city which bordered on the sea and flung him down; and there the corpses would be thrown upon skiffs in a heap, to be conveyed wherever it might chance. At that time, too, those of the population who had formerly been members of the factions laid aside their mutual enmity and in common they attended to the burial rites of the dead, and they carried with their own hands the bodies of those who were no connections of theirs and buried them. Nay, more, those who in times past used to take delight in devoting themselves to pursuits both shameful and base, shook off the unrighteousness of their daily lives and practiced the duties of religion with diligence, not so much because they had learned wisdom at last nor because they had become all of a sudden lovers of virtue, as it were – for when qualities have become fixed in men by nature or by the training of a long period of time, it is impossible for them to lay them aside thus lightly, except, indeed, some divine influence for good has breathed upon them – but then all, so to speak, being thoroughly terrified by the things which were happening, and supposing that they would die immediately, did, as was natural, learn respectability for a season by sheer necessity. Therefore as soon as they were rid of the disease and were saved, and already supposed that they were in security, since the curse had moved on to other peoples, then they turned sharply about and reverted once more to their baseness of hearts and now, more than before, they make a display of the inconsistency of their conduct, altogether surpassing themselves in villainy and in lawlessness of every sort. For one could insist emphatically without false-hood that this disease, whether by chance or by some provi-dence, chose out with exactitude the worst men and let them go free. But these things were displayed to the world in later times.

During that time it seemed no easy thing to see any man in the streets of Byzantium, but all who had the good fortune to he in health were sitting in their houses, either attending the sick or mourning the dead. And if one did succeed in meeting a man going out, he was carrying one of the dead. And work of every description ceased, and all the trades were abandoned by the artisans, and all other work as well, such as each had in hand. Indeed in a city which was simply abounding in all good things starvation almost absolute was running riot. Certainly it seemed a difficult and very notable thing to have a sufficiency of bread or of anything else; so that with some of the sick it appeared that the end of life came about sooner than it should have come by reason of the lack of the necessities of life.

And, to put all in a word, it was not possible to see a single man in Byzantium clad in the *chlamys*, and especially when the emperor became ill (for he too had a swelling of the groin), but in a city which held dominion over the whole Roman empire every man was wearing clothes befitting private station and remaining quietly at home. Such was the course of the pestilence in the Roman empire at large as well as in Byzantium. And it fell also upon the land of the Persians and visited all the other barbarians besides.

APPENDIX

EXTRACT FROM THE SECOND SPEECH OF MARCUS TULLIUS CICERO AGAINST MARK ANTONY ("THE SECOND PHILIPPIC"), 44 BC

Oratory was more than one of the arts of Ancient Rome, it was the prerequisite of public life. Any career in politics or the law demanded the skilled employment of spoken Latin; for this reason rhetoric was an essential, elaborate part of the education of young patrician men.

Cicero was arguably the greatest exponent of Latin oratory, close-run by Caesar and Cato the Elder. Cicero's Second Speech against Mark Antony is his oratorical masterwork, even though it was not actually spoken; Cicero was persuaded against attending the Senate and delivering the speech by friends who, rightly, feared that the would-be dictator Mark Antony would proceed to violence against him. Instead Cicero published the speech as a pamphlet.

There is more to the Second Philippic than oratorical brilliance. As a reflection of the tumultuous last days of the Republic it has little to rival it.

The preliminary part of the speech is Cicero's defence of his own consulship (impugned by Mark Antony). Cicero then proceeds to assassinate Antony's character:

Shall we then examine your conduct from the time when you were a boy? I think so. Let us begin at the beginning. Do you recollect that, while you were still clad in the praetexta, you became a bankrupt? That was the fault of your father, you will say. I admit that. In truth such a defence is full of filial affection. But it is peculiarly suited to your own audacity, that you sat among the fourteen rows of the knights, though by the Roscian law there was a place appointed for bankrupts, even if any one had become such by the fault of fortune and not by his own. You assumed the manly gown, which you soon made a womanly one: at first a public prostitute, with a regular price for your wickedness, and that not a low one. But very soon Curio stepped in, who carried you off from your public trade, and, as if he had bestowed a matron's robe upon you, settled you in a steady and durable wedlock.

No boy bought for the gratification of passion was ever so wholly in the power of his master as you were in Curio's. How often has his father turned you out of his house? How often has he placed guards to prevent you from entering? while you, with night for your accomplice, lust for your encourager, and wages for your compeller, were let down through the roof. That house could no longer endure your wickedness. Do you not know that I am speaking of matters with which I am thoroughly acquainted? Remember that time when Curio, the father, lay weeping in his bed; his son throwing himself at my feet with tears recommended to me you; he entreated me to defend you against his own father, if he demanded six millions of sesterces of you; for that he had been bail for you to that amount. And he himself, burning with love, declared positively that because he was unable to bear the misery of being separated from you, he should go into banishment.

And at that time what misery of that most flourishing family did I allay, or rather did I remove! I persuaded the father to pay the son's debts; to release the young man, endowed as he was with great promise of courage and ability, by the sacrifice of part of his family estate; and to use his privileges and authority as a father to prohibit him not only from all intimacy with, but from every opportunity of meeting you. When you recollected that all this was done by me, would you have dared to provoke me by abuse if you had not been trusting to those swords which we behold?

But let us say no more of your profligacy and debauchery. There are things which it is not possible for me to mention with honour; but you are all the more free for that, inasmuch as you have not scrupled to be an actor in scenes which a modest enemy can not bring himself to mention.

Mark now, O conscript fathers, the rest of his life, which I will touch upon rapidly. For my inclination hastens to arrive at those things which he did in the time of the civil war, amid the greatest miseries of the republic and at those things which he does every day. And I beg of you, though they are far better known to you than they are to me, still to listen attentively, as you are doing to my relation of them. For in such cases as this, it is not the mere knowledge of such actions that ought to excite the mind, but the recollection of them also. Although we must at once go into the middle of them, lest otherwise we should be too long in coming to the end.

He was very intimate with Clodius at the time of his tribune-ship; he, who now enumerates the kindnesses which he did me. He was the firebrand to handle all conflagrations; and even in his house he attempted something. He himself well knows what I allude to. From thence he made a journey to Alexandria, in defiance of the authority of the senator and against the interests of the republic, and in spite of religious obstacles; but he had Gabinius for his lender, with whom whatever he did was sure to be right. What were the circumstances of his return from thence? What sort of return was it? He went from Egypt to the farthest extremity of Gaul before he returned home. And what was his home! For at that time every man had possession of his own house; and you had no house anywhere, O Antonius. House, do you say? What place was there in the whole world where you could set your foot on any thing that belonged to you, except Mienum, which you farmed with your partners, as if it had been Sisapo?

You came from Gaul to stand for the quaestorship. Dare to say that you went to your own father before you came to me. I had already received Caesar's letters, begging me to allow myself to accept of your excuses; and therefore, I did not allow you even to mention thanks. After that, I was treated with respect by you, and you received attentions from me in your canvass for the quaestorship. And it was at that time, indeed, that you endeavoured to slay Publius Clodius in the forum, with the approbation of the Roman people; and though you made the attempt of your own accord, and not at my instigation, still you clearly alleged that you did not think, unless you slew him, that you could possibly make amends to me for all the injuries which you had done me. And this makes me wonder why you should say that Milo did that deed at my instigation; when I never once exhorted you to do it, who of your own accord attempted to do me the same service. Although, if you had persisted in it, I should have preferred allowing the action to be set down entirely to your own love of glory rather than to my influence.

You were elected quaestor. On this, immediately, without any resolution of the senate authorizing such a step, without drawing lots, without procuring any law to be passed, you hastened to Caesar. For you thought the camp the only refuge on earth for indigence, and debt, and profligacy, – for all men, in short, who were in a state of utter ruin. Then, when you had recruited your resources again by his largesses and your own robberies (if, indeed, a person can be said to recruit, who only acquires something which he may immediately squander), you hastened, being again a beggar, to the tribuneship, in order that in that magistracy you might, if possible, behave like your friend.

Listen now, I beseech you, O conscript fathers, not to those things which he did indecently and profligately to his own injury and to his own disgrace as a private individual; but to the actions which he did impiously and wickedly against us and our fortunes, – that is to say, against the whole republic. For it is from his wickedness that you will find that the beginning of all these evils has arisen.

For when, in the consulship of Lucius Lentulus and Marcus Marcellus, you, on the first of January, were anxious to prop up the republic, which was tottering and almost falling, and were willing to consult the interests of Caius Caesar himself, if he would have acted like a man in his senses, then this fellow opposed to your counsels his tribuneship, which he had sold and handed over to the purchaser, and exposed his own neck to that axe under which many have suffered for smaller crimes. It was against you, O Marcus Antonius, that the senate, while still in the possession of its rights, before so many of its luminaries were extinguished, passed that decree which, in accordance with the usage of our ancestors, is at times passed against an enemy who is a citizen. And have you dared, before these conscript fathers, to say any thing against me, when I have been pronounced by this order to be the saviour of my country, and when you have been declared by it to be an enemy of the republic? The mention of that wickedness of yours has been interrupted, but the recollection of it has not been effaced. As long as the race of men, as long as the name of the Roman people shall exist (and that, unless it is prevented from being so by your means, will be everlasting), so long will that most mischievous interposition of your veto be spoken of.

What was there that was being done by the senate either ambitiously or rashly, when you, one single young man, forbade the whole order to pass decrees concerning the safety of the republic? And when you did so, not once only, but repeatedly? Nor would you allow any one to plead with you in behalf of the authority of the senate; and yet, what did anyone entreat of you, except that you would not desire the republic to be entirely overthrown and destroyed; when neither the chief men of the state by their entreaties, nor the elders by their warnings, nor the senate in a full house by pleading with you, could move you from the determination which you had already sold and as it were delivered to the purchaser? Then it was, after having tried many other expedients previously, that a blow was of necessity struck at you which had been struck at only few men before you, and which none of them had ever survived.

Then it was that this order armed the consuls, and the rest of the magistrates who were invested with either military or civil command, against you, and you never would have escaped them, if you had not taken refuge in the camp of Caesar.

It was you, you, I say, O Marcus Antonius, who gave Caius Caesar, desirous as he already was to throw everything into confusion, the principal pretext for waging war against his country. For what other pretence did he allege? What cause did he give for his own most frantic resolution and action, except that the power of interposition by the veto had been disregarded, the privileges of the tribunes taken away, and

Antonius' rights abridged by the senate? I say nothing of how false, how trivial these pretences were; especially when there could not possibly be any reasonable cause whatever to justify any one in taking up arms against his country. But I have nothing to do with Caesar. You must unquestionably allow that the cause of that ruinous war existed in your person.

O miserable man if you are aware, more miserable still if you are not aware, that this is recorded in writings, is handed down to men's recollection, that our very latest posterity in the most distant ages will never forget this fact, that the consuls were expelled from Italy, and with them Cnaeus Pompeius, who was the glory and light of the empire of the Roman people; that all the men of consular rank, whose health would allow them to share in that disaster and that flight, and the praetors, and men of praetorian rank, and the tribunes of the people, and a great part of the senate, and all the flower of the youth of the city, and, in a word, the republic itself was driven out and expelled from its abode.

As, then, there is in seeds the cause which produces trees and plants, so of this most lamentable war you were the seed. Do you, O conscript fathers, grieve that these armies of the Roman people have been slain? It is Antonius who slew them. Do you regret your most illustrious citizens? It is Antonius, again, who has deprived you of them. The authority of this order is overthrown; it is Antonius who has overthrown it. Everything, in short, which we have seen since that time (and what misfortune is there that we have not seen?) we shall, if we argue rightly, attribute wholly to Antonius. As Helen was to the Trojans, so has that man been to this republic, – the cause of war the cause of mischief the cause of ruin The rest of his tribuneship was like the beginning. He did everything which the senate had laboured to prevent, as being impossible to be done consistently with the safety of the republic. And see, now, how gratuitously wicked he was even in accomplishing his wickedness.

He restored many men who had fallen under misfortune. Among them no mention was made of his uncle. If he was severe, why was he not so to everyone? If he was merciful, why was he not merciful to his own relations? But I say nothing of the rest. He restored Licinius Lenticula, a man who had been condemned for gambling, and who was a fellow-gamester of his own. As if he could not play with a condemned man; but in reality, in order to pay by a straining of the law in his favour, what he had lost by the dice. What reason did you allege to the Roman people why it was desirable that he should be restored? I suppose you said that he was absent when the prosecution was instituted against him; that the cause was decided without his having been heard in his defence; that there was not by a law any judicial proceeding established with reference to gambling; that he had been put down by violence or by arms; or lastly, as was said in the case of your uncle, that the tribunal had been bribed with money. Nothing of this sort was said. Then he was a good man, and one worthy of the republic. That, indeed, would have been nothing to the purpose, but still, since being condemned does not go for much, I would forgive you if that were the truth. Does not he restore to the full possession of his former privileges the most worthless man possible, – one who would not hesitate to play at dice even in the forum, and who had been convicted under the law which exists respecting gambling, – does not he declare in the most open manner his own propensities?

Then in this same tribuneship, when Caesar while on his way into Spain had given him Italy to trample on, what journeys did he make in every direction! How did he visit the municipal towns! I know that I am only speaking of matters which have been discussed in everyone's conversation, and that the things which I am saying and am going to say are better known to every one who was in Italy at that time, than to me, who was not. Still I mention the particulars of his conduct, although my speech can not possibly come up to your own personal knowledge. When was such wickedness ever heard of as existing upon earth? Or shamelessness? Or such open infamy?

The tribune of the people was borne along in a chariot, lictors crowned with laurel preceded him; among whom, on an open litter, was carried an actress; whom honourable men, citizens of the different municipalities, coming out from their towns under compulsion to meet him, saluted not by the name by which she was well known on the stage, but by that of Volumnia. A car followed full of pimps; then a lot of debauched companions; and then his mother, utterly neglected, followed the mistress of her profligate son, as if she had been her daughter-in-law. O the disastrous fecundity of that miserable woman! With the marks of such wickedness as this did that fellow stamp every municipality, and prefecture, and colony, and, in short, the whole of Italy.

To find fault with the rest of his actions, O conscript fathers, is difficult, and somewhat unsafe. He was occupied in war; he glutted himself with the slaughter of citizens who bore no resemblance to himself. He was fortunate – if at least there can be any good fortune in wickedness. But since we wish to show a regard for the veterans, although the cause of the soldiers is very different from yours; they followed their chief; you went to seek for a leader; still (that I may not give you any pretense for stirring up odium against me among them), I will say nothing of the nature of the war.

When victorious, you returned with the legions from Thessaly to Brundusium. There you did not put me to death. It was a great kindness! For I confess that you could have done it. Although there was no one of those men who were with you at that time, who did not think that I ought to be spared.

For so great is men's affection for their country; that I was sacred even in the eyes of your legions, because they recollected that the country had been saved by me. However, grant that you did give me what you did not take away from me; and that I have my life as a present from you, since it was not taken from me by you; was it possible for me, after all your insults, to regard that kindness of yours as I regarded it at first, especially after you saw that you must hear this reply from me?

You came to Brundusium, to the bosom and embraces of your actress. What is the matter? Am I speaking falsely? How miserable is it not to be able to deny a fact which it is disgraceful to confess! If you had no shame before the municipal towns, had you none even before your veteran army? For what soldier was there who did not see her at Brundusium? Who was there who did not know that she had come so many days' journey to congratulate you? Who was there who did not grieve that he was so late in finding out how worthless a man he had been following?

Again you made a tour through Italy, with that same actress for your companion. Cruel and miserable was the way in which you led your soldiers into the towns; shameful was the pillager in every city, of gold and silver, and above all, of wine. And besides all this, while Caesar knew nothing about it, as he was at Alexandria, Antonius, by the kindness of Caesar's friends, was appointed his master of the horse. Then he thought that you could live with Hippia by virtue of his office, and that he might give horses which were the property of the state to Sergius the buffoon. At that time he had elected for himself to live in, not the house which he now dishonours, but that of Marcus Piso. Why need I mention his decrees, his robberies, the possessions of inheritances which were given him, and those too which were seized by him? Want compelled him; he did not know where to turn. That great inheritance from Lucius Rubrius, and that other from Lucius Turselius, had not yet come to him. He had not yet succeeded as an unexpected heir to the place of Cnaeus Pompeius, and of many others who were absent. He was forced to live like a robber, having nothing beyond what he could plunder from others.

However, we will say nothing of these things, which are acts of a more hardy sort of villainy. Let us speak rather of his meaner descriptions of worthlessness. You, with those jaws of yours, and those sides of yours, and that strength of body suited to a gladiator, drank such quantities of wine at the marriage of Hippia, that you were forced to vomit the next day in the sight of the Roman people. O action disgraceful not merely to see, but even to hear of! If this had happened to you at supper amid those vast drinking-cups of yours, who would not have thought it scandalous? But in an assembly of the Roman people, a man holding a public office, a master of the horse, to whom it would have been disgraceful even to belch, vomiting filled his own bosom and the whole tribunal with fragments of what he had been eating reeking with wine. But he himself confesses this among his other disgraceful acts. Let us proceed to his more splendid offences.

Caesar came back from Alexandria, fortunate, as he seemed at least to himself; but in my opinion no one can be fortunate who is unfortunate for the republic. The spear was set up in front of the temple of Jupiter Stator, and the property of Cnaeus

Pompeius Magnus – (miserable that I am, for even now that my tears have ceased to flow, my grief remains deeply implanted in my heart) – the property, I say, of Cnaeus Pompeius the Great was submitted to the pitiless voice of the auctioneer. On that one occasion the state forgot its slavery, and groaned aloud; and though men's minds were enslaved, as every thing was kept under by fear, still the groans of the Roman people were free. While all men were waiting to see who would be so impious, who would be so mad, who would be so declared an enemy to gods and to men as to dare to mix himself up with that wicked auction, no one was found except Antonius, even though there were plenty of men collected round that spear who would have dared any thing else.

One man alone was found to dare to do that which the audacity of every one else had shrunk from and shuddered at. Were you, then, seized with such stupidity, – or, I should rather say, with such insanity – as not to see that if you, being of the rank in which you were born, acted as a broker at all, and above all as a broker in the case of Pompeius property, you would be execrated and hated by the Roman people, and that all gods and all men must at once become and for ever continue hostile to you? But with what violence did that glutton immediately proceed to take possession of the property of that man, to whose valour it had been owing that the Roman people had been more terrible to foreign nations, while his justice had made it dearer to them.

When, therefore, this fellow had begun to wallow in the treasures of that great man, he began to exult like a buffoon in a play, who has lately been a beggar, and has become suddenly rich. But, as some poet or other says, –

"Ill-gotten gains come quickly to an end."

It is an incredible thing, and almost a miracle, how he in a few, not months, but days, squandered all that vast wealth. There was an immense quantity of wine, an excessive abundance of very valuable plate, much precious apparel, great quantities of splendid furniture, and other magnificent things in many places, such as one was likely to see belonging to a man who was not indeed luxurious but who was very wealthy. Of all this in a few days there was nothing left.

What Charybdis was ever so voracious? Charybdis, do I say? Charybdis, if she existed at all, was only one animal. The ocean I swear most solemnly, appears scarcely capable of having swallowed up such numbers of things so widely scattered and distributed in such different places with such rapidity. No thing was shut up, nothing sealed up, no list was made of any thing. Whole storehouses were abandoned to the most worthless of men. Actors seized on this, actresses on that; the house was crowded with gamblers, and full of drunken men; people were drinking all day, and that too in many places; there were added to all this expense (for this fellow was not invariably fortunate) heavy gambling losses. You might see in the cellars of the slaves, couches covered with the most richly embroidered counterpanes of Cnaeus Pompeius. Wonder not, then, that all these things were so soon consumed. Such profligacy as that could have devoured not only the patrimony of one individual, however ample it might have been (as indeed his was), but whole cities and kingdoms. And then his houses and gardens!

Oh the cruel audacity! Did you dare to enter into that house? Did you dare to cross that most sacred threshold? And to show your most profligate countenance to the household gods who protect that abode? A house which for a long time no one could behold, no one could pass by without tears! Are you not ashamed to dwell so long in that house? One in which, stupid and ignorant as you are, still you can see nothing which is not painful to you.

When you behold those beaks of ships in the vestibule, and those warlike trophies, do you fancy that you are entering into a house which belongs to you? It is impossible. Although you are devoid of all sense and all feeling, – as in truth you are, – still you are acquainted with yourself, and with your trophies, and with your friends. Nor do I believe that you, either waking or sleeping, can ever act with quiet sense. It is impossible but that, were you ever so drunk and frantic, – as in truth you are, – when the recollection of the appearance of that illustrious man comes across you, you should be roused from sleep by your fears, and often stirred up to madness if awake.

I pity even the walls and the room. For what had that house ever beheld except what was modest, except what proceeded from the purest principles and from the most virtuous practice? For that man was, O conscript fathers, as you yourselves know, not only illustrious abroad, but also admirable at home; and not more praiseworthy for his exploits in foreign countries, than for his domestic arrangements. Now in his house every bedchamber is a brothel, and every dining-room a cookshop. Although he denies this:- – Do not, do not make enquiries. He is become economic. He desired that mistress of his to take possession of whatever belonged to her, according to the laws of the Twelve Tables. He has taken his keys from her, and turned her out of doors. What a well-tried citizen! Of what proved virtue is he! The most honourable passage in whose life is the one when he divorced himself from this actress.

But how constantly does he harp on the expression "the consul Antonius!" This amounts to say "that most debauched consul," "that most worthless of men, the consul." For what else is Antonius? For if any dignity were implied the name, then, I imagine, your grandfather would sometime have called himself "the consul Antonius." But he never did. My colleague too, your own uncle, would have call himself so. Unless you are the only Antonius. But I pass over those offences which have no peculiar connection with the part you took in harassing the republic; I return to that in which you bore so principal a share, – that is, to the civil war; and it is mainly owing to you that that was originated, and brought to a head, and carried on.

Though you yourself took no personal share in it, partly through timidity, partly through profligacy, you had tasted, or rather had sucked in, the blood of fellow-citizens: you had been in the battle of Pharsalia as a leader; you had slain Lucius Dormitius, a most illustrious and high-born man; you had pursued and put to death in the most barbarous manner many men who had escaped from the battle, and whom Caesar would perhaps have saved, as he did some others.

And after having performed these exploits, what was the reason why you did not follow Caesar into Africa; especially when so large a portion of the war was still remaining? And accordingly, what place did you obtain about Caesar's person after his return from Africa? What was your rank? He whose quaestor you had been when general, whose master of the horse when he was dictator, to whom you had been the chief cause of war, the chief instigator of cruelty, the sharer of his plunder, his son, as you yourself said, by inheritance, proceeded against you for the money which you owed for the house and gardens, and for the other property which you had bought at that sale.

At first you answered fiercely enough; and that I may not appear prejudiced against you in every particular, you used a tolerably just and reasonable argument. "What does Caius Caesar demand money of me? Why should he do so, any more than I should claim it of him? Was he victorious without my assistance? No; and he never could have been. It was I who supplied him with a pretext for civil war; it was I who proposed mischievous laws; it was I who took up arms against the consuls and generals of the Roman people, against the senate and people of Rome, against the gods of the country, against its altars and hearths, against the country itself. Has he conquered for himself alone? Why should not those men whose common work the achievement is, have the booty also in common?" You were only claiming your right, but what had that to do with it? He was the more powerful of the two.

Therefore, stopping all your expostulations, he sent his soldiers to you, and to your sureties; when all on a sudden out came that splendid catalogue of yours. How men did laugh! That there should be so vast a catalogue, that there should be such a numerous and various list of possessions, of all of which, with the exception of a portion of Misenum, there was nothing which the man who was putting them up to sale could call his own. And what a miserable sight was the auction. A little apparel of Pompeius', and that stained; a few silver vessels belonging to the same man, all battered, some slaves in wretched condition; so that we grieved that there was any thing remaining to be seen of these miserable relics.

This auction, however, the heirs of Lucius Rubrius prevented from proceeding, being armed with a decree of Caesar to that effect. The spendthrift was embarrassed. He did not know which way to turn. It was at this very time that an assassin sent by him was said to have been detected with a dagger in the house of Caesar. And of this Caesar himself complained in the senate, inveighing openly against you. Caesar departs to Spain, having granted you a few days delay for making the payment, on account of your poverty. Even then you do not follow him. Had so good a gladiator as you retired from business so early? Can any one then fear a man who was as timid as this man in upholding his party, that is, in upholding his own fortunes?

After some time he at last went into Spain; but, as he says, he could not arrive there in safety. How then did Dolabella manage to arrive there? Either, O Antonius, that cause ought never to have been undertaken, or when you had undertaken it, it should have been maintained to the end. Thrice did Caesar fight against his fellow-citizens; in Thessaly, in Africa, and in Spain. Dolabella was present at all these battles. In the battle in Spain he even received a wound. If you ask my opinion, I wish he had not been there. But still, if his design at first was blamable, his consistency and firmness were praiseworthy. But what shall we say of you? In the first place, the children of Cnaeus Pompeius sought to be restored to their country. Well, this concerned the common interests of the whole party. Besides that, they sought to recover their household gods, the gods of their country, their altars, their hearths, the tutelar gods of their family; all of which you had seized upon. And when they sought to recover those things by force of arms which belonged to them by the laws, who was it most natural – (although in unjust and unnatural proceedings what can there be that is natural?) – still, who was it most natural to expect would fight against the children of Cnaeus Pompeius? Who? Why, you who had bought their property.

Were you at Narbo to be sick over the tables of your entertainers while Dolabella was fighting your battles in Spain?

And what return was that of yours from Narbo? He even asked why I had returned so suddenly from my expedition. I have just briefly explained to you, O conscript fathers, the reason of my return. I was desirous, if I could, to be of service to the republic even before the first of January. For, as to your question, how I had returned in the first place, I returned by daylight, not in the dark, in the second place, I returned in shoes, and in my Roman gown, not in any Gallic slippers, or barbarian mantle. And even now you keep looking at me; and, as it seems, with great anger. Surely you would be reconciled to me if you knew how ashamed I am of your worthlessness, which you yourself are not ashamed of. Of all the profligate conduct of all the world, I never saw, I never heard of any more shameful than yours. You, who fancied yourself a master of the horse, when you were standing for, or I should rather say begging for, the consulship for the ensuing year, ran in Gallic slippers and a barbarian mantle about the municipal towns and colonies of Gaul, from which we used to demand the consulship when the consulship was stood for and not begged for.

But mark now the trifling character of the fellow. When about the tenth hour of the day he had arrived at Red Rocks, he skulked into a little petty wine-shop, and, hidden there, kept on drinking till evening. And from thence getting into a gig and being driven rapidly to the city, he came to his own house with his head veiled. "Who are you?" says the porter. "An express from Marcus." He is at once taken to the woman for whose sake he had come; and he delivered the letter to her. And when she had read it with tears (for it was written in a very amorous style, but the main subject of the letter was that he would have nothing to do with that actress for the future; that he had discarded all his love for her, and transferred it to his correspondent), when she, I say, wept plentifully, this soft-hearted man could bear it no longer; he uncovered his head and threw himself on her neck. Oh the worthless man (for what else can I call him? there is no more suitable expression for me to use)! Was it for this that you disturbed the city by nocturnal alarms, and Italy with fears of many days' duration, in order that you might show yourself unexpectedly, and that a woman might see you before she hoped to do so?

And he had at home a pretence of love; but out of doors a cause more discreditable still, namely, lest Lucius Plancus should sell up his sureties. But after you had been produced in the assembly by one of the tribunes of the people, and had replied that you had come on your own private business, you made even the people full of jokes against you. But, however, we have said too much about trifles. Let us come to more important subjects.

You went a great distance to meet Caesar on his return from Spain. You went rapidly, you returned rapidly, in order that we might see that, if you were not brave, you were at least active. You again became intimate with him; I am sure I do not know how. Caesar had this peculiar characteristic; whoever he knew to be utterly ruined by debt, and needy, even if he knew him also to be an audacious and worthless man, he willingly admitted him to his intimacy. You then, being admirably recommended to him by these circumstances, were ordered to be appointed consul, and that too as his own colleague.

I do not make any complaint against Dolabella, who was at that time acting under compulsion, and was cajoled and deceived, But who is there who does not know with what great perfidy both of you treated Dolabella in that business? Caesar induced him to stand for the consulship. After having promised it to him, and pledged himself to aid him, he prevented his getting it, and transferred it to himself. And you endorsed his treachery with your own eagerness.

The first of January arrives. We are convened in the senate. Dolabella inveighed against him with much more fluency and premeditation than I am doing now.

And what things were they which he said in his anger, O ye good gods! First of all, after Caesar had declared that before he departed he would order Dolabella to be made consul (and they deny that he was a king who was always doing and saying something of this sort) – but after Caesar had said this, then this virtuous augur said that he was invested with a pontificate of that sort that he was able, by means of the auspices, either to hinder or to vitiate the comitia, just as he pleased; and he declared that he would do so.

And here, in the first place, remark the incredible stupidity of the man. For what do you mean? Could you not just as well have done what you said you had now the power to do by the privileges with which that pontificate had invested you, even if you were not an augur, if you were consul? Perhaps you could even do it more easily. For we augurs have only the power of announcing that the auspices are being observed, but the consuls and other magistrates have the right also of observing them whenever they choose. Be it so. You said this out of ignorance. For one must not demand prudence from a man who is never sober. But still remark his impudence. Many months before, he said in the senate that he would either prevent the comitia from assembling for the election of Dolabella by means of the auspices, or that he would do what he actually did do. Can any one divine beforehand what defect there will be in the auspices, except the man who has already determined to observe the heavens? Which in the first place it is forbidden by law to do at the time of the comitia. And if any one has; been observing the heavens, he is bound to give notice of it, not after the comitia are assembled, but before they are held. But this man's ignorance is joined to impudence, nor does he know what an augur ought to know, nor do what a modest man ought to do.

And just recollect the whole of his conduct during his consulship from that day up to the ides of March. What lictor was ever so humble, so abject? He himself had no power at all; he begged every thing of others; and thrusting his head into the hind part of his litter, he begged favours of his colleagues, to sell them himself afterwards.

Behold, the day of the comitia for the election of Dolabella arrives The prerogative century draws its lot. He is quiet. The vote is declared; he is still silent. The first class is called. Its vote is declared. Then, as is the usual course, the votes are announced. Then the second class. And all this is done faster than I have told it. When the business is over, that excellent augur (you would say he must be Caius Laelius) says, – "We adjourn it to another day."

Oh the monstrous impudence of such a proceeding! What had you seen? What had you perceived? What had you heard? For you did not say that you had been observing the heavens, and indeed you do not say so this day. That defect then has arisen, which you on the first of January had already foreseen would arise, and which you had predicted so long before. Therefore, in truth, you have made a false declaration respecting the auspices, to your own great misfortune, I hope, rather than to that of the republic. You laid the Roman people under the obligations of religion; you as augurs interrupted an augur;

you as consul interrupted a consul by a false declaration concerning the auspices.

I will say no more, lest I should seem to be pulling to pieces the acts of Dolabella; which must inevitably sometime or other be brought before our college.

But take notice of the arrogance and insolence of the fellow. As long as you please, Dolabella is a consul irregularly elected; again, while you please, he is a consul elected with all proper regard to the auspices. If it means nothing when an augur gives this notice in those words in which you gave notice, then confess that you, when you said, – "We adjourn this to another day," – were not sober. But if those words have any meaning, then I, an augur, demand of my colleague to know what that meaning is.

But, lest by any chance, while enumerating his numerous exploits, our speech should pass over the finest action of Marcus Antonius, let us come to the Lupercalia.

He does not dissemble, O conscript fathers; it is plain that he is agitated; he perspires; he turns pale. Let him do what he pleases, provided he is not sick, and does not behave as be did in the Minucian colonnade. What defence can be made for such beastly behaviour? I wish to hear, that I may see the fruit of those high wages of that rhetorician, of that land given in Leontini.

Your colleague was sitting in the rostra, clothed in purple robe, on a golden chair, wearing a crown. You mount the steps; you approach his chair, (if you were a priest of Pan, you ought to have recollected that you were consul too;) you display a diadem. There is a groan over the whole forum. Where did the diadem come from? For you had not picked it up when lying on the ground, but you had brought it from home with you, a pre-meditated and deliberately planned wickedness. You placed the diadem on his head amid the groans of the people; he rejected it amid great applause. You then alone, O wicked man, were found both to advise the assumption of kingly power, and to wish to have him for your master who was your colleague and also to try what the Roman people might be able to bear and to endure.

Moreover, you even sought to move his pity; you threw yourself at his feet as a suppliant; begging for what? To be a slave? You might beg it for yourself, when you had lived in such a way from the time that you were a boy that you could bear everything, and would find no difficulty in being a slave; but certainly you had no commission from the Roman people to try for such a thing for them.

Oh how splendid was that eloquence of yours, when you harangued the people stark naked! What could be more foul than this? More shameful than this? More deserving of every sort of punishment? Are you waiting for me to prick you more? This that I am saying must tear you and bring blood enough if you have any feeling at all. I am afraid that I may be detracting from the glory of some most eminent men. Still my indignation shall find a voice. What can be more scandalous than for that man to live who placed a diadem on a man's head, when everyone confesses that that man was deservedly slain who rejected it?

And, moreover, he caused it to be recorded in the annals, under the head of Lupercalia, "That Marcus Antonius, the consul, by command of the people, had offered the kingdom to Caius Caesar, perpetual dictator; and that Caesar had refused to accept it." I now am not much surprised at your seeking to disturb the general tranquillity; at your hating not only the city but the light of day; and at your living with a pack of abandoned robbers, disregarding the day, and yet regarding nothing beyond the day. For where can you be safe in peace? What place can there be for you where laws and courts of justice have sway, both of which you, as far as in you lay, destroyed by the substitution of kingly power? Was it for this that Lucius Tarquinius was driven out; that Spurius Cassius, and Spurius Maelius, and Marcus Manlius were slain; that many years afterwards a king might be established at Rome by Marcus Antonius though the bare idea was impiety? However, let us return to the auspices.

With respect to all the things which Caesar was intending to do in the senate on the ides of March, I ask whether you have done anything? I heard, indeed, that you had come down prepared, because you thought that I intended to speak about your having made a false statement respecting the auspices, though it was still necessary for us to respect them. The fortune of the Roman people saved us from that day. Did the death of

Caesar also put an end to your opinion respecting the auspices? But I have come to mention that occasion which must be allowed to precede those matters which I had begun to discuss. What a flight was that of yours! What alarm was yours on that memorable day! How, from the consciousness of your wickedness, did you despair of your life! How, while flying, were you enabled secretly to get home by the kindness of those men who wished to save you, thinking you would show more sense than you do!

O how vain have at all times been my too true predictions of the future! I told those deliverers of ours in the Capitol, when they wished me to go to you to exhort you to defend the republic, that as long as you were in fear you would promise every thing, but that as soon as you had emancipated yourself from alarm you would be yourself again. Therefore, while the rest of the men of consular rank were going backward and forward to you, I adhered to my opinion, nor did I see you at all that day, or the next; nor did I think it possible for an alliance between virtuous citizens and a most unprincipled enemy to be made, so as to last, by any treaty or engagement whatever. The third day I came into the temple of Tellus, even then very much against my will, as armed men were blockading all the approaches.

What a day was that for you, O Marcus Antonius! Although you showed yourself all on a sudden an enemy to me; still I pity you for having envied yourself.

What a man, O ye immortal gods! And how great a man might you have been, if you had been able to preserve the inclination you displayed that day; – we should still have peace which was made then by the pledge of a hostage, a boy of noble birth, the grandson of Marcus Bamballo. Although was fear that was then making you a good citizen, which is never a lasting teacher of duty; your own audacity, which never departs from you as long as you are free from fear, has made you a worthless one. Although even at that time, when they thought you an excellent man, though I indeed differed from that opinion, you behaved with the greatest wickedness while presiding at the funeral of the tyrant, if that ought to be called a funeral.

All that fine panegyric was yours, that commiseration was yours, that exhortation was yours. It was you – you, I say – who hurled those firebrands, both those with which your friend himself was nearly burned, and those by which the house of Lucius Bellienus was set on fire and destroyed. It was you who let loose those attacks of abandoned men, slaves for the most part, which we repelled by violence and our own personal exertions; it was you who set them on to attack our houses. And yet you, as if you had wiped off all the soot and smoke in the ensuing days, carried those excellent resolutions in the Capitol, that no document conferring any exemption, or granting any favour, should be published after the ides of March. You recollect yourself, what you said about the exiles; you know what you said about the exemption; but the best thing of all was, that you forever abolished the name of the dictatorship in the republic. Which act appeared to show that you had conceived such a hatred of kingly power that you took away all fear of it for the future, on account of him who had been the last dictator.

To other men the republic now seemed established, but it did not appear so at all to me, as I was afraid of every sort of shipwreck, as long as you were at the helm. Have I been deceived? Or, was it possible for that man long to continue unlike himself? While you were all looking on, documents were fixed up over the whole Capitol, and exemptions were being sold, not merely to individuals, but to entire states. The freedom of the city was also being given now not to single persons only, but to whole provinces. Therefore, if these acts are to stand, – and stand they can not if the republic stands too, – then, O conscript fathers, you have lost whole provinces; and not the revenues only, but the actual empire of the Roman people has been diminished by a market this man held in his own house.

Where are the seven hundred millions of sesterces which were entered in the account-books which are in the temple of Ops? A sum lamentable indeed, as to the means by which it was procured, but still one which, if it were not restored to those to whom it belonged, might save us from taxes. And how was it, that when you owed forty millions of sesterces on the fifteenth of March, you had ceased to owe them by the first of April? Those things are quite countless which were purchased of different people, not without your knowledge; but there was one excellent decree posted up in the Capitol affecting king Deiotarus, a most devoted friend to the Roman people. And when that decree was posted up, there was no one who, amid all his indignation, could restrain his laughter.

For who ever was a more bitter enemy to another than Caesar was to Deiotarus? He was as hostile to him as he was to this order, to the equestrian order, to the people of Massilia, and to all men whom he knew to look on the republic of the Roman people with attachment. But this man, who neither present nor absent could ever obtain from him any favour or justice while he was alive, became quite an influential man with him when he was dead. When present with him in his house, he had called for him though he was his host, he had made him give in his accounts of his revenue, he had exacted money from him; he had established one of his Greek retainers in his tetrarchy, and he had taken Armenia from him, which had been given to him by the senate. While he was alive he deprived him of all these things; now that he is dead, he gives them back again.

And in what words? At one time he says, "that it appears to him to be just, . . ." at another, "that it appears not to be unjust . . ." What a strange combination of words! But while alive (I know this, for I always supported Deiotarus, who was at a distance), he never said that anything which we were asking for, for him, appeared just to him. A bond for ten millions of sesterces was entered into in the women's apartment (where many things have been sold, and are still being sold), by his ambassadors, well-meaning men, but timid and inexperienced in business, without my advice or that of the rest of the hereditary friends of the monarch. And I advise you to consider carefully what you intend to do with reference to this bond. For the king himself, of his own accord, without waiting for any of Caesar's memoranda, the moment that her heard of his death, recovered his own rights by his own courage and energy.

He, like a wise man, knew that this was always the law, that those men from whom the things which tyrants had taken away had been taken, might recover them when the tyrants were slain. No lawyer, therefore, not even he who is your lawyer and yours alone, and by whose advice you do all these things, will say that any thing is due to you by virtue of that bond for those things which had been recovered before that bond was executed. For he did not purchase them of you; but, before you undertook to sell him his own property, be had taken possession of it. He was a man – we, indeed, deserve to be despised, who hate the author of the actions, but uphold the actions themselves.

Why need I mention the countless mass of papers, the innumerable autographs which have been brought forward? Writings of which there are imitators who sell their forgeries as openly as if they were gladiators playbills. Therefore, there are now such heaps of money piled up in that man's house, that it is weighed out instead of being counted. But how blind is avarice! Lately, too, a document has been posted up by which the most wealthy cities of the Cretans are released from tribute; and by which it is ordained that after the expiration of the consulship of Marcus Brutus, Crete shall cease to be a province. Are you in your senses? Ought you not to be put in confinement? Was it possible for there really to be a decree of Caesar's exempting Crete after the departure of Marcus Brutus, when Brutus had no connection whatever with Crete while Caesar was alive? But by the sale of this decree (that you may not, O conscript fathers, think it wholly ineffectual) you have lost the province of Crete. There was nothing in the whole world which any one wanted to buy that this fellow was not ready to sell.

Caesar too, I suppose, made the law about the exiles which you have posted up. I do not wish to press upon any one in misfortune; I only complain, in the first place, that the return of those men has had discredit thrown upon it, whose cause Caesar judged to be different from that of the rest; and in the second place, I do not know why you do not mete out the same measure to all. For there can not be more than three or four left. Why do not they who are in similar misfortune enjoy a similar degree of your mercy? Why do you treat them as you treated your uncle? About whom you refused to pass a law when you were passing one about all the rest; and whom at the same time you encouraged to stand for the censorship, and instigated him to a canvass, which excited the ridicule and the complaint of everyone.

But why did you not hold that comitia? Was it because a tribune of the people announced that there had been an ill-omened flash of lightning seen? When you have any interest of your own to serve, then auspices are all nothing; but when it is only your friends who are concerned, then you become scrupulous. What more? Did you not also desert him in the matter of the septemvirate? "Yes, for he interfered with me." What were you afraid of? I suppose you were afraid that you would be able to refuse him nothing if he were restored to the full possession of his rights. You loaded him with every species of insult, a man whom you ought to have considered in the place of a father to you, if you had had any piety or natural affection at all. You put away his daughter, your own cousin, having already looked out and provided yourself beforehand with another. That was not enough. You accused a most chaste woman of misconduct. What can go beyond this? Yet you were not content with this. In a very full senate held on the first of January, while your uncle was present, you dared to say that this was your reason for hatred of Dolabella, that you had ascertained that he had committed adultery with your cousin and your wife. Who can decide whether it was more shameless of you to make such profligate and such impious statements against that unhappy woman in the senate, or more wicked to make them against Dolabella, or more scandalous to make them in the presence of her father, or more cruel to make them at all?

However, let us return to the subject of Caesar's written papers. How were they verified by you? For the acts of Caesar were for peace's sake confirmed by the senate; that is to say, the acts which Caesar had really done, not those which Antonius said that Caesar had done. Where do all these come from? By whom are they produced and vouched for? If they are false, why are they ratified? If they are true, why are they sold? But the vote which was come to enjoined you, after the first of June, to make an examination of Caesar's acts with the assistance of a council. What council did you consult? Whom did you ever invite to help you? What was the first of June that you waited for? Was it that day on which you, having travelled all through the colonies where the veterans were settled, returned escorted by a band of armed men?

Oh what a splendid progress of yours was that in the months of April and May, when you attempted even to lead a colony to Capua! How you made your escape from thence, or rather how you barely made your escape, we all know.

And now you are still threatening that city. I wish you would try, and we should not then be forced to say "barely." However, what a splendid progress of yours that was! Why need I mention your preparations for banquets, why your frantic hard drinking? Those things are only an injury to yourself; these are injuries to us. We thought that a great blow was inflicted on the republic when the Campanian district was released from the payment of taxes, in order to be given to the soldiery; but you have divided it among your partners in drunkenness and gambling. I tell you, O conscript fathers, that a lot of buffoons and actresses have been settled in the district of Campania. Why should I now complain of what has been done in the district of Leontini? Although formerly these lands of Campania and Leontini were considered part of the patrimony of the Roman people, and were productive of great revenue, and very fertile. You gave your physician three thousand acres; what would you have done if he had cured you? And two thousand to your master of oratory; what would you have done if he had been able to make you eloquent? However, let us return to your progress, and to Italy.

You led a colony to Casilinum, a place to which Caesar had previously led one. You did indeed consult me by letter about the colony of Capua (but I should have given you the same answer about Casilinum), whether you could legally lead a new colony to a place where there was a colony already. I said that a new colony could not be legally conducted to an existing colony, which had been established with a due observance of the auspices, as long as it remained in a flourishing state; but I wrote you word that new colonists might be enrolled among the old ones. But you, elated and insolent, disregarding all the respect due to the auspices, led a colony to Casilinum, whither one had been previously led a few years before; in order to erect your standard there, and to mark out the line of the new colony with a plough. And by that plough you almost grazed the gate of Capua, so as to diminish the territory of that flourishing colony.

After this violation of all religious observances, you hasten off to the estate of Marcus Varro, a most conscientious and upright man, at Casinum. By what right? With what face do you do this? By just the same, you will say, as that by which you entered on the estates of the heirs of Lucius Rubrius, or of the heirs of Lucius Turselius, or of other innumerable possessions. If you got the right from any auction, let the auction have all the force to which it is entitled; let writings be of force, provided they are the writings of Caesar, and not your own; writings by which you are bound, not those by which you have released yourself from obligation.

But who says that the estate of Varro at Casinum was ever sold at all? Who ever saw any notice of that auction? Who ever heard the voice of the auctioneer? You say that you sent a man to Alexandria to buy it of Caesar. It was too long to wait for Caesar himself to come! But who ever heard (and there was no man about whose safety more people were anxious) that any part whatever of Varro's property had been confiscated? What? What shall we say if Caesar even wrote you that you were to give it up? What can be said strong enough for such enormous impudence? Remove for a while those swords which we see around us. You shall now see that the cause of Caesar's auctions is one thing and that of your confidence and rashness is another. For not only shall the owner drive you from that estate, but any one of his friends, or neighbours, or hereditary connections, and any agent, will have the right to do so.

But how many days did he spend revelling in the most scandalous manner in that villa! From the third hour there was one scene of drinking, gambling, and vomiting. Alas for the unhappy house itself! How different a master from its former one has it fallen to the share of! Although, how is he the master at all? But still by how different a person has it been occupied! For Marcus Varro used it as a place of retirement for his studies, not as a theatre for his lusts.

What noble discussions used to take place in that villa! What ideas were originated there! What writings were composed there! The laws of the Roman people, the memorials of our ancestors, the consideration of all wisdom and all learning, were the topics that used to be dwelt on then; – but now, while you were the intruder there (for I will not call you the master), every place was resounding with the voices of drunken men; the pavements were floating with wine; the walls were dripping; nobly born boys were mixing with the basest hirelings; prostitutes with mothers of families. Men came from Casinum, from Aquinum, from Interamna to salute him. No one was admitted. That, indeed, was proper. For the ordinary marks of respect were unsuited to the most profligate of men.

When going from thence to Rome he approached Aquinum, a pretty numerous company (for it is a populous municipality) came out to meet him. But he was carried through the town in a covered litter, as if he had been dead. The people of Aquinum acted foolishly, no doubt; but still they were in his road. What did the people of Anagnia do? Who, although they were out of his line of road, came down to meet him, in order to pay him their respects, as if he were consul. It is an incredible thing to say, but still it was only too notorious at the time, that he returned nobody's salutation; especially as he had two men of Anagnia with him, Mustela and Laco; one of whom had the care of his swords, and the other of his drinking-cups.

Why should I mention the threats and insults with which he inveighed against the people of Teanum Sidicinum, with which he harassed the men of Puteoli, because they had adopted Caius Cassius and the Bruti as their patrons? A choice dictated, in truth, by great wisdom, and great zeal, benevolence, and affection for them; not by violence and force of arms, by which men have been compelled to choose you, and Basilus, and others like you both, – men whom no one would choose to have for his own clients, much less to be their client himself.

In the meantime, while you yourself were absent, what a day was that for your colleague when he overturned that tomb in the forum, which you were accustomed to regard with veneration! And when that action was announced to you, you – as is agreed upon by all who were with you at the time – fainted away. What happened afterwards I know not. I imagine that terror and arms got the mastery. At all events, you dragged your colleague down from his heaven; and you rendered him, not even now like yourself, at all events very unlike his own former self.

After that what a return was that of yours to Rome! How great was the agitation of the whole city! We recollected Cinna being too powerful; after him we had seen Sulla with absolute authority, and we had lately beheld Caesar acting as king. There were perhaps swords, but they were sheathed, and they were not very numerous. But how great and how barbaric a procession is yours! Men follow you in battle array with drawn swords; we see whole litters full of shields borne along. And yet by custom, O conscript fathers, we have become inured and callous to these things. When on the first of June we wished to come to the senate, as it had been ordained, we were suddenly frightened and forced to flee.

But he, as having no need of a senate, did not miss any of us, and rather rejoiced at our departure, and immediately proceeded to those marvellous exploits of his. He who had defended the memoranda of Caesar for the sake of his own profit, overturned the laws of Caesar – and good laws too – for the sake of being able to agitate the republic. He increased the number of years that magistrates were to enjoy their provinces; moreover, though he was bound to be the defender of the acts of Caesar, he rescinded them both with reference to public and private transactions.

In public transactions nothing is more authoritative than law; in private affairs the most valid of all deeds is a will. Of the laws, some he abolished without giving the least notice; others he gave notice of bills to abolish. Wills he annulled; though they have been at all times held sacred even in the case of the very meanest of the citizens. As for the statues and pictures which Caesar bequeathed to the people, together with his gardens, those he carried away, some to the house which belonged to Pompeius, and some to Scipio's villa.

And are you then diligent in doing honour to Caesar's memory? Do you love him even now that he is dead? What greater honour had he obtained than that of having a holy cushion, an image, a temple, and a priest? As then Jupiter, and Mars, and Quirinus have priests, so Marcus. Antonius is the priest of the god Julius. Why then do you delay? Why are not you inaugurated? Choose a day; select someone to inaugurate you; we are colleagues; no one will refuse. O you detestable man, whether you are the priest of a tyrant, or of a dead man! I ask you then, whether you are ignorant what day this is? Are you ignorant that yesterday was the fourth day of the Roman games in the Circus? And that you yourself submitted a motion to the people, that a fifth day should be added besides, in honour of Caesar? Why are we not all clad in the praetexta? Why are we permitting the honour which by your law was appointed for Caesar to be deserted? Had you no objection to so holy a day being polluted by the addition of supplications, while you did not choose it to be so by the addition of ceremonies connected with a sacred cushion? Either take away religion in every case, or preserve it in every case.

You will ask whether I approve of his having a sacred cushion, a temple and a priest? I approve of none of those things. But you, who are defending the acts of Caesar, what reason can you give for defending some, and disregarding others? Unless, indeed, you choose to admit that you measure everything by your own gain, and not by his dignity. What will you now reply to these arguments – (for I am waiting to witness your eloquence; I knew your grandfather, who was a most eloquent man, but I know you to be a more undisguised speaker than he was; he never harangued the people naked; but we have seen your breast, man, without disguise as you are)? Will you make any reply to these statements? Will you dare to open your mouth at all? Can you find one single article in this long speech of mine, to which you trust that you can make any answer? However, we will say no more of what is past.

But this single day, this very day that now is, this very moment while I am speaking, defend your conduct during this very moment, if you can. Why has the senate been surrounded with a belt of armed men? Why are your satellites listening to me sword in hand? Why are not the folding-doors of the temple of Concord open? Why do you bring men of all nations the most barbarous, Ityrcans, armed with arrows, into the forum? He says that he does so as a guard. Is it not then better to perish a thousand times than to be unable to live in one's own city without a guard of armed men? But believe me, there is no protection in that; – a man must be defended by the affection and good will of his fellow-citizens, not by arms.

The Roman people will take them from you, will wrest them from our hands. I wish that they may do so while we are still safe. But however you treat us, as long as you adopt those counsels it is impossible for you, believe me, to last long. In truth, that wife of yours, who is so far removed from covetousness, and whom I mention without intending any slight to her, has been too long owing her third payment to the state. The Roman people has men to whom it can entrust the helm of the state; and wherever they are, there is all the defense of the republic, or rather, there is the republic itself; which as yet has only avenged, but has not reestablished itself. Truly and surely has the republic most high-born youths ready to defend it, – though they may for a time keep in the background from a desire for tranquillity, still they can be recalled by the republic at any time.

The name of peace is sweet, the thing itself is most salutary. But between peace and slavery there is a wide difference. Peace is liberty in tranquillity; slavery is the worst of all evils, – to be repelled, if need be, not only by war, but even by death.

But if those deliverers of ours have taken themselves away out of our sight, still they have left behind the example of their conduct. They have done what no one else had done. Brutus pursued Tarquinius with war; who was a king when it was lawful for a king to exist in Rome. Spurius Cassius, Spurius Maelius, and Marcus Manlius were all slain because they were suspected of aiming at regal power. These are the first men who have ever ventured to attack, sword in hand, a man who was not aiming at regal power, but actually reigning. And their action is not only of itself a glorious and godlike exploit, but it is also one put forth for our imitation; especially since by it they have acquired such glory as appears hardly to be bounded by heaven itself. For although in the very consciousness of a glorious action there is a certain reward, still I do not consider immortality of glory a thing to be despised by one who is himself mortal.

Recollect then, O Marcus Antonius, that day on which you abolished the dictatorship. Set before you the joy of the senate and people of Rome; compare it with this infamous market held by you and by your friends; and then you will understand how great is the difference between praise and profit. But in truth, just as some people, through some disease which has blunted the senses, have no conception of the niceness of food, so men who are lustful, avaricious, and criminal, have no taste for true glory. But if praise can not allure you to act rightly, still can not even fear turn you away from the most shameful actions? You are not afraid of the courts of justice. If it is because you are innocent, I praise you; if because you trust in your power of overbearing them by violence, are you ignorant of what that man has to fear, who on such an account as that does not fear the courts of justice?

But if you are not afraid of brave men and illustrious citizens, because they are prevented from attacking you by your armed retinue, still, believe me, your own fellows will not long endure you. And what a life is it, day and night to be fearing danger from one's own people! Unless, indeed, you have men who are bound to you by greater kindnesses than some of those men by whom he was slain were bound to Caesar; or unless there are points in which you can be compared with him.

In that man were combined genius, method, memory, literature, prudence, deliberation, and industry. He had performed exploits in war which, though calamitous for the republic, were nevertheless mighty deeds. Having for many years aimed at being a king, he had with great labour, and much personal danger, accomplished what he intended. He had conciliated the ignorant multitude by presents, by monuments, by largesses of food, and by banquets; he had bound his own party to him by rewards, his adversaries by the appearances of clemency. Why need I say much on such a subject? He had already brought a free city, partly by fear, partly by patience, into a habit of slavery.

With him I can, indeed, compare you as to your desire to reign; but in all other respects you are in no degree to be compared to him. But from the many evils which by him have been burned into the republic, there is still this good, that the Roman people has now learned how much to believe every one, to whom to trust itself, and against whom to guard. Do you never think on these things? And do you not understand-that it is enough for brave men to have learned how noble a thing it is as to the act, how grateful it is as to the benefit done, how glorious as to the fame acquired, to slay a tyrant?

When men could not bear him, do you think they will bear you? Believe me, the time will come when men will race with one another to do this deed, and when no one will wait for the tardy arrival of an opportunity.

Consider, I beg you, Marcus Antonius, do some time or other consider the republic: think of the family of which you are born, not of the men with whom you are living. Be reconciled to the republic. However, do you decide on your conduct. As to mine, I myself will declare what that shall be. I defended the republic as a young man, I will not abandon it now that I am old. I scorned the sword of Catiline, I will not quail before yours. No, I will rather cheerfully expose my own person, if the liberty of the city can her restored by my death.

May the indignation of the Roman people at last bring forth what it has been so long labouring with. In truth, if twenty years ago in this very temple I asserted that death could not come prematurely upon a man of consular rank, with how much more truth must I now say the same of an old man? To me, indeed, O conscript fathers, death is now even desirable, after all the honors which I have gained, and the deeds which I have done. I only pray for these two things: one, that dying I may leave the Roman people free. No greater boon than this can be granted me by the immortal gods. The other, that every one may meet with a fate suitable to his deserts and conduct toward the republic.

Source: *The Orations of Marcus Tullius Cicero*, trans CD Yonge, George Bell & Sons, 1903.

SOURCES

The editor has made every effort to locate all persons owning rights in the selections which appear in this volume, and to secure permission for use from the holders of such rights. Queries regarding the use of material should be addressed to the editor c/o the publishers. If any errors have inadvertently been made corrections will, of course, be made in future editions.

PART ONE

Anon, "Instructions on farming", quoted in *Readings in Ancient History*, Vol. II, *Rome and the West* ed. William Stearns Davis, Allyn & Bacon, 1946.

Anon, "Reward for capture: runaway slaves", quoted in *They Saw It Happen in Classical Times*, ed. BK Workman, Basil Blackwell & Mott, 1964. Copyright © 1964 Basil Blackwell & Mott, Ltd.

Anon, "The Twelve Tables", *The Library of Original Sources*, Vol. III, ed Oliver J Thatcher, University Research Extension Co., 1901.

Anon, "I appeal to you to elect . . .", nos 1–7, *Remains of Old Latin*, Vol. IV, trans. EH Warmington, Harvard University Press, 1967; nos 8–10, *A Selection of Latin Inscriptions*, RH Barrow, Clarendon, 1934.

Anon, "Punic Wars: Hannibal addresses his soldiers", from *The World's Great Speeches*, ed. Lewis Copeland, Lawrence W. Lamm & Stephen J. McKenna, Dover Publications; Inc., 1999.

Antony, Mark, "On going to bed with Cleopatra", quoted in *The Life of Augustus* by Suetonius, trans. JC Rolfe, Loeb Classical Library, Harvard University Press, 1952.

Appian, "Pompey enters Rome in triumph", *Civil and Foreign Wars*, trans. Horace White, Bohn's Classical Library, 1899.

Caelius, "An aedile requests panthers", *Letters of Cicero*, trans. LP Wilkinson, Geoffrey Bles, 1949.

Caesar, Julius, "Julius Caesar defeats the Nervii", "The Britons", "Druids in Gaul", *The Conquest of Gaul*, trans. SA Handford, Penguin 1951. Copyright © 1951 SA Handford.

Caesar, Julius "Julius Caesar invades Britain", "A Chariot Fight", *Commentaries on the Gallic War*, trans. W. McDevitte and W. Bohn, 1872.

Catilina, Lucius, "The Catiline Conspiracy: Catiline rouses his accomplices", from *The World's Great Speeches*, ed. Lewis Copeland, Lawrence W. Lamm & Stephen J. McKenna, Dover Publications, Inc., 1999.

Cato the Elder, "How to keep a slave", quoted in *Readings in Ancient History*, Vol. II, *Rome and the West* ed. William Stearns Davis, Allyn & Bacon, 1946.

Cato the Elder, "Purchasing a farm" from *De Agri Cultura*, trans. BK Workman *They Saw It Happen in Classical Times*, ed. BK Workman, Basil Blackwell & Mott, Ltd., 1964. Copyright © 1964 Basil Blackwell & Mott, Ltd.

Cicero, Marcus, "Piracy in Sicily", from *Against Verres*, trans. BK Workman in *They Saw It Happen in Classical Times*, ed. BK Workman, Basil Blackwell & Mott, Ltd., 1964. Copyright © 1964 Basil Blackwell & Mott, Ltd., 1964.

Cicero, Marcus, "Gang-warfare in Rome", "Cicero takes Pindenissum", *Cicero's Letters to Atticus*, trans. DR Shackleton Bailey, Cambridge University Press, 1965–8. Copyright © 1978 DR Shackleton Bailey.

Cicero, Marcus, "Electoral bribery", *Letters*, ES Shuckburgh, G. Bell & Sons, 1899.

Cicero, "Surely nothing can be sweeter than liberty", from *De Republica*, I, trans. CW Keyes *De Republica, De Legibus*, Harvard University Press, 1959.

Cicero, "A dictator comes to dinner", "Jury Corruption", *Life and Letters of Cicero*, GE Jeans, Macmillan, 1880.

Cicero, "After the deed: The conspirators meet", *Cicero: Selected Works*, trans. Michael Grant, Penguin 1960. Copyright © 1960, 1965, 1971 Michael Grant.

Cicero, Marcus Tullius II, "Everyday life: A Roman student writes home", quoted in *The World's Story*, Vol. IV, ed. Eva March Tappan, Houghton Mifflin, 1914.

Cicero, "Queen Cleopatra in Rome", quoted in *Private Letters: Pagan and Christian*, ed. Dorothy Brooke, Ernest Benn Ltd., 1929.

Ennius, Quintus, "Punic Wars: The view of a soldier-poet", *Annales*, trans. EH Warmington in *Remains of Old Latin* I, Harvard University Press, 1967.

Horace, "A Journey to Brundusium", *Satires*, I, trans. C Smart in *The Complete Works of Horace*, Dent, 1911.

Horace, "Octavian's Victory at Actium" (originally "Cleopatra"), *Odes*, trans. John Marshall in *The Complete Works of Horace*, Dent, 1911.

Macrobius, "Field Fares stuffed with asparagus, fattened fowls . . .", quoted in *Readings in Ancient History*, Vol. II, *Rome and the West* ed. William Stearns Davis, Allyn & Bacon, 1946.

Nicolaus of Damascus, "The assassination of Julius Caesar", from *Historici Graeci Minores* ed. Dindorff, trans. BK Workman in *They Saw It Happen in Classical Times*, ed. BK Workman, Basil Blackwell & Mott, Ltd., 1964. Copyright © 1964 Basil Blackwell & Mott, Ltd., 1964.

Plautus, Titus, "The conduct and treatment of slaves", *Comedies*, trans. HT Riley, Bohn's Classical Library, 1852.

Plutarch, "Spartacus revolts", from *Life of Crassus* in *Lives of Illustrious Men*, trans. John Dryden & A. Clough, Sampson Low & Co., 1876.

Plutarch, "Numa ordains the Vestal Virgins", from *Life of Numa* in *Lives of Illustrious Men*, trans. John Dryden & A. Clough, Sampson Low & Co., 1876.

Polybius, "Punic Wars: A portrait of Hannibal", "Scipio delivers the final attack on Carthage", "Men ready to endure anything", from The *Histories of Polybius*, Book IX, trans. Evelyn S. Shuckburgh, Macmillan, 1889.

Sallust, "The Catiline Conspiracy: The character and career of Catiline", quoted in *Readings in Ancient History*, Vol. II, *Rome and the West* ed. William Stearns Davis, Allyn & Bacon, 1946.

Sallust, "Cicero speaks to the Senate", "The last stand of Catiline", *The Conspiracy of Cataline*, trans. JC Rolfe in *Sallust*, Harvard University Press, 1955.

Sallust, "Letter of Mithridates", from *Histories* Book IV, trans. John C Rolfe in *Sallust*, Harvard University Press, 1955.

Suetonius, "Every woman's husband and every man's wife", *The Lives of the Twelve Caesars*, trans. HM Bird, Wordsworth Classical Library, 1997.

Terence, "Bringing up children", *The Brothers*, trans. John Sargeaunt, Harvard University Press, 1912.

Virgil, "Civil War: A poet celebrates an outbreak of peace", Eclogue IV, *The Eclogues and Georgics of Virgil*, trans. C Day-Lewis, Doubleday, 1964. Copyright © C Day-Lewis 1963.

PART TWO

Agrippina the Younger, "Agrippina the Younger pleads for her life", quoted in *Treasury of the World's Greatest Letters*, ed. M. Lincoln Shuster, Simon & Schuster, 1948.

Anon, "Messages of love", quoted in *Readings in Ancient History*, Vol. II, *Rome and the West* ed. William Stearns Davis, Allyn & Bacon, 1946.

Anon, "Advertisements for gladiatorial shows", quoted in *Readings in Ancient History*, Vol. II, *Rome and the West* ed. William Stearns Davis, Allyn & Bacon, 1946.

Anon, "The martyrdom of Polycarp", quoted in *Voices from the Past*, ed. James & Janet Maclean Todd, Readers Union, 1956.

Anon, "Housekeeping record", trans. BK Workman in *They Saw It Happen in Classical Times*, ed. BK Workman, Basil Blackwell & Mott, 1964. Copyright © 1964 Basil Blackwell & Mott, Ltd.

Anon, "Roll call of the First Cohort of Tungrians", *Life and Letters on the Roman Frontier*, Alan K. Bowman, British Museum Press, 1994. Copyright © Alan K. Bowman.

Anon, "The Pumpkinification of Claudius", from *Apocolocyntosis*, trans. WHD Rouse, in *Petronius, Seneca, Apocolocyntosis*, Harvard University Press, 1956.

Aristides, Aelius, "The golden age: an oration to Rome", *Roman Oration* trans. James H. Oliver in *The Ruling Power*, The American Philosophical Society, 1953.

Augustus, "The deeds of Augustus", quoted in *Readings in Ancient History*, Vol. II, *Rome and the West* ed. William Stearns Davis, Allyn & Bacon, 1946.

Augustus, "The education of Claudius", from Suetonius *Lives of the Twelve Caesars*, trans HM Bird, Wordsworth, 1997.

Augustus, "Augustus at the gaming board", quoted in *Private Letters: Pagan and Christian*, ed. Dorothy Brooke, Ernest Benn Ltd., 1929.

Aurelius, Marcus, "Two days in the life of an emperor's son", quoted in *Private Letters: Pagan and Christian*, ed. Dorothy Brooke, Ernest Benn Ltd., 1929.

Aurelius, Marcus, "Marcus Aurelius Meditates", *Meditations*, trans. Maxwell Staniforth in *Marcus Aurelius Meditations*, Penguin Books, 1964.

Aurelius, Marcus, "The virtues of Antoninus Pius", quoted in *Readings in Ancient History*, Vol. II, *Rome and the West* ed. William Stearns Davis, Allyn & Bacon, 1946.

Cassius, Avidius "A governor plots insurrection", quoted in *Private Letters: Pagan and Christian*, ed. Dorothy Brooke, Ernest Benn Ltd., 1929.

Claudius, "Claudius harangues the Conscript Fathers", quoted in *Readings in Ancient History*, Vol. II, *Rome and the West* ed. William Sterns Davis, Allyn & Bacon, 1946.

Frontinus, "The pilfering of water", from *de Aquis*, trans BK Workman in *They Saw It Happen in Classical Times*, ed. BK Workman, Basil Blackwell & Mott, 1964. Copyright © 1964 Basil Blackwell & Mott, Ltd.

Isidorus, Gaius, "An estate owner's will", quoted in *Readings in Ancient History*, Vol. II, *Rome and the West* ed. William Stearns Davis, Allyn & Bacon, 1946.

Josephus, "Vespasian marches against the Jews", "The siege of Jerusalem", "The destruction of the Temple at Jerusalem", "A Roman military camp", from *The Wars of the Jews*, trans. William Whiston in *The Genuine Works of Flavius, Josephus*, Thomas & John Turnbull, 1801.

Juvenal, "Messalina prostitutes herself", "On the City of Rome", *Satires*, trans. William Gifford, JM Dent & Sons Ltd, 1954.

Juvenal, "One prolongs his eyebrows with some damp soot staining the edge of a needle", *Juvenal and Persius*, trans. GG Ramsay, Harvard University Press, 1912.

Juvenal, "Domitian and the yes-men", Satire IV, from *The Satires of Juvenal*, trans. Hubert Creekmore, Mentor Books, 1963.

Martial, "Window shopping", "Immigrants", *Epigrams*, IX, trans. various, Bohn Library, 1860.

Masclus, "An appeal for beer", *Life and Letters on the Roman Frontier*, Alan K. Bowman, British Museum Press, 1994. Copyright © Alan K. Bowman.

Papirianus, P. Lucinius, "Charity", Quoted in *Charities and Social Aid in Greece and Rome*, Arthur Robinson Hands, Cornell University Press, 1968.

Paterculus, Velleius, "Arminius forces the Roman eagles back", quoted in *Readings in Ancient History*, Vol. II, *Rome and the West* ed. William Stearns Davis, Allyn & Bacon, 1946.

Petronius, "The Banquet of Trimalchio", quoted in *Readings in Ancient History*, Vol. II, *Rome and the West* ed. William Stearns Davis, Allyn & Bacon, 1946.

Philo, "A personal audience with Caligula", from *They Saw It Happen in Classical Times*, ed. BK Workman, Basil Blackwell & Mott, 1964. Copyright © 1964 Basil Blackwell & Mott, Ltd.

Pliny the Elder, "Recipe for honey wine", from *Pliny the Elder: Natural History*, H. Rackham, Heinemann, 1938–47.

Pliny the Elder, "The great buildings of Rome", "A portrait of Italy", *Natural History*, trans. J. Bostock & H. Riley, Bohn, 1856.

Pliny the Younger, "The life of a Roman gentleman", *Letters*, trans. JB Firth, Scott Library, 1900.

Pliny the Younger, "The persecution of the Christians", Should I found a fire-brigade?", *Letters*, trans W. Melmoth and WML Hutchinson, Loeb Classical Library, Harvard University Press, 1915.

Pliny the Younger, "The eruption of Vesuvius", "Summer in Tuscany", "Slaves murder their master", "A love letter", "Chariot-racing", *The Letters of the Younger Pliny*, trans. Betty Radice, Penguin, 1969. Trans copyright © Betty Radice 1963, 1969.

Saint John, "Jesus Christ is crucified", from "The Gospel According to St John", *The Holy Bible*, RSV.

Seneca, "Gladiatorial shows", *Seneca: Letters from a Stoic*, trans. Robin Campbell, Penguin, 1969. Copyright © 1968 Robin Alexander Campbell. Addendum on suicides of gladiators is from *Seneca*, trans. Richard M. Gummere, Harvard University Press, 1970–1.

Seneca, "Baths", quoted in *Aspects of Western Civilization, Problems & Sources in History*, ed. Perry M. Rogers, Prentice Hall, 1997.

Severa, Claudia, "A birthday invitation", *Life and Letters on the Roman Frontier*, Alan K. Bowman, British Museum Press, 1994. Copyright © 1994 Alan K. Bowman.

Soranus, "Conception, contraception and abortion", *Gynaecology*, trans. Owsei Temkin, Johns Hopkins Press, 1956.

Strabo, "A picture of Rome", *Geography*, trans. HC Hamilton & W. Falconer, Bohn's Classical Library, 1854.

Strabo, "Collapsing houses", "Egypt under the rule of Rome", quoted in *Readings in Ancient History*, Vol. II, *Rome and the West* ed. William Stearns Davis, Allyn & Bacon, 1946.

Suetonius, "The gluttony of Vitellius", "Vitellius: The end", "Tyranny, bed-wrestling and entertainments for the people", "The whimsical cruelties of Caligula", *The Lives of the Twelve Caesars*, trans. HM Bird, Wordsworth Classics of World Literature, 1997.

Tacitus, "Nero murders Britannicus", "After the fire: Nero rebuilds Rome", "After the Fire: Nero persecutes the Christians", *Annals*, trans. Alfred John Church & William Jackson Broadribb, Macmillan, 1877.

Tacitus, "The manners and customs of the Germans", "Agricola in action at Mons Graupius", *The Agricola and The Germania*, trans. H. Mattingly (revised SA Handford), Penguin, 1970. Copyright © 1948, 1970 the estate of H. Mattingly; Copyright © 1970 SA Handford.

Tacitus, "The great fire of Rome", "The suicide of Seneca", "The vanity of Nero", "Boudicca revolts", *The Annals of Imperial Rome*, trans. Michael Grant, Penguin, 1956. Trans. copyright © Michael Grant, 1956, 1971.

Theon, "A boy complains", quoted in *Private Letters: Pagan and Christian*, ed. Dorothy Brooke, Ernest Benn Ltd., 1929.

Various, "Petty crime in Roman Egypt", quoted in *Readings in Ancient History*, Vol. II, *Rome and the West* ed. William Stearns Davis, Allyn & Bacon, 1946.

PART THREE

Ammianus Marcellinus, "Delinquency in Rome: The rich", "Delinquency in Rome: The common people", *Amminanus Marcellinus I*, trans. John C. Rolfe, Harvard University Press, 1956.

Ammianus Marcellinus, "The Emperor as pilgrim: Constantius II visits Rome", "So destructive a slaughter: The battle of Adrianople", *The Roman History*, trans. CD Yonge, Bohn's Classical Library, 1887.

Anon. "Diocletian seizes the Christians' books", from "The Deeds of Zenophilus", trans. HB Workman, *Persecutions in the Early Church*, Epworth Press, 1923.

Apion, "A soldier writes home", quoted in *Private Letters: Pagan and Christian*, ed. Dorothy Brooke, Ernest Benn Ltd., 1929.

Apollinaris, Sidonius, "A portrait of Theodoric the Visigoth", "A country house party", "The magnificence of the barbarian Prince Sigismer", *The Letters of Sidonius*, trans. OM Dalton, OUP, 1915.

Claudius II, "The defeat of the Goths: The emperor reports", quoted in *Private Letters: Pagan and Christian*, ed. Dorothy Brooke, Ernest Benn Ltd., 1929.

Constantine, "Constantine orders the building of the Church of the Holy Sepulchre", quoted in *Private Letters: Pagan and Christian*, ed. Dorothy Brooke, Ernest Benn Ltd., 1929.

Eusebius, "Constantine the Great overthrows Maxentius", *Life of Constantine*, trans. CF Cruse, Samuel Bagster & Sons, 1842.

Hero of Alexandria, "A proto-type jet engine", quoted in *Voices of the Past*, ed. James and Janet maclean Todd, Readers Union, 1956.

Herodian, "Didius Julianus Buys the Empire at Auction", quoted in *Readings in Ancient History*, Vol. II, *Rome and the West* ed. William Stearns Davis, Allyn & Bacon, 1946.

Herodian, "The Emperor Septimius Severus is made a god", "Mob insurrection", from *Histories*, trans. BK Workman in *They Saw It Happen in Classical Times*, ed. BK Workman, Basil Blackwell & Mott, 1964. Copyright © 1964 Basil Blackwell & Mott, Ltd.

Jordanes, "Alaric the Visigoth sacks Rome", "The battle of the Catalaunian Plains", *The Origin and Deeds of the Goths*, trans. Charles C Mierow, University Press (Princetown), 1908.

Julian, "Julian is proclaimed Augustus", quoted in *Private Letters: Pagan and Christian*, ed. Dorothy Brooke, Ernest Benn Ltd., 1929.

Julian, "An emperor's gift", quoted in *Private Letters: Pagan and Christian*, ed. Dorothy Brooke, Ernest Benn Ltd., 1929.

Psenymis, Aurelius, "A Flute-Player's Contract", quoted in *They Saw It Happen in Classical Times*, ed. BK Workman, Basil Blackwell & Mott, 1964. Copyright © 1964 Basil Blackwell & Mott, Ltd.

Priscus, "Priscus at the Court of Attila the Hun", from *Fragmenta Historicorum Graecorum*, trans. JB Bury. Reproduced from *Internet Medieval Sourcebook*.

St Augustine, "The conversion of Augustine", *Confessions & Enchridon*, trans. Albert C. Outler, SCM Press, 1955.

St Jerome, "A churchman laments the sack of Rome", quoted in *Voices of the Past*, ed. James and Janet Maclean Todd, Readers Union, 1956.

Serenus, "A cuckold laments", quoted in *Private Letters: Pagan and Christian*, ed. Dorothy Brooke, Ernest Benn Ltd., 1929.

Sozomen, "Constantine founds Constaninople", quoted in *Readings in Ancient History*, Vol. II, *Rome and the West* ed. William Stearns Davis, Allyn & Bacon, 1946.

Synesius, "Embarrassing relatives", "Buying summer clothes", "The hazards of sea travel". *Letters of Synesius of Cyrene*, trans. Augustine FitzGerald, Oxford University Press, 1926.

Vopiscus, "Aurelian conquers Zenobia", quoted in *Readings in Ancient History*, Vol. II, *Rome and the West* ed. William Stearns Davis, Allyn & Bacon, 1946.

PART FOUR: EPILOGUE

Procopius, "The secret history of the Empress Theodora", *The Secret History*, trans. GA Williamson, Penguin, 1966. Copyright © 1955 GA Williamson.

Procopius, "Justinian suppresses the Nika revolt", "Belisarius reconquers Africa", "The Plague", *History of the Wars*, trans. HB Dewing, Harvard University Press/Macmillan, 1914.